Authenticity in English Language Teaching

Münchener Arbeiten zur Fremdsprachen-Forschung

edited by

Friederike Klippel

Volume 38

Leo Will

Authenticity in English Language Teaching

An analysis of academic discourse

Waxmann 2018
Münster • New York

Diese Arbeit wurde im Jahr 2017 von der
Ludwig-Maximilians-Universität München als Dissertation angenommen.

Bibliographic information published by die Deutsche Nationalbibliothek
Die Deutsche Nationalbibliothek lists this publication in the
Deutsche Nationalbibliografie; detailed bibliographic data
are available in the internet at http://dnb.dnb.de.

Münchener Arbeiten zur Fremdsprachen-Forschung, Band 38
edited by Friederike Klippel

ISSN 2196-4343
Print-ISBN 978-3-8309-3558-2
E-Book-ISBN 978-3-8309-8558-7

© Waxmann Verlag GmbH, 2018
www.waxmann.com
info@waxmann.com

Cover Design: Anne Breitenbach, Münster
Print: CPI books GmbH, Leck
Printed on age-resistant paper, acid-free as per ISO

MIX
Papier aus verantwor-
tungsvollen Quellen
FSC® C083411

Preface

I would like to thank my supervisor Prof. Dr. Dr. h.c. Friederike Klippel, to whom I am most deeply indebted. To learn from her has meant to develop judgment in areas that extend far beyond ELT. I would also like to thank all members of *DocNet Language Education*, an international cooperation of critical friends founded by Friederike Klippel, Christiane Lütge, and Sarah Mercer.

Munich, 04/01/2018

Leo Will

Contents

1 Introduction

Much has been written about authenticity in EFL (English as a Foreign Language). The word has different meanings and many authors see a need to provide a definition before using the term in their writings. Definitions vary in length and rigor. Some of the more elaborate definitions span entire publications and are more appropriately referred to as conceptualizations. In this study, all such definitions and conceptualizations are subsumed under what I call *explicit negotiation of authenticity* (cf. chapter 4.4.3). These instances of explicit negotiation are so common in the literature that they can be considered to constitute a discursive formation (Foucault 1969: 91). Although authors have offered insightful synopses of the different meanings of authenticity, a systematic and extensive discourse analysis has not yet been conducted. With the study at hand I endeavor to fill this void. This work scrutinizes and categorizes the precise concepts that are referred to as authentic in the academic EFL discourse. I am interested in the discursive dynamics that determine which concepts of authenticity are widely accepted and which ones remain marginal. Discourse analytical tools help reveal patterns that tend to stay beneath the surface in common literature reviews.

1.1 Problem statement

The terms *authentic* and *authenticity* are frequently used in the EFL discourse. However, they denote numerous different concepts, which is problematic because, in academic discourses, terminological precision is important. Even for experts, it has become increasingly difficult to identify and keep apart all the different notions conjured up by the term *authentic/authenticity*: "The notion of 'authenticity' is commonly invoked in language learning, yet the field's understanding of its meaning is to a large extent purely intuitive" (Johnston 1999: 60).

The vagueness of the term is not the only problem. A potentially distortive factor is the term's connotation: "When we try to define 'authenticity', however, we notice that it is one of those words like 'real' (as in 'He's really real') that sounds good but leaves us wondering exactly what it means" (Bachman 1991: 689). Badger/MacDonald conclude that "the discourse related to authenticity is problematic. [...] [T]he concept of authenticity is used to justify more than it should" (Badger/MacDonald 2010: 578-579). Indeed, the highly positive connotation that the term carries may exert an impact on the EFL discourse, potentially leading to an ideology according to Waters:

> [D]iscourse promotes or proscribes language teaching ideas on the basis of ideological belief rather than pedagogical value. The debate about 'authenticity' vs. 'artificiality' in language teaching is a representative example of this tendency. (Waters 2009: 138)

The risk of ideology influencing the EFL discourse is a prime motive for this study.

Whereas the connotation of authenticity appears to be consistently positive, the denotation of the term is extremely volatile. Even the seemingly straightforward concept of textual authenticity, as in authentic texts and materials, is defined differently by different authors. Richards et al. describe authenticity as "the degree to which language teaching materials have the qualities of natural speech or writing" (Richards/Platt/Weber 1985: 22). This allows for contrived text to be called *authentic* provided that "qualities of natural speech or writing" (ibid.) are identified. The following definition contradicts Richards et al. (1985): "Authentic texts (either written or spoken) are those which are designed for native speakers: they are real texts designed not for language students, but for the speakers of the language in question" (Harmer 1983: 146). For Harmer, authentic texts must have a communicative origin as opposed to an origin that prioritizes language learning. The following statement by Grellet narrows the definition even further:

> Authenticity means that nothing of the original text is changed and also that its presentation and layout are retained. A newspaper article, for instance, should be presented as it first appeared in the paper; with the same typeface, the same space devoted to the headlines, the same accompanying picture. (Grellet 1981: 8)

These discrepancies of definition apply only to one concept of authenticity. The denotational diversity is far greater if other concepts are taken into account. After all, the term *authentic/authenticity* is not only used to describe certain kinds of written and spoken text. Authors apply the term to tasks, to individual behavior, to instances of interaction, and to topics discussed in the classroom, to name but a few aspects.

The conceptual diversification of authenticity has grown over the decades. In conjunction with the consistently positive connotation of *authentic/authenticity*, there exists a constant threat of ideology emanating from whatever concept is invoked by the term. The phenomenon has been referred to as the "cult of authenticity" (Day/Bamford 1998: 233).

1.2 Current state of research

Authenticity remains a hot topic in EFL. In 2016, Richard Pinner publishes a 200-page monograph titled "Reconceptualising authenticity for English as a global language". Reinterpretations of authenticity are thus ongoing, begging a diachronic analysis of the term and its concepts.

In the literature, some publications display an awareness of how authenticity has developed as a term in academic EFL. Authenticity is increasingly perceived as an EFL topic by the authors in the discourse, and a certain self-consciousness – or meta-discursiveness (cf. chapter 5.2.4) – is identifiable. I present a short selection of publication titles. The respective phrasings suggest that authenticity is treated as the main subject:

- *Some points about 'authenticity'* (Lee 1983)
- *Authenticity in the language classroom* (Breen 1985)
- *Authentizität als fremdsprachendidaktischer Begriff* (Beile 1986)

- *Authenticity revisited: How real is real?* (Arnold 1991)
- *Inauthentic authenticity or authentic inauthenticity?* (Taylor 1994)
- *What is authenticity?* (Tatsuki 2006)
- *Authentic materials and authenticity in foreign language learning* (Gilmore 2007)
- *Authenticity in CALL: three domains of 'realness'* (Buendgens-Kosten 2013)

Most of such publications feature insightful literature reviews of the discourse. I conceive of a literature review as an approximation to discourse analysis in that a number of contributions to a single topic are invoked. However, literature reviews are more selective than a discourse analysis and they rarely feature explanations as to why some sources are cited while others are not. What is more, they seldom give insight into diachronic developments and relations within the discourse. The brevity of a journal article hardly allows for a systematic and rigorous scrutiny of discourse. Arguably, Gilmore's article (2007) offers the most differentiated representation of conceptual authenticity, drawing on an impressive body of sources. His publication includes a categorization of concepts which serves as a starting point for my study. In the opening passages, Gilmore states:

> There is a considerable range of meanings associated with authenticity, and therefore it is little surprise if the term remains ambiguous in most teachers' minds. What is more, it is impossible to engage in a meaningful debate over the pros and cons of authenticity until we agree on what we are talking about. (Gilmore 2007: 98)

With these words, Gilmore introduces his categorization that is part of his investigation of authenticity, but he also announces a "debate over the pros and cons of authenticity" (ibid.). This reflects a typical structure of the publications in the discourse: A descriptive review of the literature is followed by more conceptual thoughts on what kind of authenticity is most conducive to language learning and teaching. The descriptive part of Gilmore's article (2007) may be considered a meta-study of authenticity but, as is customary in literature reviews, it does not describe the methodology pursued in selecting the sources nor does it discuss structural patterns found in the discourse.

More recent descriptions of the discourse are provided by Joy (2011), and Buendgens-Kosten (2014). The former observes that

> [...] the attempts made to define authenticity, on the one hand, have deepened its complexity, and have widened its scope, on the other. The complexity has deepened due to the plethora of attempts made to define authenticity from various perspectives. Interestingly, this variety has led to different types of authenticity. (Joy 2011: 10)

Buendgens-Kosten (2014) equally emphasizes the complexity mentioned by Joy (2011). She actually refers to the categorization by Gilmore (2007):

> In its widest sense, 'authenticity' is related to notions of 'realness' or 'trueness to origin'. As a technical term in the field of ELT, authenticity has been used to characterize texts (both written and spoken), learning material, tasks, cultural artefacts, multimedia products, forms of assessment, and even types of teacher and audience. Unsurprisingly, a variety of definitions co-exist, and Gilmore (2007) outlines a total of eight different meanings [...]. (Buendgens-Kosten 2014: 457)

Gilmore (2007), Joy (2011), and Buendgens-Kosten (2014) can be considered discourse analytical approximations. Especially Gilmore (2007), with his categorization, provides connectivity for the upcoming analysis of the academic EFL discourse on authenticity. Unlike Gilmore (2007), Joy (2011), and Buendgens-Kosten (2014), I investigate the discourse taking into account aspects of authorial stance, authorial style, author status, and bibliometrics. My interest lies not only in the question of what is considered authentic, but also how those concepts have come about and how they have prevailed over other concepts that may have been labeled authentic by single authors but may not have resonated in the discourse.

1.3   Outline

In the first part of this study, a systematic – as opposed to chronological – overview of the different meanings is given (chapter 2). This overview leads to a conceptual taxonomy (chapter 3) that differs from other categorizations – e.g. Breen (1985), Decke-Cornill (2004), and Gilmore (2007) – in that it classifies authenticity solely based on the different concepts attached to the term by different authors. Gilmore (2007), for example, bases his list at least partially on collocations, meaning that two authors speaking of *authentic tasks* fall in the same category even if their understandings are at odds. A particularly differentiated analysis is conducted for textual authenticity (chapter 2.2) which is the most commonly invoked concept of authenticity in the discourse. Because authors put forth divergent definitions of authentic texts and materials, a very close look is taken to identify areas of conceptual consensus and areas of disagreement. The analysis concludes in an extrapolation of the defining criteria and in a concrete application of these, thus yielding specific text genres that are considered authentic by a vast majority in the discourse (chapter 2.2.3).

Chapters 2 and 3 precede the methodological chapters because the latter apply primarily to the discourse analytical part of this study (chapter 5). Thus, the systematic overview provides important preliminary knowledge of the concepts, with the conceptual taxonomy serving as a means of structure to draw upon in the later proceedings.

Chapter 4 lays out in detail the research methods used. The assets of a discourse analysis over a basic literature review are described in relation to the research interest of this study. This interest lies in finding out what is (and what has been) considered authentic in EFL (English as a Foreign Language). Equally important are the underlying dynamics that appear to shape the discourse. I explain the notion of discourse as such, drawing on the groundwork performed by Michel Foucault (chapter 4.1). Then, I demarcate the discourse under scrutiny from other discourses, highlighting its specificities (chapter 4.4). One particularity of my approach is the integration of a bibliometric analysis to complement the discourse analytical method (chapter 4.5.3). The use of this method is made possible by previously compiling a document selection that essentially constitutes the academic EFL discourse on authenticity.

What follows in chapter 5 is the core element of this study, namely the chronological analysis of the discourse. Conceptual developments are presented decade by decade, taking into account various discourse analytical aspects. The conceptual taxonomy serves as a backdrop to the analysis.

Finally, chapter 6 traces different concepts of authenticity in the history of EFL. This approach is taken to counteract a potential fallacy, namely that concepts are new or innovative simply because they carry a new label that is *authenticity*.

2   Authenticity in EFL – a systematic overview

This opening chapter provides a systematic synopsis of the different concepts of authenticity that are prevalent in the field of English as a Foreign Language (henceforth EFL) today. Although this chapter is not centrally concerned with the historical geneses of these concepts, it is necessary to sketch certain developments at least roughly instead of merely presenting a catalogue of concepts. A more detailed and rigorous diachronic analysis is undertaken in chapter 5. The methodological tools leading to the following overview are explained in chapter 4.

In the 1970s the adjective *authentic* along with the noun *authenticity* became prolific in the field of foreign language teaching and learning (Decke-Cornill 2004: 17; Gilmore 2007: 97). Precisely what these words meant at the time and how frequently they were used is not yet of concern at this point. Henry G. Widdowson was the first to devote a publication to authenticity in 1976 – *The authenticity of language data*. The opening lines of Widdowson's article refer to a development in the preceding years which has brought authenticity to the fore:

> Over recent years we have witnessed an increasing concern on the part of the linguist with the communicative functioning of language. There is a feeling abroad that for a linguistic description to be adequate it must not reduce natural language to an algebraic system but should attempt to account for 'authentic' data, the language user's own experience of language in contexts of use. This movement towards an approximation to authenticity has its dangers: it can lead to a linguistics of anecdote, ad hoc observation, and a neglect of methodological principles upon which any systematic account must depend. (Widdowson 1976: 261)

Widdowson's critique of the "movement towards an approximation to authenticity" (ibid.) marks the beginning of an interesting discourse. Since the two words *authentic* and *authenticity* are members of the same word family and since a functional differentiation between the two is not yet necessary, I will refer to them often as *authentic/authenticity*, or simply as *the term*. This includes the noun *authentication* and the adverb *authentically*, which are considerably less frequent.

The emergence of the term in scholarly literature coincided with the emergence of what is today known as the communicative turn – a movement in language pedagogy that sees language primarily as a means of communication and consequently prioritizes materials that have been created to this very end, and not with the purpose of teaching the English language to speakers of other languages (Wilkins 1976: 79; Morrow 1977: 13; Harmer 1983: 146).[1] Until the late 1970s it was scarcely used to describe anything other than such materials. This denotation is still prolific today.

It is important to mention at this point that the idea of using authentic texts and materials for language teaching was by no means new. For example Offelen's *A double grammar for Germans [...]* (1687), one of the earliest English textbooks, contains numerous

---

[1]   This is merely a preliminary definition of authentic materials. Two of the three authors state that authentic materials should also be created by native speakers and/or be directed at native speakers. Such details are discussed in chapter 2.2.

literary and scholarly texts by English writers. Much later than that – but still well ahead of CLT (Communicative Language Teaching) – language learning theorists made statements about the assets of authentic texts:

> The great advantage of natural, idiomatic texts over artificial 'methods' or 'series' is that they do justice to every feature of the language ... The artificial systems, on the other hand, tend to cause incessant repetition of certain grammatical constructions, certain elements of the vocabulary, certain combinations of words to the almost total exclusion of others which are equally, or perhaps even more, essential. (Sweet 1899: 177)

Offelen and Sweet shall serve as very brief examples. What can be seen is that authentic text was used to facilitate English language learning long before the communicative turn. It was used not only for lack of other materials but for diverse motives, of which Sweet illustrates just one. A more elaborate description of the historical developments is given in chapter 6.

Note that Sweet does not speak of texts in terms of *authentic*. Before the communicative approach became gradually prevalent in the 1970s, language learning approaches such as the New Method and the Audiolingual Method had relied heavily on the use of contrived[2] materials (Gilmore 2007: 97; Schröder 1985: 51-52). The communicative turn, therefore, can be seen as the partial rediscovery of authentic text for language learning purposes, if under new prevailing circumstances. The new terminology of *authentic/authenticity* is a reflection of a zeitgeist which had promoted the term in other academic fields and helped it make its way into colloquial usage (Noetzel 1999: 19-40; Rosenbloom 2011: 1).

What becomes clear is that one needs to distinguish between *authentic/authenticity* as a term and authenticity as a concept. I look at the term and at the various concepts attached to it bearing in mind that there can be different words for the same concept and *vice versa*. This chapter is specifically confined to accounts of *authentic/authenticity* as a technical term within EFL and does not include instances of its use that are rather colloquial, even if they occur in academic writing. Apart from the finding that the concept of authentic text existed long before the corresponding term, as mentioned above, this chapter will also omit all accounts of authenticity as a potential concept when the term *authentic/authenticity* is not applied.

Authentic materials played a pivotal role in CLT as of the 1970s (Wilkins 1983: 24; Porter 1983: 38-39; Little/Devitt/Singleton 1988: foreword; Lewkowicz 2000: 43; Wesche/Skehan 2002: 208; Larsen-Freeman/Anderson 2011: 126).[3] Some authors felt that "[a]uthentic language should be used in instruction wherever possible" (Omaggio Hadley 1993: 80). Deploying authentic materials in the language classroom was seen as an essential means to foster communicative competence through the learner's exposure

---

2   The term *contrived* as the opposite of *authentic materials* is only one among a couple of adjectives used by English-speaking authors to denote what in German is more uniformly called *didaktische Materialien*.

3   The connection between CLT and authentic materials is undeniable to some extent. Yet, the intricacies of this connection must be scrutinized more closely. Chapter 4.5.5.2 provides important insights in this regard.

to idiomatic and naturally occurring language. This naturalness of language was purportedly accompanied by a cultural value of the materials and a concomitant upside in terms of learner motivation:

> Precisely because [authentic texts] come complete with all the savour, stench and rough edges of life beyond the school walls, they are likely to be markedly more successful in provoking pupil reaction and interaction than the somewhat anaemic texts that one so often finds between the covers of textbooks. For similar reasons, authentic texts, even when used in a non-social mode – as private reading matter or as a basis for individual language practice – are likely to give rise to a greater depth of psychological processing, and thus more learning, than specially written or simplified texts. (Little/Devitt/Singleton 1988: 6-7)

Henry G. Widdowson's seminal article *The authenticity of language data* (1976) calls into question the seemingly inherent positive qualities of authentic texts. Widdowson does not really dispel the newly gained enthusiasm with authentic texts but introduces a completely new way of thinking when stating the following:

> I am not suce [sic] that it is meaningful to talk about authentic language as such at all. I think it is probably better to consider authenticity not as a quality residing in instances of language but as a quality which is bestowed upon them, created by the response of the receiver. Authenticity in this view is a function of the interaction between the reader/hearer and the discourse as incorporating the intentions of the writer/speaker. (Widdowson 1976: 263)

Widdowson is not very specific in his early writings about how to achieve authenticity in the language classroom but he asserts that authenticity should be about the reader's "appropriate response" (Widdowson 1976: 263) to a text. It would for example be inappropriate to have learners underline all the adjectives in a newspaper article, since the author of the article did not have any such activity in mind when creating the text. Widdowson goes so far as to disengage the term *authentic/authenticity* from materials calling the latter "genuine" (1978: 80) if certain textual features apply. It appears, however, that genuine text, for Widdowson, remains a pre-condition of authenticity. Genuineness (i.e. authentic text) is necessary but not sufficient for authenticity to occur. This, at least, was Widdowson's proposition in 1976. In later publications he modified this formula.

Widdowson's (1976) statement was ground-breaking in that it sparked a lengthy debate about what would conclusively qualify as authentic. The debate is part of the scholarly discourse. As such it is depicted and closely analyzed in the discourse analytical chapters. This debate yielded a diversification of concepts attached to the term *authentic/authenticity*. The distinction between *genuineness* and *authenticity* allowed scholars to apply the term *authentic/authenticity* to other entities, for it was no longer tied to texts and materials.

An overview of the different concepts of authenticity is best provided in the form of categorizations. The following chapter presents three categorizations coming from three different authors. Such pithy approaches are rare in the literature. The three typologies which follow are in fact the only ones my research has quarried. They are unique in that they are put forth either in the clear-cut form of a list (Breen 1985; Gilmore 2007) or in the form of chapter titles (Decke-Cornill 2004).

2.1 A comparison of three categorizations: Breen (1985), Decke-Cornill (2004), Gilmore (2007)

Helene Decke-Cornill (2004) and Alex Gilmore (2007) are among the more contemporary authors to give synoptic accounts of the different concepts. Gilmore lists as many as eight categories of authenticity in EFL (Gilmore 2007: 98):

> At least eight possible inter-related meanings emerge from the literature. Authenticity relates to:
>
> (i) the language produced by native speakers for native speakers in a particular language community (Porter & Roberts 1981; Little, Devitt & Singleton 1989[4]);
>
> (ii) the language produced by a real speaker/writer for a real audience, conveying a real message (Morrow 1977; Porter & Roberts 1981; Swaffar 1985; Nunan 1988/9; Benson & Voller 1997);
>
> (iii) the qualities bestowed on a text by the receiver, in that it is not seen as something inherent in a text itself, but is imparted on it by the reader/listener (Widdowson 1978/9; Breen 1985);
>
> (iv) the interaction between students and teachers and is a 'personal process of engagement' (van Lier 1996: 128);
>
> (v) the types of task chosen (Breen 1985; Bachman 1991; van Lier 1996; Benson & Voller 1997; Lewkowicz 2000; Guariento & Morley 2001);
>
> (vi) the social situation of the classroom (Breen 1985; Arnold 1991; Lee 1995; Guariento & Morley 2001; Rost 2002);
>
> (vii) assessment (Bachman 1991; Bachman & Palmer 1996; Lewkowicz 2000);
>
> (viii) culture, and the ability to behave or think like a target language group in order to be recognized and validated by them (Kramsch 1998)

Gilmore's list serves as a good starting point for a categorization. It is a descriptive overview as opposed to being conceptual, or even normative, contribution to the discourse. The list does not provide a differentiation in terms of impact within the discourse. By listing as many as eight items its coverage of conceptual authenticity is almost exhaustive. However, the list may suggest equal status of its elements. The order of the components listed hints at a certain prioritization that is not explained by Gilmore. What might be insightful for the more knowledgeable reader are the references given in parentheses. Point (iii), for example, references Widdowson and Breen, who are among the most influential authors in the discourse.

Before taking a closer look at the single concepts a graphic lineup of Gilmore's list (2007) and Decke-Cornill's categorization (2004) is given. The latter categorization consists of only three concepts. The third column is a representation of Breen's "four types

---

4   This title is a reprint of the book *Authentic texts in foreign language teaching* (Little/Devitt/Singleton 1988).

of authenticity" (Breen 1985: 61). Figure 1 shows which of the respective categories correspond to each other – at least roughly.[5]

In the remainder of this chapter, I explain what insights are to be derived from the graphic overview beginning with the most apparent points. To avoid pitfalls, it is important to provide information about the nature and the context of the three categorizations at hand, since they are published in different articles with potentially different aims and foci, and at different points in time. Explanations of the individual categories are subsequently put forward in the respective subchapters.

What meets the eye is that authentic assessment is neither covered by Decke-Cornill's categories nor by Breen's.[6] It is indeed a rather ancillary category which could be seen as a subcategory of *authentic task*. Another straightforward feature of this table is the fact that *authentic language/text* appears in all three categorizations. This is not surprising since it used to be, and is to date, the dominant meaning of the term.

Whether Gilmore's first or second category is more compatible with Decke-Cornill's and Breen's notions of authentic text remains to be examined. These two points, authentic text and authentic assessment, suggest that the order of Gilmore's categorization is not arbitrary. However, there is at least one feature which seems to contradict the assumption of prioritization: One would not expect Gilmore's last category to be echoed by Decke-Cornill or Breen after the one before, authentic assessment, was not. Gilmore appears to rank authentic assessment as slightly more important than cultural authenticity. In this case the superficial look at the table is deceiving. The category of cultural authenticity is neither championed by Decke-Cornill nor by Kramsch (1993), who Gilmore refers to. Unlike, say, category three, which is clearly defined by Widdowson (1976; 1978), cultural authenticity is mentioned by Kramsch (Kramsch 1993: 178) as a probationary concept she eventually dismisses. She specifically does not make a case for cultural authenticity as a relevant concept but concludes to "leave aside questions of 'authenticity'" (Kramsch 1993: 184) in her writing which centers around cultural aspects of language learning. Decke-Cornill is even more forthright about her category of cultural authenticity, eventually denying it the label *authenticity* and calling it the "simulation of authenticity" ("Authentizität simulierendes Handeln im Unterricht"). An example given by Decke-Cornill is the activity of baking scones in an EFL classroom to foster intercultural competence. Such practices are harshly critiqued for being folkloristic (Decke-Cornill 2004: 20).

---

5   The table does not include Widdowson (or any other author of the discourse) because he does not provide a synopsis of existing concepts but pursues a specific understanding of authenticity. Widdowson's views are of course represented within the three categorizations in the table.

6   Whenever Breen, Decke-Cornill, and Gilmore are mentioned with reference to figure 1, the publications in question are Breen (1985), Decke-Cornill (2004), Gilmore (2007).

Concept of authenticity[7]	Gilmore (2007)	Decke-Cornill (2004)	Breen (1985)
Text	Language produced by native speakers for native speakers in a particular language community	Authentic texts and materials ("Authentische Texte und Materialien")	Authenticity of the texts which we may use as input data for our learners
	Language produced by a real speaker/writer for a real audience, conveying a real message		
Text reception	Qualities bestowed on a text by the receiver, in that it is not seen as something inherent in a text itself, but is imparted on it by the reader/listener		Authenticity of the learners' own interpretations of texts
Individual behavior	Personal process of engagement	Learners acting authentically as themselves ("Authentizität als selbst-identisches Schülerhandeln")	
Task	Types of task chosen		Authenticity of tasks conducive to language learning
Social situation	Social situation of the classroom		Authenticity of the actual social situation of the language classroom
Assessment	Assessment		
Culture	Culture, and the ability to behave or think like a target language group in order to be recognized and validated by them	Simulation of authenticity ("Authentizität simulierendes Handeln im Unterricht")	

Figure 1: Comparison of three categorizations

---

7 In this column I give a short label to every category. Concepts grouped under one label are identical or at least very similar. This should already be evident by the wording, except for Decke-Cornill's *simulation of authenticity* being labeled *culture*. The category is explained on the following pages.

This closer look at cultural authenticity supports the assumption that Gilmore's sequential order is not arbitrary. The comparison of Gilmore's list with the more restricted categorizations of Decke-Cornill and Breen shows that authentic text is a central category and that authentic assessment is rather marginal. Cultural authenticity as a concept appears to be particularly controversial. The three authors do not only give synopses of conceptual and terminological authenticity but are eager to comment on them incorporating practical implications and expressions of approval or disapproval regarding single concepts of authenticity. Interestingly, such comments can amount to a dismissal of certain concepts with the consequence of not granting them the label *authentic*, as seen with Decke-Cornill ("simulation of authenticity"). Such a denial is rooted in a terminological idiosyncrasy of authenticity: The term possesses a strongly positive connotation, which furthers its use in benevolent contexts and hinders it in critical ones (Gilmore 2007: 98; Waters 2009: 139).

A number of differences exist between the three categorizations. These pertain to context as well as authorial style. Some commonalities are presented before elaborating on these differences. All three categorizations, respectively, are embedded in a short publication format. Breen's article is published in the journal *Applied Linguistics*, Gilmore's article in *Language Teaching*. Decke-Cornill's categorization is extrapolated from an article that is a contribution to a collected volume. The three articles have the term *authentic/authenticity* featuring prominently in their titles, which suggests a certain focus on the topic at hand:

- *Authenticity in the language classroom* (Breen 1985)
- *Die Kategorie der Authentizität im mediendidaktischen Diskurs (The category of authenticity in the CALL[8] discourse* – Decke-Cornill 2004)
- *Authentic materials and authenticity in foreign language learning* (Gilmore 2007)

With respect to the categorizations, their main common feature naturally lies in the approach itself, namely to discuss authenticity in terms of different categories. What is more, corresponding elements are easily identified. Not only do all three typologies contain authentic text, but all three list this category first. Such a consensus does not exist for cultural authenticity which is listed last by Gilmore but not by Decke-Cornill so the latter's list had to be rearranged to suit the table above.

As for the differences between the categorizations, a disparity of author status exists between Breen, Decke-Cornill, and Gilmore, which impinges on their exposure in the scholarly discourse on authenticity.[9] Breen is by far the most influential author in the field out of the three. While this aspect has discourse analytical implications, what is of interest here is not the impact of the publication itself but the way in which the concepts are presented. The second difference is the year of publication. This aspect has strong implications. While Decke-Cornill (2004) and Gilmore (2007) are not too far apart, Breen's

---

8 Computer-assisted language learning
9 The implications of author status are explained in chapter 4.2.2.

article is published as early as in 1985. Obviously, the authors are only able to describe concepts labeled authentic by the time they put forth their writings.

Authentic assessment is not yet a common concept or term in 1985 but receives growing attention during the 1990s (Bachman 1990; Bachman/Palmer 1996; O'Malley/Pierce 1996; Lewkowicz 2000). It is a truism that the later a synopsis is given the more concepts may have accumulated over time. What is surprising, then, is that Decke-Cornill only names three concepts. This, however, is owed to another important discrepancy between the three publications: the authorial approach. This is where the table is potentially deceptive. It may create the impression that all three authors are equally concerned with giving an exhaustive and descriptive depiction of concepts tied to authenticity. Thus, it is important to remark that Gilmore takes a significantly more descriptive approach to providing a catalogue than Breen and Decke-Cornill do. Gilmore presents his list speaking of "eight possible inter-related meanings [which] emerge from the literature" (Gilmore 2007: 98). He is anxious to cover all the concepts "[a]uthenticity relates to" (ibid.) – note how vaguely he formulates the linkage to authenticity. He is also aware of the term's connotation:

> Authenticity doesn't necessarily mean 'good', just as contrivance doesn't necessarily mean 'bad' [...] [T]erms such as 'authentic', 'genuine', 'real' or 'natural' and their opposites 'fake', 'unreal' or 'contrived' are emotionally loaded and indicate approval or disapproval whilst remaining ill-defined. (Gilmore 2007: 98)

Gilmore's text features many references and the author himself remains largely non-committal to any of the schools of thought he portrays. His list of sources is impressive (approx. 250 works cited).

As mentioned, the reason for Decke-Cornill listing only three concepts as opposed to eight (Gilmore) lies in the difference of authorial approach. First of all, she does not present a list. She does claim to reflect in her categories the main concepts of authenticity in chronological order, but only a few references are used to trace the development:

> In the EFL discourse the term was first used for texts and materials [...]. The term then saw an expansion and a shift toward classroom activities. [...] Another expansion led to the term's application to persons and the actions of learners. These three levels are dealt with in the following elaborations. (Decke-Cornill 2004: 17-18)[10]

Instead, Decke-Cornill weighs the pros and cons of the different concepts from a pedagogical perspective. She is at times quite candid in her commitment to certain ideas and her dismissal of others. It is possible that additional concepts are purposely omitted due to focus or due to perceived irrelevance. I have shown how the author is critical of cultural

---

10   Original: "In der fremdsprachendidaktischen Diskussion ist der Begriff zunächst auf Texte und Materialien angewendet und auf deren Herkunft aus zielkulturellen Kontexten bezogen worden. In diesem Zusammenhang spielt das Konstrukt des ‚native speaker' eine besondere Rolle. Der Begriff der Authentizität hat dann eine Ausdehnung und Verschiebung erfahren, bei der das Unterrichtsgeschehen ins Zentrum der Aufmerksamkeit geriet. In einer dritten Erweiterung wird auch er in Bezug auf die Personen und das Handeln von Schülerinnen und Schülern verwendet. Mit diesen drei Ebenen beschäftigen sich die folgenden Ausführungen." (Decke-Cornill 2004: 17–18)

authenticity. She still devotes a chapter to the concept because she acknowledges its role in the discourse. Gilmore remains largely non-committal and avoids a personal stance.

One parenthetical aspect which sets Decke-Cornill apart is obviously the fact that she writes in German. This matters in terms of how influential the publication is but not so much with regard to the different concepts presented. Her article (2004) appears at a time when the English-speaking discourse and the German-speaking discourse have largely coalesced, as is depicted in chapter 5.3.2.3. This means that the meanings of the words *authenticity* and *Authentizität* are virtually identical.

Decke-Cornill's style can be seen as located somewhere between Gilmore's and Breen's on a continuum from descriptive to conceptual, the latter of which includes personal positioning and pedagogic reasoning (cf. chapter 4.3.1). Breen (1985), whose text appears almost two decades before Decke-Cornill's (2004), makes strong statements and uses very little referencing. In fact, his bibliography consists of only nine sources, two of which are by himself, two are by Widdowson, one is a poem.[11] Breen's list of concepts is introduced with the words:

> In the daily life of the classroom, the teacher is continually concerned with four types of authenticity. These may be summarized as follows (Breen 1985: 60-61):
>
> 1 Authenticity of the texts which we may use as input data for our learners.
> 2 Authenticity of the learners' own interpretations of such texts.
> 3 Authenticity of tasks conducive to language learning.
> 4 Authenticity of the actual social situation of the language classroom.

At the time, Breen does not have such a vast body of literature to draw on. The term has not become as pervasive as it is today. Concepts 3 and 4 of the list are actually his own inventions. Gilmore picks up on these and references Breen when listing them. In the light of historical context, Breen's list is actually quite long considering how early it appears. It works towards a diversification of concepts. While a more elaborate description of the stylistic continuum (descriptive vs. conceptual) is deferred to the methodological chapters of this study, what is roughly meant by *conceptual* can be explained using Breen's approach as an example. Unlike the descriptive and analytical approach taken by Gilmore, Breen's self-assigned role appears to be that of a commentator guided by pedagogical deliberations. He takes the liberties to make bold statements and create new concepts. Decke-Cornill, if more moderately, takes a similar approach. She, however, uses these liberties to omit certain concepts instead of expanding the catalogue. She is also not quite as outspoken as Breen, who states:

> Learning is the main psychological and social function of a classroom. [...] [G]iven the actual social potential of a classroom, the contrivance of 'other worlds' within it may not only be inauthentic but also quite unnecessary. (Breen 1985: 67)
>
> [I]t may be quite unnecessary to adapt texts in any way or to devise 'pedagogic' texts at all! (Breen 1985: 69)

---

11   Breen's bibliography is scrutinized more closely in chapter 5.2.2.

Breen's list, despite its innovations, is relevant because two of its concepts draw on pre-existing literature and the other two continue to evolve in the discourse and are taken up by authors like Gilmore. If Breen's creation of new concepts was not echoed in the discourse, the relevance of his list could be called into question.

In conclusion, the three categorizations are worth comparing because they pursue the same general approach of creating a typology while featuring interesting discrepancies, e.g. time of publication and authorial style. Furthermore, they are not overly connected to one another. Gilmore, for example, cites Breen but does not appear to engage with his categorization. Gilmore does not cite Decke-Cornill, and Decke-Cornill does not cite Breen.

The following chapters elaborate on the different concepts of authenticity as represented in the far left column of figure 1. Knowing all the concepts and their implications is instrumental in understanding the discourse that is under scrutiny in the later course of this study. Once the concepts are roughly explained it is possible to trace them historically. Many of the concepts played a role in language teaching before they were referred to as *authentic*. The ensuing categories are synthetically derived from the three lists by Breen (1985), Decke-Cornill (2004), and Gilmore (2007). They correspond to the left column of figure 1.

2.2 Text

The most common concept of authenticity in EFL, undoubtedly, is textual authenticity as in authentic materials. I differentiate between text and materials. My distinction is in accord with Klippel/Doff (2006: 146) who refer to materials as physical written textual documents. Text encompasses all kinds of produced language – oral or written. Materials are not to be confused with media. The word *media* will be used to denote all channels transporting text such as overhead projection, websites, films, audio recordings etc. The distinction becomes difficult where these channels are physical of nature such as a book or a white board. The white board itself is a medium. Written on it is text. The combination of the whiteboard and the text written on it can be seen as material (physical written textual document) just like a book which, by definition, combines text and medium.

How prevalent the concept of textual authenticity is and has been can be gleaned from the following statement by Joachim Appel:

> Authenticity has for a long time been a buzzword in language teaching. It usually means using written or spoken texts not specifically designed for language teaching. Such material can be very stimulating. At the same time it should not be forgotten that there is another aspect of authenticity: the realness of the teacher. (Appel 1995: 52)

The aspect of teacher realness is not important at this point. What is notable about Appel's words is that the reader has to be reminded to think beyond texts and materials when thinking of authenticity. In the following chapters, authenticity is discussed relating to text. An important terminological distinction is drawn between authenticity and genuineness before various definitions are presented.

2.2.1 The issue of authenticity versus genuineness

The quote above (Appel 1995: 52) is indicative of how Widdowson's term *genuineness* (cf. chapter 2) has failed to catch on in the EFL discourse:

> Genuineness is a characteristic of the passage itself and is an absolute quality. Authenticity is a characteristic of the relationship between the passage and the reader and it has to do with appropriate response. One of the difficulties about extracts, then, is that although they are genuine, the fact that they are presented 'as' extracts imposed on the learner for language learning purposes necessarily reduces their authenticity. (Widdowson 1978: 80)

Rather few instances can be found where *genuine* is used to denote text of non-pedagogic origin. These instances typically occur with authors who have delved deeply into the subject of authenticity such as the following:

> We [...] need to specify in some detail [...] how the traditional view of authenticity as the use of **genuine materials** is compatible with a more expanded and process-oriented view of authentication. (van Lier 1996: 133)

> The teacher's task is not necessarily to provide '**genuineness**' but to be concerned, among many other things, with classroom authenticity, with authenticity of social setting, interaction, purpose and interpretation. (Amor 2002: 74) (emphases added by L.W.)

Stuart Amor, like van Lier, discusses authenticity in his publication. He strongly engages with Widdowson's ideas. Amor's use of the term *genuineness* is taken directly from Widdowson (1978). Other authors, however, avoid using the term in this sense and must be assumed to intentionally do so. Breen (1985), for example, quotes the same passage from Widdowson (genuine vs. authentic – Widdowson 1978: 80). Yet, he prefers to speak of *authentic texts* (at least 12 times in his 11-page paper) despite Widdowson's assertion that "[t]here is no such thing as authentic language data" (Widdowson 1976: 270). What is more, Breen uses *genuine* in collocations with *communication* at least five times, which is contrary to Widdowson's idea.

Similarly to Breen, Gilmore (2007) seems to be fully aware of Widdowson's case for a distinction. He actually quotes Widdowson (1978) (cf. category (iii) of his list – chapter 2.1). Yet, he also does not use the term *genuine/genuineness*. He employs the term *authentic/authenticity* as many as 147 times on 23 pages, for a large part denoting texts, materials, and language. Only four instances of *genuine* can be found, one of which relating to text – an inadvertence or a stylistic variation, it seems.

Almost all other publications that deal explicitly with the subject of authenticity in foreign language learning display very similar proportions of the two distinctive terms (e.g. Arnold 1991; Lee 1995; Long 1996; Day/Bamford 2009; Mishan 2010; Joy 2011; Buendgens-Kosten 2013; Buendgens-Kosten 2014). These texts are chosen randomly. How the term is used in these publications is discussed in the chronological discourse analysis (chapter 5).

Not surprisingly, the term *authentic/authenticity* prevails in writings where the very word appears in the title. However, these publications appear to be familiar with the dichotomy of *authenticity* and *genuineness*, some of them even mention it (e.g. Breen). What is more, *genuine/genuineness* appears not to figure in the title of any publication in

EFL. In my research, using it as a search word has not yielded any results. The term is equally absent in all EFL dictionaries (chapter 4.5.4) I have had access to.

One final note on this issue is that in the German body of literature, the adjective *authentisch* in combination with *Texte* or *Materialien* is omnipresent as opposed to German *genuin*. This is so, to a large extent, because German *genuin* is a rarely used word in general. In conclusion, Widdowson's (Widdowson 1978: 80) terminological proposition appears not to have materialized in the EFL discourse.

2.2.2 Definitions and underlying criteria of authentic text

In this chapter, the term *genuine/genuineness* is avoided, even though Widdowson would apply this term to all the concepts about to be presented. What is outlined is the muddled field of authenticity as a more or less inherent characteristic of text. Ironically, it covers all the concepts that Widdowson refuses to call *authentic* (e.g. Widdowson 1976: 270). On the preceding pages I have shown how some of the most prolific commentators on authenticity attach the term to text and materials instead of seeing it as a matter of appropriate response to a given passage, as Widdowson (1976; 1978) does. Textual authenticity is also the most wide-spread concept of authenticity in publications that do not explicitly focus on the subject of authenticity. The term is then used in a seemingly consolidated manner mostly in collocations with *texts* and/or *materials*. When used in such a way, the term is often not introduced with a definition. Authors speak of *authentic text, authentic materials* or *authentic language* without explaining the term.[12] At first glance, the concept of authentic text is neat and distinct unlike Widdowson's (1976; 1978) rather abstract notion of authenticity as the result of appropriate response. However, a closer look reveals strong conceptual variations. In this chapter authentic text is approached in a purely descriptive manner. No statements are made about the implications of single definitions for classroom practice.

Many writers have tried to pinpoint what is meant by *authentic text* so that more or less clear definitions can be found, many of which are presented in the course of this chapter. Curiously, these definitions tend to differ greatly – at times to the extent of being mutually exclusive. Looking at figure 1, Gilmore's (2007) list is the only one to distinguish two kinds of concepts for textual authenticity. His first category describes authentic text as language produced by a native-speaker to communicate within a native-speaker community. His second category describes authentic text as language produced to convey a real message. Gilmore's first category is thus included in category two because communicating within a native-speaker community usually implies the conveyance of a real message. The first definition is narrower because it stipulates the language production of a native-speaker.

Taylor (1994) compiles definitions of authentic teaching materials that are underpinned by the same variance that leads to Gilmore's (2007) distinction:

---

12   In chapter 4.4.3, I explain the difference between implicit and explicit negotiation of the term. Here, I discuss definitions or partial definitions of authentic text.

Here are some definitions of authenticity of text or teaching materials (Taylor 1994: 2):

'An authentic text is a stretch of real language, produced by a real speaker or writer for a real audience and designed to convey a real message of some sort.' (Morrow, 1977, p. 13)

'Authentic texts (either written or spoken) are those which are designed for native speakers: they are real texts designed not for language students, but for the speakers of the language in question.' (Harmer, 1983, p. 146)

'A rule of thumb for authentic here is any material which has not been specifically produced for the purposes of language teaching.' (Nunan, 1989, p. 54)

Wilkins (1976, p. 79) talks in a similar vein about authentic materials as being materials which were originally directed at a native-speaking audience.[13]

Two of these – Harmer (1983) and Wilkins (1976) – include the aspect of native-speakerism. What is interesting is that in both cases this aspect applies to the intended receiver, not the producer of the text. Gilmore's (2007) first category, however, includes the native-speaker aspect on part of both the receiver and the producer: "the language produced by native speakers for native speakers in a particular language community" (Gilmore 2007: 98). This must be said to be inaccurately referenced. None of Gilmore's sources bears out the bilateral native-speaker aspect (receiver and producer). Gilmore's category reads:

(i) the language produced by native speakers for native speakers in a particular language community (Porter & Roberts 1981; Little, Devitt & Singleton 1989[14])

The two sources cited lack page numbers but they probably refer to the following statements:

We shall call this 'real' language not intended for non-native learners 'authentic'. (Porter/Roberts 1981: 37)

Essentially an authentic text is a text that was created to fulfil some social purpose in the language community in which it was produced. (Little/Devitt/Singleton 1989: 25)

It is slightly interpretative on Gilmore's part that these definitions stipulate a native-speaker author or speaker. Native-speaker production may be a common idea when talking about authentic text. However, this idea is hardly ever made explicit. With most authors, authentic text is defined via the intended receivers being native speakers, while nothing is said about who produces the text, e.g.: "The definition of an authentic text used in this study [...] is a text that is intended for the native speaker of the target language" (Young 1993: 452). This may be due to the fact that many EFL textbooks are actually written by native speakers, yet the purpose of highlighting specific language forms bars them from being authentic. Harmer is most explicit about textbook language not being authentic – irrespective of the writer's origin:

A non-authentic text, in language teaching terms, is one that has been written especially for language students, but here again there is a distinction to be made between texts written to

---

13   Wilkins verbatim: "[...] authentic language materials. By this is meant materials which have not been specially written or recorded for the foreign learner, but which were originally directed at a native-speaking audience." (Wilkins 1976: 79)

14   This title is a reprint of the book *Authentic texts in foreign language teaching* (Little/Devitt/Singleton 1988).

illustrate particular language points for presentation […] and those written to appear authentic, even though there has been some language control of the 'rough-tuning' type. The justification for the latter is that beginner students will probably not be able to handle genuinely authentic texts, but should nevertheless be given practice in reading and listening to texts that look authentic […]. (Harmer 1983: 146)

It is important to note that both categories, the native speaker category (Gilmore's first) and the real message category (Gilmore's second), are defined by the provenance of the text, and not by inherent textual qualities – even though a correlation may be assumed by the respective proponents (Decke-Cornill 2004: 18-19).

Provenance is one of four potential criteria one can extrapolate from definitions of authentic text:

a) Provenance
  1. Intention (real message; intended receiver)
  2. Producer (native speaker or not)
b) Inherent textual qualities
c) Aspects of post-production
d) Use of the text (appropriate response)

In the following subchapters, the four criteria are presented and elaborated in detail. Chapter 2.2.2.5 presents criteria that are found in the discourse but are rather unique.

2.2.2.1 Provenance

Provenance can lead to a broad definition that is based on the producer's communicative intention, which means the intention to convey a real message. Nearly all authors in the discourse agree on this core element. Definitions based on communicative intention are often formulated *ex negativo* (Decke-Cornill 2004: 18-19): They state what is not authentic instead of stating what is, namely anything produced for the purpose of teaching a foreign language instead of conveying a real message. The broad definition, then, goes: *An authentic text is one that is not produced for the purpose of teaching a foreign language.* Or in Davies's words: "[S]implification is a pedagogic device and […] therefore what is authentic is what is not simplified and what is not pedagogic" (Davies 1984: 184). A narrower definition is yielded if native-speakerism comes into play. Either the producer or the intended receiver (or both) must then be native speakers. In the following elaborations I distinguish between the *real message criterion* and the *native speaker criterion*.

2.2.2.2 Inherent textual qualities

Studies have tried to analyze the linguistic differences between *real* language and so-called textbook language. The results have been quite insightful. Gilmore (2004) for example compares dialogues in textbooks with what he calls "authentic service encounters" and identifies a tendency of the former to underrepresent typical features of spoken discourse such as false starts, repetition, latching, hesitation devices, and back-channeling. Paran summarizes:

> [A] productive and provocative area of research has been comparing corpus data and the representation of spoken language in coursebooks and classrooms. Many studies focus on elements that are missing and are not taught; for example how complaints are presented, teaching learners to mitigate requests, the pedagogical presentation of reported speech compared with its occurrence in language corpora, or the use of vague language [...]. All of these studies also contribute important insights to the debate about the meaning and role of authenticity in the language classroom. (Paran 2012: 451)

Such investigations require large quantities of text and the findings reveal typical characteristics rather than hard-and-fast phenomena that apply to every text of a given origin. A statement such as the following is therefore questionable:

> Native speakers or teachers of English as a foreign language are able with little hesitation and considerable accuracy to distinguish between [...] texts which have been specially prepared for ELT and 'the real thing' – instances of [...] language which were 'not' initiated for the purpose of teaching. (Porter/Roberts 1981: 37)

Motherese might be one example where textual features approximate those of pedagogic text: This term refers to the opposite of authentic text. The different authors use a wide range of terms to denote pedagogic text. Some of these terms are: *textbook language, nonauthentic text, inauthentic text, contrived text, didactic text, simplified text.*

Even though the provenance will guarantee textual authenticity according to many authors, the language itself might be very difficult to tell apart from pedagogic text. The native-speaker category is no less susceptible to criticism, considering the ongoing controversy about clear-cut distinctions between native-speaker and non-native-speaker language norms. What is more, pieces of text might be too short to display any of those alleged native-speaker or real message qualities. It simply cannot be ruled out that stretches of text will not give away their origin.

Most authors seem aware that categories based on provenance or intention cannot be said to have fully reliable textual qualities. As a consequence, Gilmore's (2007) list does not feature a definition of authentic text that is based on such qualities. However, a few definitions of that kind can be found in the literature, e.g.:

> [...] [T]he term 'authentic' is used to refer to language samples – both oral and written – that reflect a naturalness of form, and an appropriateness of cultural and situational context that would be found in the language as used by native speakers. (Rogers/Medley 1988: 468)

The following entry is contained in the *Longman dictionary of language teaching and applied linguistics* under *authenticity/authentic*: "the degree to which language teaching materials have the qualities of natural speech or writing" (Richards/Platt/Weber 1985: 22).

The provenance of text no longer works as an absolute defining factor but merely provides a point of reference. What is in focus is the text itself without knowing who wrote it and what the intended target group is. The question whether a text is authentic or not will be answered not absolutely but in terms of degree. This relative definition will have to rely on textual features which first have to be identified – e.g. by means of corpus analysis (Badger/MacDonald 2010: 579).

This is where potential contradictions occur: By having a relative definition of text authenticity rather than an absolute definition, one may end up with texts that are absolutely authentic because of their provenance and intention, while being relatively inauthentic according to the relative definition. I have already pointed out how stretches of text may not display certain features in spite of their authentic origin. The opposite is equally imaginable: A text produced for language learning that looks authentic by virtue of idiomatic features or a certain range of vocabulary. In addition to the narrow definition (native speaker) and the broad definition (real message / *ex negativo*), which are both absolute, there is thus a third definition, which is relative. It allows for different degrees of authenticity.

2.2.2.3 Aspects of post-production

The question of whether an authentic text (in terms of provenance) may undergo alterations, if it is to remain authentic, is an interesting one. I refer to such alterations as aspects of *post-production*. Given the absoluteness of origin, as outlined above, it would be surprising if post-production was not seen as erasing authenticity. Indeed, statements are made by some of the commentators about how post-production is not reconcilable with authenticity. The probably most common measure of post-production is the linguistic simplification of text to make it suitable to the learners' level of language proficiency: "[S]implification is a pedagogic device and [...] therefore what is authentic is what is not simplified and what is not pedagogic" (Davies 1984: 184). Davies is keen to stress that motherese and also Pidgins cannot be categorized as simplification because they are not intended to teach a foreign language (Davies 2009: 166). Both motherese and Pidgin would thus qualify as authentic. A definition of simplification is given by Lautamatti:

> The term simplification of written discourse is here used to refer to the rewriting of texts with the intention of making them more readable or more easily comprehensible. As such, simplification is practised widely as a legitimate method of language teaching and material production. It is mainly carried out in terms of simplification of vocabulary and syntactic structures. (Lautamatti 1978: 72)

Grellet goes even further. She considers simplification only one of several aspects of post-production which preclude authenticity:

> Authenticity means that nothing of the original text is changed and also that its presentation and layout are retained. A newspaper article, for instance, should be presented as it first appeared in the paper; with the same typeface, the same space devoted to the headlines, the same accompanying picture.[15] (Grellet 1981: 8)

The rigor of this statement is not matched by any other author. This may partially be owed to the gradual emergence of the copy-and-paste technique and the internet as today's main resource of authentic texts. Grellet, in 1981, may not have anticipated these developments. Truly authentic texts could hardly be found in modern day language classrooms,

---

15   This aspect evidently applies only to written documents. I am not yet distinguishing between written and spoken text here because it may obstruct clarity. A distinction is made later in this chapter.

if Grellet's definition is applied. Incidentally, her resoluteness may be rooted in an almost ethnological approach. Materials, as I have delineated them in chapter 2.2, are physical written textual documents. As such their authenticity may not only be measured by retention of the language but additionally by retention of all other tangible qualities they carry. In brief, authentic materials may contain authentic text but, just as importantly, they serve as cultural artifacts. I further pursue these thoughts dealing with the category of authentic culture in chapter 2.8.

Grellet's (ibid.) statement may be the most restrictive one in terms of post-production. However, this is only the case, if matters of decontextualization are not considered to fall within this category. Some authors make claims along the lines that authentic text cannot remain authentic once it is brought into a language classroom:

> A particular speaker talking to a particular audience at a particular time in a particular situation will use particular language […]. If the situation changes in the slightest way the language used will also change, and this fact ultimately makes the concept of 'authentic' in language teaching terms unattainable. For the language we present as 'authentic' is authentic only to the very particular situation in which it was first used. By using it in a classroom for teaching purposes, we are destroying this authenticity […]. (Morrow 1977: 14)

> A text can only be truly authentic, in other words, in the context for which it was originally written. […] [R]emoved from its original context, there can be no such thing as an authentic text […]. (Hutchinson/Waters 1987: 159)

> What any attempt to define authenticity by sampling 'real-life' language use fails to recognize, ultimately, is that instances of language use are by definition context dependent and hence unique. (Bachman 1990: 310-311)

> every text is produced in a specific context and the very act of extracting a text from its original source, even if it is left in its entirety, could be said to 'disauthenticate' it since authenticity […] is 'non-transferable'. (Lewkowicz 2000: 46)

According to this orthodoxy, the decontextualization of originally authentic text is bound to annihilate its authenticity. This goes beyond Widdowson's early idea of appropriate response, which does not lament the decontextualizing of text but merely certain inappropriate ways of dealing with the text in the classroom. It is interesting to see how nearly all of these statements (Morrow, Hutchinson/Waters, Bachman) are made at a time when internet-based technology is not as advanced as it is today. The internet has become arguably the greatest source of authentic text. Its fluid nature makes it difficult to speak of decontextualization at all. Moreover, it has become virtually impossible to intend a text solely for native speakers, if it is published online. Text uses have become much less predictable. People read text anywhere they go. Students may read on their way to school – and secretly in class. Some of this text may even be in English. Most of the citations above, however, stem from a time when bringing authentic text to the classroom usually meant bringing written documents which – beside containing authentic text – served as cultural artefacts.

2.2.2.4 Use of the text (appropriate response)

One more definition can be found that barely qualifies as a definition of authentic text. Mishan (2005) is strongly inspired by Widdowson's (1976) notion of appropriate response, laying out possible ways of using authentic texts for authentic tasks. Unlike others who advanced Widdowson's idea towards detaching authenticity completely from texts and materials (e.g. van Lier 1996), Mishan sees authentic text as a necessary – but not sufficient – precondition for task authenticity in the language classroom:

In order for tasks to be authentic, they should be designed to

1. Reflect the original communicative purpose of the text on which they are based.
2. Be appropriate to the text on which they are based.
3. Elicit response to / engagement with the text on which they are based.
4. Approximate real-life tasks.
5. Activate learners' existing knowledge of the target language and culture.
6. Involve purposeful communication between learners.

(Mishan 2005: 75)

Even though Mishan mentions various existing definitions of authentic text, she herself does not commit to one of them. Using a rather vague term she speaks of "cultural products" which she describes as "the supernym for the materials drawn from a variety of media and genres from the target culture" (Mishan 2005: XII). This reference to "the target culture", along with a cornucopia of text examples given in the book, suggests an affinity with native-speaker components in the definition of cultural products. All the samples are likely produced by native speakers and intended for native speakers. However, these cultural products are only taken as a starting point and need to be spliced with tasks encouraging appropriate response. The title of Mishan's book, *Designing authenticity into language learning materials* (2005), is indicative of this concept. Thus, Mishan's understanding combines Gilmore's (2007) first category (from native speaker to native speaker) with Gilmore's third category (appropriate response). Of all the definitions assembled in this chapter, Mishan's is the only one in line with Widdowson's (1976; 1978) initial approach to authenticity. However, the status of cultural products as an absolute prerequisite for authenticity is Mishan's idea, not Widdowson's. Widdowson – especially in his later publications – does not support such a connection.[16] Mishan's approach is taken up by Badger/MacDonald:

The authenticity of a text in the classroom depends on the similarity between the way it is used in the classroom and the way it was used in its original communicative context. (Badger/MacDonald 2010: 578)

Badger/MacDonald describe the "authenticity of a text" (ibid.) but the explanation rather applies to activities. Therefore, appropriate response is not unequivocally classified as a defining criterion of authentic text, but may ultimately form a category of its own.

---

16   I had the opportunity to talk to Prof. Widdowson in person where he was quite clear on this question.

2.2.2.5 Uncommon criteria

Some statements can be found which reveal rather unusual understandings of authenticity. Underlying these statements are defining criteria that are not shared by other authors in the discourse and that may run counter to more common definitions of authentic text. These criteria are not accommodated in the upcoming analysis of authentic text genres due to their singular occurrence and their incompatibility with the other criteria.

The first of these uncommon criteria is contained in a definition by Little/Devitt/Singleton (1988). The criterion is hidden, as it were, in the final two sentences of the following definition (the beginning of which I have quoted before):

> Essentially an authentic text is a text that was created to fulfil some social purpose in the language community in which it was produced. Thus novels, poems, newspaper and magazine articles, handbooks and manuals, recipes, and telephone directories are all examples of authentic texts; and so too are radio and television broadcasts and computer programmes. As far as language teaching is concerned, however, 'authentic text' has come to have a rather more limited meaning than this. Many attempts to implement the communicative approach have found no use for literary texts […]. (Little/Devitt/Singleton 1988: 25)

The understanding is at variance with all other approaches. As has been mentioned, the increased use of authentic texts coincides with the emergence of Communicative Language Teaching (CLT). In this quote by Little/Devitt/Singleton, however, the connection between authenticity and CLT is taken to an extreme. The compatibility with CLT starts to define what is to be considered an authentic text. Since literary texts have not been used in many communicative language classrooms, the authors are disinclined to call them authentic. This is an odd defining criterion that would cause problems in the pursuit of an operable definition of authentic text.

Little/Devitt/Singleton's observation – made in the late 1980s – corresponds with how Schröder describes the German situation of CLT in the early phase (Schröder 1985: 51-52). The traditional literary canon fell out of favor with the student movement of 1968. It was perceived as largely incompatible with the communicative approach. The role of literature in the EFL classroom remained a minor one for a while before it reemerged in the 1980s, which is the time when Little/Devitt/Singleton (1988) published their book (cf. chapter 6 for a more detailed historical description). If Little/Devitt/Singleton's defining criterion of CLT compatibility is applied today, it is likely to yield different results for literature. Literature can no longer be seen as antithetical to the communicative approach. The criterion is therefore not given further importance in this study.

Another definition that is difficult to reconcile with other criteria is the following one: "To put it simply, authentic language is language where something other than language for its own sake is being discussed" (Pinner 2013: 151). This definition includes only texts that are not metalinguistic. It may be intuitive that metalinguistic classroom discourse, for instance, is not perceived as authentic. Pinner may actually aim for something similar to the real message criterion. Still, it is questionable that speakers who convey real messages never talk about "language for its own sake" (ibid.). In fact, classroom discourse may be seen as a typical example where these two elements coincide.

Lastly, a criterion can be inferred from statements made by Tan (2005), who pleads for language produced by EFL learners to be deemed authentic:

> The impression given from learner corpora research is that learner language is flawed because it contains usages which are considered unnatural and inauthentic when compared to native language usage. However, if we were to examine the 'authenticity' criteria by which researchers base their claims, we would find that it is very much based on imperialistic assumptions about the ownership of English, rather than the present role of English as a lingua franca. (Tan 2005: 128)

Though the *lingua franca* case is also – directly or indirectly – made by Trabelsi (2010) and Kramsch (2012) (cf. chapter 5.2.5), it is still not commonly advocated and it is antithetical to the native-speaker criterion. Thus, the criterion is omitted in the following analysis of authentic text genres.

2.2.2.6 Summary of the defining criteria

In this chapter, the criteria for authentic text are laid out with greater refinement beginning with a graphic table (figure 2) that summarizes the points outlined in the preceding chapters. Such elaboration is needed in order to eventually classify individual text genres as authentic or non-authentic.

Aspects of post-production are not included as a criterion in any of the categories shown in figure 2 because this is implicit in the distinction between absolute and relative. All the absolute definitions disallow simplification and, possibly, other means of post-production. The relative definition, which is based on textual qualities, allows for post-production, especially for the kind that does not affect the language itself (changing font etc.). Simplification would be seen as a gradual diminution of authenticity. Another aspect the table does not reflect is the matter of different text genres. Here, text means language produced in writing or speaking so all potential genres are included. A differentiation in terms of text genre is made in the next chapter.

The diversification of criteria pursued here may be regarded as an over-interpretation of the statements made by the authors I referred to. What may be specifically striking is the minute differentiation of producer and intended receiver in terms of native and non-native speaker in the upper four categories. These precise categories are the consequential results inferred from the various definitions. This meticulousness is necessary in particular since so many authors imply or emphasize the importance of authentic materials. For example, when a definition is put forth which contains a native-speaker element, it is necessary to question whether this element refers to the writer/speaker (producer) or to the reader/listener (receiver) of a text. Wilkins's definition of authentic materials as "materials which have not been specially written or recorded for the foreign learner, but which were originally directed at a native-speaking audience" (Wilkins 1976: 79) is not absolutely clear about these stakeholders. It allows for text produced by non-native speakers as long as it is directed at native speakers. Whether this is intended by Wilkins is questionable and it cannot be resolved here. I thus chose to list all possible options in the table. These are for the most part inferences from authors' statements, but I decided not to give references because giving references would suggest an author's unequivocal commitment to the concept.

Criterion	Criterion type	Absolute or relative
Text conveying a real message (including communication between non-native speakers)	Provenance (intention)	Absolute
Text conveying a real message (produced by a native-speaker AND intended for one or more native-speaker receivers)	Provenance (intention and producer)	Absolute
Text conveying a real message (produced by a non-native speaker AND intended for one or more native-speaker receivers)	Provenance (intention and producer)	Absolute
Text conveying a real message (produced by a native-speaker AND intended for one or more non-native-speaker receivers)	Provenance (intention and producer)	Absolute
Text (conveying a real message) put to appropriate use	Provenance AND use of the text (appropriate response)	Absolute (text) AND relative (use)
Text displaying qualities of natural language	Inherent textual qualities	Relative

Figure 2: Defining criteria of authentic text

Definitions can also be unclear about other components than the native-speaker element. Some definitions suggest a clear intention on the part of the producer as to who should be the receiver(s). To stay with Wilkins (1976), an authentic text is described as being "directed at a native-speaking audience". Such intentions, however, can be difficult to pinpoint depending on the genre of text. In a recorded dialogue the intended receiver is clear, if for example two people are conversing and the conversation is a genuine exchange as opposed to contrived listening material.[17] The intended receiver, then, is the respective conversation partner in the exchange. On the other hand, a novel cannot be said to be

---

17   Listening materials with contrived conversation, which are readily available, are not considered authentic by any of the authors referenced.

directed at an easily identified audience. The latter example raises issues in conjunction with the native-speaker element. Wilkins (1976) – and others who define authenticity similarly – suggests that novelists produce their writings exclusively for native speakers of the given language (Wilkins 1976: 79), which is a tenuous assumption. In the case of a recorded dialogue, the receiver of an utterance is usually identified as a native or a non-native speaker by his or her accent. The speakers may also be introduced (or may be celebrities), in which case the identification is not an issue. If both or all of the participants are native speakers of English, the spoken text produced is authentic according to all definitions. If, however, one of the participants (intended receivers) is a non-native speaker – especially one with a low proficiency – the other speaker is likely to use a form of teacherese. Although a real message is conveyed, teacherese usually includes simplification, which in turn collides with Davies's (1984) definition of authenticity.[18]

I have tried to show how the intricacies of the native-speaker element are not sufficiently addressed in the different authors' definitions of authentic text. This is possibly owed to a certain conciseness which the authors aim for in their definitions. Oftentimes absolute precision may actually not be the goal because the author is more dedicated to questions of how to use authentic materials. In general, the more elaborate a definition the higher the probability that omissions are made deliberately. Here is one example:

> I use the term 'authentic text' to mean (i) the record of any communicative act in speech or writing that was originally performed in fulfilment of some personal or social function, and not in order to provide illustrative material for language teaching, and – by extension – (ii) any communicative event that can easily become such a record, for example, radio and television broadcasts and certain forms of electronic communication. Thus defined, authentic texts have the capacity to draw language learners into the communicative world of the target language community. This capacity appears to support the communicative purpose of language teaching and is responsible, at least in part, for the widely held belief that it is important to enable learners to respond authentically to authentic texts. (Little 1997: 225)

This definition is exceptionally detailed. Unlike shorter definitions it can be assumed to consciously forgo a native-speaker element. The strong focus on communication and the use of the word *any* corroborate the assumption. Swaffar (1985) is similarly conscientious.[19] Thus, definitions differ not only in content but also in scope. Few of them are comprehensive enough to address all the criteria in figure 2.

---

18   Davies (1984: 184): "[S]implification is a pedagogic device and [...] therefore what is authentic is what is not simplified and what is not pedagogic [...]."

19   Swaffar (1985: 17): "For purposes of the foreign language classroom, an authentic text, oral or written, is one whose primary intent is to communicate meaning. In other words, such a text can be one which is written for native speakers of the language to be read by other native speakers (with the intent to inform, persuade, thank etc.) or it may be a text intended for a language learner group. The relevant consideration here is not for whom it is written but that there has been an authentic communicative objective in mind. This distinction may be clarified with the assertion that most textbook materials currently at the disposal of foreign language students do not reflect communicative goals because theirs is a pseudo intent to teach language per se rather than to communicate information."

The following chapter discusses one final differentiating aspect of authentic text, which ultimately allows for a classification in terms of what types of text are considered authentic by a majority of the authors. While thus far the word *text* has been applied to both spoken and written language, the upcoming deliberations make a distinction in this regard, thereby leading to what is close to a consensus list of authentic text genres.

2.2.3 Authentic text genres

In this chapter, diverse text genres are scrutinized applying the criteria presented in the previous chapters. This analysis can lead to careful propositions as to which genres are considered authentic according to a broad consensus in the discourse. A second category is put forward containing text genres that are deemed authentic following only certain criteria. The latter category, thus, comprises genres of limited or contested authenticity.

Some of the authors, who define authentic text, do not mention different genres. Others give examples of authentic text genres. Others again limit their definitions to either written or spoken text. In this chapter, the defining criteria put forth in the preceding chapters are applied to both written and spoken text. Discrete text genres are considered. Depending on how many criteria are met by a given text genre, and depending on how prominent these criteria are in the discourse, the genre can be roughly classified as more or less authentic.

The implications of the native-speaker element for different genres are exemplified above with the discrepancies between a recorded conversation and a novel. The same is the case for the aspect of producer intention. The following definitional statements display different degrees of specificity with regard to text genre. Some of them have already been presented, but shall now be analyzed in terms of how they deal with genre.

> Authentic texts (either written or spoken) are those which are designed for native speakers: they are real texts designed not for language students, but for the speakers of the language in question. (Harmer 1983: 146)

> Essentially an authentic text is a text that was created to fulfil some social purpose in the language community in which it was produced. Thus novels, poems, newspaper and magazine articles, handbooks and manuals, recipes, and telephone directories are all examples of authentic texts; and so too are radio and television broadcasts and computer programmes. (Little/Devitt/Singleton 1988: 25)

> An authentic text is a stretch of real language, produced by a real speaker or writer for a real audience and designed to convey a real message of some sort [...]. A particular speaker talking to a particular audience at a particular time in a particular situation will use particular language [...]. If the situation changes in the slightest way the language used will also change, and this fact ultimately makes the concept of 'authentic' in language teaching terms unattainable. For the language we present as 'authentic' is authentic only to the very particular situation in which it was first used. By using it in a classroom for teaching purposes, we are destroying this authenticity [...]. (Morrow 1977: 14)

The first definition by Harmer does not mention different genres. However, the definition mentions written and spoken text, which shall be considered a very basic distinction in terms of genre. Including both written and spoken text is thus a conscious decision. The second definition by Little/Devitt/Singleton is followed by examples of genres, these being split into written and spoken genres. The third quote by Morrow begins with a short definition, which is then elaborated. While the short definition itself distinguishes between written and spoken, the elaboration pursues only the latter. It specifies implications for spoken genres. Written genres are not given equal attention. If the statements are to be equally valid for written genres, difficulties arise. The problem becomes visible when one tries to apply the following sentence to written genres: "the language we present as 'authentic' is authentic only to the very particular situation in which it was first used." One would wonder in what situation the language in a novel "was first used." Completely different rules would have to apply.

Some authors differentiate between genres by giving examples but do not elaborate on them. Others elaborate on one genre but fail to mention the limited validity of such statements (e.g. Morrow 1977: 14). The underlying problem is that any definition of authentic text that aims for conciseness is bound to group together various genres. However, most of the defining criteria are not applicable to all the genres in equal fashion.

A binary distinction between written and spoken genres is one step toward alleviating the problem. For example, the criterion of post-production can be applied to all written genres but is less imaginable with spoken language. Still, a complete differentiation would be more desirable. Sometimes a single item belonging to one genre can have qualities so idiosyncratic that the question of authenticity must be scrutinized only for the specific item at hand. For example, a radio show in English, which is broadcast by an Austrian station, raises interesting issues to be discussed in the course of this chapter. The defining criteria have been provided by the different authors: provenance, inherent textual qualities, aspects of post-production, use of the text. The interdependence of these and their contingency on questions of text genre are aspects yet to be addressed. This is done best by analyzing single genres one by one.

One final question needs clarification. Text authenticity, which is the only concept featured in all three taxonomies of figure 1, finds a distinction with Gilmore (2007) but neither with Decke-Cornill (2004) nor with Breen (1985). It may, therefore, be interesting to see what these two authors mean by authentic text. Decke-Cornill (2004: 17) quotes Tricia Hedge (2000) who is in line with the general real-message definition and emphasizes the non-acceptance of simplification. A native-speaker element is not included:

> With communicative language teaching has come pressure to use authentic materials, in other words, materials which have not been designed especially for language learners and which therefore do not have contrived or simplified language. (Hedge 2000: 67)

> The term 'authentic' [...] refers to the way language is used in non-pedagogic, natural communication. (Hedge 2000: 78)

As mentioned before, Decke-Cornill describes this sort of definition as working *ex negativo* because it states what is not authentic instead of stating what is. Indeed, quite a few authors choose this approach. Hedge's definition is potentially narrowed down when Decke-Cornill claims that such an understanding has strengthened the role of the native speaker (2004: 18). This statement by Decke-Cornill is predicated on the assumption that non-pedagogic language is used almost exclusively produced by native speakers. It remains unclear, however, whether Decke-Cornill sees a native-speaker criterion in the definition of authentic text.

An investigation into Breen's concept of text authenticity proves inconclusive. The very first sentence of his article reads: "I would like to begin by providing a particular example of an authentic text" (Breen 1985: 60). What follows is a poem by the Czech writer Miroslav Holub – in English. Holub wrote his poems in Czech and did not translate them himself. It is difficult trying to distill a definition from the circumstance that a translated piece of poetry is described as authentic. The translator is likely a native speaker of English who arguably does not convey a real message of his own when rendering an already existing text in a different language. The question would therefore be who the producer is – Holub or the translator. Whether Holub conveys a real message through the poem is another question. Breen does not explain his choice of text, nor does he explain why and how this text is authentic. At a later stage, Breen speaks of text "produced by a fluent user of the language for fluent listeners or speakers" (Breen 1985: 62). This can be seen as a moderate native-speaker criterion. Obviously, fluent speakers of a language do not necessarily have to be native speakers. Technically speaking, Breen adds a new criterion to the catalogue: fluency on part of producer and receiver. What is more, Breen is quite contradictory in defining text authenticity. He considers other aspects of authenticity as more important so that his vagueness on authentic text may actually be intentional. His focus is on task authenticity, which is achieved by utilizing the "social potential of a classroom" (Breen 1985: 67). In a footnote, however, Breen is very candid about the importance of using authentic text in the classroom:

> [I]t seems to me that [...] pedagogic or contrived texts are likely to distort the target language data and, thereby, deprive the learner of two things: first, direct access to the actual conventions of target language use and, second, the opportunity to apply his own prior knowledge of the real conventions of communication which underlie his own mother tongue. My own main point would imply that learners – because they are learners – are themselves likely to 'filter out' what is inaccessible and, indeed, to distort any particular text in order to make it serve them in the development of new knowledge. An interesting conclusion from this would be that it may be quite unnecessary to adapt texts in any way or to devise 'pedagogic' texts at all! (Breen 1985: 69)

If even Breen (1985) and Decke-Cornill (2004) are not very precise in their definitions, it is understandable how publications with a different focus use the term rather vaguely.

There exist a number of possible reasons why so many writers do not provide a precise definition of authentic text. First, the concept is perceived to be relatively straightforward. It is not as elusive as the concepts of authenticity that are under scrutiny in the following chapters. Second, the term *authentic text* is ubiquitous and the more often it occurs the more one will assume that its meaning is fixed. Third, many publications focus on how to use texts rather than on what specific qualities the texts should have. A rough distinction between authentic and pedagogic text is sufficient in most of these cases. Four, writers who have not delved deeply into the issue of authenticity may not be aware of the different possible categories of text authenticity. And if they are, they may feel that only a very small number of texts would fall within one category but not within another so that a differentiation is negligible.

It is demonstrated in figures 3 and 4, by referring to miscellaneous text genres, what the area of consensus is and where there is disagreement. In the figure 3, text genres are listed that are authentic according to nearly all definitions. The items can be stated to be almost unequivocally authentic as long as they are produced by native speakers and as long as they are not produced to teach a foreign language.

Genres of largely uncontested authenticity
Narrative texts **(written)** e.g. novels, short stories, children's books
Non-fiction and journalistic texts **(written)** e.g. guidebooks, biographies, scientific publications, newspaper articles
Poetry **(written)**
Songs, speeches, presentations, radio broadcasts, podcasts **(audio)**
Films, TV broadcasts, online videos **(audiovisual)**

Figure 3: Genres of largely uncontested authenticity

Genres of contested authenticity	
Genre	Potential restrictions
Spoken conversation **(audio)**	Native-speaker element ➔ Simplification
Written conversation **(written)** e.g. text messaging, posts in social media	Native-speaker element ➔ Simplification
Letters and e-mails **(written)**	Native-speaker element ➔ Simplification
Text translated into English **(written)**	Native-speaker element ➔ Who is the producer?

Figure 4: Genres of contested authenticity

The text types in figure 4 are either subject to disagreement due to colliding criteria or raise questions about whether a given criterion is really met. As in figure 3, the text genres in figure 4 presuppose production by a native speaker. I go on to explain the allocation of items to the two different tables and suggest possible conclusions to be drawn from the two lists. To do so, I elaborate on some of the restrictions. Most of the restrictions disappear, if all producers and recipients are native speakers. However, if only the producer is a native speaker, possible limitations occur which are marked as "native-speaker element → simplification". This is explained in due course.

The last item in figure 4 is not very likely to be deemed authentic by most authors in the discourse. It is based on Breen's claim that a Czech poem translated into English be considered authentic (Breen 1985: 60). The caveat with any translation must be that the translator cannot be clearly said to be the producer. If he or she is seen as the producer, then the message conveyed is not his/her own (real message criterion) and it is unclear whether this is acceptable in terms of authenticity. If the original author is considered the producer, then neither is the text produced by a native speaker of English nor is it produced for an English-speaking readership (native-speaker criterion).

The first three items in figure 4, i.e. spoken/written conversation and letters/e-mails, must be subjected to a more differentiated analysis in terms of who the partners in communication are. Letters and e-mails that are written by native speakers are unequivocally authentic if the receivers are also native speakers. If, however, the receiver is a non-native speaker, then the producer may choose to deploy some form of simplification. While such simplification does not fall under post-production, the effect may be similar to a written text that is simplified retroactively. The same logic applies to spoken and written conversation. In all of these categories, a non-native speaker receiver may be accommodated by the speaker or writer by means of simplification, though be it real-time simplification as opposed to post-production.

There exist singular exceptions in figure 3 where items may incur restrictions. One such exception would be English radio broadcasts on a station located in a non-English-speaking country, which is the case with Austrian radio station FM4:

> The programming of FM4 is […] notable for its high level of spoken word content, much of which is produced in the English language. Morning programmes, including the current affairs-based 'Reality Check' and 'Update', are broadcast in English while afternoon shows 'Connected' and 'Homebase' are German-speaking. News in French is also transmitted twice a day. (FM4: 2015)

On the station's homepage nothing is said about why shows are broadcast in foreign languages so there is no declared intention to teach English to the listeners. The only statement made in this regard is that "FM4's hosts and on-air guests are encouraged to follow FM4's 'Native Speaker Principle' and speak in their mother tongue" (FM4: 2015). As shown above, the native-speaker criterion for authenticity shows a tendency to focus on the intended receiver rather than the producer. Since the targeted audience of FM4 is made up primarily of German native speakers, the fulfillment of the native-speaker criterion is not guaranteed.

Songs may incur similar restrictions as the FM4 broadcasts. Pop music in English that is produced by native speakers usually does not have a clear-cut audience in terms of native or non-native speakers. The more successful an artist is, the more likely he or she is to reach a non-native-speaking audience. Still, singers may not be very inclined to use simplification, at least not to the same extent as are people who talk to non-native speakers in a conversation. Oftentimes, the musical element appears to be more important than the linguistic element of a song. All in all, simplification is probably not so common in pop songs. Therefore, lyrics should be considered authentic texts with only minor restrictions.

2.2.4 Final remarks on textual authenticity

What all these exceptions and differentiations display is how every attempt at a conclusive categorization is bound to remain slightly deficient. A consensus definition is not achieved. It is expedient to be familiar with the different criteria rather than with the different definitions of *authentic text*. Beginning with the *ex negativo* criterion of text not produced for purposes of foreign language learning more criteria can be added to arrive at an incrementally narrower definition. These include real message, native speaker (producer and/or intended receiver), post-production, inherent textual qualities, and use of the text. The most restrictive criterion, however, has not yet been mentioned: context. Statements emphasizing the role of context in authenticity read as follows:

> A particular speaker talking to a particular audience at a particular time in a particular situation will use particular language [...]. If the situation changes in the slightest way the language used will also change, and this fact ultimately makes the concept of 'authentic' in language teaching terms unattainable. For the language we present as 'authentic' is authentic only to the very particular situation in which it was first used. By using it in a classroom for teaching purposes, we are destroying this authenticity [...]. (Morrow 1977: 14)

> A text can only be truly authentic, in other words, in the context for which it was originally written. [...] [R]emoved from its original context, there can be no such thing as an authentic text [...]. (Hutchinson/Waters 1987: 159)

> [T]he language is only authentic in the original conditions of its use, it cannot be in the classroom. The authenticity is nontransferable. (Widdowson 1994: 384)

These statements change the entire conceptualization of textual authenticity. They contradict nearly all other definitions. While conventional concepts of authentic text are discarded, all language produced within the provisions of language learning and teaching, i.e. pedagogic text, becomes potentially authentic because the EFL classroom is "the context for which it was originally written" (Hutchinson/Waters 1987: 159 – see above). This reasoning all but subverts the conventional understanding of textual authenticity.

Not always is it necessary to draw such thorough distinctions between the criteria and definitions of authentic text. However, authentic text is the most widespread concept of authenticity. At the same time, definitions in the literature veer toward a certain succinctness. The deliberations in this chapter shall serve as an insight into the conceptual construction of textual authenticity, wherein the different criteria play have been laid out and analyzed. On the practical level, it is expedient to be familiar with the criteria and be aware of their implications for specific text genres and sometimes even for single samples of text.

Figures 3 and 4 emerge from an attempt at splitting text types into two broad categories: one category of high consensus and one category of rather contentious authenticity. The subsequent elaborations provide important information on potential restrictions. It is, furthermore, important to bear in mind that Widdowson would likely call all these categories *genuineness*, not *authenticity*.

Authentic text is an extremely heterogeneous category of which Gilmore's (2007) dichotomous approach is considered insufficient. The following chapter discusses Gilmore's third category. I will adhere to the order of categories in the far left column of figure 1.

2.3   Text reception

Mishan's (2005) notion of *Designing authenticity into language learning materials* (title of her book) is essentially rooted in Widdowson's concept of authenticity as text reception. In this chapter I outline Widdowson's concept and demarcate it from Mishan's. After all, the latter falls into *text* while the former is treated here as a category in its own right. Widdowson deals with the issue of authenticity in a number of publications and develops his concept gradually. It must be extrapolated from numerous statements over time. To not overly simplify but do justice to the complexity of this development I quote several statements by Widdowson. Although many other authors have borrowed single elements from Widdowson, the concept I refer to as *authentic text reception* is essentially his. Therefore, no other authors are referenced in this chapter.

What many have ignored is that Widdowson makes a clear distinction between general EFL classes and ESP classes, the latter of which he describes as a budding – and promising – discipline in 1976:

> Previously, the main effort in the teaching of English took place within the context of general primary and secondary education. English was a subject like other subjects and the learner's achievement was measured by examinations designed essentially to validate the syllabus rather than to reflect actual communicative needs. In these circumstances teaching was required to prepare learners for the examination but not (except incidentally) for an encounter with language use. [...] Recently, however, English teaching has been called upon to meet the needs of people who have to actually use the language for occupational and academic purposes. In these circumstances, it has to cope with a connection with the real world and provide for immediate communicative needs. [...] English for special purposes (ESP), whether these be occupational (EOP) or academic (EAP), requires a teaching methodology which will guide learners towards an ability to handle language in use. Its adequacy can only be measured by its success in achieving this aim. In general ELT or EFL, it is desirable to adopt a communicative approach to language teaching, but we are not likely to incur any drastic penalty if we do not do so. But in ESP such an approach is not only desirable but mandatory since if we do not satisfy the communicative requirements of the learners the penalties are likely to be severe: our methodology will be exposed as ineffective and sooner or later we are likely to be out of a job. (Widdowson 1976: 261-262)

Widdowson claims that ESP in particular requires communicative approaches to language teaching. What is more, his newly developed concept of authenticity is aimed at ESP. Widdowson seems critical of the practices in common EFL classrooms at the time. He expresses "the need to adopt a communicative perspective in the teaching of ESP, one that will develop communicative competence and prepare the learner for an authentic experience of language. But how do we set about devising procedures which will bring this about?" (Widdowson 1976: 261).

What follows is the description of appropriate response:

> I wish to argue, then, that authenticity has to do with appropriate response. But what does this appropriacy entail? [...] Let us suppose that we are confronted with a piece of written discourse. How do we establish an authentic relation with it? We do so, I suggest, by recovering the intentions of the writer. [...] So when I speak of appropriate response, I mean the reader's interpretation by reference to the conventions associated with a particular discourse type. Authenticity, then, is achieved when the reader realizes the intentions of the writer by reference to a set of shared conventions. (Widdowson 1976: 263-264)

Widdowson's conceptualization of authenticity as appropriate response may be new and generally appealing, yet its value is only claimed for ESP.

> Authenticity, then, depends on a congruence of the language producer's intentions and language receiver's interpretation, this congruence being effected through a shared knowledge of conventions. It is clear that if this view is accepted it makes no sense simply to expose learners to genuine language use unless they know the conventions which would enable them to realize it as authentic. Thus, confronted with a class of physics students wanting to learn English so as to read textbooks in their subject, I might be tempted to select passages of discourse which are thematically relevant from a whole range of sources on the assumption that I am thereby furthering the communicative purpose for which the learners need the language. But if I then exploit these passages for the traditional kind of comprehension question, structure exercise, and so on, their authentic potential remains unrealized. I might just as well have selected an extract from the Highway Code or Winnie the Pooh. The fact that the data is genuine is irrelevant. (Widdowson 1976: 264)

> How do we proceed? There are, I think, two main stages, the selection of discourse in relation to the assumed terminal behaviour of the learners, and the subjection of this material to a pedagogic processing to ensure the eventual achievement of this behaviour. (Widdowson 1976: 265)

Widdowson proposes different sorts of text for the purpose at hand. By way of illustration, he cites an ESP science course. The text genre would be either scientific or semi-scientific, i.e. targeting adults with a casual interest in science. The semi-scientific genre is to be found in newspapers when a science topic is dealt with. All texts proposed by Widdowson are *genuine* according to him. What is implicit is that such texts will be easy for the students of an ESP science course to authenticate[20] by virtue of familiarity with and interest in the topic – students have a "knowledge of conventions" (Widdowson 1976: 264). The corresponding tasks should not focus on form but be aligned with "the assumed

---

20   The term *authentication* is coined by Widdowson in 1978. The corresponding statements follow in the course of this chapter.

terminal behaviour of the learners" (Widdowson 1976: 265). Widdowson does not support such practices for general EFL courses, but this is not made sufficiently clear in the article. This lack of clarity has caused other authors to indiscriminately adopt and expand the concept into a comprehensive method.

In 1978, Widdowson starts discussing the use of genuine text in general EFL settings. In this context he coins the term *to authenticate*:

> Genuineness is a characteristic of the passage itself and is an absolute quality. Authenticity is a characteristic of the relationship between the passage and the reader and it has to do with appropriate response. One of the difficulties about extracts, then, is that although they are genuine, the fact that they are presented 'as' extracts imposed on the learner for language learning purposes necessarily reduces their authenticity. (Widdowson 1978: 80)

> [T]he learner may simply not feel himself in any way engaged by the text being presented to him and so may refuse to authenticate it by taking an interest. This means, among other things, that the topic of the discourse has to be one which will appeal to the learner in some way. (Widdowson 1978: 80-81)

Authentication is thus framed as a feasible enterprise in the EFL setting. In 1994, however, Widdowson begins to expound immense problems in terms of achieving authentication:

> Over recent years, we have heard persuasive voices insisting that the English presented in the classroom should be authentic, naturally occurring language, not produced for instructional purposes. [...] Now the obvious point about this naturally occurring language is that, inevitably, it is recipient designed and so culturally loaded. It follows that access to its meaning is limited to those insiders who share its cultural presuppositions and a sense of its idiomatic nuance. Those who do not, the outsiders, cannot ratify its authenticity. (Widdowson 1994: 384)

Whereas ESP learners may be considered insiders to a given scientific culture, it is not easy to present general EFL learners with genuine text of which they will have a knowledge of conventions. They will rather find themselves in no position to authenticate the genuine material. According to Widdowson, the category of authentic text reception has very limited benefits with genuine text in the EFL classroom. It is more likely achieved in ESP settings. However, the concept opens up possibilities for contrived text to be authenticated. After all, that may be the sort of text the typical EFL learner is familiar with.

2.4 Individual behavior

Describing individual behavior as authentic is quite different from describing text as such. The criteria of textual authenticity are not transferable: provenance, inherent textual qualities, aspects of post-production, appropriate response. The category of authentic individual behavior is primarily coined by van Lier (1996) who takes up Widdowson's notion of authentication as an individual process within the learner. Gilmore references van Lier as the only source of this category.[21] A close look at van Lier's concept shall therefore be the starting point of this chapter. He asserts that authenticity "has nothing to do with the origination of the linguistic material brought into the classroom" (van Lier 1996: 127). What authenticity is, according to van Lier, can be derived from the following statements:

> In a curious way, it seems to me that the traditional language lessons of the grammar trans-lation type which I remember from my school days might lay greater claim to that sort of authenticity than some of the so-called communicative classrooms that I have had occasion to observe in recent years. I must emphasize that the old lessons seem to have been authentic 'for me, although they may well have been inauthentic for some of my class mates.

> Authentication is basically a personal process of engagement, and it is unclear if a social setting could ever be clearly shown to be authentic for every member involved in it. How-ever, given the privileged status of the teacher, it is reasonable to suggest that a teacher's authenticity may stimulate authenticity in the students as well. In terms of language teach-ing methods, one cannot say that any particular teaching method is more likely to promote authenticity than any other, regardless of whether or not it promotes the use of 'genuine' materials. Rather, the people in the setting, each and every one individually for himself or herself, as well as in negotiation with one another, authenticate the setting and the actions in it. When such authentication occurs en masse, spontaneously or in an orchestrated fash-ion (socially constructed authentication, so to speak), we may well have the most authentic setting possible. A good teacher may be able to promote such authenticity. It may be easier to achieve it in some settings than in others. (van Lier 1996: 128)

Authenticity is seen as the result of authentication, a concept which is borrowed from Widdowson. Van Lier expands this concept beyond text reception by applying it to teach-ing methods and classroom interaction. Out of all the writers contributing to the debate on authenticity van Lier is the only one to refer to notions of authenticity outside EFL by invoking existentialist philosophy. His understanding of authenticity does not lend itself to a concise definition.

> I take as my starting point the existentialist definition of authentic: an action is authentic when it realizes a free choice and is an expression of what a person genuinely feels and believes. An authentic action is intrinsically motivated. Inauthentic action is taken because everyone else is doing them, they 'ought' to be done, or in general they are motivated by external factors. (van Lier 1996: 13)

"[W]hat a person genuinely feels" (ibid.) and what a person is "intrinsically motivated" (ibid.) to do are obviously aspects not easily observed by a teacher in the EFL classroom. The concept is still presented as worthwhile and beneficial, considering that according to van Lier a "good teacher" (van Lier 1996: 128) is able to promote such authenticity. Decke-Cornill (2004) puts forth a comparable concept of authenticity as one of her three categories (*learners acting authentically as themselves* – "Authentizität als selbst-iden-tisches Schülerhandeln"). Unlike van Lier, she outlines some practical implications of the concept's wholesale implementation in the foreign language classroom. One such impli-

---

21   Gilmore choses a longer title for this category than I do: "the interaction between students and teachers [i.e.] a 'personal process of engagement'" (Gilmore 2007: 98).

cation would be that, during group work activities, learners tend to speak their first language because they are not intrinsically motivated to speak English.[22] A teacher who prioritizes individual authenticity will pander to the learners' moods, even if they jar with classroom objectives. The inherent value of the concept is thus called into question. For Decke-Cornill the concept of authentic individual behavior seems to include excrescences causing friction with institutional provisions as well as with obvious language learning objectives (Decke-Cornill 2004: 20-21).

Van Lier's concept, as well as Decke-Cornill's, is entirely learner-centered. The teacher's behavior is regarded only insofar as it influences processes of authentication on the learner's part. Little is said about teacher behavior in concrete terms. A notion similar to van Lier's underlies Johnston's concept of authenticity. However, he specifically focuses on how the teacher reacts to learner utterances:

> An authentic audience is an audience that is concerned exclusively with the meaning of the speaker's message. This criterion discounts the teacher as audience insofar as the teacher is really interested in what forms the learner can produce in native-like ways. When teachers are indeed interested in the meaning of what their students write and say, then they may be seen as an authentic audience. (Johnston 1999: 60-61)

The interplay between teacher and learner is also central to Scrivener/Thornbury (2012) who apply the term *authenticity* to very general patterns of teacher behavior. They suggest it is critical to "find an authentic classroom persona. [...] Authenticity means behaving in a way that is appropriately real, appropriately you – letting the students see something of your genuine reactions to things, your moods and your natural behaviour, rather than covering everything up in a performance" (Scrivener 2012: 36). The question what effect such teacher behavior has on processes of authentication is left untouched. All in all, both Johnston (1999) and Scrivener/Thornbury (2012) may refer to a more non-academic meaning of *authenticity*.

The concept of authentication clearly hearkens back to philosophical notions of authenticity as introduced by Rousseau and developed further by Sartre and Heidegger (Noetzel 1999: 19-40). Its adoption in EFL is heralded by Widdowson's idea of appropriate response (1976). Whereas in Widdowson's early understanding behavior had to be appropriate to the intentions of an author of materials, authenticity is seen by van Lier and others as an individual's behavior being congruent with his or her innermost inclinations, which is a highly philosophical approach. Neither Decke-Cornill (2004) nor Johnston (1999) refer to philosophy. They probably fail to do so because this concept of authenticity has long made its way into colloquial language, as in an *authentic person*. Referencing and explaining is thus considered unnecessary by both authors. Most indicative of this influence of colloquial usage are the statements made by Scrivener/Thornbury (2012).

---

22 Original: "Beobachtungen zum Verhalten auch im bilingualen Unterricht lassen nun aber die Vermutung zu, dass die Schülerinnen und Schüler in Gruppeninteraktionen durchaus Sprachwechsel in ihre Muttersprache vornehmen. Es ist nicht auszuschließen, dass sie gerade in diesen Momenten 'als sie selbst' handeln." (Decke-Cornill 2004: 21)

2.5 Task

In chapter 2.2.2.4, Mishan's (2005) view on authenticity is presented. The essence of her approach is that genuine text must be accompanied by tasks that mirror activities the intended readership – not the language learner – would be likely to do with these texts. She thereby adheres closely to Widdowson's (1976; 1978) notion of appropriate response. Only in conjunction with these tasks does the text become authentic. I elected to categorize Mishan's concept as text authenticity partially because the title of her book, *Designing authenticity into language learning materials* (Mishan 2005), suggests such a focus. Obviously, the tasks themselves would also be described as authentic. In the present chapter, however, I focus on concepts of task authenticity which do not presuppose the use of genuine materials.

Breen (1985) is one of the most important contributors to the discourse on authenticity in EFL. His widely received article (Breen 1985) tackles the issue of task authenticity. In his eyes, after a long period of fixation on authentic materials "the focus shifts towards authenticity of tasks or learning behaviours required in relation to whatever data are offered" (Breen 1985: 64). Breen propounds two different approaches to task authenticity, but does not commit to any one of them. The two concepts are almost irreconcilable. One is the *authentic communication task*. The concept is in line with the then emerging approach of Task-Based Language Teaching (TBLT). Such authentic communication tasks are predicated on the idea that the foreign language should be used exclusively as a means to the end of conveying a message. It should not be the object of analysis. An example given by Breen (1985) is the task of filling out an income tax form. The message conveyed is, in this case, personal information given to the state by the tax payer. Clearly, such tasks lend themselves to the use of authentic materials, but Breen does not mention authentic materials as a prerequisite.

Definitions of authentic task by other authors usually include a reference to the world outside the classroom:

> The definition [...] is that authentic classroom tasks are those which are most like natural communication outside class. (Chapelle 1999: 103)

> [A] task might be said to be authentic if it has a clear relationship with real world needs. (Guariento/Morley 2001: 350)

> Task authenticity refers to tasks that closely mirror communication in the world outside the classroom. (Nunan 2004: 212)

> In order for tasks to be authentic, they should be designed to [...] approximate real-life tasks. (Mishan 2005: 75)

The approximation of real-world tasks is only one defining criterion out of six, according to Mishan (2005). Breen (1985) distances himself from such real-world tasks, yet he maintains the term *authentic communication task* to describe them. Breen's second approach to authenticity is realized in the so-called *authentic language learning task*: If the learner "is asked to do something which most people would never do in the 'real world' [...] it is possible [...] that such apparently inauthentic language-using behaviour might be authentic language learning behaviour" (Breen 1985: 65). Any grammar exercise or drill is thus included in this category. It is obvious that such a concept of authenticity is oppositional to TBLT with its real-world approaches. Breen, thus, applies the term *authentic* to two irreconcilable concepts (Guariento/Morley 2001: 351). While the authentic communication task is widely adopted throughout the literature, the authentic language learning task is rarely called *authentic* by other authors than Breen. Guariento/Morley (2001) provide an extensive overview of task authenticity which is, however, symptomatic of this lopsided resonance to Breen's dichotomous conception. Guariento/Morley's overview is presented at the end of this chapter. Mishan (2010) sees task authenticity as similarly heterogeneous but even she does not include form-focused activities:

> At the pedagogical end of the spectrum, 'authentic tasks' might include a range of classic information gap activities. Further along the continuum come games and play, which [...] are an intrinsic part of both the human experience and of language learning. At the 'real-life' end, come any number of everyday tasks - corresponding with 'e-pal' via email or chat, talking about the meaning or emotional impact of a film or song, making a podcast, writing a blog or story and so on. (Mishan 2010: 152)

One reason for this is the perceived artificiality which occurs when (inauthentic) language learning tasks are allotted using authentic materials, as the following caveats may illustrate:

> When in real life, for example, do people listen to the news with the purpose of noting down how many items are covered? (Guariento/Morley 2001: 349)

> [I]f we clip an article from a newspaper, and bring it to class, then this is a 'genuine' piece of language. Once introduced into the language lesson, we may proceed to ask students to do 'authentic' or 'inauthentic' things with it. Inauthentic things would presumably include such tasks as learning it by heart, conjugating all the verbs in it, or finding three synonyms for every concrete noun in it [...]. It is harder to say what might be authentic uses of the article. (van Lier 1996: 126)

As is the case with textual authenticity, there seems to be a dichotomous underpinning to the conception of task authenticity. The underlying dichotomy of textual authenticity is the producer's intention to either convey a real message or teach a foreign language, as described in chapter 2.2.2.

The complementary opposition with regard to task authenticity consists of *classroom* on the one hand and *real world* on the other. It appears that many representatives of the TBLT orthodoxy see real-world situations as inherently content-driven and genuine communication as an exclusive quality of the real world. Tasks, consequently, must be similar to the proceedings in the real world. Breen (1985) strays from this exclusive understanding. Classroom activities are seen by TBLT proponents as inherently form-focused and tend to include metalanguage. This dichotomy forms an intuitive – yet delusive – congruence with the dichotomous conception of authentic versus pedagogic materials. I have demonstrated above how authors propose the use of authentic materials for real-world activities. The final sentence in the quote above by van Lier hints at the problems of this assumed congruence. Firstly, in the so-called real world reading a newspaper article is not necessarily followed by any particular activity at all. People tend to read the news in order to catch up with the latest events. Sometimes a discussion with friends, relatives, or colleagues will ensue but very often the newly acquired information will not be put to such a tangible use. Secondly, *the real world* is never clearly defined. It appears to be merely contrasted with *the classroom*. What can be quite safely said is that these two terms refer to situations rather than locations. *Classroom* is probably more easily pin-pointed than *real world*. It likely denotes any situation where language instruction takes place – physically speaking, this does not have to be inside a classroom. A broad defini-tion of *real world*, then, works *ex negativo*: any situation where no language instruction is taking place. In this respect, the contrasting definitions display analogies with the def-initions of authentic text versus pedagogic text.

A narrower definition of *real world* may have two possible points of reference. The first possible point of reference is constituted of typical situations native speakers would find themselves in. The second possible point of reference consists of situations the learner is likely to encounter in the future. Either of these two points of reference has been used as a tacit guideline for devising tasks by proponents of TBLT. Breen's (1985) ex-ample of a real-world task, filling out an income tax form, testifies rather to the first point of reference. It is a typical activity of native speakers. The second point of reference has influenced to an enormous extent an entire branch of EFL: English for Specific Purposes (ESP).

> In an ESP group [...] all the members of the class have a common interest, the SP for which they are learning the language. [...] One of the most striking characteristics of groups of ESP learners in my experience is that they have a very clear idea of why they are learning the language, and very little tolerance of anything they consider irrelevant to this purpose. Endless sagas of the Brown family or Martin and Gillian very soon lead to disenchantment among learners whose interest in English is limited to chemical engineering or prehistoric fossils. (Morrow 1977: 14)

The more predictable future language activities are for a group of learners, the more ap-propriate it is to use these predictions as guidelines for devising real-world tasks. Learners in an ESP class are to be prepared for a certain spectrum of situations within a certain occupational field. Crew members on German railway trains, for example, are trained to make announcements in English which are quite predictable and redundant. On a basic level, they will also be expected to talk to passengers in English mainly having to answer questions concerning the train schedule or ticketing. The ESP classroom, therefore, is bound to anticipate real-world situations. It is largely characterized by activities that are authentic in the sense that they are very similar to what is probable to happen outside the classroom.

Unfortunately, future activities are not very predictable for most general EFL classes, which leads Widdowson (1998) to the conclusion that

> except in certain specific cases, there is no way of anticipating [...] encounters in any very precise way. The learners have to learn to fine-tune the appropriate patterns of contextual response for themselves. The purpose of teaching is to get learners to invest in a general capacity for further learning, not to rehearse them in communicative roles they may never be called on to play. A lot of time is wasted in trying to teach things that can only be learned

by experience. The point of pedagogy is not to replicate experience in advance but to prepare learners to learn from it. (Widdowson 1998: 715)

The terms "investing" and "rehearsing" (ibid.) are frequently used in a contrasting way
by Widdowson. While investing is never really fleshed out, rehearsing appears to describe
what I have labeled *real-world tasks*. The quote above serves as an example of how
Widdowson, in one of his later publications, combats the effects of his own former initiative towards promoting appropriate response. A dogmatic task-based implementation of
the idea is apparently not what he had envisioned, especially when applied to general EFL
settings and not ESP.

Lastly, Breen's (1985) eventual conception of task authenticity shall be outlined. As
mentioned before, he is neither in favor of the authentic communication task (real-world
task) nor of the authentic language learning task. Instead, he pleads for a combination of
both:

> [A]n authentic learning task in the language classroom will be one which requires the learn-
> ers to communicate ideas and meanings and to meta-communicate about the language and
> about the problems and solutions in the learning of the language. In sum, tasks can be cho-
> sen which involve the learners not only in authentic communication with texts and with
> others in the classroom, but also about learning and for the purpose of learning. (Breen
> 1985: 66)

> [T]he essential contribution of the classroom is that it is an almost unique social context
> where people meet for the explicit purpose of learning something—from others for them-
> selves. Learning is the main psychological and social function of a classroom. [...] [G]iven
> the actual social potential of a classroom, the contrivance of 'other worlds' within it may
> not only be inauthentic but also quite unnecessary. [...] Perhaps one of the main authentic
> activities within a language classroom is communication about how best to learn to com-
> municate. (Breen 1985: 67-68)

Breen's idea reconciles the two strands *real world* and *classroom*. *Real world* is incorporated in the form of communication. The concept owns up to the fact that language is used
communicatively rather than analytically in the so-called *real world*. Therefore, learners
are required to communicate a great deal with each other and with the teacher when learning a foreign language. *Classroom* is incorporated in the form of content. Unlike many
proponents of TBLT, Breen contends that the highest degree of authenticity is achieved
when learners communicate about topics which are classroom-inherent. The very topic
of learning the foreign language will form an authentic content for communication within
the EFL classroom.

A conceptual overview of task authenticity is provided by Guariento/Morley (2001).
It is not surprising that Breen's concept of authentic language learning task is omitted:

> Authenticity through a genuine purpose
> One of the crucial aspects of task authenticity is whether real communication takes place;
> whether the language has been used for a genuine purpose.
> [...]
> Authenticity through real world targets
> [A] task might be said to be authentic if it has a clear relationship with real world needs
> [...]
> Authenticity through classroom interaction

[...] [I]t is important that the choice and sequence of tasks are negotiated, and it is this very process of negotiation which is authentic.
[...]
Authenticity through engagement
[...] [A]uthenticity of task might be said to depend on whether or not a student is 'engaged' by the task.

(Guariento/Morley 2001: 349-350)

It is hardly conceivable how Breen's (1985) authentic language learning task would be in line with these descriptions, while his authentic communication task clearly is. This omission is a corollary considering that Breen's two initial concepts are all but mutually exclusive. Whoever devises a concept of task authenticity is bound to neglect one of the two, which is usually the authentic language learning task.

2.6 Social situation

The authenticity of a social situation is entirely dependent upon the context. Gilmore (2007) calls this category "the social situation of the classroom" and references five sources: Breen (1985), Arnold (1991), Lee (1995), Guariento/Morley (2001), Rost (2002). Breen is the initiator of this concept, as shown in the preceding chapter. All other references are either unnecessary because they refer to Breen and hardly go beyond his concept (Arnold 1991; Guariento/Morley 2001) or they are inadequate because they do not focus on the social situation (Lee 1995; Rost 2002). Lee, for instance, mentions Breen but the social situation of the classroom is not explicitly brought up. Instead, an empirical study is presented which is based on real-world tasks. Some of the tasks do not require a social setting but are carried out by the students individually, e.g. creating an interview questionnaire or writing a report for a meeting in a professional work setting (Lee 1995: 327). Consequently, it appears misguided that Gilmore would reference Lee in this context. Rost (2002) is concerned with developing the listening skill. In the context of authenticity he leans toward real-world approaches and genuine language input in Widdowson's sense (Rost 2002: 167).

Breen's (1985) understanding of authenticity in the context of tasks is presented above. It is essentially a combination of communicative activities with classroom topics: The teacher and the learners should communicate about the immediate topic of learning the foreign language or about other content considered inherent to the classroom setting. Whether this sort of communication is devised as a task or whether it comes naturally is an important detail. In fact, Breen (1985) suggests that such topics lay claim to authenticity because learners will find them relevant in the given situation. However, the concept is meant to be learner-centered, which makes Breen's assumption a tenuous one. Even though it seems plausible that such topics will be of interest to the learners, there can be no guarantee. Imposing the topic is never completely learner-oriented, even if presumably relevant content is chosen. If in a given situation the learners do not feel engaged by the topic of language learning, they must be granted the freedom to choose a different topic for communication. Breen's (1985) concept would then display a strong affinity with the alternative method of Community Language Learning where the learners are free to converse about topics they choose (Richards/Rodgers 2001: 90-99). Besides the topics to be treated in class, Breen's main emphasis is on "the authentic social potential of the classroom" (Breen 1985: 68). Communication between the stakeholders is a key element of his concept. What should take place is an active exchange of thoughts within the EFL classroom. Only then can the social situation of the classroom be called authentic. This comprehensive idea cannot be said to resonate with the other references given by Gilmore (2007) under this category. This conceptual discrepancy is in place due to the classroom element (topics) rather than due to the communicative element (which easily lends itself to real-world approaches and CLT in general).

At this juncture, one viewpoint must be mentioned which makes an even stronger case for what I call *classroom authenticity*. Van Lier disengages this concept from any aspect of communication (chapter 2.4). The central idea is that the classroom remains recognizable as such:

> [T]he classroom can be a laboratory, a window on the language world, an arena for action, a planning center, and many things besides. But in being any or all of those things, the classroom should never have to deny being a classroom. (van Lier 1996: 139)

This entails that classroom authenticity does not necessarily require social interaction. Learners may feel engaged by a grammar exercise which is done individually and does not include communication. Van Lier is thus the only author to tacitly incorporate Breen's authentic language learning task in his concept of authenticity. His statement "that the traditional language lessons of the grammar translation type which I remember from my school days might lay greater claim to that sort of authenticity than some of the so-called communicative classrooms" (van Lier 1996: 128) accords a certain degree of legitimacy to form-focused activities. Van Lier opposes the view that only real-world activities can be authentic, but attributes the classroom with its traditional tasks its own reality and authenticity.

Gilmore's (2007) categories of task authenticity and social situation of the classroom are difficult to demarcate. It would probably be more sensible if all the subsumed concepts were rearranged along the lines of real-world authenticity and classroom authenticity.

2.7 Assessment

Authentic assessment has been conceived differently within EFL, as is summarized by Bachman:

> One approach, for example has been to define it as direct, in the sense of getting at the ability without going through an intermediate representation of the ability. [...] A second approach has been to define authenticity in terms of similarity to real life. [...] A third approach to defining authenticity is to appeal to what was once called face validity, which is really nothing more than face appeal. [...] This definition refers to a purely subjective response on the part of the evaluator [...]. (Bachman 1991: 689-690)

Bachman dismiss these approaches as either difficult to implement or generally misguided. Instead, two complementary types of authenticity are propounded: situational and interactional authenticity.

> We define situational authenticity as the perceived relevance of the test method characteristics to the features of a specific target language use situation. Thus, for a test task to be perceived as situationally authentic, the characteristics of the test task need to be perceived as corresponding to the features of a target language use situation. (Bachman 1991: 690)

The author concedes a similarity between this concept and the real-world approach (Bachman: "real-life approach" – ibid.), the latter of which is rejected. He affirms situational authenticity to be more flexible than real-world approaches, which are described as prototypical and monolithic. Situational authenticity, as is claimed, responds to specific learner needs. It may actually be suited for ESP courses. However, this is not made explicit and the separation from the real-world approach remains vague.

Interactional authenticity, which is the second type proclaimed by Bachman, requires test takers to use a large array of skills and competencies. These may include non-language skills such as planning. Therefore, "[t]asks should consist of multiple, sequential subtasks" and "[g]oal setting and planning should be required at the beginning of the task" (Bachman 1991: 697). Unlike most concepts of textual authenticity, "both situational and interactional authenticity are relative, so that we speak of 'low' or 'high' authenticity, rather than 'authentic' and 'inauthentic'" (Bachman 1991: 692).

This two-pronged concept of authenticity is later adapted, as Bachman/Palmer (1996) focus on the situational aspect while devising the concept of interactiveness alongside authenticity.

> We define 'authenticity' as the degree of correspondence of the characteristics of a given language test task to the features of a TLU [target language use] task. [...] Authenticity thus provides a means for investigating the extent to which score interpretations generalize beyond performance on the test to language use in the TLU domain, or to other similar nontest language use domains. This links authenticity to construct validity, since investigating the generalizability of score interpretations is an important part of construct validation. (Bachman/Palmer 1996: 23-24)

The conceptual alignment with real-world authenticity is thus furthered. This understanding corresponds to what other authors consider to be authentic assessment (Brown 2004: 28):

> Essentially, when you make a claim for authenticity in a test task, you are saying that this task is likely to be enacted in the 'real world'. Many test item types fail to simulate real-world tasks. They may be contrived or artificial in their attempt to target a grammatical form or a lexical item. The sequencing of items that bear no relationship to one another lacks authenticity. [...]
>
> In a test, authenticity may be present in the following ways:
> - The language in the test is as natural as possible.
> - Items are contextualized rather than isolated.
> - Topics are meaningful (relevant, interesting) for the learner.
> - Some thematic organization to items is provided, such as through a story line or episode.
> - Tasks represent, or closely approximate, real-world tasks.

Lewkowicz confirms that in the context of authentic assessment the situational aspect would prove far more influential than the interactional one (Lewkowicz 2000: 48). Lewkowicz conducted a study with 72 university students who were attending academic English courses. The students were to take two tests: The first test was arguably inauthentic, designed mainly in a multiple-choice format and divided into different sections (grammar, vocabulary, written expression etc.). The second test was more integrated and consisted of note-taking while listening, writing, synthesizing – all in all, it could be called situationally authentic in that it resembled many of the tasks the students would have to master as part of their university course. The study endeavored to find out about the students' perceptions of these tests and, specifically, about the degree of authenticity they would ascribe to them. Overall, the results were quite mixed and led Lewkowicz to believe that "[a]uthenticity would appear not to be universally important for test takers" (Lewkowicz 2000: 48). In conclusion, she states that "there may be a mismatch between the importance accorded to authenticity by language testing experts and other stakeholders in the testing process. Authenticity may be of theoretical importance for language testers needing to ensure that they can generalize from test to non-test situations, but not so important for other stakeholders in the testing process" (ibid.).

While it remains unclear whether situational authenticity is desirable, it appears futile to survey test takers on their perceptions. Even if the results are such that a high degree of situational fit is perceived and confirmed by the test takers, practical implications are difficult to infer. After all, test takers may be in a position to say (a) whether authenticity is achieved – and whether they find this authenticity to be desirable – yet almost certainly they will lack the expertise to judge (b) whether authenticity is important as an objective assessment criterion (Lewkowicz 2000: 53-61).

The value of situational authenticity (or real-world authenticity) seems to be a general consensus among assessment experts. However, the term *authentic* has been used to cover various other approaches. Farrell, in deliberating on approaches to reading assessment, appears to equate authenticity with anything "out of the ordinary":

> Rather than using the more traditional approaches outlined earlier in the chapter, teachers of reading to ELLs may thus want to consider using the following authentic reading assessment methods:
>
> - Portfolios
> - Peer assessment
> - Self-reports
> - Anecdotal records
> - Attitude scales
> - Informal reading inventory
>
> [...] Another alternative and authentic reading assessment is the involvement of peers in the assessment process. ELLs evaluate each other on aspects of reading that include levels of reading participation, work samples, and behavior in class. (Farrell 2009: 95-96)

Irrespective of the exact denotation, "one feature of authenticity upon which there has been general agreement over time is that it is an important quality for test development"

(Lewkowicz 2000: 43-44) or, as Shohamy states in as early as 1985: "The topic of 'authentic tests' has become so popular in recent years that it is hard to believe that a little more than a decade ago it was not an issue at all" (Shohamy/Reves 1985: 48).

2.8 Culture

Gilmore's (2007) last category, cultural authenticity, is justifiably listed at the bottom for it is not overly present in the literature. It appears to be a concept carried over from the academic field of ethnology and possibly also from a colloquial denotation of authenticity. Among ethnographers, the idea of cultural authenticity has been controversial as of late. Van Ede explains how the concept has long been subject to an essentialist understanding:

> The idea that each culture contains a certain authentic essence and that it is the task of the researcher to lay bare this essence has long been the sine qua non of the ethnographic endeavour. [...] Cultural anthropology has inherited a conceptualisation of 'culture' as an unchangeable bounded entity that is somehow organically attached to a particular people and territory. In recent years, this 'essentialist' understanding of authenticity has been fiercely criticized in academic circles. (van Ede 2004: 5)

Geurds describes today's understanding of cultural authenticity as pliable and in constant flux (Geurds 2013: 1-2). Yet, it is the old essentialist concept that has seen some popularity in EFL. Considering that intercultural learning is a central pillar of EFL, it is quite surprising that *authentic/authenticity* is not a prolific term in this area.[23] In fact, the hackles of some EFL authors are raised by a skepticism of the essentialist approaches. To explain Gilmore's acknowledgement of cultural authenticity, I first present some of the early voices backing the concept and then go on to elaborate on the concept itself.

> The activities of a domain are framed by its culture. Their meaning and purpose are socially constructed through negotiations among present and past members. Activities thus cohere in a way that is, in theory, if not always in practice, accessible to members who move within the social framework. These coherent, meaningful, and purposeful activities are authentic, according to the definition of the term we use here. Authentic activities then, are most simply defined as the ordinary practices of the culture. (Brown/Collins/Duguid 1989: 34)

> Suppose that one of our objectives as humanists is to impart an empathic understanding of a foreign culture, and that we want to pursue authenticity to its limits. [...] Authentic examples and anecdotes can produce understanding, but only through the long process of inductive reasoning from cases to generalization about a defined universe of data. Students should certainly practice this process in both high school and college, by means of exercises where they study in depth a small, manageable corpus of authentic examples. They need to learn by experience how responsible generalizations are created. (Nostrand 1989: 50)

Nostrand's idea that generalizations on a foreign culture can be derived inductively like a grammatical structure is at least to some extent rooted in the essentialist view outlined by van Ede. Authentic materials ("corpus of authentic examples" ibid.) appear to be seen as an important means in this process. Kienbaum/Russell/Welty consider them "the raw

---

23   (Kramsch 1993: 177): "It is a truism to say that teaching a language is teaching culture."

data of a culture, and the students' ability to understand that culture will depend upon their ability to interpret that data" (Kienbaum/Russell/Welty 1986: 8). What is to be learned from them, according to the authors, is the authentic essence in activity and behavior of a given culture, as described by Stevick in an empirical study:

> As Bert reads authentic materials written by and for Chinese people, he is not only picking up how the purely linguistic elements fit together; he is also finding out what meanings exist in Chinese life that do not exist in his native culture, and how some of these meanings are connected to one another [...]. (Stevick 1989: 26-27)

Most of these advocacies of the essentialist view date from the 1980s. They may be less common today. Greater attention is devoted to this question in the chronological discourse analysis (chapter 5).

The concept is granted a category of its own by Gilmore (2007), but even Gilmore's one single reference, Kramsch (1993), is swift in describing the concept and then goes on in detail about how such an understanding is misguided.[24] Kramsch ultimately resolves to "leave aside questions of 'authenticity'" (Kramsch 1993: 184). Decke-Cornill is equally dismissive of the concept. Target culture activities (e.g. baking scones), when transferred into the classroom, will "turn into exotica, into folkloristic matter" (Decke-Cornill 2004: 20).[25]

The essentialist view on cultural authenticity in EFL appears to embrace authentic materials as valuable artefacts transporting the target culture into the classroom. The ethnographic pattern is evident here. I distinguish between texts and materials (cf. chapter 2.2). At this juncture the distinction is important. Text itself is an intangible entity until it is made into material such as a printed book. Having described authentic text as the primary concept of authenticity in EFL, authentic materials are located at the interface between textual authenticity and cultural authenticity because they combine authentic text with the culturally authentic qualities of the given artefact. Having said that cultural authenticity does not play a big role in the EFL discourse, the term *authentic materials* appears to be used frequently in a way that implies a certain cultural value, one that goes beyond purely textual authenticity. Grellet's statement is indicative of this notion:

> Authenticity means that nothing of the original text is changed and also that its presentation and layout are retained. A newspaper article, for instance, should be presented as it first appeared in the paper; with the same typeface, the same space devoted to the headlines, the same accompanying picture. (Grellet 1981: 8)

What is highlighted about authentic materials is their cultural authenticity to the same degree as the textual one. Some even use the term *cultural* in describing the materials – either in combination with the term *authentic* or without it.

---

24 Gilmore references Kramsch (1998), not Kramsch (1993), in his list but has no title from that year in his bibliography. This is probably a clerical mistake. Kramsch (1993) discusses authenticity at length.

25 Original: "Aber im Kontext einer hiesigen Schule wird das zum Exotikum, zum folkloristischen Fremdkörper." (Decke-Cornill 2004: 20)

The contexts for language practice should be devised, as much as possible, from culturally authentic sources. [...] The proficiency-oriented classroom will incorporate such material frequently and effectively at all levels. (Omaggio Hadley 1993: 80)

the concept of 'cultural products' [...] is adopted in this book as the superonym for the materials drawn from a variety of media and genres from the target culture. (Mishan 2005: XII)

Kienbaum/Russell/Welty speak of artefacts: "Authentic materials [...] are genuine artifacts such as timetables, newspapers, magazines, letters, hotel guides, restaurant menus, bills, essays, leaflets, recorded interviews, radio and television broadcasts, advertisements and films" (Kienbaum/Russell/Welty 1986: 7-8).

Incidentally, Widdowson (1994) displays notions of essentialism in his description of culture, distinguishing between insiders and outsiders to a culture. This view, however, leads him – as opposed to most other authors – to object to the use of authentic materials:

> Over recent years, we have heard persuasive voices insisting that the English presented in the classroom should be authentic, naturally occurring language [...]. Now the obvious point about this naturally occurring language is that, inevitably, it is recipient designed and so culturally loaded. It follows that access to its meaning is limited to those insiders who share its cultural presuppositions and a sense of its idiomatic nuance. Those who do not, the outsiders, cannot ratify its authenticity. In other words, the language is only authentic in the original conditions of its use, it cannot be in the classroom. The authenticity is non-transferable. And to the extent that students cannot therefore engage with the language, they cannot make it their own. It may be real language, but it is not real to them. It does not relate to their world but to a remote one they have to find out about by consulting a dictionary of culture. (Widdowson 1994: 384)

To sum up, the concept of cultural authenticity in EFL is an essentialist one and there are two strands to be distinguished: culturally authentic behavior and culturally authentic materials. The first concept has been harshly criticized and is today all but extinct, i.e. it is no longer referred to as *authentic* in the literature. The second concept is tied to the concept of authentic text, which is still the most viral concept to date. Many authors use the terms *authentic text* and *authentic materials* interchangeably. Therefore, it is often not clear whether textual authenticity or cultural authenticity is meant. All in all, authentic materials seem to be seen by many as combining the best of both worlds.

3   A conceptual taxonomy

Using Gilmore's (2007) list for orientation, a new conceptual taxonomy for authenticity in EFL is put forward in this chapter. Gilmore does not really claim to take a conceptual approach. His list is rather terminological in that it presents what authors have called authentic. Gilmore asserts to compile what "meanings emerge from the literature" (Gilmore 2007: 98) but his list is constituted of quotes from the different authors referenced. Gilmore's criterion, thus, seems to be a rather linguistic one. I have demonstrated how different terms may denote the same concept and vice versa. If two authors speak of *authentic tasks* meaning different things, they will still fall in the same category of Gilmore's list. Similarly, the term *authentic materials* may imply qualities of textual authenticity or qualities of cultural authenticity. Gilmore does not respond to these instances of mismatch between term and concept (or between *signifiant* and *signifié*).

My taxonomy is the result of a conceptual analysis of the discourse. This means that a given terminological label is not taken at face value. Rather, the underlying concepts are scrutinized and compared. However, the term *authentic/authenticity* – most typically as part of a collocation – will remain the common guideline of my analysis, meaning that I am not looking at concepts that are not described as authentic by a given author. For some categories in my taxonomy I will refer back to Gilmore and explain the possible differences from his categorization. Like Gilmore's categories, the categories in my taxonomy are interrelated, yet to a slightly lesser extent. After all, one of the main deficiencies to be identified with Gilmore's list is the lumping together of concepts based on the terminological approach taken. Areas of conceptual overlap will be of particular interest in the upcoming descriptions.

3.1   Textual authenticity

This category combines the first two of Gilmore's (2007) categories, i.e. "(i) the language produced by native speakers for native speakers in a particular language community [...]" (Gilmore 2007: 98) and "(ii) the language produced by a real speaker/writer for a real audience, conveying a real message" (ibid.). Textual authenticity could be treated in a far more differentiated manner. The intricacies of this concept are laid out extensively in chapter 2.2.2. For the sake of synopsis, however, Gilmore's dichotomous representation is rather misleading since it draws dividing lines that are difficult to justify. I thus propose a subsumption under the umbrella of *textual authenticity*. By and large, textual authenticity as a concept is quite distinct showing relatively little overlap with the other categories in this taxonomy. It is also the most wide-spread concept in the discourse to date.

3.2   Authenticity of text reception

This category is the equivalent of Gilmore's third category, i.e. "(iii) the qualities bestowed on a text by the receiver, in that it is not seen as something inherent in a text itself, but is imparted on it by the reader/listener" (Gilmore 2007: 98). Authentic text reception is a concept predicated on Widdowson's (1978) idea of authentication. Few authors have adopted this concept wholesale but it has served widely as a springboard for the conceptualization of other new concepts. Essentially, Widdowson conceives of it as a way of dealing with text in a language learning situation that does justice to the intentions of the author. In ESP courses, where authentic text is used, form-focused activities will not be considered authentic because it is assumed that the author of an authentic text has not created his/her product with such purposes in mind.

The category has a small area of overlap with textual authenticity in that some authors declare texts to be authentic only once they are put to appropriate use. A larger area of overlap is to be found with the category of real-world authenticity: If authentic text is used, the activities done with it should mirror activities typically done by the target audience of the text at hand. Mishan (2005) pursues this approach most strictly.

3.3 Real-world authenticity

At this point, Gilmore's categorization is revised. His categories of interaction, task, social situation, and assessment are each conceptually very heterogeneous and prone to interface with one another. The concept of real-world authenticity is most commonly found in the context of Task-Based Language Teaching (TBLT). As shown above, a considerable number of authors consider tasks to be authentic if they reflect procedures and situations from outside the classroom. A conceptual dichotomy between real-world and classroom is discernible. While *classroom* stands for stereotypical language learning activities such as pattern drills, *real world* refers to communicative activities. Typically, such activities mimic the activities commonly done by English native speakers in everyday situations or activities the given learners are predicted to do in the future. A weaker form of real-world authenticity is claimed for communicative activities in the classroom that lack similarity to either of these two referential schemata. For example, an information gap activity where two learners talk about pictures trying to find differences in them is not likely to be done by native speakers nor is it a likely future situation for the learners. Still, communication alone is seen as a feature of the real world as opposed to form-focused exercises. Such communication is sometimes referred to as *meaningful*.

The category of real-world authenticity has some overlap with textual authenticity in that authentic texts are intended for native speakers and thus for real-world practices (e.g. reading/listening for pleasure). The same is true for cultural authenticity because the target culture is a native-speaking culture.

3.4 Classroom authenticity

Classroom authenticity is the polar opposite of real-world authenticity. This means that activities and situations, which are typically done in the EFL classroom, are called authentic. A strong form of classroom authenticity is present in exercises with an extreme focus on the formal features of the language, specifically grammar. Only one statement in favor of this strong form can be found (van Lier 1996: 128). A weaker form is either identified in activities that cover grammar in a functional manner or in activities that are communicative and meaningful but deal with classroom-specific contents. The latter approach is championed by Breen (1985) who supports a high degree of communication in the classroom but suggests that the topics should revolve around the very processes of learning the foreign language in order to be called authentic. This concept – especially in its strong form – arguably has the least overlap with any of the other categories.

Since very few authors invoke the concept of classroom authenticity, no recurrent linguistic signifiers are found. Instead, I will exemplify how the concept is codified by quoting Breen, who is its main proponent. If a lexical pattern is observable, it is really the proximity of *authentic/authenticity* and *classroom*:

> [G]iven the actual social potential of a classroom, the contrivance of 'other worlds' within it may not only be inauthentic but also quite unnecessary. (Breen 1985: 67)

> The authenticity of the classroom is that it is a rather special social event and environment wherein people share a primary communicative purpose: learning. (Breen 1985: 67-68)

> [T]he language teacher and the language learner are immersed in the potential authenticity of the classroom 'as a classroom'. (Breen 1985: 68)

> Perhaps one of the main authentic activities within a language classroom is communication about how best to learn to communicate. (ibid.)

3.5 Authenticity of individual behavior

This concept is philosophical in origin. It corresponds to Gilmore's fourth category, i.e. "(iv) [...] 'personal process of engagement'" (Gilmore 2007: 98). An individual's behavior is deemed authentic not by virtue of conforming with the schemata of either real world or classroom. Rather, authenticity is achieved by the individual if he or she is free to be himself or herself – or if a given design caters to the inclinations of the individual. As a consequence, the concept is vague and flexible. It appears quite similar to the notion of authentication which is also an individual process.

Overlap with the other concepts is entirely contingent on what is considered likely to stimulate authentication on part of the learner. Opinions in the literature are divided on what approaches best engage the learner.

3.6 Cultural authenticity

The concept of cultural authenticity instantiates in two possible ways, both of which are predicated on an essentialist understanding of culture. The first refers to patterns of behavior stereotypically ascribed to a target culture (behavioral cultural authenticity). The second is ethnographic in that it refers to materials from the target culture (ethnographic cultural authenticity). Such materials are considered authentic not so much because of their linguistic qualities but because they are assumed to function as an ethnic artefact transporting the target culture into the EFL classroom.

One primary area of overlap can be identified for each of the two understandings of cultural authenticity, the behavioral one and the ethnographic one. Behavioral cultural authenticity tallies with one of the two schemata of real-world authenticity, namely with the schema of prototypical native-speaker behavior. Ethnographic cultural authenticity, i.e. the idea of cultural artefacts, is prone to interface with textual authenticity because authors tend to confound the terms *authentic text* and *authentic materials*, as mentioned in chapter 2.8.

3.7 Elaborations on the conceptual taxonomy

It is important to quarry the concepts that lie underneath the term *authentic/authenticity*. The term itself merely acts as an overarching signifier that marks my field of research. Unlike Gilmore's (2007) rather terminological approach, I use the linguistic criterion only insofar as the term *authentic/authenticity* (also *authentication*) must be included in the signifying code in order for me to investigate the corresponding *signifié*. The process of categorization itself is purely conceptual, having yielded a taxonomy of all those concepts commonly referred to as authentic in EFL. The conceptual focus is considered expedient because the relation between term and concept is inconsistent in many instances throughout the literature. As a consequence, some of the newly developed categories carry titles that are not to be found with any of the authors. In the case of classroom authenticity, for example, longer stretches are quoted to evidence a codified pattern linking the term *authentic/authenticity* with the given concept. Breen (1985) himself never uses the specific term *classroom authenticity*.

The conceptual approach has also yielded the omission of Gilmore's (2007) category of authentic assessment. *Authentic assessment* and *authentic testing* have been identified as signifiers denoting a concept which is almost entirely covered by the category of real-world authenticity. The terms themselves loom large in the discourse creating the impression of a distinct concept. The conceptual kinship, however, suggests a merging of categories. While Bachman (1991) propounds a rather complex concept of authentic assessment, the dominant understanding in the discourse is still too close to the real-world approaches to grant authentic assessment a category of its own.

For the sake of visual ease the taxonomy is presented in the form of a graphic table (figure 5). To exemplify areas of overlap I have highlighted two subcategories which are almost identical. All other instances of overlap are too subtle or intricate to be represented visually without making the table considerably more complex. They are explained in the descriptions of the respective categories above.

Concept	Subdivision	
1. Textual authenticity		
2. Authenticity of text reception		
3. Real-world authenticity	a) Typical activities of native-speakers	
	b) Typical activities of the learners in the future	
4. Classroom authenticity		
5. Authenticity of individual behavior		
6. Cultural authenticity	a) Behavioral cultural authenticity	
	b) Ethnographic cultural authenticity	

Figure 5: A taxonomy of conceptual authenticity in EFL

The order of the categories in the taxonomy needs explaining. The precise reasons for ranking one concept before another is best expounded after a detailed chronological analysis of the discourse, which affords additional insights. The following points are kept purposely simple to give just an overall understanding of the sequencing factors. Three criteria have led to the decisions made in this regard:

1. Relevance
2. Affinity to adjacent categories
3. Chronology

It may be assumed that the same factors influenced Gilmore's (2007) order of listing, although this cannot be verified. After all, my taxonomy is not too different from his as regards the order of the categories.

Relevance of the individual concept is the most important criterion. The question is how prolific a given concept has been in the discourse in terms of explicit and implicit negotiation. In other words, to what an extent do authors refer to the concept of textual authenticity as opposed to, say, cultural authenticity? The second criterion, affinity to adjacent categories, guarantees a certain coherence within the taxonomy. It allowed me to explain the categories one by one without having to change topics beyond a certain degree of smooth readability. The third criterion, chronology, refers to the point in time when the corresponding concept came up or was most present.

Picking textual authenticity as the first concept of the list is a straightforward choice based on relevance and chronology. I illustrate in the chronological discourse analysis (chapter 5) how robust the concept has stayed over time. At no point can it be said to have lost its foremost presence in the discourse. It is also one of the earliest concepts to be consistently denoted as authentic, if not the first. The second concept, authenticity of text reception, is markedly less relevant than the first. The lone criterion of relevance would probably not justify its second position in the taxonomy. However, its initiator, Widdowson, is anxious to link the concept to that of textual authenticity. It can actually be seen as an adaptation of textual authenticity so its affinity to the adjacent category plays a role. Even though the relevance of the concept in and of itself is little, its influence on the discourse should be considered enormous. The concept was put forth as early as in 1976 by Widdowson. Thus, the chronological criterion applies to a certain extent. The third concept, real-world authenticity, is arguably the second most relevant one. However, it bears little affinity with textual authenticity and emerged after authenticity of text reception, leading me to list it in third position. Classroom authenticity follows up real-world authenticity despite its rather marginal status. Proponents of the concept contrast it with the preceding category, which makes it expedient to mention the two concepts in immediate succession. What is more, both concepts are often codified along the lines of authentic tasks and activities, which reinforces the connection. Authenticity of individual behavior is one of the more ancillary concepts. Lastly, cultural authenticity as a concept is seldom invoked. In its behavioral form, specifically, it is met with strong criticism. The ethnographic aspect is potentially implied in *authentic materials* but rarely is it made explicit.

4   Methodology

In this study, I have chosen to start out *medias in res*, as outlined in the introduction. It is essential that the concepts of authenticity be known to the reader prior to the explanations on how the underlying discourse is structured. The upcoming methodological elaborations presuppose this knowledge on the reader's part so that, henceforth, single patterns and developments can be exemplified with the concepts already established. Thus far, findings have been presented in a traditional manner, i.e. accompanied by only a few indications as to how they transpired. Such approaches are common practice in scholarly discourse, as will be demonstrated. The lack of systematicity refers to a negligence of analytical rigor and transparency regarding the discourse under scrutiny. This negligence may lead to an uneven representation of works cited where obscure publications receive the same weight as mainstream ones, leaving important aspects such as power relations and authorial stance unaccounted for. That is why a more in-depth analysis of the discourse is called-for.

The research interest of this study can therefore be phrased in terms of the following questions:

1) What is/was considered authentic in EFL (English as a Foreign Language)?
2) How have these concepts of authenticity evolved over time?
3) What concepts of authenticity were pursued in the history of EFL, including those times when the term itself did not exist?

Questions 1) and 2) are largely dealt with by means of discourse analysis. This method allows for deeper insights than a common literature review. My discourse analytical approach systematically analyzes such aspects as authorial stance (chapter 4.3.1), power relations (chapter 4.2.2), authorial style (chapter 4.3.1), and citations (chapter 4.3.2).

Question 3) is focused on those concepts, which are commonly referred to as *authentic* in the EFL discourse but which actually existed before the term was coined. These concepts are traced by means of historical research to find out how prevalent they were in different periods of time prior to their christening as *authenticity*. As a starting point of the historical research, the year 1668 is chosen, which marks the earliest documented account of institutional English teaching in Germany.

A mixed methods approach is thus taken. However, the different methods used are not pursued to an equal degree. There is a strong slant towards discourse analysis because this method is specifically fit to reveal information pertaining to the questions of what the term *authentic/authenticity* means in EFL and of how these meanings are negotiated – questions 1) and 2) above. A minor part of the study is conducted by means of historical research – question 3). Technically speaking, my discourse analytical research is also historical because, in most cases, the point in time when a statement was made is of central interest. This puts me in a position to trace temporal developments in the discourse instead of just linking statements thematically regardless of when they were made.

By researching scholarly literature I try to extrapolate denotations and connotations of the term *authentic/authenticity* within the academic field of EFL. However, the EFL discourse goes beyond academic publications. The term is equally used by EFL teachers as well as by EFL textbook publishers advertising their products. These two groups of people are assumed to have some connection with the scholarly discourse, e.g. during their studies at university. Consequently, interrelations between their use of the term and the EFL scholars' use of the term are probable. Teachers and textbook publishers are therefore considered to form a discourse adjacent to the scholarly discourse. As mentioned, the term is widely used beyond EFL. Everyday language avails itself of it as well as various academic disciplines. A graphic representation of the discourses is given in chapter 4.4.4.

Different analytical tools are needed for each of the discourses just described. The differences lie in the idiosyncratic qualities of each discourse but also in the research interest of the study at hand. Since the scholarly EFL discourse is of primary concern, the corresponding research method must yield more detailed and more rigorous results than the methods used to investigate the other discourses. The latter are analyzed with the aim of gleaning the most common denotations and connotations of the term so the concepts can be compared to those within the EFL scholarly discourse. After all, one can safely assume interrelations between all these discourses.

In the upcoming chapters, I present and elaborate on those methods which are essentially discourse analytical. Methods of historical research, which pertain to question 3), are explained at a later point. Finally, no interest is taken in any sort of practical evaluation of teaching methods. No classroom action has been observed to see whether, for instance, authentic communication takes place. Equally, no teachers have been interviewed about their views on different concepts of authenticity and perceived practical benefits. The study at hand is, therefore, not empirical in the conventional sense. Still, my discourse analytical tools include sampling (chapter 4.5.1). The sample is mainly constituted of academic publications in the field of foreign language education, especially EFL.

4.1 Discourse analysis as theory and method

In the present chapter, discourse analysis is presented as an overarching means of investigation. Since the discourse under scrutiny is highly idiosyncratic, a progression is pursued from the general to the specific, and from the theoretical to the practical. The chapter at hand forms the starting point of this sequence by outlining the most generally applicable theories.

The aim of discourse analysis is to reveal structures of form and content within written and spoken processes of communication (Landwehr 2008: 15-16).[26] My focus is on these

---

26   Original: "[…] [O]bwohl die allgemeinen Verwendungsweisen von ‚Diskurs' sehr weit gestreut sind, richtet sich sein (reflektierter) wissenschaftlicher Einsatz immer auf Untersuchungen des Sprach- und Zeichengebrauchs, ob es sich dabei nun um mündliche oder schriftliche Aussagen, konkrete Kommunikationsprozesse, die Analyse größerer Textkorpora oder die Untersuchung bildlicher und akustischer Medien handelt." (Landwehr 2008: 15–16)

structures only insofar as they apply to statements on authenticity. My general approach to discourse analysis is guided by what Jørgensen/Phillips suggest in a concise manner:

> In discourse analytical research, the primary exercise is not to sort out which of the statements about the world in the research material are right and which are wrong (**although a critical evaluation can be carried out at a later stage in the analysis [1]**). On the contrary, the analyst has to work with what has actually been said or written, **exploring patterns in and across the statements [2]** and identifying the social consequences of different discursive representations of reality. In working with discourses close to oneself with which one is very familiar, it is particularly difficult to treat them 'as' discourses, that is, as socially constructed meaning-systems that could have been different. Because analysts are often part of the culture under study, they share many of the taken-for-granted, common-sense understandings expressed in the material. The difficulty is that it is precisely the common-sense understandings that are to be investigated: analysis focuses on how some statements are accepted as true or 'naturalised', and others are not. Consequently, **it is fruitful to try to distance oneself from one's material and, for instance, imagine oneself as an anthropologist who is exploring a foreign universe of meaning in order to find out what makes sense there [3]**. (Jørgensen/Phillips 2002: 21) (emphases added by L.W.)

I have put three passages in bold print – [1], [2] and [3]:

- [2] encapsulates my general approach.
- [1], which refers to a personal evaluation of the discourse (and potentially a personal contribution to it), will be considered only in the final part of this study.
- [3] is important for I am not only the analyst but at the same time a member of the discourse community. Firstly, the aspect of distancing is a way of avoiding the possibility of bias. Secondly, to assure transparency about my position in the discourse I provide some relevant information about myself in chapter 5.1.

My methodology is predicated on Saussure's dichotomous model of *signifiant* and *signifié* (1916) (Jørgensen/Phillips 2002: 9-10). The many concepts of authenticity are described applying this theory. The approach is considered particularly appropriate because I do not focus on one single concept, but endeavor to provide a holistic analysis. However, some concepts of authenticity – like Widdowson's notion of authentication – are too complex to be adequately represented using Saussure's dichotomy. Badger/MacDonald (2010), therefore, state that their "conceptualization of authenticity [...] is hard to reconcile with a Saussurean [...] view of language as comprising a signifier and a signified. It fits in better with a Piercean view [...] of language as something which stands to somebody for something in some respect or capacity" (Badger/MacDonald 2010: 581). The Piercean model appears serviceable for the single case analysis of certain concepts like Widdowson's concept of authentication. The study at hand, however, envisions a comparison of multiple concepts that are each tied to one overarching signifier. Saussure's model provides the clarity of structure needed for a comprehensive representation of the discourse. As regards the signified, which is indeed vague or fleeting in many cases, a flexible approach must be adopted. Pierce's theory is considered helpful in that regard.

The most prominent theorist associated with discourse as an investigative field is Michel Foucault. Any rigorous deliberation on discourse is bound to draw on the works of Foucault, who has provided the theoretical groundwork for discourse analytical practices. His thoughts on the topic are prolific. An understanding of discourse must be derived from his many writings, which include vast conceptual elaborations and multiple modifications over time (Landwehr 2008: 66).[27] Foucault identified overarching regularities in the behavior of natural scientists, economists, and grammarians. These regularities apply to acts of defining and investigating objects, constructing terminology, and building theories in the respective fields. By way of approximation, discourse can be described as the pattern allowing these people concerted acts in thinking, speaking, and acting (Landwehr 2008: 67).[28] Discourses are institutionalized ways of communicating which are not of interest as objects, e.g. their language, but as actions. Foucault stresses the facilitating function of discourse that comes with institutionalization:

> The desire says: 'I don't want to have to enter into this unpredictable structure of discourse.' [...]
>
> And the institution responds: 'You don't have to make the start. We are all here to show you that the discourse follows rules; that for a long time we have been taking care of its appearance; that a place has been made for it, which honors it but also disarms it; and that if it were to gain some power, this power is invested by us and by us only.[29] (Foucault 1971: 9)

Discourse is thus not governed by one central power but by the myriad of individuals contributing to it (Landwehr 2008: 76).[30] Foucault speaks of discursive formations when a certain number of utterances can be ascribed to a system of diffusion and when the objects of discourse reveal a certain pattern:

> A discursive formation will be identified if we can define the system within which a formation of different strategies spreads out; in other words, if we can show how all of them derive from the same game of relations (despite their extreme diversity at times and despite their dispersion in time) [...].[31] (Foucault 1969: 91)

---

27 Original: "Foucault selbst ist von einer gewissen Verantwortung für [die Beliebigkeit des Diskursbegriffs] nicht frei zu sprechen, da er als Theoretiker nicht unbedingt bekannt dafür ist, in klassische philosophischer Manier eindeutige Definitionen seiner zentralen Begriffe vorgelegt zu haben. Im Gegenteil war es Eigenart seines Arbeitens, mit einer offenen, Kritiker mögen sagen: beliebigen Begrifflichkeit zu operieren, die sich seinen eigenen, stetig wandelnden Interessen anpasste [...]." (Landwehr 2008: 71)

28 Original: "Demnach lässt sich der Diskurs also in einem ersten Schritt als eine Ordnung begreifen, die den mit diesem Diskurs vertrauten Subjekten das gemeinsame Denken, Sprechen und Handeln erlaubt" (Landwehr 2008: 67).

29 Original: "Le désir dit: 'Je ne voudrais pas avoir à entrer moi-même dans cet ordre hasardeux du discours [...]' Et l'institution répond: 'Tu n'as pas à craindre de commencer; nous sommes tous là pour te montrer que le discours est dans l'ordre des lois; qu'on veille depuis longtemps sur son apparition; qu'une place lui a été faite, qui l'honore mais le désarme; et que, s'il lui arrive d'avoir quelque pouvoir, c'est bien de nous, et de nous seulement, qu'il le tient.'" (Foucault 1971: 9)

30 Original: "Der Diskurs wird nicht von einer übermächtigen Zentrale gesteuert, sondern zeichnet sich durch eine Vielzahl von Urhebern aus" (Landwehr 2008: 76).

31 Original: "Une formation discursive sera individualisée si on peut définir le système de formation des différentes stratégies qui s'y déploient; en d'autres termes, si on peut montrer

In his conclusive definition of discourse, Foucault stresses the historical nature of discourse in that it cannot be planned or designed after a given ideal form:

> We shall call discourse a group of statements in so far as they belong to the same discursive formation [...] [Discourse] is made up of a limited number of statements for which a group of conditions of existence can be defined. Discourse in this sense is not an ideal, timeless form [...] it is, from beginning to end, historical – a fragment of history [...] posing its own limits, its divisions, its transformations, the specific modes of its temporality.[32] (Foucault 1969: 154)

The constitutive element of discourse is, therefore, the statement (*fr.* énoncé). In discourse analysis, statements are investigated with regard to the impact they inherently exert by virtue of their contextualized signification:

> A statement belongs to a discursive formation like a sentence belongs to a text, and like a proposition belongs to a cluster of meanings. But whereas the regularity of a sentence is defined by the rules of a language, and that of a proposition by the rules of a logic, the regularity of statements is defined by the discursive formation itself. [...] because the discursive formation is characterized [...] by an actual dispersion, and the statements [abide] by a rule of coexistence [...].[33] (Foucault 1969: 152-153)

For Foucault, a statement is not of interest when scrutinized in isolation. He stresses the importance of context:

> The statement [...] cannot be isolated in the same way as a sentence or a proposition or an act of formulation. To describe a statement does not mean to insulate and characterize a segment horizontally; but to define the conditions under which a series of signs [...] has come into existence – into a specific kind of existence. [...] The description of statements, in a vertical manner of sorts, aims at the conditions for the existence of the different groups of signifiers.[34] (Foucault 1969: 142-143)

For the research interest of this study the purely contextual understanding of *statement* is not expedient. What is called *sentence* and *proposition* by Foucault above, namely the

---

comment elles dérivent toutes (malgré leur diversité parfois extrême, malgré leur dispersion dans le temps) d'un même jeu de relations [...]." (Foucault 1969: 91)

32 Original: "On appellera discours un ensemble d'énoncés en tant qu'ils relèvent de la même formation discursive [...] [Le discours] est constitué d'un nombre limité d'énoncés pour lesquels on peut définir un ensemble de conditions d'existence. Le discours ainsi entendu n'est pas une forme idéale et intemporelle [...] il est, de part en part, historique - fragment d'histoire [...] posant le problème de ses propres limites, de ses coupures, de ses transformations, des modes spécifiques de sa temporalité [...]." (Foucault 1969: 154)

33 Original: "Un énoncé appartient à une formation discursive comme une phrase appartient à un texte, et une proposition à un ensemble déductif. Mais alors que la régularité d'une phrase est définie par les lois d'une langue, et celle d'une proposition par les lois d'une logique, la régularité des énoncés est définie par la formation discursive elle-même [...] puisque la formation discursive se caractérise [...] par une dispersion de fait, qu'elle est pour les énoncés [...] une loi de coexistence [...]." (Foucault 1969: 152–153)

34 Original: "L'énoncé [...] ne peut pas être isolé au même titre qu'une phrase, une proposition ou un acte de formulation. Décrire un énoncé ne revient pas à isoler et à caractériser un segment horizontal; mais à définir les conditions dans lesquelles s'est exercée la fonction qui a donné à une série de signes [...] une existence, et une existence spécifique. [...] La description des énoncés s'adresse, selon une dimension en quelque sorte verticale, aux conditions d'existence des différents ensembles signifiants." (Foucault 1969: 142–143)

qualities of a statement in terms of form (sentence) and content (proposition), are in many cases of equal importance. The term *statement* is therefore used in this book as a broad signifier encompassing all three aspects: context, form, and content. Almost all statements consist of linguistic signifiers, the signs. In my case, the sign *authentic/authenticity* plays an outstanding role. The signs have meanings attributed to them, which is merely a terminological modification of Saussure's pairing of *signifiant* and *signifié* (Jørgensen/Phillips 2002: 9-10). What is crucial in discourse theory is that the connection between a given sign and its meaning is permanently challenged by the forces of the discourse. Consequently, the discourse itself is seen as being in constant flux.

> Discourses are incomplete structures in the same undecidable terrain that never quite become completely structured. Hence there is always room for 'struggles' over what the structure should look like, what discourses should prevail, and how meaning should be ascribed to the individual signs. (Jørgensen/Phillips 2002: 29)

In most cases, the connection between a sign and its meaning is considered erratic. The sign is then referred to as a *floating signifier*. If, however, a certain fixation is observed, then the sign is spoken of in terms of a *moment*:

> [W]hat signs have a privileged status, and how are they defined in relation to the other signs in the discourse? When we have identified the signs that are nodal points, we can then investigate how other discourses define the same signs (floating signifiers) in alternative ways. And by examining the competing ascriptions of content to the floating signifiers, we can begin to identify the struggles taking place over meaning. In that way, we can gradually map the partial structuring by the discourses of specific domains. What signs are the objects of struggle over meaning between competing discourses (floating signifiers); and what signs have relatively fixed and undisputed meanings (moments)? (Jørgensen/Phillips 2002: 30)

> [A]ll moments stay potentially polysemic, which means that the moments are always potentially elements. Specific articulations reproduce or challenge the existing discourses by fixing meaning in particular ways. And because of the perpetual potential polysemy, every verbal or written expression [...] is also, to some extent, an articulation or innovation; [...] every expression is an active reduction of the possibilities of meaning because it positions the signs in relation to one another in only one way, thus excluding alternative forms of organisation. (Jørgensen/Phillips 2002: 29)

Jørgensen/Phillips exemplify the struggles within a discourse by the meaning of the word *body* in medicine. Its status as a moment, i.e. an expression of fixed meaning, has been challenged by alternative treatment discourses which ascribe the word a different content. The discourse of traditional medicine competes with the discourse of alternative treatment methods so that the ongoing struggle makes a floating signifier out of what was once close to being a moment. Every articulation of *body* in either discourse is prone to either confirm or challenge the traditional content (Jørgensen/Phillips 2002: 24-30). Analogies can be drawn between this struggle and the struggle over *authentic/authenticity* in EFL. However, the authenticity struggle features multiple aberrations from the one expounded by Jørgensen/Phillips (2002). Firstly, it is improbable that the status of *moment* has ever been remotely attained for *authentic/authenticity* (both within and beyond EFL). This might be due to the fact that, unlike *body*, the *signifiés* for authenticity are more abstract in that they rarely consist only of physical qualities. Physical objects such as the body appear to be more likely to approximate the status of moment than abstract concepts like authenticity. Secondly, the opposing discourses outlined for *body* are not as clear-cut for *authenticity*. Multiple forces seem to be at work here probably causing a higher complexity of struggle. These forces include external discourses where *authentic/authenticity* is prolific, e.g. colloquial language.

Jørgensen/Phillips stress the social dimension of discourse:

> [L]anguage is a 'machine' that generates, and as a result constitutes, the social world. This also extends to the constitution of social identities and social relations. It means that 'changes' in discourse are a means by which the social world is changed. (Jørgensen/Phillips 2002: 9)

Discourse as the force field between language and society is also addressed by Bhatia:

> '[D]iscourse as text' [refers to] the analysis of language use that is confined to the surface level properties of discourse, which include formal as well as functional aspects of discourse – that is phonological, lexico-grammatical, semantic, organizational (including cohesion), and other aspects of text structure [...] 'Discourse as genre', in contrast, extends the analysis beyond the textual product to incorporate context in a broader sense to account not only for the way text is constructed, but also for the way it is often interpreted, used, and exploited in specific institutional, or more narrowly professional contexts to achieve specific disciplinary goals. The nature of questions addressed in this kind of analysis may often be not only linguistic, but also socio-cognitive and ethnographic. (Bhatia 2012: 246-247)

Foucault is not interested in grammar but in the statement and in the role statements play in the social construction of discourse. A statement is marked by context and by repetitive occurrence, it is not of interest as a singular utterance (Landwehr 2008: 71).[35] Unlike Foucault, I do not conceive of statement as a necessarily repetitive element. In my field of research, which may be more restricted than what Foucault envisions, it is serviceable to allow for a single utterance to form a statement.

In a discourse, rules apply. The rules relate mainly to topic, meaning that a finite number of topics are discussed within a single discourse. The rules allow for slightly more variance in other areas. There will be statements in the same discourse, although they may differ greatly with regard to time, location, social context etc. (Keller 2008: 205).[36] The topic functioning as common denominator entails that a considerable number of statements, which involve the term *authentic/authenticity*, is identified as one discourse.

---

35 Original: "[...] Bestimmungsmerkmale für eine Aussage: Einerseits ist sie immer eingebettet in bestimmte Zusammenhänge [...]. Andererseits zeichnen sich Aussagen durch ihr regelmäßiges und wiederholtes Auftauchen aus [...]" (Landwehr 2008: 71).

36 Original: "Kommunikative Äußerungen [...] können an zeit-räumlich und sozial sehr weit auseinander liegenden Orten erscheinen, von unterschiedlichsten sozialen Akteuren für diverse Publika hergestellt sein und dennoch einen typisierbaren Kerngehalt, eine typische ‚Aussage' im Sinne Foucaults enthalten, also Teil ein und desselben Diskurses sein." (Keller 2008: 205)

Although concepts of authenticity vary, the topic is bounded to some degree by this terminological precept. Variance is allowed for as regards time, institutional context etc.

The discourse structure is a result of all the past processes of shaping this discourse. The structure provides boundaries for future discursive events. While every single discursive event will have to stay within the boundaries, it has the power to transform the discourse structure (Keller 2008: 206).[37] Irrespective of the specific nature of a given discourse, its rules of formation consist of the following points:

- normative rules for making statements
- rules for signifying concerning the constitution of meaning for single phenomena
- performative resources and material resources (*dispositif*) for the creation and dissemination of meaning

These rules constitutive of discourse are exclusive in selecting speakers and content over other speakers and other content. Discourse structures are therefore always power structures (Keller 2008: 208).[38] The second point above is of special interest in the study at hand, for it essentially refers to the connections between *signifiant* and *signifié*. These rules for signifying are scrutinized regarding the term *authentic/authenticity* with all its corresponding concepts.

4.2 The academic discourse

Academic discourse is a specific kind of discourse, which EFL belongs to. Some basic thoughts on what Morris calls the *scientific discourse* are applicable to the EFL discourse:

> Scientific discourse illustrates the most specialized form of designative-informative discourse. [...] As science advances, its statements become more purely designative, more general, better confirmed, and better systematized. Scientific discourse is therefore made up of those statements which constitute the best knowledge of a given time, that is, those statements for which the evidence is highest that the statements are true. [...]
>
> The scientific statement does not approve or disapprove of the conditions it states, nor of any particular act under these conditions [...]. (Morris 1946: 126-128)

---

37 Original: "Eine solche Struktur ist strukturiert – also Ergebnis vergangener Prozesse der Strukturbildung – und strukturierend im Hinblick auf die Spielräume zukünftiger diskursiver Ereignisse. Das tatsächliche Geschehen ist keine direkte Folge der Strukturmuster und Regeln, sondern Ergebnis des aktiv-interpretierenden Umgangs sozialer Akteure mit diesen Orientierungsmustern. [...] Giddens (1992) definiert Strukturen als Regeln und Ressourcen, die konkreten Handlungsereignissen (Praktiken) sowohl zugrunde liegen als auch in diesen immer wieder erzeugt werden [...]." (Keller 2008: 206)

38 Original: "Diskurskonstitutive Regeln der Selektion von Sprechern und Inhalten sind immer auch Regeln der Exklusion. Nicht jede(r) erfüllt die Kriterien und verfügt über die Ressourcen oder Kapitalien, die für die Teilnahme an einem spezifischen Diskurs vorausgesetzt sind. Und auch die spezifische Definition der Wirklichkeit, die ein Diskurs vorgibt, schließt andere Varianten aus. Insoweit verweist der Diskursbegriff unmittelbar auf den Begriff der Macht. Diskursstrukturen sind zugleich Machtstrukturen [...]." (Keller 2008: 208)

While the quote predates Foucault, the role of the statement as core element of discourse is equally emphasized. A unifying element of all scientific discourses is the absence of overt approval or disapproval based on personal preference, as Morris points out. It is not made clear whether Morris has only natural science in mind, but the absence of overt approval or disapproval is a fundamental characteristic that is transferable to EFL.

In more recent research, the term *academic discourse* has been employed to include all research disciplines. An entire branch of discourse analysis deals with the genre of academic discourse (see among others: Biber 1996; Hyland 2000; Del Lungo Camiciotti / Tognini Bonelli 2004; Hyland/Guinda 2012; Pho 2013; Basturkmen 2014).

The following chapters deal with specific elements of academic discourse. The first two, authorial stance and exclusiveness, apply to all disciplines. After a discussion of these two points, the focus is further narrowed to the EFL discourse.

4.2.1 Authorial stance

The question of approval and disapproval ties in with what is commonly referred to as *stance* or *authorial stance*. One thinks this is irrelevant for academic discourse. After all, the difference to other registers is significant:

> [C]omparative register research shows that the old stereotypes about the stanceless nature of academic writing are to some extent accurate. [...] [S]tudies have shown that stance is much more commonly expressed in other spoken and interpersonal written registers, and that it is comparatively rare in academic writing. (Gray/Biber 2012: 24-25)

Such empirical findings are based on a comparison with colloquial discourse structures, which inevitably causes a stark contrast. It is not the case that a complete absence of personal positioning in academic discourse can be affirmed. Researchers agree that a differentiated approach to measuring stance and subjectivity is called for because any communicative act is inherently egocentric:

> One of the properties distinguishing scientific from nonscientific communication is the apparent lack of subjectivity in scientific discourse. Its nature is philosophical rather than pragmatic, but it should be considered in more detail because of linguistic implications. Since most instances of naturally occurring communication are egocentric and since subjectivity is a natural feature of any speaker- or situation-dependent discourse, we should really be speaking of varying degrees of subjectivity. (Cecchetto/Stoinska 1997: 142)

> According to one idealized representation of university language, there would be no need for stance expressions. Rather, lecturers and textbook writers would communicate only the facts and propositional information that students need to know. However, this ideal is far from reality; in fact, in some cases speakers and writers in university registers seem more concerned with the expression of stance than with the communication of 'facts'. (Biber 2006: 87)

Biber's statement includes spoken registers at university, but he refers to lectures, not to casual conversation within university walls. The genre of lecture is actually closer to written academic publications than to most spoken registers. One shortcoming of Morris's (1946) descriptions is his indiscriminate approach to scientific discourse. Whereas Morris does not specify disciplines, Hyland distinguishes "between the sciences and engineering as hard knowledge and the social sciences/humanities as soft disciplines" (Hyland 2000: 29). He is aware that this binary distinction still bears weaknesses:

> The concept of hard and soft domains of knowledge is obviously not without problems, partly because these are everyday terms which carry connotations of clear-cut antithetical divisions. As a result, the use of these terms to characterise academic disciplines by types of knowledge forms clearly runs the risk of reductionism, or even reification, by packing a multitude of complex abstractions into a few simple opposites. Moreover, for some the terms may seem ideologically loaded, privileging a particular mode of knowing based on the structural perspectives, symbolic representations and model-building methods of the natural sciences. However, the hard-soft scheme is more directly related to established disciplinary groupings than some more abstract categorisations [...].

> Obviously such broad distinctions cannot capture the full complexity of disciplinary differences, and may only be acceptable at a general level of analysis, but they do provide a useful basis for identifying dimensions of variability between these fields. If the hard-soft distinction is conceived as a continuum rather than as unidimensional scales, I believe it offers a convenient way of examining general similarities and differences between fields without positing rigidly demarcated categories. (Hyland 2000: 29-30)

EFL falls into what Hyland calls the soft disciplines. These disciplines are distinguishable from the sciences by one elementary point:

> In the humanities and social sciences [...] the fabric of established understandings has a wider weave. Problem areas and topics are generally more diffuse and range over wider academic and historical territory, and there is less assurance that questions can be answered by following a single path. (Hyland 2000: 32)

In the humanities, the truth is often relative rather than absolute:

> If 'truth' does not lie exclusively in the external world, there is always going to be more than one way of looking at a certain problem. This plurality of competing interpretations, with no objective means of absolutely distinguishing the actual from the plausible, means that while readers may be persuaded to judge a claim acceptable, they always have the option of rejecting it. (Hyland 2000: 13)

The relativity of truth makes the academic discourse in the humanities susceptible to the approval or the disapproval of authors and readers. This contentiousness appears to be in place with questions of authenticity. The essential question in the context of authenticity lies in the definition of the term. A definition usually marks a starting point from which investigation and argumentation ensue. Definitions are necessary procedures in academic discourse and they are incumbent on the author. They are in many cases not expected to cause controversy because they are not in themselves statements about the world but merely provide tools for such statements by linking a *signifiant* with a *signifié*. The *signifiant* is either a word or a short compound or collocation. The *signifié*, in the humanities, is for the most part intangible. It is a concept, a process, a pattern, an activity etc. Often a *signifié* is nameless until a definition is put forth. Giving it a *signifiant* is in itself a validation unless it is made clear that the newly christened concept is undesirable. The latter is the case, for example, if the *signifiant* carries a negative connotation. If, however, there is a positive connotation to the *signifiant*, the validating effect is reinforced even further.

Authenticity, as a term, holds a very strong positive connotation, so to define it means to greatly validate a given concept. This idiosyncrasy of authenticity causes its definition to become more than a mere starting point of a discussion. In some instances, the definition of authenticity is the actual object of discussion. Authorial stance, therefore, is of eminent significance. To give a brief example of a nameless *signifié* that is accorded the *signifiant* of *authentic/authenticity*: There has been no term denoting discussions in the EFL classroom on the very subject of how to learn the foreign language. Breen (1985), by means of definition, grants this concept the *signifiant* that is *authenticity*: "[O]ne of the main authentic activities within a language classroom is communication about how best to learn to communicate" (Breen 1985: 68).

According to Hyland, authors constantly anticipate potential opposition on the part of the reader and have to create strategies of pre-empting them.

> [T]he social interactions in academic writing stem from the writer's attempts to anticipate possible negative reactions to his or her persuasive goals. The writer will choose to respond to the potential negatability of his or her claims through a series of rhetorical choices to galvanise support, express collegiality, resolve difficulties and avoid disagreement in ways which most closely correspond to the community's assumptions, theories, methods and bodies of knowledge. (Hyland 2000: 13)

Many of these mechanisms apply to authors engaging in definitions of authenticity. I present Hyland's dichotomous conceptualization of reader opposition before proceeding to his thoughts on how authors deal with them.

> Opposition to statements can come from two principal sources [...]. First, readers may reject a statement on the grounds that it fails to correspond to what the world is thought to be like, i.e. it fails to meet 'adequacy conditions'. [...]

> Second, statements have to incorporate an awareness of interpersonal factors, addressing 'acceptability conditions', with the writer attending to the affective expectations of participants in the interaction. Theoretical strategies for social interaction are employed here to help the writer to create a professionally acceptable persona and an appropriate attitude, both to readers and the information being discussed. This means representing one's self in a text in a way that demonstrates one's flawless disciplinary credentials; showing yourself to be a reasonable, intelligent, co-player in the community's efforts to construct knowledge and well versed in its tribal lore. Critical here is the ability to display proper respect for colleagues and give due regard for their views and reputations. (Hyland 2000: 13)

The two-pronged notion of reader opposition lends itself to a schematic distinction between content and form. Meeting "adequacy conditions" (ibid.) means to pursue a compelling line of argumentation so as to convince the reader that the statements made are true. In other words, the content of what is delivered must display substance and epistemic value. "Acceptability conditions" (ibid.) are essentially social in nature. They are met when a high level of discursive conformity is achieved on the different levels mentioned by Hyland. The effect of such conformity is a positive affective impression on the reader, which will influence the way statements are perceived. Adequacy and acceptability are difficult to keep apart once practical examples are considered. Hyland himself does not reify the distinction. Instead, he propounds the following general rules for creating a good research article (Hyland 2000: 12):

- establish the novelty of one's position
- make a suitable level of claim
- acknowledge prior work and situate claims in a disciplinary context
- offer warrants for one's view based on community-specific arguments and procedures
- demonstrate an appropriate disciplinary ethos and willingness to negotiate with peers.

I will henceforth refer to these rules in the merged form of *adequacy/acceptability conditions*.

While these are the general conditions, the concrete strategies of achieving them tend to manifest themselves partly in the linguistic form of authorial stance. Here are two complementary definitions:

> The ways that writers chose [sic] to represent themselves, their readers and their world, how they seek to advance knowledge, how they maintain the authority of their discipline and the processes whereby they establish what is to be accepted as substantiated truth, a useful contribution and a valid argument are all culturally-influenced practical actions and matters for community agreement. These practices are not simply a matter of personal stylistic preference, but community-recognised ways of adopting a position and expressing a stance. (Hyland 2000: 11)

> [Stance] can be seen as an attitudinal dimension and includes features which refer to the ways writers present themselves and convey their judgements, opinions, and commitments. It is the ways that writers intrude to stamp their personal authority onto their arguments or step back and disguise their involvement. (Hyland 2005: 176)

Essentially, the expression of stance aims at striking a balance between tentativeness and assertion (Hyland 2000: 13-14). While tentativeness is expressed through so-called hedges, assertion is typically accompanied by boosters:

> Hedges are devices like 'possible', 'might' and 'perhaps', that indicate the writer's decision to withhold complete commitment to a proposition, allowing information to be presented as an opinion rather than accredited fact. Because all statements are evaluated and interpreted through a prism of disciplinary assumptions, writers must calculate what weight to give to an assertion, attesting to the degree of precision or reliability that they want it to carry and perhaps claiming protection in the event of its eventual overthrow [...].

> Boosters, on the other hand, are words like 'clearly', 'obviously' and 'demonstrate', which allow writers to express their certainty in what they say and to mark involvement with the topic [...]. (Hyland 2005: 178-179)

The function of hedging and boosting is summed up by Hyland as follows:

> Hedges and boosters [...] show writers weighting (a) the expression of their commitment depending on how they judge the epistemic status of their statements, as facts or interpretations, and (b) the effect they anticipate this commitment might have on readers' responses. [...] [The] distinction between 'what we say' and 'what we say about what we say' is at the root of choice and subtlety in language use. (Hyland 2000: 88)

In the following chapters, select instances of hedging and boosting are discussed as they occur in the discourse under scrutiny.

Another aspect of stance, alongside hedging and boosting, is self-mention.

> In the humanities and social sciences, [...] the use of the first person is closely related to the desire to both strongly identify oneself with a particular argument and to gain credit for

an individual perspective. Personal reference is a clear indication of the perspective from which a statement should be interpreted, enabling writers to emphasize their own contribution to the field and to seek agreement for it [...]. (Hyland 2005: 181)

Self-mention is further detailed at a point in this book when concrete dependencies and implications of self-mention can be worked out, which requires the prior introduction of author status (chapter 4.2.2) and authorial style (chapter 4.3.1).

According to Hyland, hedging, boosting, and self-mention are strategies employed by authors to express their stance. These elements are surface features of text and their function is to frame the content of what is expressed. The content itself is seen as separate from stance. It may, however, be more plausible to conceive of stance as the interplay of content and form/surface. A statement consisting of content and form expresses stance in large parts by virtue of what is said over how it is said. Content which meets the adequacy/acceptability conditions cannot be purely judged by epistemic value because, in the humanities, much of the content expressed is not objectively true or false. Very often, the content itself is controversial, thereby in itself displaying authorial stance. The form of the statement, will then merely modify the content by means of hedging or boosting. In many cases, content of particular contentiousness is put forth accompanied by forms of hedging so as to meet adequacy/acceptability conditions in spite of the controversial content. The following statement exemplifies this strategy:

> [T]he essential contribution of the classroom is that it is an **almost** unique social context where people meet for the explicit purpose of learning something—from others for themselves. Learning is the main psychological and social function of a classroom. [...] [G]iven the actual social potential of a classroom, the contrivance of 'other worlds' within it **may** not only be inauthentic but also **quite** unnecessary.

> [...] The authenticity of the classroom is that it is a **rather** special social event and environment wherein people share a primary communicative purpose: learning. The language classroom can exploit this social potential by expecting and encouraging learners to share their own learning processes and experiences. **Perhaps** one of the main authentic activities within a language classroom is communication about how best to learn to communicate. (Breen 1985: 67-68) (emphases added by L.W.)

The words highlighted are typical hedges. They are employed here to allay the potential controversy caused by the content of the statement. An omission of these elements would lead to a phrasing such as: "The contrivance of 'other worlds' is unnecessary." If boosting is applied instead of hedging, the result could be: "The contrivance of 'other worlds' is **absolutely** unnecessary." These three versions – hedged, neutral, boosted – arguably display a gradual decrement of conformity to adequacy/acceptability conditions. Due to the high degree of possible dissension over the content, boosting would be all but unacceptable.

In sum, I plead for a modified conceptualization of authorial stance as the interplay of content and form in all of those instances where content cannot be measured by epistemic value. Such instances abound in the EFL discourse on authenticity.

4.2.2 Exclusiveness and author status

In this chapter, questions are broached about who partakes in the academic discourse and about what governs the power relations within the discourse community. I begin with the binary aspects of including or excluding individuals before proceeding to an analysis of hierarchy amongst those who get included. The chapter at hand is a sub-chapter of academic discourse because the EFL discourse on authenticity does not differ greatly from the general rules which apply to the bulk of academic fields. At times, however, digressions are made to point out specifics of EFL in this regard.

Adequacy/acceptability conditions, tying in with authorial stance, have strong social implications within the academic discourse. They are inevitably embedded in a complex web of contingency factors pertaining to the contextual structures of the discourse at hand. Most notably, these structures have to do with power and hierarchy, which are aspects covered by the overarching theories of critical discourse analysis (CDA):

> An approach to the analysis of discourse which views language as a social practice and is interested in the ways that ideologies and power relations are expressed through language. Critical discourse analysts are particularly interested in issues of inequality, sometimes keeping in mind the question 'who benefits?' when carrying out analysis. [...] The approach was first developed by Norman Fairclough (1989). (Baker/Ellece 2011: 26)

For the purpose at hand, it is sufficient to limit the scope to what has been propounded in the specific context of academic discourse studies.

One feature of what Keller calls special discourses as opposed to public discourses is its exclusiveness with regard to the selection of participating actors:

> 'Public discourse' denotes political-argumentative controversy about social problems, in which the civic public participates through mass media and different other public arenas. [...]

> Discourse research of Symbolic Interactionism, unlike Foucault, dealt with rather small-scale mechanisms of such discourses, with their participating actors, their strategies and resources, and with their fixed contents and their institutional consequences. [...] [The latter are] institutional – and therefore in a way semi-public – special discourses [...].[39] (Keller 2008: 229-230)

This social exclusiveness is the case for the EFL discourse. The publishing houses as mediating institutions take on a gatekeeping function, if an essentially bureaucratic one. What is more decisive in the selection process is the self-regulatory mechanism inherent to any academic community, a mechanism marked by the mostly meritocratic dynamics

---

[39]   Original: "'Public Discourse' bezeichnet hier politisch-argumentative Auseinandersetzungen über gesellschaftliche Problemfelder, an denen sich, vermittelt über die Massenmedien und diverse andere öffentliche Arenen, die zivilgesellschaftliche Öffentlichkeit beteiligt. [...] Die entsprechende Diskursforschung des Symbolischen Interaktionismus hat sich dann im Unterschied zu Foucault mit historisch 'kleinformatigeren' Karrieremechanismen solcher Diskurse, mit den beteiligten Akteuren, ihren Strategien und Ressourcen sowie mit den festgeschriebenen Inhalten und deren institutionellen Konsequenzen beschäftigt. [...] [Letztere sind] institutionelle – also in gewissem Sinne teilöffentliche – Spezialdiskurse [...]." (Keller 2008: 229–230)

of professional hierarchy (employment) on the one hand and the fulfilment of ade-
quacy/acceptability conditions (publishing) on the other. In most countries, the minimum
prerequisite for an individual to enter into the academic discourse community is a master's degree in EFL or in a cognate discipline (linguistics, literature, education). The degree qualifies for an employment at university. During the subsequent pursuit of a doc-
torate degree articles can already be published. In general, employment and publishing
go hand in hand. Work contracts tend to include a combination of teaching, researching,
and organizational work within the institution. The institutional requirements just outlined are accompanied by the appraisal of a supervisor who will or will not accept some-
one as a doctoral student, and who may also function as a mentor and facilitate early
publications by virtue of her/his connections within the academic world and within the
publishing industry.

Once access to the discourse community is gained by an individual, various factors
come into play determining what I refer to as *author status*. High author status is achieved
when a "writer receives the reward of recognition. This can take the form of promotion,
substantiation, or simply a reputation among one's peers" (Hyland 2000: 168). The following depictions by Hyland largely apply to EFL thereby underpinning also the EFL
discourse on authenticity:

> Many fields of science are characterised by fierce rivalry as the rewards of reputation, in-
> cluding the funding to continue one's research, are often tied to establishing one's priority
> by reaching publication before others. (Hyland 2000: 85)

> Utility tends not to be a strong point of humanities disciplines, although once again wide
> differences are evident, but the kind of knowledge soft fields create is often respected by
> outsiders as 'scholarship'. The ideology that learning should be pursued for its own sake,
> however, is now perhaps archaic […]. Attracting research funding, consultancy contracts
> and students is a highly competitive business and this kind of competition invariably brings
> Mammon closer to the academy, and marketing norms into university discourses […]. This
> increasing external interference challenges the ways disciplinary communities govern
> themselves, ask questions, decide research problems, reward success and value the pursuit
> of knowledge […]. (Hyland 2000: 166-167)

The motives for publishing an article or a monograph are, thus, highly extrinsic. I will
refer back to these outer circumstances as they become potentially pertinent within my
analysis. Hyland interviewed researchers and received candid answers:

> While my informants spoke of advancing knowledge and genuine curiosity about specific
> research issues, most admitted that recognition was an important source of professional
> gratification for them. However, because reputation becomes translated into concrete con-
> sequences, and because both material and symbolic capital are scarce, participation in the
> system of academic exchange is often fiercely competitive. (Hyland 2000: 169)

The general principle of *publish-or-perish* thus continues to dominate the academic discourse and drives individual careers. An interesting mechanism is in place where processes of peer review determine what will be printed and what will not.

The process is typically based on an anonymous vetting of written contributions to a
journal, thereby pursuing the meritocratic principle and attempting to minimize favorit-
ism. It is also applied to book formats. The most desirable scenario plays out, if "editors,

referees, proposal readers, conference attendees and journal readers regard [a contribution] as original and significant, allow it to be published, cite it in their own work, and develop it further" (Hyland 2000: 168). Peer review would be expected to promote young professionals with little name recognition by affording them equal opportunities in the competitive field of academic publishing. Hyland challenges this view:

> [T]hrough peer review and editorial intervention, disciplines seek to ensure that accounts of new knowledge conform to the broad generic practices they have established, while writers are often willing to employ these practices because of a desire to get published and achieve recognition. This desire to gain a reputation therefore acts as a system of social control as it encourages conformity to the approved discursive practices of the discipline. To put it bluntly, the ideological and discursive system which reproduces knowledge also reproduces a particular arrangement of social relations. (Hyland 2000: 170)

Authors who are versed in these "approved discursive practices" (ibid.) by virtue of experience are, thus, put at an advantage. While this appears reasonable, Hyland fails to address the aspect of name recognition. I shall argue that the advantage experienced authors gain through conformity to discursive conventions are easily off-set by the removal of name recognition as a determining factor. Obviously, other publication formats allow authors of high rank to benefit greatly from their past accomplishments. Monographs and collected works will be published depending on the position of the author within the institution and/or depending on the renown of the institution itself. Publishing houses, as well, are marked by different levels of reputation. An author, whose writings are distributed by a prestigious publisher, makes more influential contributions to the discourse. The general access to publication opportunities of a given author usually corresponds with the person's author status, at least with regard to the publishing of book formats where peer review processes are often forgone. Thus, an established relationship with publishing houses is likely the most reliable means of guaranteeing the permanent possibility of having one's writings printed and distributed. This and other past accomplishments will work together in furthering one author's status and will ultimately create what I call *name recognition*. Cecchetto/Stoinska refer to this phenomenon as *appearance*:

> Appearance may be understood as referring to the stimuli that function to tell us of the performer's (author's) social status and position in the social or, more narrowly, professional hierarchy. In scientific texts, the appearance aspect can be reduced to the biographical information about the author, or even to the author's name and affiliation. This information usually provides enough background to determine the author's status and position in the field. (Cecchetto/Stoinska 1997: 150-151)

I use the term *author status*, instead of *appearance*, partly because it allows for gradation in terms of high and low. A high author status usually coincides with a high level of name recognition. Cecchetto/Stoinska see a correlation between author status and style of writing, the latter being referred to as *manner*:

> Manner may then be understood [...] as referring to those stimuli that function as a source of information about the interaction role the performer will expect to play in the upcoming situation. We naturally expect some consistency between appearance and manner. (Cecchetto/Stoinska 1997: 150-151)

This correlation is visible in the EFL discourse on authenticity. It is, however, unilaterally suspended during processes of peer review when the reader does not know the identity of the writer and, therefore, cannot expect consistency between appearance and manner. It may of course be the case that reviewers can guess by the style of writing who the author is. Authors of high status are more likely to be recognized than those of low status because their past writings have usually had more exposure. What this element of guesswork engenders has not been investigated.

Cecchetto/Stoinska allude to the fact that past accomplishments do not have to be confined to publications in order to impact the author's appearance ("biographical information", "affiliation") (1997: 150-151). Indeed, academia is a field where author status is closely tied to what may be termed *institutional status*. The latter is, for example, furthered through a high position at a reputable institution. Various other kinds of personal credentials could be listed. After all, some professors may have a reputation for being versed in politics and public relations while being mediocre at writing. The two kinds of status are strongly interwoven so that a permanent terminological distinction is not considered expedient. It is, however, important to note that author status is not solely dependent on the individual's skills in research and writing.

All things considered, publications likely constitute the central pillar of repute. In the humanities, a single contribution to the discourse may achieve seminal status and heighten immensely its author's status and/or name recognition. To do so, it must fulfill adequacy/acceptability conditions to an unusually high degree. These effects are possible, according to Hyland, because "good theory doesn't date ... Durkheim is a cottage industry. People promote or pan his ideas but he's still there because we can't say for sure whether he's right or wrong" (Hyland 2000: 32). In more abstract terms:

> [O]ld ground is re-crossed and reinterpreted rather than suppressed. The process of coming to terms with the complexity of human behaviour is perceived as less obviously progressive and therefore less likely to discard older ideas as obsolete or irrelevant. [...] As a result, disciplinary giants are frequently encountered in the soft papers, particularly in 'pure' knowledge fields, where the pathfinders' stocks of relevance are clearly greater. (Hyland 2000: 32)

Very clear examples of such developments can be found in the EFL discourse on authenticity.

One important differentiation must be made: The status level of a given author may differ depending on the scope of the discourse. Some authors have a high status within the specific EFL discourse on authenticity, meaning that they have made substantial contributions to this one topic of authenticity but not necessarily to other topics. These will be spoken of as having high (*small-scale*) author status. If, however, an author is well-known throughout the field of EFL or even beyond for miscellaneous contributions, I explicitly speak of high *general* or *large-scale* author status.

4.3 The EFL discourse

I have narrowed down the scope of discourse from very general theories via the genre of academic writing to the field of academic writing in the humanities. The final two steps will be a further specialization toward the general EFL discourse and ultimately toward the EFL discourse on authenticity. This progression of step-by-step narrowing is pursued because

> [...] specialized languages must be taken into consideration separately or grouped by level, genre etc. The latter view is arguably confirmed by the findings of several studies and authors working with different texts, fields and specialized genres. The results drawn from one field cannot 'per se' be extended to others; the findings for a given genre call for adjustment and additions if applied to another. (Gotti 2003: 10)

What is stated by Gotti regarding language is equally true regarding the organization of any specialized discourse. The EFL discourse on authenticity is such a specialized discourse and it is embedded in the general EFL discourse. What thus far has been referred to as the EFL discourse is a discursive formation that is institutionally confined to scholarly writing within the academy. However, it is accompanied by an influential guild of practitioners constituted mainly of teachers and textbook writers. Not all academic discourses are so closely connected to a practical field.

> The effects of professional and workplace contexts on academic literacy practices are largely unknown, but are clearly pertinent. [...] Academic 'forums of competition' [...], within which new concepts are appraised, become blurred with those of a more applied orientation as members are influenced by the problems, procedures and criteria of evaluation which emerge from, and are relevant to, workplace concerns and practices. (Hyland 2000: 35-36)

It is not easy to demarcate the academic discourse from the practical discourse in a field where individuals tend to be active as both theorists and practitioners. The institutional make-up of EFL is such that scholars are often at the same time teacher trainers. They may have worked in schools for some time before being employed in academia. In turn, university students get in touch with scholarly writing during their course of studies and little is known as to how much of this knowledge is maintained as they move on to become language teachers at school. A consequence of this meshwork is that scholarly literature in EFL addresses different types of audience.

4.3.1 Authorial style

The different types of audience within EFL may contribute to a variance in what I call *authorial style*. This collocation is sometimes used in literary studies where it denotes the writing style of a given author of literature. The term is usually employed when the uniqueness of an individual author's style is emphasized: "There is widespread consensus that a major aspect of James Kelman's authorial style is his unique use of voice" (Murphy 2006: 183). Another example shows how attempts are made to measure this uniqueness linguistically:

Most statistically or computationally supported research into authorship attribution is now-adays style-based, convinced that by measuring some textual features we can distinguish between texts written by different authors. The basic assumption of such stylometric re-search is consequently that each author has a unique set of linguistic characteristics or a 'stylome' that can be quantitatively distinguished from any other author's style. (Keste-mont/Daelemans/Sandra 2012: 54-55)

For the aim of this study, uniqueness is not of primary interest. Yet, the descriptions by Kestemont/Daelemans/Sandra (2012) are pertinent to the conceptualization of authorial style that is about to be presented. Since I am uncertain to what extent the following elaborations apply to other academic fields, I am presenting them in the exclusive context of the EFL discourse, unlike authorial stance and author status.

Much of what has been said about stance and adequacy/acceptability conditions is actually located on one end of a stylistic spectrum, which I refer to as the *conceptual* end. Here, new theories are forged. Readers must be convinced – partly through authorial stance – that new concepts are valuable and beneficial for the endeavor of learning and teaching a foreign language. The presumptive readership, then, is primarily one of fellow academics who are themselves in a position to discursively respond to the statements made. Hyland's remarks on reader opposition are essentially predicated on this assump-tion of possible response. However, certain publications cater to a different type of audi-ence. One example would be what Hyland calls *textbooks*. In the context of EFL, this term is already used for language teaching materials so, in the following citation, the word *textbook* shall be thought of as referring to EFL manuals or introductions to EFL:

[T]extbooks are conservative exemplars of current disciplinary paradigms. They are seen as places where we find the tamed and accepted theories of a discipline, where 'normal science' is defined and acknowledged fact is represented. [...]

This purpose, and a student target audience, seems to set textbooks apart from the more prestigious genres through which academics exchange research findings, dispute theories and accumulate professional credit. Thus, while the research article is a highly valued genre central to the disciplinary construction of new knowledge, the textbook simply represents an attempt to reduce the multivocity of past texts to a single voice of authority. (Hyland 2000: 105)

If the conceptual style of writing forms one end of a spectrum, the style typically deployed in the genre of EFL manuals forms the opposite end. I refer to this end as *descriptive* style. Authorial style includes linguistic features, yet it is not confined to them. For in-stance, descriptive style is all but devoid of boosting.

Figure 6 illustrates a continuum between descriptive and conceptual authorial style. A single publication can be placed on a certain spot along the continuum. However, just like Hyland's conception of stance is spelled out on the micro-level (hedges and boosters), authorial style can literally vary from one sentence to another.

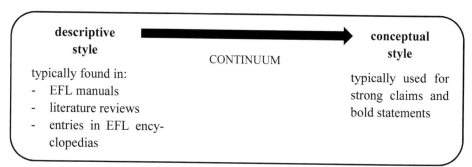

Figure 6: Authorial styles in EFL

In practice, single publications in EFL will feature chapters of literature review providing a synopsis of existing research and theory on the given topic. Such passages are more likely to be written in a descriptive style than those where novel conclusions are drawn or where practical implications are suggested. To say that one publication is more descriptive than conceptual is to express that the number of descriptive sentences and passages is higher than that of conceptual ones. All in all, authorial style on the micro-level can be determined almost dichotomously between conceptual and descriptive, whereas an entire publication is to be positioned somewhere along the continuum.

Even notionally descriptive genres do not necessarily display a homogeneous stylistic approach. For instance, some entries in EFL encyclopedias feature strong stance instead of consistent self-effacement, as will be shown in the in-depth analysis of the discourse. Such outliers may be ascribed to different causes. The author may be negligent in her/his catering to readership and adhere to stylistic habits. The author may also consider the fact that fellow authors could read the text, although they are not the primary target group. Then, potential reader opposition will be preempted.

4.3.2 Citations

Citation practices are strongly linked to questions of style. Hyland presents an elaborate analysis of citation techniques (Hyland 2000: 20-40). In the context of authorial style, a more contingent approach is taken. The following descriptions will be exemplified as I proceed to the analysis of the discourse.

I have suggested that EFL manuals are usually written in descriptive style. Such monographs must be concise and comprehensive. The resulting lack of space causes a tendency to avoid quotations. Often, only the publication is indicated with or without a page number. Similar conditions concerning aim and space apply to EFL encyclopedias. Direct citations are equally rare in most cases. Both genres, manuals and encyclopedias, tend to work with indirect referencing and very often no page numbers are indicated for references. This method is appropriate when holistic concepts are presented or when a publication is referred to in its entirety. It is an expedient approach to treating topics that are too big to be expounded in detail. A similar means is the interspersing of short thematic bibliographies under a caption like *Further reading*. These sections are found at the end of chapters in EFL manuals or at the end of entries in EFL encyclopedias.

Hyland does not account for descriptive styles when theorizing on stance, citation, and adequacy/acceptability conditions. His remarks tend to focus on the author's intention of convincing the reader with arguments:

> Citation is central to the social context of persuasion as it can provide justification for arguments and demonstrate the novelty of one's position [...]. (Hyland 2000: 20)

> The inclusion of explicit references to the work of other authors is thus seen as a central feature of academic research writing, helping writers to establish a persuasive epistemological and social framework for the acceptance of their arguments. (Hyland 2000: 22)

Serving the purpose of bolstering the arguments presented, citation practices would be expected to lend themselves to conceptual style. However, some of the most conceptual writings on authenticity feature little to no references at all (e.g. Breen 1985: nine references; Widdowson 1998: three references; Widdowson 1994: one reference; Widdowson 1976: no references). Sometimes, only well-known authors are invoked, and indirect citations are favored over direct ones. Moreover, these references are often interdisciplinary conferring an air of grand theory on the text. Authors referenced will be e.g. Chomsky, Goffman, Halliday, Piaget etc. Ultimately, there is an aspect of name-dropping that comes with referencing (e.g. van Lier 1996):

> [C]iting the work of others is not simply an issue of accurate attribution, but also a significant means of constructing an authorial self. Writing in the humanities stresses the individual creative thinker, but always within the context of a canon of disciplinary knowledge. Foregrounding the names of those whose work we engage with enables us to establish a professional persona. (Hyland 2000: 37)

Genuine or innovative ideas are, by nature, unprecedented and may be so new that little literature is available for reference. Note however that even if literature is available, the ideas may appear diminished, if they draw on too many prior works.

Sparse use of citations is a strategy typically employed by authors of high status. Conceptual style, as well, appears to be accepted within the discourse community if it is practiced by renowned authors. This correlation tallies with the thoughts on appearance and manner which are formulated by Cecchetto/Stoinska.[40] I demonstrate in chapter 4.3.3 how the combination of high status and conceptual style can yield effects which cement the author's status in the discourse.

4.3.3 The relations between adequacy, style, stance, author status, and citation

In this chapter, the different connections between adequacy, style, stance, author status, and citation are highlighted. Some of these connections have already been discussed in

---

40   Cecchetto/Stoinska (1997: 150–151): "Manner may then be understood [...] as referring to those stimuli that function as a source of information about the interaction role the performer will expect to play in the upcoming situation. We naturally expect some consistency between appearance and manner [...]."

the previous chapters. Therefore, a condensed overview afforded by means of triangulating the different factors is given here. Out of the five factors, adequacy is the only one which has not been expounded. It is also the only factor functioning as an ultimate value. The term is extrapolated from Hyland's adequacy conditions denoting epistemic value and logical reasoning:

> [R]eaders may reject a statement on the grounds that it fails to correspond to what the world is thought to be like, i.e. it fails to meet 'adequacy conditions'. Claims have to display a plausible relationship with reality (the discipline's epistemological framework) [...]. (Hyland 2000: 13)

It thus refers to questions of *What?* rather than *How?* A perfect fulfilment of adequacy conditions equals the highest possible degree of truth and logic. Since in the humanities truth is often relative and dependent on logic, adequacy is more appropriately conceived of as the content of a statement being commonly accepted in the discourse. Style, stance, and author status – as well as citation to a lesser degree – are each contingent on adequacy.

Adequacy and style are contingent in that adequacy is achieved differently for descriptive texts than it is for conceptual texts. The adequacy of an EFL manual (descriptive), for example, will be measured by how correctly and comprehensively the different aspects of EFL are presented and not by how genuine and innovative its discrete contents are. The manual as a whole must be adequate by providing an accurate overview of concepts and approaches. The single components must be coherently explained and related, but since they are already established in the field, the reader need not be convinced of their value. In conceptual texts, adequacy is achieved through a compelling line of argumentation, which creates plausibility and, ultimately, a perceived notion of truth on the reader's part. This notion of truth may be reinforced by the judicious use of stance. It may also depend on the author's status.

Adequacy and stance are contingent in that statements of controversial content tend to be accompanied by strategies of hedging, so as to meet adequacy/acceptability conditions. In chapter 4.2.1 an example is given where a statement by Breen (1985) displays such connections.

Adequacy and author status are contingent in that authors of high status appear to show a greater tendency to express thoughts which may be seen as highly genuine but also as quite contentious. Their so-called appearance (Cecchetto/Stoinska 1997: 150-151) allows them to proceed in this manner. Thus, well-known authors are free to choose their style from anywhere on the stylistic spectrum between very conceptual and very descriptive. Low status authors may find it harder to work conceptually and still find their works accepted by fellow academics.

Adequacy and citation practices are not directly connected. The amount of citation appears not to differ greatly between styles, except for some outliers on the conceptual end of the stylistic spectrum (e.g. Breen 1985: only nine references; Widdowson 1998: three references; Widdowson 1994: one reference; Widdowson 1976: no references). Not only is the stylistic dichotomy (descriptive/conceptual) insufficient for predicting the number of citations, the quantitative approach itself is not always insightful. Citations are quite versatile. While Hyland underscores their persuasive value, it is important to acknowledge how citations support descriptive genres by providing information or by outsourcing relevant literature due to spatial constraints.

The connection between style and stance is quite straight-forward in that boosting is mainly used in texts of conceptual style but appears rather out of place in descriptive writings. Note that I refer to Hyland's notion of stance, which focuses on formal features such as hedging, boosting, and self-mention. I argued in chapter 4.2.1 that an author's true stance can only be gauged weighing these formal features against the content of a statement. Formal features of hedging may be used to conceal the author's true stance when a statement of controversial content is made. If true stance was considered, which includes content, even texts of highly descriptive style would become potential objects of analysis because the mere arrangement of content, e.g. in an EFL manual, can be indicative of the author's true stance. Such analyses would have to look at instances of overrepresentation and underrepresentation of single topics. Specific elements of stance are contingent upon other factors, and some of these contingencies are rather counterintuitive. For example, it is not the case that authors of high status necessarily use a high number of boosters, which one might expect. Rather, they tend to make statements of such genuine (and controversial) content that they are all but compelled to deploy hedging in order to meet acceptability conditions.

One other element of stance has been introduced rather briefly: The aspect of self-mention, which "refers to the use of first person pronouns and possessive adjectives to present propositional, affective and interpersonal information" (Hyland 2005: 181), is most consistently tied to conceptual writing as opposed to descriptive writing where it appears to be all but non-existent. The genre of encyclopedic entries, for instance, is completely devoid of self-mention.

4.4 The academic EFL discourse on authenticity

Thus far, the descriptions of discourse have led from a look at general discourse theories to a focus on the academic discourse to a further focus on the EFL discourse. The final step is now one of conclusive demarcation in various respects.

On the surface, the only distinctive factor between the EFL discourse at large and the academic EFL discourse on authenticity is that the latter revolves around questions of authenticity, which entails a narrowing of focus compared to the general EFL discourse. The focus is a choice made by the discourse analyst and it leads to a definition of the research object. In other fields and with other methodological approaches, the research object is often pre-defined and does not have to be picked out and demarcated from what can be seen as a vast contextual mass. Before discourse analysis can take place, the discourse under scrutiny must be clearly defined. For the purpose at hand, such a definition of the research object is all but tantamount to questions of focus and, thus, to questions of demarcation.

4.4.1 Demarcation – preliminary thoughts

A discursive formation is distinct when its rules of formation differ from those of other discursive formations. Foucault, however, theorizes about general overarching rules which are constitutive of any discursive formation:

> The investigation of discursive formations is designed as a process of typologizing, which can be conducted in more or less depth depending on the research questions. [...] Foucault was scarcely interested in a concrete content analysis of the single discourses in jurisdiction, for example. At least he rarely expressed [...] an interest in a contrastive analysis and confrontation of the phenomena within different discourses. His general view was directed at the rules of formation and at the power implications that are common to all discourses, regardless of the discrete forms of implementation on the content level.[41] (Keller 2008: 229)

Following Keller's typological approach, the question is how the academic EFL discourse on authenticity can be separated from adjacent discursive formations.

4.4.2 Demarcation – mode, field, and tenor

To demarcate the academic EFL discourse on authenticity, I draw on the concepts of *mode, field* and *tenor*, as put forth by Halliday (1976: 62-64) and Gregory/Carroll (1978: 27-63). These concepts, which are claimed to apply to any spoken or written register, are encapsulated by Gotti:

> [Halliday and Gregory/Carroll] classify all registers according to three parameters: mode, field, and tenor. The first concerns chiefly the channel and medium of communication and the third the relationship between participants, while the second (field) regards the object of communication, i.e. its topic [...]. (Gotti 2003: 24)

"The categories of field, tenor and mode are thus determinants and not components of speaking" (Halliday 1976: 62). For the research purpose at hand, they are deployed as demarcating criteria.

Mode, which refers to "the channel and medium of communication" (Gotti 2003: 24), differs markedly between the academic EFL discourse and the semi-informed EFL discourse, let alone the colloquial discourse. Communication in the academic EFL discourse takes place primarily via the medium of academic publications. Teachers and materials designers are all but institutionally debarred from this conduit due to the lower academic qualifications required for teachers than for researchers. What is more, many teachers – even if sufficiently qualified – will find it difficult to engage in scholarly publishing while maintaining a teaching job at school. It is easier for a member of a cognate academic

---

41   Original: "Diese Beispiele machen deutlich, dass die Untersuchung diskursiver Formationen als Typisierungsprozess angelegt ist, der in Abhängigkeit von den jeweiligen Fragestellungen der Analyse mit unterschiedlicher Tiefenschärfe betrieben werden kann. Unabhängig davon, auf welcher Ebene der Feinanalyse diskursive Formationen rekonstruiert werden, bleibt festzuhalten, dass Foucault sich kaum für konkrete inhaltliche Auseinandersetzungen bspw. zwischen einzelnen Teildiskursen des Rechts interessierte – zumindest hat er nur selten [...] explizit sein Interesse an der phänomenbezogenen Gegenüberstellung und Konfrontation unterschiedlicher Diskurse geäußert (Foucault 1975). Sein generalisierender Blick zielte auf die allen gemeinsamen Formationsregeln und deren 'Machtwirkungen', unabhängig von den singulären inhaltlichen Ausführungen." (Keller 2008: 229)

discipline to make a relevant contribution to the academic EFL discourse on authenticity than for any non-academic. Aspects of authorial stance (chapter 4.2.1), authorial style (chapter 4.3.1), and citations (chapter 4.3.2) are elements of mode.

Tenor, which refers to "the relationship between participants" (Gotti 2003: 24), is largely conjoined with mode. Due to the mode of scholarly writing most participants never interact with one another face to face but are colleagues by virtue of working in the same trade. Tenor in the academy is marked by a high degree of hierarchical structuring, so all questions of author status (chapter 4.2.2) are considered elements of tenor. These power implications are considerably less prolific amongst teachers and materials designers. Both mode and tenor are essentially institutional criteria.

Field, which refers to "the object of communication, i.e. its topic" (Gotti 2003: 24), is a thematic criterion. It is normally a useful means to demarcate special discourses within EFL from one another. Examples of EFL topics would be TBLT, pronunciation, assessment, vocabulary etc. A certain degree of interface is normal between the topics. In the case of authenticity, however, field fails to function as a reliable criterion. Denotations of *authentic/authenticity* stretch across various EFL topics, e.g. TBLT (authentic tasks) or assessment (authentic assessment). Consequently, the criterion of field must be complemented – if not replaced – by another criterion: the explicit negotiation of terminology.

4.4.3 Demarcation – explicit negotiation of terminology

When investigating authenticity in EFL, it soon becomes evident that two kinds of statements must be distinguished: statements in which the term *authentic/authenticity* happens to be used, and statements which comment on the term itself. The former kind is certainly interesting to look at, yet the vast number of statements makes it virtually impossible for a single scholar to analyze with due diligence. Even more interesting is the latter kind, which I refer to as statements which explicitly negotiate authenticity.

The following words by Norman Fairclough are valid and important in the context of authenticity:

> Most of the time, we treat the meaning of a word (and other linguistic expressions) as a simple matter of fact, and if there is any question about 'the facts' we see the dictionary as the place where we can check up on them. For words we are all perfectly familiar with, it's a matter of mere common sense that they mean what they mean! I shall suggest below that common sense is as suspect here as elsewhere. [...]

> Because of the considerable status accorded by common sense to 'the dictionary', there is a tendency to generally underestimate the extent of variation in meaning systems within a society. [...] It is easy to demonstrate that meanings [...] vary 'ideologically': one respect in which discourse types differ is in their meaning systems. [...]

> [T]he meaning of a word is not an isolated and independent thing. Words and other linguistic expressions enter into many sorts of relationship – relationships of similarity, contrast, overlap and inclusion. And the meaning of a single word depends very much on the relationship of that word to others. So instead of the vocabulary of a language consisting of an unordered list of isolated words each with its own meaning, it consists of clusters of words associated with 'meaning systems'. (Fairclough 2015: 114-115)

A word which denotes a tangible object, say *cucumber*, may be less contingent on those "relationships of similarity, contrast, overlap and inclusion" (ibid.) than is the word *authentic/authenticity*. As mentioned before, *authentic/authenticity* is a floating signifier (Jørgensen/Phillips 2002: 30), and in the academic field of EFL this terminological idiosyncrasy has led to a high amount of explicit negotiation.

The term 'terminology' denotes:

a) the inventory of technical terms, that is, lexical items which designate a defined concept in a particular subject field, and

b) the theoretical categories, principles and rules for correlating words and phrases to defined concepts, and the recommendations for the lexical material thought suitable for this naming process [...]. (Gläser 1995: 37)

The EFL discourse on authenticity differs from other EFL discourses by its terminological focus. Of interest are all the statements which include or surround the signifiers *authentic, authenticity, authentication, (to) authenticate*.[42] These lexemes are to be considered technical terms according to the definition above. Under investigation are stretches of text which explicitly negotiate at least one of them. Thus, my sampling method follows a partially technical – since lexical – criterion, which facilitates the selection process for the texts to be investigated.

To consider *authentic/authenticity* a *terminus technicus* of EFL is a corollary of the fact that academic discourses are marked by a high degree of specialization, which usually has strong terminological implications. The implications are highlighted in the following description by Swales:

This specialization may involve using lexical items known to the wider speech communities in special and technical ways, as in information technology discourse communities, or using highly technical terminology as in medical communities. [...] It is hard to conceive, at least in the contemporary English-speaking world, of a group of well-established members of a discourse community communicating among themselves on topics relevant to the goals of the community and not using lexical items puzzling to outsiders. (Swales 1990: 26)

EFL does not really feature this lexical exclusiveness. Large parts of EFL terminology are not as technical and opaque to outsiders as may be the case in other academic discourses. Many publications are fairly comprehensible for the layman. The denotative and connotative value of *authentic/authenticity*, for example, scarcely differs from what the colloquial use of the term transports. In fact, *authentic/authenticity* is among those words moving most freely between special discourse and public discourse (Keller 2008: 229-230). All in all, rather few technical terms can really be said to be confined to the field of EFL. The lack of technical terminology in EFL exists due to a lack of signifiers that are really exclusive. This means that, unlike in medicine for example, there are hardly any signifiers that would not be at least remotely understood by people external to the field.

42　As I stated before, I do not conceive of statement as a necessarily repetitive element, thereby contradicting Foucault. In my field of research, which may be more restricted than what Foucault envisions, it is serviceable to allow for a single utterance to form a statement, provided that criteria of substance and relevance are fulfilled.

The fact that EFL terminology is often borrowed from other fields or from everyday language does not preclude the existence of technical terminology per se. By virtue of rigorous processes of defining words and expressions – and at times by virtue of mere redundancy of a term – the terminology may be seen as technical and exclusive. Yet, by sharing terms with other discursive formations the meanings of the terms are subject to constant flux, as Jørgensen/Phillips point out:

> [B]ecause a discourse is always constituted in relation to an outside, it is always in danger of being undermined by it, that is its unity of meaning is in danger of being disrupted by other ways of fixing the meaning of the signs. Here, the concept of 'element' becomes relevant. Elements are the signs whose meanings have not yet been fixed; signs that have multiple, potential meanings (i.e. they are 'polysemic'). Using this concept, we can now reformulate the concept of discourse: a discourse attempts to transform elements into moments by reducing their polysemy to a fully fixed meaning. [...] [T]he discourse establishes a 'closure', a temporary stop to the fluctuations in the meaning of the signs. But closure is never definitive [...]. (Jørgensen/Phillips 2002: 27-28)

Fairclough sees the closure on the lexical level as concomitant with the closure on the macrostructural level of the discourse. Once a dominant discourse type is established, the fluctuation of word meanings will cease. This process is called *naturalization*:

> [I]f a discourse type so dominates an institution that dominated types are more or less entirely suppressed or contained, then it will cease to be seen as arbitrary (in the sense of being one among several possible ways of 'seeing' things) and will come to be seen as 'natural', and legitimate because it is simply 'the' way of conducting oneself. I will refer to this, as others have done, as the 'naturalization' of a discourse type. (Fairclough 2015: 113)

This danger of being undermined by an outside is specifically present in the academic EFL discourse on authenticity.

Different authors have expounded the problem with terminology in the humanities. While the first of the following two observations characterizes the situation at large, the second one is true for *authentic/authenticity* in particular:

> The absence of standardization of terminology in the social sciences, as opposed to that of the natural sciences and the technological disciplines, has resulted in an outcrop of new terms in a number of fields. In linguistics, in particular, the flowering of terminology has reached new dimensions, and its striking feature is a host of neologisms and polysemy of existent linguistic terms in different concepts and approaches. (Gläser 1995: 1)

> Clearly, it is typical rather than untypical of many humanities fields that their concepts are not used in a particular uniform manner, and perhaps a strict demand to achieve a common terminology and sharp definitions is too much to ask. It is nevertheless important not to accept that anything goes, and buy loose or random use of terms and concepts under the general guise of fuzziness and indeterminacy characterising the conceptual domain of our field. (Mauranen 2004: 204)

The problem outlined necessitates a discourse analytical approach to understanding *authentic/authenticity*.

A discourse based on a single term is dynamic, …

a)   … if the denotation of the term is one, which people have different opinions about (while finding it highly relevant).

or

b)   … if the term itself is a floating signifier, i.e. people disagree about what the term means (while finding the presumptive meanings highly relevant).

In the public and political discourse, an example of a) would be the term *refugee*. The denotation itself is relatively clear but people have different attitudes toward refugees. An example of b) would be the term *freedom*. Because it refers to rather vague concepts, the denotation of the term is never completely fixed but is contingent upon a myriad of factors. Curiously, very few people seem to have negative attitudes toward freedom, which is similarly the case with authenticity.

I argue that the term *authentic/authenticity* is close to b), but also features elements of a). The similarity to a word like *freedom* can be explained by the conceptual abstractness and by the connotation of the term. These characteristics expose *authentic/authenticity* to disagreement over its denotation.

The common ground *authentic/authenticity* shares with *refugee* is that even if the denotation is clear, people disagree on topics surrounding it. In the EFL discourse on authenticity, the term has adopted at least one denotation that is largely consolidated: authentic texts and materials. Once the meaning is clear, it becomes susceptible to dissent not on a terminological basis but on a practical one because authors differ over the use of such materials. Similarly to discussions on refugees, opinions vary as to how useful authentic materials are, what one should do with them, or whether they even may cause harm.

The academic EFL discourse on authenticity is so dynamic because both a) (e.g. *refugee*) and b) (e.g. *freedom*) apply to a very high degree. a) causes what I call *implicit* negotiation of the term, b) causes what I call *explicit* negotiation of the term. Looking at the discourse, texts are of no interest if they do not feature the term *authentic/authenticity*. Texts are of limited interest if they use the term casually rather than with explicit focus. Therefore, a distinction is made between texts which negotiate authenticity rather implicitly and those which negotiate it explicitly. To be precise, by *academic EFL discourse on authenticity* I refer to all the statements contributing to an explicit negotiation of the term within the discursive formation in question. This explicit negotiation of terminology is a common feature of academic discourse in general, which is a reification of Morris's very basic explanation that scientific discourse "attempts to gain greater precision […] by the introduction of carefully defined designators which signify characteristics of the environment neglected or unnoticed at simpler levels of observation" (Morris 1946: 126-128). Text level examples to illustrate the difference between implicit and explicit negotiation are given in chapter 4.5.1.

The difficulties attendant on a) (qualities of *refugee*) and b) (qualities of *freedom*) are exacerbated by a particular circumstance, which applies to *authentic/authenticity* more than to most other terms:

> The interrelation between terminology and phraseology is a more intricate problem than it appears at first sight. Phrases may become terms once they have been allocated to a defined concept which represents a phenomenon or a complex state of affairs in the notional system of a particular subject area. [...]

> Collocations are always the point of departure and the initial stage of phrase formation [...]. As a rule, they originate from a textual environment of spoken or written discourse and are thus closer to syntax than to lexicology and phraseology. Undoubtedly, collocations continue to be a source for new set expressions which, by stipulation of their structure and meaning, may acquire the status of terms. (Gläser 1995: 55-56)

Particularly the adjective *authentic* eagerly enters into diverse collocations creating combinations of adjective and noun as varied as *authentic materials, ... language, ... text, ... task, ... activity, ... classroom, ... setting, ... testing* etc. The noun *authenticity* is more limited in this regard. Still, it forms collocations or compounds such as *cultural authenticity, task authenticity* etc. The noun *authentication* does not appear to lend itself to collocations. It is also considerably less frequent in discourses outside of academic EFL. The adverb *authentically* is used rarely. Some of the collocations are referred to as terms based on my perception of them as "set expressions" (Gläser 1995: 55-56). For example, *authentic material(s)* and *authentic text(s)* are considered terms. A quantitative analysis might be insightful to determine which collocations are most common and which ones are marginal.

The issue of collocation is arguably an additional source of "struggle over meaning" (Jørgensen/Phillips 2002: 30) (cf. chapter 4.1). The possible combinations are so vast that a multitude of denotations is promoted by mere virtue of syntactical flexibility.

The research interest of this study entails the terminological focus. Every single statement in the discourse to contain the term *authentic/authenticity* contributes to a negotiation of the term. If, however, the term is used without explaining what it means, the negotiation is considered implicit. In academic discourses, which tend to define terminology in a rigorous and explicit manner, implicit negotiation through the mere use of a term is mostly negligible. Even a high author status is unlikely to make up for a low degree of explicit negotiation when it comes to forming powerful statements in the discourse under scrutiny. Therefore, the ultimate sampling criterion complementing mode and tenor (chapter 4.4.2) is explicit negotiation of the term *authentic/authenticity*.

To reiterate, mode refers to "the channel and medium of communication" (Gotti 2003: 24). It therefore contains the contingent elements of authorial stance (chapter 4.2.1), authorial style (chapter 4.3.1), and citations (chapter 4.3.2). Tenor, which refers to "the relationship between participants" (Gotti 2003: 24), is marked among other things by hierarchical structures. It therefore contains the element of author status. Both mode and tenor are subject to the institutional principles that govern academia. Instead of complementing mode and tenor with field, which would serve as a thematic sampling criterion, I propose explicit negotiation of terminology as a criterion because the academic EFL discourse on authenticity revolves around a term rather than revolving around a single topic.

4.4.4 Adjacent discourses

Mode, tenor, and explicit negotiation of authenticity are the three aspects that allow for a demarcation of the academic EFL discourse on authenticity. The discourse can thus be demarcated from various adjacent discourses. Two complementary graphic representations (figures 7 and 8) shall serve to illustrate the constellations within which the discourse is embedded.

Figure 7 shows different discursive formations based on Keller's typological approach (Keller 2008: 229). All the formations are special discourses in the following sense:

> Discourse research of Symbolic Interactionism, unlike Foucault, dealt with rather small-scale mechanisms of [special] discourses, with their participating actors, their strategies and resources, and with their fixed contents and their institutional consequences. [...] [The latter are] institutional – and therefore in a way semi-public – special discourses [...].[43] (Keller 2008: 229-230)

A binary distinction is made between academic discourse (arrow pointing to the top) and non-academic discourse (arrow pointing to the left). This distinction is largely institutional and not thematic because nearly all topics are discussed in both academic and non-academic contexts. The two contexts thus differ in mode and tenor but not in field (cf. chapter 4.4.2). After the binary distinction, a vast thematic diversification – i.e. a diversification in terms of field – is yielded in both spaces. In the academic field, the diversification is clearly structured by research disciplines so the graphic representation in the form of boxes is considered largely adequate: academic discourse in medicine, academic discourse in engineering etc.

---

43   Original: "Die entsprechende Diskursforschung des Symbolischen Interaktionismus hat sich dann im Unterschied zu Foucault mit historisch ‚kleinformatigeren' Karrieremechanismen solcher Diskurse, mit den beteiligten Akteuren, ihren Strategien und Ressourcen sowie mit den festgeschriebenen Inhalten und deren institutionellen Konsequenzen beschäftigt. [...] [Letztere sind] institutionelle – also in gewissem Sinne teilöffentliche – Spezialdiskurse [...]." (Keller 2008: 229–230)

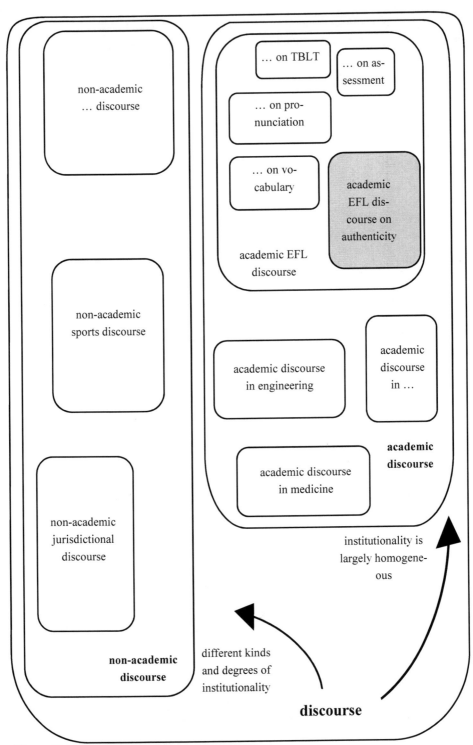

non-academic
... discourse

non-academic
sports discourse

non-academic
jurisdictional
discourse

... on TBLT

... on as-
sessment

... on pro-
nunciation

... on vo-
cabulary

academic
EFL dis-
course on
authenticity

academic EFL
discourse

academic discourse
in engineering

academic
discourse
in ...

academic discourse
in medicine

**academic
discourse**

institutionality is
largely homogene-
ous

**non-academic
discourse**

different kinds
and degrees of
institutionality

discourse

Figure 7: Different types of discourse

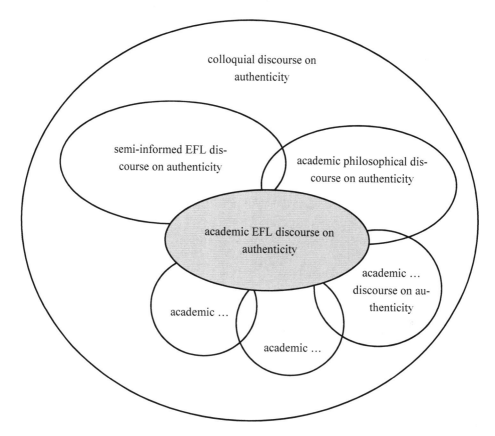

Figure 8: The academic EFL discourse on authenticity with its adjacent discourses

Such a clear structure is not in place for non-academic contexts, where some formations are more institutionalized than others. The graphic representation by means of thematic boxes is therefore slightly simplistic. For example, the sports discourse is heterogeneous in many respects. It is a thematic discourse, in which many different individuals participate and which is subject to varying forms of institutionalization. People watch basketball games in their spare time and talk about players, teams etc. In a more institutionalized framework, officials meet in exclusive circles to discuss organizational matters of the national basketball league. Consequently, there exists a wide range of institutionality.

This range of institutionality is considerably smaller in the non-academic jurisdictional discourse. People participating in this discourse are for the most part professionals who were influenced by the academic discourse during their studies at university. The degree of institutionality is consistently high, thus comparable to academic discourses. It is decreased in rare cases, namely when lawsuits draw a wide public interest due to scandals being investigated. The discourse is then opened up to the public through media coverage. Comparable scenarios are hardly imaginable for a topic like nuclear physics, where the non-academic discourse all but equals its academic counterpart. Topics of nuclear physics are not frequently discussed in casual settings but exist almost exclusively in highly institutionalized contexts that are professional and/or academic.

Public interest is a general determinant of heterogeneous institutionality. Topics that are of interest to a broad public usually do not remain within the institutional confines of a professional field. Beside sport (and law to a lesser degree), politics is another example of heterogeneous institutionality. Such heterogeneity lends itself to an institutional splitting of discourses. In the case of politics, the splitting could yield a professional discourse, a journalistic discourse, a popular discourse etc. In figure 7, institutional splitting is not represented beyond the academic/non-academic distinction. Thematic splitting, however, is made visible within both academic and non-academic spaces.

In the academic discourse, thematic splitting ultimately leads to what I have termed *academic EFL discourse on authenticity*, which is a highly specialized discourse. In figure 7, such a degree of specialization is not visually represented for the other academic and non-academic fields. What makes the fields thematically distinct is their compartmentalized organization within universities. The academic publishing industry is equally split into disciplines, which is most tangible in disciplinary journals. Obviously, *ELT Journal* will not accept contributions from disciplines that have no bearing on the topics of language teaching and learning. On the academic macro level, thematic splitting is thus institutionally reinforced.

Within each discipline, further specialization takes place but it may not be so clearly structured. Thematic splitting within disciplines is usually less institutionalized than on the academic macro level. A university does not have a department of TBLT, a chair of vocabulary learning etc. This makes it difficult to draw dividing lines between topics. Many topics are shaped by the dynamics of the discourse. In EFL, some topics are arguably: Task-Based Language Teaching (TBLT), pronunciation, assessment, vocabulary, authenticity etc.

As mentioned before, to see authenticity as a topic would imply a certain thematic homogeneity within the corresponding discourse. The terminological focus, however, sets the discourse on authenticity apart from more thematic discourses, e.g. TBLT. In figure 7, the academic EFL discourse on authenticity is placed alongside TBLT, pronunciation, assessment etc. This is not meant to suggest that distinctions between the discourses are solely based on field, i.e. based on thematic differences.

Each topic forms its own discursive formation, yet these are often interwoven because the topics are cognate and the rules of formation are virtually identical. In most cases, the demarcation of different EFL discourses runs along thematic lines. The academic EFL discourse on authenticity is idiosyncratic in that it is fixated on a term rather than on a single theme. The term *authentic/authenticity* tends to become the very object of analysis, which is a phenomenon I refer to as *explicit negotiation*. Few other terms in EFL are explicitly negotiated at a comparable rate. *Creativity* or *autonomy* (e.g. Schmenk 2008) come to mind. The terminological fixation means that, for the purpose of this study, explicit negotiation can be made a criterion of demarcation. It also means that in order for a contribution to belong to the discourse, it must feature the term. To give a counterexample, the discourse on vocabulary may include contributions that do not display the term *vocabulary* but rely on terminology such as *mental lexicon, words, lexemes, items etc.* A contribution may still put forth pertinent ideas on how vocabulary is learned.

The academic EFL discourse on authenticity is one of many EFL discourses, as is represented in figure 7. Its terminological focus, which is an idiosyncrasy, renders it cognate not only with academic EFL discourses but also with discourses outside of EFL where the term is equally present. Figure 8 thus complements figure 7 by showing what other discursive formations (outside of academic EFL) may influence the academic EFL discourse on authenticity. The primary connection between the different circles in figure 8 is the presence of the term *authentic/authenticity*. The primary criterion of demarcation is the institutional one. The term transcends institutional limits like few others. It appears that any context in which the term is used has the power to transform the term's meaning not only in the same context but far beyond. This assumption is based on the following line of argumentation:

The academic EFL discourse on authenticity, which in figure 8 is represented as a grey circle, borders on and interfaces with a number of discursive formations. It is also embedded in one very large discourse, which is the colloquial discourse on authenticity. Since the term *authentic/authenticity* is used by speakers colloquially without reference to any academic discipline, it is part of everyday language. Every person in academia or in any other professional field is at the same time a member of the public colloquial discourse. When the term *authentic/authenticity* is used in the public discourse, the receiver cannot be expected to be familiar with technical definitions. Furthermore, a person in academia who is familiar with certain definitions has likely used the word before encountering it in form of a technical term. It can therefore be assumed that the public colloquial discourse on authenticity has a bearing on all other professional and academic contexts where the term is used.

The preposition *on* in the expression *colloquial discourse on authenticity* may suggest an explicit negotiation of authenticity, i.e. definitions and metadiscursive elements. Scholars in the academy make statements as to how the term is defined, what it refers to, or what it should refer to. Unlike in academic contexts, however, explicit negotiation is rare in the public domain. The mere use of the term, which is referred to as *implicit negotiation*, is still considered to have an impact given how pervasive the colloquial discourse is. The preposition *on* is used for the sake of consistency and for the lack of a better expression.

The influence which the colloquial discourse exerts on the EFL discourse is a logical assumption, but it becomes evident and tangible in instances where EFL authors cite general dictionaries such as the Oxford English Dictionary (OED) (e.g. Beile 1986: 145-146; Kramsch 1993: 179-180). The creators of dictionaries are clear about their endeavor to present naturally occurring language: "One of the guiding principles of [...] lexicography is that entries should be based on the 'real' facts of the language, drawn principally from examples illustrating contemporary usage" (Oxford English Dictionary 2016).

The academic EFL discourse on authenticity is touched by several other academic discourses in which the term is prevalent (cf. figure 8). The academy, as an institution that overarches many disciplines, has arguably a unifying effect. Researchers from different fields are likely to see each other as co-workers and the discursive rules of formation are similar in all disciplines. These conditions facilitate contact and exchange between disciplinary discourses. A lexeme like *authenticity* is subject of explicit negotiation in different academic fields and, at times, authors consult definitions from neighboring disciplines. Van Lier (1996), for instance, invokes philosophical notions of authenticity as he puts forth his views on the term and its concepts. In figure 8, various academic discourses that negotiate authenticity are placed around their EFL equivalent to illustrate the discursive cognateness.

Lastly, figure 8 features a circle that has a considerable area of overlap with the academic EFL discourse on authenticity. This circle represents the discourse formed by statements that are made not by EFL scholars but by EFL teachers. These people may have been in contact with the scholarly literature and they are generally interested in and concerned with questions of learning and teaching EFL. Still, the assumption is that their understanding of the term is informed to a large degree by colloquial denotations and connotations. Teachers are thus considered *semi-informed* in that they are concerned with the topic in a less than academic manner. Equally included in the semi-informed EFL discourse are statements made by publishers of textbooks and learning materials. Such statements are usually to be found in the context of marketing where the term *authentic/authenticity* is used to advertise the given materials. The interface between the semi-informed EFL circle and the academic EFL circle is owed in part to an assumed portion of individuals who are teachers (or textbook designers) and researchers at the same time. The demarcation between the two circles, albeit a blurry one, is chiefly institutional in nature because EFL as an academic field is subject to gatekeeping mechanisms (cf. chapter 4.2.2). It is important to mention that no evaluative prioritization is made between the discourses. The terminology of semi-informed versus academic circle may falsely suggest hierarchical implications.

Some graphic aspects of figure 8 must be elaborated on. The sizes of the circles are not *to scale*. The dimensions are not completely arbitrary but they are rather intuitive and shall not be considered accurate or representative. More important than those questions of proportion are the interfacing parts of the circles. They are intended to hint at the fluid nature of discourse as such. The academic discourses forming a cluster of sorts is a result from the unifying effects that are arguably at play in institutions of higher education, as expounded above. The semi-informed EFL circle interfaces considerably with its academic counterpart but just barely so with the other academic disciplines. Non-academics – in this case teachers – are not very likely to engage in discourses that are both institutionally and thematically remote. One intentional detail in figure 8 is that the academic EFL circle is not entirely surrounded by the adjacent discourses but features a stretch at the left that is exposed to the all-encompassing colloquial discourse. Otherwise a false impression of insulation would be created. Although terminology is explicitly negotiated within the academic EFL circle, the colloquial understanding of words is bound to exert an influence.

A very basic characteristic of the academic EFL discourse on authenticity is that it unfolds largely in written form, which is typical of any academic discourse. Consequently, the demarcation from adjacent discourses implies that certain texts belong to the discourse while others are not part of it. In the following chapter, this demarcation is pursued in more practical terms leading to a selection of documents that constitute the academic EFL discourse on authenticity.

4.5 Compiling a document selection of authenticity in EFL

Having demarcated the academic EFL discourse on authenticity, it is possible to identify documents that fall within this discourse and separate them from other documents that do not meet the relevant criteria. In what follows, texts are selected which explicitly negotiate authenticity.

This excludes all texts which …

- do not belong to the academic field of EFL.
- do not feature the term *authentic/authenticity*.
- negotiate the term *authentic/authenticity* implicitly rather than explicitly (cf. chapter 4.4.3).
- are written in a language other than English or German.
- are not officially published, hence difficult to find and/or access, e.g. master's theses, internet blog posts, oral formats such as presentations at conferences etc.

To elaborate on the fourth point, the research at hand focuses on texts written in English, since the discourse is most prolifically maintained in this language. My own first language being German, I decided to include German texts as well. The difference between the English term and the German term (*authentisch/Authentizität*) is negligible in denotation and in connotation. Including two languages has some benefits. Firstly, the German discourse functions as a control group of sorts: What can be seen is whether certain discursive patterns differ between the languages. Secondly, the quantitative proportion between the two languages is insightful: English texts generally outnumber German texts and may, consequently, be expected to show similar supremacy over other languages. Thirdly, cross-references between the two languages can be investigated.

The last one of the points above – texts which are not published and generally accessible – implies the exclusion of any spoken discourse, extending to presentations at conferences. I have been able to speak in person to some of the most important participants in the discourse and will refer to the implications of these conversations in due course. Oral formats are, however, omitted in the data collection for two reasons: One, they are impossible to cover in a remotely comprehensive manner. Two, they are ancillary to the written formats in terms of discursive impact due to their more transient nature.

4.5.1 From demarcation to sampling – practical examples of explicit negotiation

The five points above, which describe the characteristics of texts not to be examined, are of course inversely derived from the aspects of demarcation, as expounded in chapter 4.4. These aspects – mode, tenor, and explicit negotiation of authenticity – are apt to serve as sampling criteria for the compilation of a document selection. The one criterion that demands special attention is explicit negotiation because it is often difficult to decide whether the criterion applies or not. Later in this chapter, text samples are provided to illustrate the threshold between implicit and explicit negotiation.

A selection of documents, as compiled in this study, allows for a certain degree of transparency and accountability. Every text relevant for the analysis appears in the corresponding bibliographic list. The document selection is useful, in particular, if bibliometric insights are to be drawn in addition to the qualitative findings of discourse analysis.

In historical research, the heuristic approach of creating a body of sources is commonly pursued. It allows for transparency in both qualitative and quantitative analysis. Unlike purely historical researchers I prefer to speak of *texts*, not of *sources*, in part because some of them are so recent that the latter term would be misleading. Furthermore, the discourse analytical focus foregrounds the linguistic element to some extent and to speak of *texts* is traditional in this field. The historical analysis of sources is guided by principles of hermeneutics. Ruisz (2004), who researches US reeducation policy in postwar Germany, takes such a hermeneutic approach gaining insights from her sources and inferring from them political and societal facts of a given era (Ruisz 2014: 21). To that end a heterogeneous body of sources, which encompasses a variety of text genres, is compiled. Ruisz is meticulous in listing and describing her sources. The primary research interest of the study at hand differs from Ruisz's in that a clearly defined discourse is in focus. Thus, the document selection to be developed is relatively homogeneous.

As explained, the document selection is confined to academic publications. These include monographs, articles in edited volumes, and articles in journals. An additional genre to be covered are entries in encyclopedias of EFL or applied linguistics. These entries are naturally found under the headword *authentic/authenticity* and they give a definition of the term within a relatively short format. For the first three types of publications mentioned it is not always easy to identify those texts which meet the criterion of explicit negotiation. A viable means to start with is the selection of publications which carry the term in the title. Such texts have been found to use the term in a usually quite conscious and reflected manner. It is rare that an author uses the term in the title without extensively addressing it in the text. In most cases even a definition – partial or comprehensive, more or less explicit – can be derived.

However, a few exceptions to the rule must be mentioned:

Dunn, Opal (2006). Do boys as young learners of English need different language learning opportunities from girls? Can **authentic picture books** help? In: Enever/Schmid-Schönbein (eds.), 115-122.

Kierepka, Adelheid (2006). Children's approaches to **authentic picture books** in the primary EFL classroom. In: Enever/Schmid-Schönbein (eds.), 123-130.

Hughes, Annie (2006). The 'why', 'what' and 'how' of using **authentic picture books** and stories in the EYL classroom. Some practical considerations. In: Enever/Schmid-Schönbein (eds.), 151-163. (emphases added by L.W.)

These three articles are contributions to the same book edited by Janet Enever and Gisela Schmid-Schönbein (2006). It seems that the term *authentic picture book* has been agreed upon by the authors and that an elaboration on what is meant by *authentic* is seen as unnecessary. None of the authors comment on the term or explain it. Therefore, these three titles are not included in the document selection. Another instance where texts are purposely omitted is one issue of the journal *Language Testing* from 1985. The issue is dedicated exclusively to the topic of authentic assessment and contains as many as five articles which feature the term in the title. Instead of listing all five articles, however, I have decided to include the issue of the journal as one publication. There are two reasons for proceeding in this manner. First, none of the articles has a high qualitative relevance for the discourse in terms of cross reference, author status, and substance. Second, a full representation in the document selection would distort the bibliometric picture with regard to its quantitative validity (cf. chapter 4.5.3 for an explanation of bibliometrics). The following publications are thus all contained in one reference:[44]

Klein-Braley, Christine (1985). A cloze-up on the C-Test: a study in the construct validation of **authentic tests**. *Language Testing,* 2(1), 76-104.

Seliger, Herbert W. (1985). Testing **authentic language**: the problem of meaning. *Language Testing,* 2(1), 1-15.

Shohamy, E.; Reves, T. (1985). **Authentic language tests**: where from and where to? *Language Testing,* 2(1), 48-59.

Spolsky, Bernard (1985). The limits of **authenticity in language testing**. *Language Testing,* 2(1), 31-40.

Stevenson, Douglas K. (1985). **Authenticity**, validity and a tea party. *Language Testing,* 2(1), 41-47. (emphases added by L.W.)

One more example rebuts the use in the title as reliable criterion. The edited volume *Stories matter. The complexity of cultural authenticity in children's literature* (Fox/Short 2003) contains nine contributions, which respectively feature the term in their title. As in Enever/Schmid-Schönbein (2006), there seems to be an agreement between the authors on a certain understanding of authenticity. The common theme revolves around questions of culture so *cultural authenticity* is a prolific collocation throughout the volume. At no point is a definition provided:

> We found ourselves agreeing with Rudine Sims Bishop, who argues that cultural authenticity cannot be defined, although 'you know it when you see it' as an insider reading a book about your own culture. [...] The reader's sense of truth in how a specific cultural

---

44   In the upcoming document selection, the author indicated is Seliger et al. (1985). The publication is titled *Language Testing* 2(1).

experience has been represented within a book, particularly when the reader is an insider to the culture portrayed in that book, is probably the most common understanding of cultural authenticity. (Short/Fox 2003: 4-5)

The book is, in fact, an example of how the negotiation of authenticity can remain below the threshold of explicitness while using the term prolifically. To give a sense of this threshold, a text level illustration is seen as called-for. The following quote from the book is an example of implicit negotiation approximating the threshold of explicitness but not crossing it. This rather long extract is provided to show the constant absence of explicit negotiation. The extract displays the highest degree of negotiation found within the whole book:

> In my own early work (Sims, 1982), I implicitly defined authenticity in relation to two dimensions. The first had to do with which aspects of the cultural, physical, or social environment the authors chose to emphasize, for example whether the ghetto was 'place of sudden violence, sordid poverty, and crime' (Etter, 1969) or simply 'home' as Lucille Clifton (1987) characterized the 'inner city' in one of her poems. Noting the elements of the environment emphasized by the text provided an indication of the extent to which the work reflected the cultural perspective or worldview of the people whose lives are reflected in the work or that of someone passing through and projecting their own sensibilities onto the book.
>
> The second dimension was the accuracy of what I called 'authenticating details'. It was my contention that such details as the grammatical and lexical accuracy of the characters' dialect, and taken-for-granted information possessed by members of a cultural group, help to determine authenticity. For example, some authors tried to represent Black vernacular by seemingly sprinkling 'be' constructions or expressions such as 'I is' randomly throughout the dialogue. One book described an African Methodist Episcopal (A.M.E.) church service in a way that was inaccurate and offensive, indicating both an ignorance of the facts and an insensitivity to the meanings that the service holds for church members. I described the differences as those between writing as an 'insider' or as an 'outsider' to the cultural environment in which the story was set. That description was not original with me (e.g., Shepard used the terms in his 1971 article), but the 'insider/outsider' dichotomy is still at the core of arguments over cultural authenticity. (Bishop 2003: 27-28)

The extract serves as a benchmark for the distinction between implicit and explicit negotiation of authenticity. The negotiation here is slightly too long-winded and indirect to be considered a definition of authenticity. It rests barely underneath the threshold of explicitness. The negotiation not only lacks succinctness but also conclusiveness. The passage above, which would be expected to provide a conclusive definition, begins with the following formulation: "I implicitly defined authenticity in relation to two dimensions. The first had to do with [...]" (ibid.). Markers of inconclusiveness are: *implicitly, in relation to, had to do with*. The ensuing description merely provides examples of what "has to do with" (ibid.) authenticity, thereby remaining rather vague. A reference to another author, who defines authenticity more concisely, would likely put the descriptions on the side of explicitness. Many texts in the document selection about to be presented actually quote definitions by others before commenting on them.

To contrast the extract by Bishop (2003), here is an example of a statement that is considered barely above the threshold of explicit negotiation:

In the context of foreign language pedagogy, the need for authenticity is well recognized. The dominant approach to language teaching – the communicative method – demands that the use of 'real life' language is promoted in the classroom. In order for the real world language to emerge there is a need to create authentic learning situations. As Sildus (2006) observes, "[R]eal life language always happens in a context, and it would be logical to design classroom activities to resemble real language use" (p.55). (Nikitina 2011: 34)

The definition of authenticity here is still somewhat indirect, but it is considered sufficiently specific to qualify as explicit negotiation. Moreover, the term *authentic* figures prominently in the title of the publication: *Creating an authentic learning environment in the foreign language classroom*. Nikitina (2011) is therefore included in the document selection.

It must, ultimately, be reaffirmed that the term *authentic/authenticity* being featured in the title is only a starting point of the sampling process. While it is not a guarantee for texts to be included, there are also a number of texts which negotiate the term explicitly without making this visible in the title of the publication. Often these publications contain a chapter dedicated to authenticity or, in rare cases, they broach the topic without announcing it in a caption. Ultimately, the decisive criterion for including a text in the document selection is that it deals with the term in an explicit and reflective manner. The term being part of the title is but an indication that such explicit negotiation is to be found.

Mode, tenor, and explicit negotiation of authenticity are the underlying criteria for selecting the documents. These criteria can now be reified as follows:

Sampling criteria:

- Text features explicit negotiation of the term *authentic/authenticity*
- Text belongs to academic EFL[45]
- Text is written in English or German
- Text is officially published (which excludes master's theses, internet blog posts, oral formats such as presentations at conferences etc.)

The goal of creating a comprehensive selection of documents bears the risk of missing out on relevant publications. The approximative method of looking for texts with the term contained in the title prevents an extensive failure in this regard. Electronic search engines of library catalogues, online databases, and the world-wide web at large, were useful devices at the early stages of my sampling method. Typing in the word *authentic* would yield results containing either the adjective or the noun. At times, filtering functions were in place to narrow down the search according to scientific discipline or other components. The following search words yielded positive results in combination with *authentic*: *English, foreign, language, learning, teaching, classroom, applied linguistics, EFL, ELT.* These electronic means are more common for book formats than for journal articles, since

---

45   In a few cases, texts are included from the fields of German as a Foreign Language and French as a Foreign Language. This is considered acceptable as long as the conceptualizations of authenticity are not influenced by the fact that they apply to the learning of a language other than English.

no all-encompassing database with a search engine was available to search for single journal articles by title. Articles in journals are, thus, more prone to stay under the radar.

The use of search engines was only the very first step. Once a number of texts had been found, I employed what is sometimes referred to as the snowball method: looking at the bibliography of a given publication to find more texts relevant for the topic. The downside of the snowball method is its retrospective design, meaning that a given bibliography can only contain texts older than the publication at hand. To keep up with the latest publications I had to stay alert and also rely on an academic circle of colleagues. Time and again colleagues from various contexts would point out new texts to me, of which I am enormously thankful. Discovering relevant texts which do not display the term in the title was another challenge. The terminological index at the end of monographs was often helpful. Yet, to find the book in the first place, I was dependent on the snowball method, on recommendations, or on author status. For example, I decided to search nearly every text written by Widdowson. I have pursued these approaches to compiling the documents over a period of roughly three years, eventually having reached a point of saturation where most texts that cropped up were already in the list. Although the possibility of sporadic blind spots cannot be excluded, I hope to have found nearly all texts germane to the research interest. The sampling method inherently yields a certain time frame within which all items are located. The minutiae of determining the starting point of the discourse are presented in chapter 4.5.5.

I now present the document selection within which the term *authentic/authenticity* is explicitly negotiated. It is in bibliographic form and it contains the four publication formats mentioned: monographs, articles in edited volumes, articles in journals, encyclopedic entries. The order of representation is chronological and divided by decade for a better overview. Texts published later than 2014 are not included because I finished my search for literature in late 2015.

4.5.2 The academic EFL discourse on authenticity – a document selection

(German publications highlighted in grey)

Number of citations received from other works within the document selection

	Publication	Citations given (= works cited within the document selection)	Type of publica-tion
0	Stevick, Earl W. (1971). *Adapting and writing language lessons*. Washington, DC: Foreign Service Institute.	None	Book
28	Widdowson, Henry G. (1976). The authenticity of language data. In: Fanselow, John F.; Crymes, Ruth H. *On TESOL '76*. Washington, D.C.: TESOL, 261-270.	None – no bibliography	Article in edited volume[46]
8	Wilkins, David A. (1976). *Notional syllabuses. London*. Oxford: Oxford University Press.	None	Book
5	Gutschow, Harald (1977). 'Authentizität' und 'Aktualität' in Texten für den Fremdsprachen-unterricht. *Zielsprache Deutsch* 4/1977, 2-11.	None	Article in journal
10	Morrow, Keith (1977). Authentic texts and ESP. In: Holden, Susan. *English for specific purposes*. London: Modern English Publications, 13-15.	None – no bibliography	Article in journal
4	Geddes, Marion; White, Ron (1978). The use of semi-scripted simulated authentic speech and listening comprehension. *Audio-Visual Language Journal* 16 (3), 137-145.	Wilkins (1976)	Article in journal
28	Widdowson, Henry G. (1978). *Teaching language as communication*. Oxford: Oxford University Press.	None	Book
2	Beile, Werner (1979). Authentizität und Hörverstehen. In: Heuer, Helmut (ed.). *Dortmunder Diskussionen zur Fremdsprachendidaktik. Kongressdokumentation der 8. Arbeitstagung*	None – no bibliography	Article in edited volume

---

46 Reprinted in Widdowson (1979) as well as in Hedge/Andon/Dewey (eds.); most authors actually cite the reprint of 1979.

	d. Fremdsprachendidaktiker Dort-mund 1978. Dortmund: Lensing, 232-234.		
2	Henrici, Gert (1980). Authentischer Fremsprachenunterricht. Einige An-merkungen. *Bielefelder Beiträge zur Sprachlehrforschung* 2, 123-134.	None	Article in journal
2	Petersen, Hans (1980). Objektivierung und Vergegenwärtigung als Katego-rien des Fremdsprachenunterrichts. In: Authentizität und Lehrbarkeit [thematic issue]. *Der fremdsprachli-che Unterricht* 14/1980, Heft 55, 193-205.	None	Article in journal
3	Weijenberg, Jan (1980). *Authentizität gesprochener Sprache in Lehrwer-ken für Deutsch als Fremdsprache.* Heidelberg: Groos.	Beile (1979), Gutschow (1977)	Book
2	Beile, Werner (1981): Authentizität aus anderer Sicht. *Der fremdsprachliche Unterricht*, 15 (57), 61-62.	None – no bibliography	Article in journal
8	Grellet, Françoise (1981). *Developing reading skills. A practical guide to reading comprehension exercises.* Cambridge, New York: Cambridge University Press.	None	Book
5	Porter, Don; Roberts, Jon (1981). Au-thentic listening activities. *ELT Journal,* 36(1), 37-47.	None	Article in Journal
1	Beeching, Kate (1982). Authentic mate-rial 1. *British Journal of Language Teaching* 20 (2), 17-20.	Widdowson (1976)	Article in journal[47]
5	Candlin, Christopher N.; Edelhoff, Christoph (1982). *Challenges: Teacher's Guide.* London: Long-man.	Widdowson (1978)	Book
2	Lynch, Anthony J. (1982). 'Authentic-ity' in language teaching: Some im-plications for the design of listening materials. *British Journal of Lan-guage Teaching* 20 (2), 9-16.	Widdowson (1976)	Article in journal
1	Alexander, Richard (1983). How au-thentic can (and should) 'authentic' texts be? In: Kühlwein, Wolfgang (ed.). *Texte in der Sprachwissen-schaft, Sprachunterricht und*	None	Article in edited vol-ume

---

47 "Authentic material 2", which appears one issue later, is not as explicit in its negotiation of authenticity.

	Sprachtherapie. Bd. 4. Tübingen: Narr, 87-88.		
1	Lee, William R. (1983). Some points about 'authenticity'. *World Language English*, 2(1), 10-14.	None – no bibliography	Article in journal
1	Rivers, Wilga M. (1983). *Communicating naturally in a second language*. New York: Cambridge University Press. Not available!		Book
4	Widdowson, Henry G. (1983). *Learning purpose and language use*. Oxford, New York: Oxford University Press.	Widdowson (1976; 1978)	Book
7	Davies, Alan (1984). Simple, simplified and simplification. What is authentic? In: Alderson, Charles J.; Urquhart, A. H. (eds.). *Reading in a foreign language*. Harlow: Longman, 181-195.	Widdowson (1976; 1978)	Article in edited volume
1	Joiner, Elizabeth G. (1984). Authentic texts in the foreign language classroom: Focus on listening and reading. Monterey, CA: Defense Language Institute. *ERIC Document Reproduction Service No. ED 274153*, 3-24.	Rivers (1983)	Article via ERIC
3	Löschmann, Marianne & Löschmann, Martin (1984). Authentisches im Fremdsprachenunterricht. *Deutsch als Fremdsprache* 21/1984, 41-47.	Beile (1981), Edelhoff (1985)[48], Gutschow (1977)	Article in journal
36	Breen, Michael P. (1985). Authenticity in the language classroom. *Applied Linguistics,* 6(1), 60-70.	Candlin/Edelhoff (1982), Widdowson (1976; 1978)	Article in journal
5	Edelhoff, Christoph (1985). Authentizität im Fremdsprachenunterricht. In: Edelhoff, Christoph (ed.). *Authentische Texte im Deutschunterricht.* München: Hueber, 7-30.	None	Article in edited volume
1	Richards, Jack C.; Platt, John Talbot; Weber, Heidi (1985). *Longman dictionary of applied linguistics*. Harlow: Longman.	None – no bibliography	Entry in dictionary
3	Seliger et al. (1985). *Language Testing* 2(1).	None	Approx. 7 articles in journal[49]

---

48   Löschmann/Löschmann (1984) had access to Edelhoff (1985) prior to its publication.
49   This issue of the journal *Language Testing* has a focus on authenticity. A listing of all the single articles would yield an undue representation.

107

9	Swaffar, Janet K. (1985). Reading authentic texts in a foreign language: A cognitive model. *Modern Language Journal* (69.1), 15-34.	Grellet (1981), Rivers (1983)	Article in journal
2	Beile, Werner (1986). Authentizität als fremdsprachendidaktischer Begriff. Zum Problemfeld von Texten gesprochener Sprache. In: Ehnert, Rolf; Piepho, Hans-Eberhard (eds.). *Fremdsprachen lernen mit Medien.* München: Hueber, 145-162.	Beile (1979; 1981), Edelhoff (1985), Gutschow (1977), Henrici (1980), Petersen (1980), Piepho (1977), Weijenberg (1979, 1980)	Article in edited volume
7	Rings, Lana (1986). Authentic language and authentic conversational texts. *Foreign Language Annals* 19 (3), 201-208.	Wilkins (1976), Swaffar (1985), Löschmann/Löschmann (1984), Weijenberg (1980)	Article in journal
1	Rück, Heribert (1986). Fetisch ‚authentischer Text'? *Neusprachliche Mitteilungen aus Wissenschaft und Praxis,* 39(3), 165.	None – no bibliography	Article in journal
8	Kienbaum, Barbara E.; Russell, A. J.; Welty, S. (1986). Communicative competence in foreign language learning with authentic materials. Calumet, Indiana. *ERIC Document Reproduction Service No. ED 275200,* 2-36.	None – no bibliography	Article via ERIC
9	Hutchinson, Tom; Waters, Alan (1987). *English for specific purposes. A learning-centred approach.* Cambridge: Cambridge University Press.	None	Book
12	Little, David; Devitt, Seán; Singleton, David (1988). *Authentic texts in foreign language teaching. Theory and practice.* Dublin: Authentik.	Suggestions for further reading but no citations and no bibliography	Book
2	Little, David; Singleton, David M. (1988). Authentic materials and the role of fixed support in language teaching: Towards a manual for language learners. Dublin: Trinity College. *ERIC Document Reproduction Service No. ED 316033,* 3-30.	None	Article via ERIC
4	Nunan, David (1988b). *The learner-centred curriculum. A study in second language teaching.* Cambridge, New York: Cambridge University Press.	Candlin/Edelhoff (1982)	Book
10	Rogers, Carmen Villegas; Medley, Frank W. (1988). Language with a purpose. Using authentic materials in the foreign language classroom.	Geddes/White (1978), Grellet (1981), Joiner (1984), Rings (1986)	Article in journal

	Foreign Language Annals 21 (5), 467-478.		
6	Clarke, David F. (1989). Communicative theory and its influence on materials production. *Language Teaching,* 22(2), 73-86.	Breen (1985), Davies (1984), Geddes/White (1978), Grellet (1981), Hutchinson/Waters (1987), Widdowson (1976; 1978), Wilkins (1976)	Article in journal
8	Nostrand, Howard Lee (1989). Authentic texts and cultural authenticity: An editorial. *Modern Language Journal* 73 (1), 45-52.	None	Article in journal
12	Nunan, David (1989). *Designing tasks for the communicative classroom.* Cambridge; New York: Cambridge University Press.	Candlin/Edelhoff (1982), Porter/Roberts (1981)	Book
21	Widdowson, Henry G. (1990). *Aspects of language teaching.* Oxford: Oxford University Press.	Breen (1985), Widdowson (1976)	Book[50]
6	Bachman, Lyle F. (1990). *Fundamental considerations in language testing.* Oxford: Oxford University Press.	Seliger et al. (1985)	Book
11	Bacon, Susan M.; Finnemann, Michael D. (1990). A study of the attitudes, motives, and strategies of university foreign language students and their disposition to authentic oral and written input. *The Modern Language Journal* 74 (4), 459.	Nostrand (1989), Kienbaum/Russell/Welty (1986), Rogers/Medley (1988)	Article in journal
5	Arnold, Ewen (1991). Authenticity revisited: How real is real? *English for Specific Purposes,* 10, 237-244.	Breen (1985), Hutchinson/Waters (1987), Nunan (1989), Widdowson (1978)	Aricle in journal
1	Bachman, Lyle F. (1991). What does language testing have to offer. *TESOL Quarterly* 25 (4), 671-704.	Bachman (1990), Widdowson (1978)	Article in journal
3	Herron, Carol; Seay, Irene (1991). The effect of authentic oral texts on student listening comprehension in the foreign language classroom. *Foreign Language Annals* 24 (6), 487-495.	Bacon/Finneman (1990), Kienbaum/Russell/Welty (1986), Nostrand (1989), Rogers/Medley (1988)	Article in journal
0	Weller, Franz Rudolf (1992). Wie ‚authentisch' ist ‚idiomatisches' Französisch? Anmerkungen zu zwei un-	Alexander (1983), Beile (1986), Gutschow (1977), Henrici (1980), Little/Devitt/Singleton (1988), Löschmann/Löschmann	Article in journal

---

50   This book is a compilation of articles – some published, some unpublished – from the 1980s.

	klaren Begriffen der Fremdsprachendidaktik. *Fremdsprachen Lehren und Lernen* 21, 117-139.[51]	(1984), Petersen (1980), Piepho (1977), Rück (1986), Widdowson (1976)	
7	Kramsch, Claire J. (1993). *Context and culture in language teaching*. Oxford: Oxford University Press.	Breen (1985), Little/Singleton (1988), Löschmann/Löschmann (1984), Nostrand (1989), (Widdowson 1976; 1990)	Book
2	Young, Dolly J. (1993). Processing strategies of foreign language readers: Authentic and edited input. *Foreign Language Annals* 26 (4), 451-468.	Davies (1984), Kienbaum/Russell/Welty (1986), Swaffar (1985)	Article in journal
3	McNeill, Arthur (1994). What makes authentic materials different? The case of English language materials for educational television. In: n.a. *Papers presented at the Annual International Language in Education Conference, Hong Kong*. n.a., 314-326.	Bacon/Finnemann (1990), Beeching (1982), Lynch (1982), Kienbaum/Russell/Welty (1986), Little/Devitt/Singleton (1988), Nostrand (1989), Widdowson (1976)	Article in edited volume
11	Taylor, David (1994). Inauthentic authenticity or authentic inauthenticity? http://www.tesl-ej.org/wordpress/issues/volume1/ej02/ej02a1/, access date: 08/15/2014.	Bachman (1990), Breen (1985), Kramsch (1993), Morrow (1977), Nunan (1989), Seliger et al. (1985), Widdowson (1976; 1990), Wilkins (1976)	Article in online journal
4	Widdowson, Henry G. (1994). The ownership of English. *TESOL Quarterly* (28/2), 377-389.	None	Article in journal
2	Adams, Thomas W. (1995). What makes materials authentic? *ERIC Document Reproduction Service No. ED 391389*, 1-8.	Breen (1985), Geddes/White (1978), Morrow (1977), Nunan (1989), Rogers/Medley (1988), Taylor (1994), Widdowson (1976)	Article via ERIC
1	Dunkel, P.A. (1995). Authentic second/foreign language listening texts: Issues of definition, operationalization, and application. In: Byrd, Patricia (ed.). *Material writers' guide*. Boston: Heinle and Heinle, 95-106.	Geddes/White (1978), Herron/Seay (1991), Nostrand (1989), Porter/Roberts (1981), Rings (1986), Rogers/Medley (1988), Weijenberg (1980)	Article in edited volume
13	Lee, Winnie Yuk-chun (1995). Authenticity revisited: text authenticity and learner authenticity. *ELT Journal*, 49(4), 323-328.	Bachman (1990), Bacon/Finneman (1990), Breen (1985), Widdowson (1976)	Article in journal

---

51   Weller (1995) is included, although it belongs to the field of French as a Foreign Language. Texts do not strictly have to belong to EFL, if their conceptualizations of authenticity are not influenced by the fact that they apply to the learning of a language other than English.

4	Bachman, Lyle F.; Palmer, Adrian S. (1996). *Language testing in practice. Designing and developing useful language tests.* Oxford; New York: Oxford University Press.	Widdowson (1978; 1983)	Book
0	Kramsch, Claire (1996). Wem gehört die deutsche Sprache? *Die Unterrichtspraxis / Teaching German* 29 (1), 1.	Widdowson (1990; 1994)	Article in journal
0	Long, Michael H. (1996). Authenticity and learning potential in L2 classroom discourse. *University of Hawaii Working Papers in ESL,* 14(2), 127-149.	Arnold (1991), Breen (1985), van Lier (1996), Widdowson (1976; 1996), Wilkins (1976)	Article in journal
1	O'Malley, J. Michael; Pierce, Lorraine Valdez (1996). *Authentic assessment for English language learners.* Reading, Massachusetts: Addison-Wesley Pub. Co.	None	Book
11	van Lier, Leo (1996). *Interaction in the language curriculum. Awareness, autonomy and authenticity.* New York: Longman.	Breen (1985), Widdowson (1976; 1990)	Book
10	Widdowson, Henry G. (1996). Comment: authenticity and autonomy in ELT. *ELT Journal,* 50(1), 67-68.	None	Article in journal
4	Cook, Guy (1997). Language play, language learning. *ELT Journal,* 51, 224-231.	None	Article in journal
1	Little, David (1997). Responding authentically to authentic texts: A problem for self-access language learning? In: Phil Benson; Peter Voller (eds.). *Autonomy and independence in language learning.* London; New York: Longman, 225-236.	Breen (1985), Widdowson (1978)	Article in edited volume
11	Peacock, Matthew (1997). The effect of authentic materials on the motivation of EFL learners. *ELT Journal,* 51(2), 144-156.	Bacon/Finneman (1990), Kienbaum/Russell/Welty (1986), Little/Devitt/Singleton (1988), Morrison (1989), Swaffar (1985)	Article in journal
4	Chavez, Monika (1998). Learner's perspectives on authenticity. *IRAL – In-*	Bacon/Finneman (1990), Davies (1984), Nostrand	Article in journal[52]

---

52 This is an adapted reprint of an article published in 1994. Chavez (1998) contains more references than Chavez (1994), e.g. Davies (1984). What is more, Chavez (1998) is referenced by four authors, while Chavez (1994) is referenced by no one. Therefore, Chavez (1994) is not in the list.

	ternational Review of Applied Linguistics in Language Teaching 36 (4), 277-306.	(1989), Rings (1986), Rogers/Medley (1988), Swaffar (1985), Weijenberg (1980), Young (1993)	
1	Day, Richard; Bamford, Julian (1998/2009). The cult of authenticity and the myth of simplification. In: Hedge, Tricia; Andon, Nick; Dewey, Martin (eds.). *English Language Teaching 5.* 233-245.	Breen (1985), Davies (1984), Grellet (1981), Lee (1983), Richards/Platt/Weber (1985), Swaffar (1985), Widdowson (1976; 1978)	Chapter in a book[53]
1	Widdowson, Henry G. (1998a). Communication and community: The pragmatics of ESP. *English for Specific Purposes* 17 (1), 3-14.	Widdowson (1983; 1990; 1994)	Article in journal
11	Widdowson, Henry G. (1998b). Context, community, and authentic language. *TESOL Quarterly* (32/4), 705-716.	Cook (1997), Widdowson (1990)	Article in journal
0	Chapelle, Carol A. (1999). Theory and research: Investigation of 'authentic' language learning tasks. In: Egbert, Joy; Hanson-Smith, Elizabeth (eds.). *CALL environments.* Alexandria, VA: TESOL. 101-115.	None	Article in edited volume
0	Johnson, Keith (1999). Authenticity. In: Johnson, Keith; Johnson, Helen (eds.). *Encyclopedic dictionary of applied linguistics.*Oxford: Blackwell, 24-25.	Breen (1985), Widdowson (1976; 1990)	Entry in encyclopedia
1	Kohonen, Viljo (1999). Authentic assessment in affective foreign language education. In: Arnold, Jane (ed.). *Affect in language learning.* Cambridge: Cambridge University Press, 279-294.	O'Malley/Pierce (1996)	Article in edited volume
2	Kramsch, Claire J.; A'Ness, Francine; Lam, Wan Shun Eva (2000). Authenticity and authorship in the computer-mediated acquisition of L2 literacy. *Language Learning & Technology* 4 (2), 78-104.	Breen (1985), Grellet (1981), Hutchinson/Waters (1987), Kramsch (1993), Nunan (1989), Widdowson (1990)	Article in journal
1	Lewkowicz, Jo A. (2000). Authenticity in language testing: some outstanding questions. *Language Testing,* 17(1), 43-64.	Bachman (1990; 1991), Bachman/Palmer (1996), Breen (1985), Lynch (1982), Peacock (1997), Seliger et al. (1985), van Lier (1996), Widdowson (1976; 1978; 1990; 1996; 1998b)	Article in journal

---

53 Originally a chapter in a book (Day/Bamford 1998), reprinted as an article in a multi-volume series (Hedge/Andon/Dewey 2009, eds.)

1	MacDonald, Malcolm N.; Badger, Richard; White, Goodith (2000). The real thing? Authenticity and academic listening. *English for Specific Purposes* 19(3), 253-267.	Breen (1985), Cook (1997), Hutchinson/Waters (1987), Lee (1995), Nunan (1989), Taylor (1994), Widdowson (1976, 1978, 1996)	Article in journal
0	Rixon, Shelagh (2000). Authenticity. In: Michael Byram et al. (eds.). *Routledge encyclopedia of language teaching and learning.* London; New York: Routledge, 68-69.	Breen (1985), Candlin/Edelhoff (1982), Widdowson (1978)	Entry in encyclopedia
3	Widdowson, Henry G. (2000). On the limitations of linguistics applied. *Applied Linguistics* 21 (1), 3-25.	None	Article in journal
16	Guariento, William; Morley, John (2001). Text and task authenticity in the EFL classroom. *ELT Journal,* 55(4), 347-353.	Breen (1985), Little/Devitt/Singleton (1988), Porter/Roberts (1981), Wilkins (1976), Widdowson (1978)	Article in journal
0	Nation, I.S.P.; Deweerdt, Jean Paul (2001). A defence of simplification. *Prospect* 16 (3), 55-65.	Widdowson (1976)	Article in journal
3	Alptekin, Cem (2002). Towards intercultural communicative competence in ELT. *ELT Journal* 56 (1), 57-64.	Widdowson (1998b)	Article in journal
0	Amor, Stuart (2002). *Authenticity and authentication in language learning.* Frankfurt am Main; New York: Peter Lang.	Bachman (1990), Beile (1986), Breen (1985), Edelhoff (1985), Gutschow (1977), Kramsch (1993), Morrison (1989), Nunan (1989), Peacock (1997), van Lier (1996), Widdowson (1978; 1990; 1996)	Book
5	Rost, Michael (2002). *Teaching and researching listening.* Harlow, New York: Longman/Pearson.	Breen (1985), Taylor (1994)	Book
1	Day, Richard (2003). Authenticity in the design and development of materials. In: Renandya, Willy A. (ed.). *Methodology and materials design in language teaching.* Singapore: SEAMEO Regional Language Centre, 1-11. Not available!		Article in edited volume
1	Ellis, Rod (2003). *Task-based language learning and teaching.* Oxford, U.K., New York: Oxford University Press.	Bachman (1990), Bachman/Palmer (1996), Widdowson (1976)	
3	Widdowson, Henry G. (2003). *Defining issues in English language teaching.* Oxford: Oxford University Press.	None	Book

0	Brown, H. Douglas (2004). *Language assessment*. New York: Pearson/Longman.	Bachman/Palmer (1996)	Book
2	Day, Richard (2004). A critical look at authentic materials. *The Journal of AsiaTEFL* 1 (1), 101-114.	Bacon/Finnemann (1990), Clarke (1989), Day/Bamford (1998), Lee (1995), Little/Devitt/Singleton (1988), Morrison (1989), Nunan (1988b), Peacock (1997), Swaffar (1985)	Article in journal
0	Decke-Cornill, Helene (2004). Die Kategorie der Authentizität im mediendidaktischen Diskurs der Fremdsprachendidaktik. In: Bosenius, Petra (ed.). *Interaktive Medien und Fremdsprachenlernen*. Frankfurt am Main: Peter Lang. 17-27.	Breen (1985), Kramsch (1993), Little/Singleton (1988), Widdowson (1976)	Article in edited volume
8	Gilmore, Alex (2004). A comparison of textbook and authentic interactions. *ELT Journal,* 58(4), 363-374.	Widdowson (1998b)	Article in journal
3	Kilickaya, Ferit (2004). Authentic materials and cultural content in EFL classrooms. *ITESLJ* 10 (7). http://iteslj.org/Techniques/Kilickaya-AutenticMaterial.html, access date: 06/20/2016.	Chavez (1998), Guariento/Morley (2001)	Article in online journal
2	Mishan, Freda (2004). Authenticating corpora for language learning. *ELT Journal,* 58(3), 219-227.	Hutchinson/Waters (1987), Morrow (1977), van Lier (1996), Widdowson (1978, 1983, 1998b, 2000)	Article in journal
1	Nunan, David (2004). *Task-based language teaching*. Cambridge (UK); New York (NY): Cambridge University Press.	Candlin/Edelhoff (1982), Porter/Roberts (1981)	Book
0	Davies, Alan (2005). *A glossary of applied linguistics*. Edinburgh: Edinburgh University Press.	None – no bibliography	Entry in encyclopedia
9	Mishan, Freda (2005). *Designing authenticity into language learning materials*. Bristol, UK; Portland, OR: Intellect.	Arnold (1991), Breen (1985), Clarke (1989), Davies (1984), Grellet (1981), Hutchinson/Waters (1987), Kramsch/A'Ness/Lam (2000), Lee (1995), Little (1997), Little/Devitt/Singleton (1988), Morrow (1977), Nostrand (1989), Swaffar (1985), Taylor (1994), van Lier (1996), Widdowson (1978, 1983, 1990, 1998, 2000)	Book

1	Seargeant, Philip (2005). More English than England itself. The simulation of authenticity in foreign language practice in Japan. *International Journal of Applied Linguistics* 15 (3), 326-345.	Breen (1985), Lee (1995), van Lier (1996), Widdowson (1976, 1978, 1996)	Article in journal
2	Tan, Melinda (2005). Authentic language or language errors? *ELT Journal,* 59(2), 126-134.	None	Article in journal
3	Berardo, Sacha Anthony (2006). The use of authentic materials in the teaching of reading. *The Reading Matrix* 6 (2), 60-69.	Breen (1985), Davies (1984), Guariento/Morley (2001), Peacock (1997), Widdowson (1990)	Article in journal
3	MacDonald, Malcolm N.; Badger, Richard; Dasli, Maria (2006). Authenticity, culture and language learning. *Language and Intercultural Communication,* 6(3-4), 250-261.	Alptekin (2002), Breen (1985), Gilmore (2004), Guariento/Morley (2001), Lee (1995), Taylor (1994), Widdowson (1976; 1990)	Article in journal
2	Tatsuki, Donna (2006). What is authenticity? In: Newfields, Tim (ed.). *Authentic communication: Proceedings of the 5th Annual JALT Pan-SIG Conference.* Shizuoka, Japan: n.a., 1-15.	Breen (1985), Day (2004), Guariento/Morley (2001), Lee (1995), MacDonald/Badger/Dasli (2006), Nunan (1988b), Taylor (1994), Widdowson (1990; 1998b)	Article in journal
1	Thornbury, Scott (2006). *An A-Z of ELT.* Oxford: Macmillan Education.	None – no bibliography	Entry in encyclopedia
10	Gilmore, Alex (2007). Authentic materials and authenticity in foreign language learning. *Language Teaching,* 40(02), 97-118.	Arnold (1991), Bachman/Palmer (1996), Bacon/Finneman (1990), Breen (1985), Clarke (1989), Cook (1997), Gilmore (2004), Grellet (1981), Guariento/Morley (2001), Hutchinson/Waters (1987), Kienbaum/Russell/Welty (1986), Kohonen (1999), Kramsch (1993), Lee (1995), Lewkowicz (2000), Little/Devitt/Singleton (1988), Mishan (2005), Morrison (1989), Morrow (1977), Nunan (1989), Peacock (1997), Porter/Roberts (1981), Rings (1986), Rogers/Medley (1988), Rost (2002), Swaffar (1985), van Lier (1996), Widdowson	Article in journal

		(1976; 1978; 1994; 1996; 1998b; 2003)	
0	Shomoossi, Nematullah; Ketabi, Saeed (2007). A critical look at the concept of authenticity. *Electronic Journal of Foreign Language Teaching* 4 (1), 149-155.	Breen (1995), Day (2004), Dunkel (1995), Guariento/Morley (2001), Lee (1995), MacDonald/Badger/ Dasli (2006), Nunan (1988b), Rings (1986), Rogers/Medley (1988), Taylor (1994), Tatsuki (2006), Widdowson (1998b)	Article in online journal
0	Allan, Rachel (2008). Can a graded reader corpus provide 'authentic' input? *ELT Journal,* 63(1), 23-32.	Mishan (2004)	Article in journal
1	Dantas-Whitney, Maria; Rilling, Sarah; Savova, Lilia (2009). *Authenticity in the language classroom and beyond: adult learners.* Alexandria, VA: TESOL.	Gilmore (2007), Grellet (1981), Guariento/Morley (2001), Mishan (2005), Morrow (1977), Seargeant (2005), Widdowson (1998b; 2003)	Book
0	Farrell, Thomas S. C. (2009). *Teaching reading to English language learners.* Thousand Oaks: Corwin Press.	None	Book
1	Roberts, Celia; Cooke, Melanie (2009). Authenticity in the adult ESOL classroom and beyond. *TESOL Quarterly* 43 (4), 620-642.	Breen (1985), Cook (1997), Kramsch (1993), Taylor (1994), Widdowson (1998b)	Article in journal
1	Tamo, Daniela (2009). The use of authentic materials in classrooms. *Linguistic and Communicative Performance Journal* 2 (1), 74-78.	Clarke (1989), Guariento/Morley (2001), Widdowson (1990)	Article in journal
1	Waters, Alan (2009). Ideology in applied linguistics for language teaching. *Applied Linguistics* 30 (1), 138-143.	Clarke (1989), Hutchinson/Waters (1987), Widdowson (2003), Wilkins (1976)	Article in journal
0	Badger, Richard; MacDonald, Malcolm N. (2010). Making it real: Authenticity, process and pedagogy. *Applied Linguistics,* 31(4), 578-582.	Badger (2006), Breen (1985), Gilmore (2007), Roberts (2009), Waters (2007), Widdowson (1976)	Article in journal
1	Dantas-Whitney, Maria; Rilling, Sarah (2010). *Authenticity in the language classroom and beyond: children and adolescent learners.* Alexandria, VA: TESOL. Not available!		Book
0	Leitzke-Ungerer, Eva (2010). Authentizität. In: Surkamp, Carola (ed.). *Metzler-Lexikon Fremdsprachendidaktik.* Stuttgart; Weimar: Metzler, 10-11.	Gilmore (2007), Widdowson (1978)	Entry in encyclopedia

0	Mishan, Freda (2010). Task and task authenticity: Paradigms for language learning in the digital era. In: Mishan, Freda; Chambers, Angela (eds.). *Perspectives on language learning materials development.* Oxford; New York: Peter Lang, 149-172.	Davies (1984), Gilmore (2007), Guariento/Morley (2001), Mishan (2005), Nunan (1989, 2004), van Lier (1996), Widdowson (1978; 1998)	Article in edited volume
0	Trabelsi, Soufiane (2010). Developing and trialling authentic materials for business English students at a Tunisian university. In: Tomlinson, Brian; Masuhara, Hitomi (eds.). *Research for materials development in language learning.* London: Continuum, 103-120.	Bachman (1990), Bacon/Finneman (1990), Breen (1985), Kramsch (1993), Kramsch/A'Ness/Lam (2000), Little/Devitt/Singleton (1988), Mishan (2005), Swaffar (1985)	Article in edited volume
0	Nikitina, Larisa (2011). Creating an authentic learning environment in the foreign language classroom. *International Journal of Instruction,* 4(1), 33-46.	None	Article in journal
0	Joy, John L. (2011). The duality of authenticity in ELT. *Journal of Language and Linguistic Studies,* 7(2), 7-23.	Arnold (1991), Breen (1985), Chavez (1998), Davies (1984), Guariento/Morley (2001), Kim (2000), Lee (1995), Little/Devitt/Singleton (1988), Mishan (2004), Morrow (1977), Nunan (1989), Rogers/Medley (1988), Taylor (1994), Thornbury (2006), van Lier (1996), Widdowson (1976; 1978)	Article in journal
1	Khalili Sabet, Masoud (2012). The impact of authentic listening materials on elementary EFL learners' listening skills. *IJALEL* 1 (4), 216-229.	Adams (1995), Bacon/Finnemann (1990), Berardo (2006), Breen (1985), Chavez (1998), Gilmore (2004), Guariento/Morley (2001), Herron/Seay (1991), Kilickaya (2004), Kim (2000), Lee (1995), McNeill (1994), Mishan (2005), Morton (1999), Peacock (1997), Rings (1986), Rogers/Medley (1988), Rost (2002), Widdowson (1978; 1996)	Article in journal
1	Kramsch, Claire (2012). Authenticity and legitimacy in multilingual SLA. *Critical Multilingualism Studies* 1 (1), 107-128.	Widdowson (1994)	Article in journal

0	Henry, Alastair (2013). Digital games and ELT: Bridging the authenticity gap. In: Ushioda, Ema (ed.). *International perspectives on motivation*. Basingstoke, Hampshire: Palgrave Macmillan, 133-155.	Gilmore (2007)	Article in edited volume
1	Buendgens-Kosten, Judith (2013). Authenticity in CALL: three domains of 'realness'. *ReCALL,* 25(02), 1-14.	Breen (1985), Edelhoff (1985), Mishan (2005), Widdowson (1998a)	Article in journal
0	Chan, Jim Yee Him (2013). The role of situational authenticity in English language textbooks. *RELC Journal* 44 (3), 303-317.	Ellis (2003), Gilmore (2004), Guariento/Morley (2001)	Article in journal
0	Liddicoat, Anthony; Scarino, Angela (2013). *Intercultural language teaching and learning*. Chichester, West Sussex, UK; Malden, MA: Wiley-Blackwell.	Alptekin (2002), Arnold (1991), Widdowson (1978)	Book
0	McKay, Sandra (2013). Authenticity in the language teaching curriculum. In: Chapelle, Carol (ed.). *The encyclopedia of applied linguistics*. Oxford: Blackwell, 299-302.	Dantas-Whitney/Rilling/Savova (2009), Dantas-Whitney/Rilling (2010), Day (2003), Mishan (2005), Nunan (1989), Roberts/Cooke (2009), Widdowson (1998), Wilkins (1976)	Entry in encyclopedia
1	Pinner, Richard (2013a). Authenticity and CLIL: Examining authenticity from an international CLIL perspective. *International CLIL Research Journal* 2 (1), 44-45.	Gilmore (2007), Little/Devitt/Singleton (1988), Morrow (1977), Peacock (1997), Widdowson (1990)	Article in journal
1	Pinner, Richard (2013b). Authenticity of purpose: CLIL as a way to bring meaning and motivation into EFL contexts. *Asian EFL Journal* 15 (4), 138-159.	Bachman/Palmer (1996), Gilmore (2007), Morrow (1977), Peacock (1997), van Lier (1996), Widdowson (1990)	Article in journal
0	Barekat, Behzad; Nobakhti, Hamed (2014). The effect of authentic and inauthentic materials in cultural awareness training on EFL learners' listening comprehension ability. *TPLS* 4(5), 1058-1065.	Guariento/Morley (2001), Rogers/Medley (1988), Rost (2002)	Article in journal
0	Buendgens-Kosten, Judith (2014). Key concepts in ELT. Authenticity. *ELT Journal,* 68(4), 457-459.	Alptekin (2002), Breen (1985), Buendgens-Kosten (2013), Edelhoff (1985), Mishan (2005), Gilmore (2004), Gilmore (2007), Lee (1995), Tan (2005), Widdowson (1976; 1978)	Article in journal

0	Clavel-Arroitia, Begona; Fuster-Marquez, Miguel (2014). The authenticity of real texts in advanced English language textbooks. *ELT Journal,* 68(2), 124-134.	Guariento/Morley (2001), Gilmore (2004), Hutchinson/Waters (1987), Little/Devitt/Singleton (1988), Tamo (2009), Widdowson (1978; 1998b; 2000)	Article in journal
0	Al Azri, Rahid Hamed; Al-Rashdi, Majid Hilal (2014). The effect of using authentic materials in teaching. *International journal of scientific and technology research,* 3(10), 249-254.	Bacon/Finneman (1990), Baniabdelrahman (2006), Berardo (2006), Breen (1985), Gilmore (2007), Guariento/Morley (2001), Kienbaum/Russell/Welty (1986), Kilickaya (2004), Kim (2000), Lee (1995), Little/Devitt/Singleton (1988), MacDonald/Badger/Dasli (2006), McNeill (1994), Mishan (2005), Nunan (1988b), Peacock (1997), Rost (2002), Tatsuki (2006), Taylor (1994), Widdowson (1990; 1996)	Article in journal
0	Siegel, Aki (2014). What should we talk about? The authenticity of textbook topics. *ELT Journal,* 68(4), 363-375.	Gilmore (2004), Widdowson (1990)	Article in journal
0	Pinner, Richard (2014). The authenticity continuum: Towards a definition incorporating international voices. *English Today,* 30(04), 22-27.	Gilmore (2007), Morrow (1977), Peacock (1997), Pinner (2013a), Pinner (2013b), Tan (2005), van Lier (1996), Widdowson (1978; 1990; 1996)	Article in journal
0	Creese, Angela; Blackledge, Adrian; Takhi, Jaspreet Kaur (2014). The ideal 'native speaker' teacher: Negotiating authenticity and legitimacy in the language classroom. *Modern Language Journal,* 98(4), 937-951.	Kramsch (1998; 2012)	Article in journal
0	Zhafarghandi, Amir Mahdavi; Barekat, Behzad; Homaei, Sepideh (2014). A survey of Iranian EFL teachers' and learners' perceptions toward authentic listening materials at university level. *Advances in Language and Literary Studies* 5 (4), 184-197.	Adams (1995), Bacon/Finnemann (1990), MacDonald/Badger/White (2000), Berardo (2006), Breen (1985), Chavez (1998), Clarke (1989), Gilmore (2004), Guariento/Morley (2001), Herron/Seay (1991), Khalili Sabet (2012), Kilickaya (2004), Kienbaum/Russell/Welty (1986), Kim (2000), Lee (1995), McNeill	Article in journal

		(1994), Nostrand (1989), Nunan (1989), Peacock (1997), Rings (1986), Rost (2002), Taylor (1994), Widdowson (1976; 1978; 1990; 1996; 1998b), Young (1993)	

Figure 9: Document selection constituting the academic EFL discourse on authenticity

4.5.3 Bibliometric analysis of the documents – productivity analysis and citation analysis

The discourse under scrutiny is investigated predominantly on the text level applying the various discourse analytical tools which have been described in chapters 4.2 and 4.3. However, since a document selection is compiled, some surface features of the data lend themselves to a bibliometric analysis. Bibliometrics is defined as the "application of mathematical and statistical methods to books and other media of communication" (Andrés 2009: 2). A basic bibliometric interest is the overall productivity of a given discourse:

> [S]cientific productivity can be analysed in any research field, whether it be from natural science or the social sciences and humanities. The only requirement is to gather a set of publications about a given field. [...] It is important to begin with a clear topic definition. [...] [W]e must be sure that the documents included in our study are truly representative of the research field. As such, the documents gathered have to cover the whole domain of the field being analysed.

> It should be noted that the topic definition will depend on the field we are studying, and therefore it will influence both the documents to be gathered and the analysis to be carried out.

> Although a bibliometric study can be applied to define general productivity in a given area it may also be used to evaluate the productivity of individual researchers, journals, countries or any other levels of performance. Therefore it is also necessary to define at the outset the kind of data which will be assessed. [...]

> Having selected the level of productivity to be assessed (authors, research groups, journals, countries, a particular field etc.) the next step is to conduct a bibliographic search in order to collect the representative documents for our study. Since the documents selected and their content form the basis of our analysis, the bibliographic search is a key stage in this process. (Andrés 2009: 9-10)

The sampling process, which is laid out in the previous chapters, can be equated with what Andrés refers to as the "bibliographic search" (ibid.).

Productivity analysis is one methodological approach within bibliometrics. Another method is citation analysis, which is explained in due course. Both methods have obvious weaknesses. Andrés (2009) devotes one chapter to "the main limitations associated with bibliometric studies" (Andrés 2009: 121). Many of the problems arise from the practice of working with electronic databases and search engines. After all, the breakthrough of bibliometrics "came as a result of new technological developments during the 1990s" (Andrés 2009: 3).

> Working with the large databases used in bibliometric studies implies multiple data from different sources and these will obviously contain mistakes or incomplete entries. At times the source of the error will be difficult to identify, as one is dealing with large amounts of information about authors, institutions and countries etc. (Andrés 2009: 122)

Specific difficulties are encountered because "many authors will have the same surname, or even the same initials" (ibid.) or because "the same author may have his or her name written differently in articles, a common source of bias in this regard being the use of a middle name" (ibid.). Such challenges are largely canceled out in this study since most of the procedures are conducted manually. The data used here is considerably smaller than what is exemplified in Andrés (2009). The limitations attendant on purely electronic sampling are thus alleviated.

A very general problem is the overestimation of bibliometrics in general. Many temptations of this sort relate to citation analysis They will be discussed as that method becomes relevant in the later course of this chapter. However, some aspects of productivity are equally problematic if interpreted with too little rigor. A single author's productivity, for example, may be considered to be indicative of author status. Meara points out why such a correlation is problematic:

> Some authors only publish full length books; this gives them a low publication rate, but the work tends to be influential when it does appear. Some authors only publish journal articles, while others prefer to publish chapters in edited volumes; the former tend to have a longer shelf-life and be more widely cited than the latter. Some authors publish finely polished papers in major journals, while others like to produce speculative think pieces in out of the way places, where the reviewing procedures are perhaps less rigorous, and the publishing timetable somewhat shorter. (Meara 2012: 14)

Such intricacies must be taken into account if the productivity of a given author is to be used as an indicator of author status.

In EFL, few bibliometric studies have been conducted. Paul Meara (2012) uses bibliometrics to investigate publications on the topic of vocabulary acquisition. His data is used here for comparative purposes, if with many caveats. Firstly, the topic Meara investigates is so extensive, he confines his study to the time frame of one single year, 2006. 84 relevant papers appeared in that year. Secondly, Meara seeks homogeneity of format counting only articles in academic journals. Note that his study is exclusively bibliometric, so the content of the articles is not of interest as long as the general topic is vocabulary acquisition. Missing out on important contributions to the discourse is, therefore, not so much of an issue. In discourse analysis, however, influential statements must be identified and investigated irrespective of the form in which they are communicated. Consequently, my selection of documents comprises other publication formats as well.

Meara begins with a productivity analysis:

> The first thing that we can do with this data is count the number of authors contributing to the database, and the number of items that they contribute. Surprisingly, perhaps, a count of this sort is not as simple as it looks, since only a minority of the papers are produced by a single author. A significant number of the texts have several co-authors, and we need to make a decision as to how co-authorship should be handled. The procedure followed here

is that every co-author is counted separately, and given full credit for the papers they are co-authors of. (Meara 2012: 9)

In my study, co-authorship is treated in the same manner. This increases the overall number of authors as well as the number of authors who contribute to two or more publications. "[A]uthors are 'prolific' in the sense that they make a contribution to a number of papers" (Meara 2012: 9). The proportion between *simple* contributors and prolific contributors is described in what is known as *Lotka's Law*:

> [T]here are a lot of authors who publish only one study, while a small group of prolific authors contribute with a large number of publications. This premise is the basis of Lotka's law, also known as the 'inverse square law' on author productivity. The law takes the number of authors who have contributed with a single study and then predicts how many authors would have published x studies, according to this inverse square law. In summary, the number of authors who produce x studies is proportional to $1/x^2$. (Andrés 2009: 23)

> Thus if we have 100 authors who make a single contribution, then we would expect 100 x 1/2 [sic! – should be $1/2^2$] = 25 people to contribute two papers, 100 x $1/3^2$ = 9 people to contribute three papers, 100 x $1/4^2$ = 6 people to contribute four papers, and 100 x $1/5^2$ = 4 people to contribute five papers. (Meara 2012: 12-13)

Having looked at productivity of and within the academic EFL discourse on authenticity, a second bibliometric method is now presented: citation analysis. This method allows for greater insights than productivity analysis but, to best serve the research interest of this study, it is applied in conjunction with the discourse analytical procedures that follow in chapter 5.2. In the present chapter, the method is explained but not yet implemented:

> Citation analysis is a tool to identify relationships between authors or journals [...]. When an author publishes a study, this will include references to previous studies by other authors which are related to it. These citations reveal a connection between authors, groups of researchers, topics of study or counties. Furthermore, the impact and relevance that authors, studies or journals have on a scientific community can be measured by means of citation analysis. (Andrés 2009: 55)

> Citation measures can be as simple as a count of the number of citations received by an author, a publication or a journal during a given period of time [...]. At face value, citations are treated as uniformly positive recognitions of the contribution made by the author or work being cited, so the greater the number of citations and author, work or journal receives, the greater is the recognition (Andrés 2009: 56-57)

The recognition, which Andrés speaks of, corresponds to author status (cf. chapter 4.2.2). For an author it is generally desirable to receive a high number of citations. Even if the content of the citation is critiqued by the citing author, the person cited is implicitly given credit for having published a work that is worth mentioning. This general rule leads to the assumption that the number of citations received by an author or by a single article is an indication of status, importance, and relevance. However, extreme caution must be exercised when dealing with citation counts. Andrés remarks: "[T]he quality of a publication, for instance, should not only be based on the number of times it is cited, but also on other analyses" (Andrés 2009: 56-57); "it is not advisable to use [citation analysis] as a single and absolute criterion for judging the importance of a publication" (Andrés 2009: 55). This is the case because citation counts "do net tell us about work which is not cited but ought to be, or work which was forgotten because it was years ahead of its time, too far beyond the existing paradigms of people to grasp its significance" (Meara 2012: 21). Meara actually asserts that those works which are not frequently cited demand special attention because a given article may be "influential in its own terms, but has not been widely absorbed by the research community" (ibid.). For the research interest of this study, it would thus be a misguided approach to use citation analysis as a sampling method determining which texts are to be investigated and which are not. Some items of the document selection are not cited by any one of the authors but the explicit negotiation of authenticity makes them important items. Meara concludes:

> What citation analysis is good for is identifying work which forms a central part of the reading of anyone with claims to be an active scholar, and helping us find a way through the huge entities of research which need to be evaluated and assessed. (Meara 2012: 21)

Citation analysis, in this study, is conducted using a combination of two approaches:

> There are two main ways of approaching citation data. The first method is to look at which papers are most cited in a specific set of outputs [...]. [The second method] is different in that rather than focussing on individual papers, it looks instead at authors, and does not differentiate between the different parts of an author's ouevre. (Meara 2012: 14)

Meara's bibliometric study of vocabulary acquisition looks only at authors. This practice can be serviceable to identify important individuals in the discourse. For discourse analytical purposes, however, it is important to know which particular publication is cited. For instance, Widdowson changes his position over time and writes about different aspects of authenticity in the many works he contributes to the discourse. In some cases it is not only insightful to know which of his publications is cited but which statements are quoted specifically.

It has been stated that to receive citations from other authors is a sign of recognition. Oftentimes a publication is cited in the years shortly after it came out but receives less and less attention over time. In rare cases, attention persists and ultimately makes the publication what Andrés calls a *classic article*:

> While the productivity of a given field is advancing, the citations received for a given document usually decline over time. Finally, if the document is no longer cited it will become obsolete. Only a small group of articles will remain frequently cited over time, and these will become classics due to the fact that authors continue to cite them in recognition of their contribution. However, very few documents will achieve the status of classic articles (Andrés 2009: 9)

Note that the humanities are generally more likely to produce classics than the sciences are, as Hyland analyses contrastively:

> The process of coming to terms with the complexity of human behaviour is perceived as less obviously progressive and therefore less likely to discard older ideas as obsolete or irrelevant. [...] As a result, disciplinary giants are frequently encountered in the soft papers, particularly in 'pure' knowledge fields, where the pathfinders' stocks of relevance are clearly greater. (Hyland 2000: 32)

Therefore, the concept of classic is applicable to a single article but also to a single author. In the academic EFL discourse on authenticity, it appears that citation is a more reliable determinant in this regard than productivity is. Some authors contribute multiple articles but are not cited as often as Breen is, who wrote only one article on authenticity (1985). A combination of both productivity and citation (e.g. Widdowson) is usually an indication that a person can be called a classic author.

Prolific authors are at an advantage when citation analysis is practiced because they tend to cite their own previous works:

> There is no consensus about the role of author self-citations in the literature. Some authors claim that self-citations are a potential means of artificially inflating citation rates and, therefore, the author's own standing within the scientific community. However, others consider self-citations to be a natural part of scientific communication and argue that a complete lack of self-citations over a long period of time would be as pathological as an always overwhelming share [...]. (Andrés 2009: 60)

In any case, a database consisting of prolific and non-prolific authors will feature an undesirable factor of variance. This factor is to be considered because it diminishes the validity of citation counts.

An important phenomenon is the existence of invisible colleges:

> [I]nvisible colleges are networks of researchers working in a similar area and who maintain informal contacts. Authors from an invisible college will refer to each other in their documents without being linked by formal organisational relationships [...]. (Andrés 2009: 77)

This entails that a given text is cited by an author not exclusively on the grounds of topical fit and perceived quality, but that personal relations play a role. The phenomenon of invisible colleges must be born in mind when interpreting bibliometric data.

For the purpose of this study, it is important to consider which authors and which publications are cited considerably more often than others. Bibliometric findings serve as a backdrop to a more thorough investigation on the text level. They form only one tool of the discourse analytical proceedings and must be interpreted with caution given the limitations mentioned. Bibliometric aspects are integrated into the upcoming chronological analysis of the discourse (chapter 5). Findings are presented at stages when they serve the research interest and afford deeper insights. In chapters 5.3.1 and 5.3.2, the bibliometric findings are presented in a more condensed and isolated manner.

4.5.4 Text classification within the document selection

In spite of the sampling criteria applied, the documents are still diverse in many regards. Different formal criteria can be used to classify the documents. A segmentation by publication format reveals diachronic patterns. A rough distinction between short formats (mainly articles in journals or edited books) and monographs fails to offer major insights. It is not surprising that the discourse remains confined to short formats for a considerable period of time before the first monograph is published (Kienbaum/Russell/Welty 1986).[54] The overall ratio between short formats and monographs probably mirrors that of EFL

---

54 Note that monographs, which do not feature the term in the title, are not counted here. If anything, they would qualify as short formats because only single chapters or paragraphs negotiate authenticity.

publications at large. The preponderance of journal articles in EFL allows Meara to disregard all other formats in his bibliometric study of vocabulary acquisition (2012) and still attain insightful results. In the academic EFL discourse on authenticity, journal articles outnumber other formats from the beginning to the present. From the mid-1980s, a sporadic but consistent output of monographs underscores the robustness of the discourse. After all, monographs can be seen as an indication that a topic deserves more attention than the capacity of a short format allows. A similar indication can be attributed to the presence of *authentic/authenticity* in the relevant encyclopedias. Beginning in 1985, all of these books contain an entry for the term:

Richards, Jack C.; Platt, John Talbot; Weber, Heidi (eds.) (1985). *Longman dictionary of language teaching and applied linguistics*. Harlow: Longman.

Johnson, Keith; Johnson, Helen (eds.) (1999). *Encyclopedic dictionary of applied linguistics*. Oxford: Blackwell.

Byram, Michael et al. (eds.) (2000). *Routledge encyclopedia of language teaching and learning*. London: Routledge.

Davies, Alan (2005). *A glossary of applied linguistics*. Edinburgh: Edinburgh University Press.

Thornbury, Scott (2006). *An A-Z of ELT. A dictionary of terms and concepts*. Oxford: Macmillan.

Surkamp, Carola (ed.) (2010). *Metzler-Lexikon Fremdsprachendidaktik*. Stuttgart: Metzler.

Chapelle, Carol (ed.) (2013). *The encyclopedia of applied linguistics*. Oxford: Blackwell.

These encyclopedias differ considerably in terms of shape and conception. Most notably, however, they differ in their descriptions of authenticity (cf. chapter 5.3.2.2). The most important commonalities lie in their intended comprehensiveness and in the alphabetical order of the headwords, along with the inherent aim of covering the technical terminology of the field. These points imply that *authentic/authenticity* is granted the status of a technical term, which is solidified by the continual presence of the term throughout all these publications. No encyclopedia of EFL or applied linguistics has been found lacking the term post 1970. Encyclopedias of general linguistics are not considered.

4.5.5 Temporal demarcation

Three sampling criteria – mode, tenor, and explicit negotiation of authenticity (chapter 4.4) – have been laid out for the selection of the documents, but since a historical discourse is under scrutiny, a decision is called-for on when to start and when to end. The end point of the investigated discourse is the present, though it will likely continue in the future. For reasons of feasibility, I have resolved to investigate the discourse up to the year 2014. The starting point of the discourse is much more difficult to determine. The decision of compiling a document selection entails the necessity of such a starting point, although it is essentially an illusion to demarcate the discourse as such. The primary question is which publication is the first to appear in the chronology. Authors, who look at the authenticity discourse from a historical perspective, are rare. A few give rather imprecise hints as to when the term and the concept came up. Lewkowicz states that in "applied linguistics the notion emerged in the late 1970s at the time when communicative methodology was gaining momentum and there was a growing interest in teaching and testing 'real-life' language" (Lewkowicz 2000: 43). Gilmore is equally vague, but in line with Lewkowicz, asserting that the "issue of authenticity reappeared in the 1970s [...] This culminated in the approach which, at least in EFL circles, still holds sway today – Communicative Language Teaching – and paved the way for the reintroduction of authentic texts" (Gilmore 2007: 97). Not only are both authors vague in terms of fixing a concrete starting point, they are also vague about whether the time period mentioned refers to the emergence of the term or to the emergence of a certain orthodoxy, as they, respectively, speak of "the notion" and "the issue" of authenticity. No conclusive line of demarcation is to be derived from these statements. The connection with Communicative Language Teaching, which is made by both authors, is scrutinized in chapter 4.5.5.2.

In my research process, it seemed for a long time that Widdowson (1976) would be the starting point. It is the first publication to feature the term in the title and many later publications refer to statements made in this text. It also falls within the period mentioned by Lewkowicz and Gilmore above. Curiously, the text has no bibliography and no references whatsoever. It is written rather intuitively or conceptually, as it were. Thus, the snowball method of searching the bibliography for earlier publications of relevance cannot apply here. What is more, other bibliographies do not feature relevant literature from before the year 1976 so the method comes to naught entirely. Breen references a source from 1970 titled *Textes et documents authentiques au niveau 2* (Breen 1985: 70). It may be one of the earliest accounts of the term, and it obviously predates Widdowson (1976) as the first publication with the term in the title. The reason for not including it in the document selection is primarily the language being French.

A text level analysis of Widdowson's article, however, shows that the text is likely not the inception of authenticity but that it is meant to add to an existing discourse. This conclusion can be drawn from the opening statement:

> Over recent years we have witnessed an increasing concern on the part of the linguist with the communicative functioning of language. There is a feeling abroad that for a linguistic description to be adequate it must not reduce natural language to an algebraic system but should attempt to account for 'authentic' data, the language user's own experience of language in contexts of use. This movement towards an approximation to authenticity has its dangers: it can lead to a linguistics of anecdote, ad hoc observation, and a neglect of methodological principles upon which any systematic account must depend. (Widdowson 1976: 264)

Widdowson describes a development which is already underway and there is no indication that *authentic/authenticity* is being used as a new term to denote it.

4.5.5.1 An analysis of *TESOL Quarterly*

The challenge at hand is, thus, to investigate the discourse before 1976. The central interest is to find out whether the term itself is present and, more importantly, to what extent it is explicitly negotiated. With the snowball method having stalled, new sources must be found from which new references can be pursued.[55]

Gilmore does reference two texts, which are pre 1976, as evidence that authenticity gains momentum in the 1970s: O'Neill/Scott (1974) and Crystal/Davy (1975). Gilmore states that "the issue of authenticity" appears in the 1970s but he is unspecific about whether this refers to an emergence of the term or of a certain concept in EFL (Gilmore 2007: 97). Both references, O'Neill/Scott (1974) and Crystal/Davy (1975), are learners' books accompanying taped audio material of authentic spoken English. Respectively, the authors praise the value of natural unedited speech, yet they do not use the word *authentic*.

> Since it is true that in order to understand English spoken at normal speed, the student must be exposed to 'real' English, it must also be true that the structures, patterns and vocabulary cannot be artificially graded. [...] Students' experience of spoken English is frequently confined to recordings of rehearsed conversations spoken below normal speed by trained actors. This is not what the student hears when he arrives in an English speaking country. Students need a truly representative sample of real spoken English. 'Viewpoints' provide this. (O'Neill/Scott 1974: vi)

> We attach particular importance to the naturalness of our data, which has not been edited in any way. We have not come across commercially available material that is so informal or realistic, and it is in this respect that we hope the main contribution of this book will lie. (Crystal/Davy 1975: ix–x)

It is improbable that such promotional texts, if written today, should not contain the word *authentic*, especially since the very concept of authentic text is praised. What Gilmore means is evidently not an increased use of the term but an upsurge of authentic language as a concept. Invoking learning materials instead of scholarly writings is a potential indication that Gilmore did not find any of the latter – regardless of whether he looked for the term or the concept. This is of course tenuous evidence at best that no instances of *authentic/authenticity* can be found before 1976.

I have therefore looked into the possibility of completely combing EFL journals of the time. The ideal method would be to sift through all issues of a journal which is duly deemed representative of the EFL discourse by virtue of topical comprehensiveness and by virtue of reputation within the scientific community. Questions of efficiency and feasibility are chiefly about whether all texts can be accessed in digital format so they would lend themselves to an electronic word search function. At my institution, LMU Munich, *TESOL Quarterly* is accessible in this way. Methodologically speaking, a corpus analyt-

---

55 Incidentally, Dell Hymes's seminal article "On communicative competence" (1972) does not speak of authenticity, although it might be expected to do so based on the topic it discusses. Hymes is dealt with more thoroughly in the chapter on Communicative Language Teaching (CLT).

ical study is conducted searching an extensive body of text for concordances of *authentic/authenticity*. This would hardly be possible without the electronic tools just mentioned.

The very first issue of *TESOL Quarterly* appeared in 1967 so the analysis covers approximately ten years up to Widdowson's publication. I am allowing for a latency period of roughly three years after 1976 because to read Widdowson and publish a text referring to him is not realistic within one year. The analysis of *TESOL Quarterly*, therefore, continues until the late 1970s. Since *TESOL Quarterly* is US-based, an analogous study of a British journal would be insightful in case little or no discursive exchange was in place between the two countries at the time. The fact that Widdowson – who is British and worked in Edinburgh – published via *TESOL* (1976) may serve to dispel the idea of two completely separated EFL discourses between the USA and Great Britain. Even so, the British *ELT Journal* is considered a viable source as a control group, all the more as its first publication dates back to 1946 which is twenty years prior to *TESOL Quarterly*.

Unfortunately, using the word search tool in the *ELTJ* articles via the databases of our library requires previous downloading of every single document, which makes it a very tedious process. Therefore, *ELTJ* is investigated in a less than comprehensive manner. For each year three articles are picked out at random and are word-searched for concordances of *authentic/authenticity*. To be precise, in both *TESOL Quarterly* and *ELTJ* the word search is conducted inserting the shortened lexeme *authent* which yields hits for either of the two words – *authentic* or *authenticity* – but excludes words like *author*. In summary, searching *ELTJ* serves two purposes: one, covering the British discourse in case there was a discursive divide between Great Britain and the US, two, analyzing a journal that goes further back than 1967 (first issue of *TESOL Quarterly*). *ELTJ* is investigated until 1971, which is the year Stevick (1971) appears.

My corpus analytical research process began with *TESOL Quarterly*, which unexpectedly yielded Stevick (1971) as the first element in the discourse. This finding meant that the first element occurs only four years after the inception of *TESOL Quarterly*. Four years without an explicit negotiation of authenticity in one journal was not considered a satisfactory indication that no explicit negotiation took place before Stevick (1971), although the snowball method had long come to naught. Therefore, the decision was made to dig deeper into the time before 1971 by looking into *ELTJ* (1946-1971).

The first result is that no article before 1976 in both journals carries *authentic/authenticity* in its title, which is not really new because, otherwise, it would probably appear in the document selection. On the text level, though, the term occurs a couple of times. One of these instances has led to my discovery of Stevick (1971), which I expand in chapter 4.5.5.1.2. Overall, the term is used in 15 articles of *TESOL Quarterly* over these 10 years. All of the authors tend to negotiate the term implicitly relying on a rather colloquial/intuitive understanding of it. This is henceforth referred to as *casual use*. The random sample study of *ELTJ* yields one article from 1968 containing the term, which is presented in the following chapter.

4.5.5.1.1 Casual use of *authentic/authenticity* before Widdowson (1976)

Not all instances of casual use can be displayed here, but a few shall illustrate in what way the term is used. The order of presentation is chronological, except where such sequencing obstructs the display of certain patterns.

Prator (1969) speaks of the advantages a first language learner has over a second language learner saying that he "constantly hears authentic models of the type of speech he needs to learn and can usually afford to listen or not as he pleases" (Prator 1969: 99). The use is in line with the concept of authentic (spoken) text but Prator deploys the word only once in his article instead of using it systematically. The degree of negotiation, hence, is minimal. Finocchiaro (1971), in her article, uses the word four times but each time a bit differently and each time she elaborates to clarify the meaning using an additional adjective. Here are two examples, the second of which refers to textual authenticity:

> In our programs both types of motivation should be fostered. Instrumental orientation would result from numerous activities in which students use language as a tool of communication, **meaningfully and authentically** to express needs, desires, concerns and aspirations. (Finocchiaro 1971: 12)

> Grammatical items should be clarified and drilled in **authentic, natural sentences**. Unless additional words are added or they are used in a meaningful context, sentences such as 'Don't I see the plane?' or 'Does she speak to me everyday?' should not be practiced since they would never be said by a native speaker. (Finocchiaro 1971: 12) (emphases added by L.W.)

The lack of explicitness and consistency in the instances of use is, again, a sign of weak negotiation. The first identifiable pattern is that textual authenticity appears to be a concept invoked by a number of authors. Adding to Prator and Finocchiaro in this regard are Whitman (1974) and White (1974):

> The resulting sentences are, in some cases, recognizably **non-authentic**, but any teacher will recognize the formidable difficulties of achieving authenticity at the very beginning [...]. (Whitman 1974: 258)

> the teaching of English for Special Purposes should be informed by frequency studies of **authentic textual material** from the appropriate subject areas. [...] The account which follows results from attempts to use a systemic description of English in order to discover salient features of authentic language use. (White 1974: 401)

> if the teacher's aim is to teach **authentic language**, he will need to consider frequency as a criterion in the selection of verb forms and tenses for the TESL course [...]. (White 1974: 413) (emphases added by L.W.)

Whereas Whitman strays a bit from the conventional notion of authentic text as input by applying it to student utterances (output), White uses the term with an understanding that clearly antedates later conceptions of textual authenticity. What is more, he is consistent over the length of his article employing the term as many as 14 times. The article is actually a viable candidate to be added to the document selection based on explicit negotiation. In *TESOL Quarterly*, the general pattern of referring to textual authenticity remains a tentative one, as the following examples shall illustrate:

The ideal is to [...] acquire an **authentic native-speaker pronunciation** [...]. (Bowen 1972: 84)

Elements of social studies such as folk tales and **authentic cultural items** form the basis for the content of these lessons. (Sancho 1972: 335)

Cultural corners, displaying **authentic linguistic and cultural items,** provide the appropriate setting for these lessons. (*ibid.*)

These short (4 or 5 line) plays, which use only one language within any one class period, present **authentic language and culture**. (*ibid.*)

Appealing activities with **cultural and linguistic authenticity** [...] motivate the children to use both languages in meaningful contexts [...]. (Sancho 1972: 336) (emphases added by L.W.)

Bowen's collocation "authentic native-speaker pronunciation" appears familiar at first glance, which is due to the native-speaker element as it is present in many conceptualizations of textual authenticity. However, the linkage of authenticity and pronunciation jars with any of the concepts I have categorized under textual authenticity. In the scholarly discourse, the idea of authenticity pertaining to pronunciation remains inconsequential. Sancho displays a high rate of consistency in his use of the word. The focus is on cultural authenticity equally as it is on textual authenticity suggesting an inextricable connection. While the lack of explicit negotiation speaks against the article's adoption into the document selection, a concept pursued by Mishan (2005) is foreshadowed. Sancho, by systematicity of use, may be considered as marginally contributing to the evolving pattern of textual authenticity as the primary concept in the EFL discourse.

One other conceptual pattern should be mentioned on a side note here: Palmer highlights the importance of "authentic translation" as opposed to a dogged adherence to the Direct Method: "Cases occur in which the absence of an authentic and officially given translation gives rise to the most absurd misconceptions" (Palmer 1968: 64). He sees a high risk of false friends and negative interference leading learners to erroneous assumptions: "Let us recognize frankly that the withholding of an 'official' or authentic translation does not prevent the student from forming faulty associations, but that, on the contrary, such withholding may often engender them" (Palmer 1968: 65). An authentic translation, thus, is one provided by the teacher in a specific context instead of a translation assumed by the learner. According to Palmer, inauthentic translations are often subject to the learners' simplistic thinking in patterns of reliable one-to-one equivalences. Authentic translation should include explanations which raise the learners' awareness of ambiguity: "When telling him that 'prendre' is generally the equivalent of 'take', we must warn him that this does not include 'take' in the sense of 'carry', 'convey', or 'conduct'" (Palmer 1968: 65). Palmer's thoughts are picked up and expanded by Thomas, making the concept of authentic translation a discursive pattern (Thomas 1976: 409-410). However, given the lack of resonance in the subsequent discourse, this pattern must be considered short-lived. An adoption into the document selection would be an overrepresentation.

4.5.5.1.2 Focus on Stevick

As has been alluded to above, the corpus study of *TESOL Quarterly* has quarried Stevick (1971) as the very first text in the academic EFL discourse on authenticity. Two statements in Paulston (1974) led to the discovery:

> There is a very high degree of the social use of language in such a brief encounter and the authenticity, in Stevick's sense (1971), of the situation is remarkably conducive to language learning. (Paulston 1974: 359)

> I [...] informed my students that they would have to call my neighbor, a monolingual English speaker, for their next week's assignment. Suddenly there was authenticity in making a telephone conversation in English [...]. It would be unrealistic to demand that all lessons feature such authentic exercises, but if we want to teach our students to function in another language, we would do very well to systematically steer our teaching towards such activities which serve to teach not only language but also the social use of language. (Paulston 1974: 360)

The first quote explicitly invokes Stevick (1971) as the originator of a certain concept of authenticity. This concept is exemplified in the second quote. The reference is imprecise in not indicating a page number but a book in general (*Adapting and writing language lessons*). To justify Stevick (1971) as the starting point of the academic EFL discourse on authenticity, it is important to illustrate some instances of his usage:

> Swahili-language materials [...] were drawn principally from East African newspapers [...] They are authentic, in the sense that they were written by East Africans for East Africans [...]. (Stevick 1971: 190)

> One advantage in texts taken from such sources is that students know that they are working with something which was intended as communication among speakers of the language, and which therefore carries an unquestionable authenticity. (Stevick 1971: 369)

The degree and amount of explicit negotiation is high enough to justify Stevick (1971) as the inceptive element of the academic EFL discourse on authenticity.

Having identified Stevick as a contributor to the academic EFL discourse on authenticity, it appears promising to look at some more of his writings from the time. The following excerpt is taken from a publication in *TESOL Quarterly* four years prior to Stevick's book (1971). It is revealing with respect to both terminology and teaching methodology at the time:

> Mind you, these are texts, either spoken or written, which originated in real live communication among native speakers. The idea of using such texts unedited, unmitigated and unembalmed sounds a bit revolutionary. Won't it lead to chaos? Until recently, I had always assumed that it would. But it need not. Natural texts can be used very early if they are short, and if they conform to the three R's of relevance (to the interests of the class), realism, and recurrence (of vocabulary). But where are these texts to come from? Short, genuine texts with a high rate of vocabulary recurrence can be found for almost any special interest, if you look in the right place. (Stevick 1967: 8)

As for terminology, it is remarkable that these descriptions lack the word *authentic*. "[T]exts, either spoken or written, which originated in real live communication among native speakers" (ibid.) are exactly what Stevick denotes as *authentic* only four years later in his monograph (see above). Here, he refers to them as "natural texts" and "genuine texts" (ibid.). Before proceeding to the insights into teaching methodology, another example of Stevicks early writings is presented which confirms the impression that he changed his mind over time about what words to use in describing textual authenticity:

> One choice is between sequenced and unsequenced materials. Sequenced materials are those in which vocabulary or grammatical patterns, or both, are introduced at a controlled rate; and each lesson uses only what has previously been learned plus a small amount of new material. Once your students have gotten started in one of these sequences, they have to deal with only a few new problems in each lesson. This is obviously an advantage. (Stevick 1957: 61-62)

The synonymous use of *natural, genuine,* and *unsequenced* – but not yet *authentic* – shows that Stevick varied his terminology before 1971. The variations point to a relatively low degree of terminological negotiation in the EFL discourse at the time. It is unlikely that Stevick knew about any claims made by other authors about the use of *authentic/authenticity*.

As for the insights into teaching methodology to be derived from Stevick's (1967) quote: His statement that the "idea of using such texts unedited, unmitigated and unembalmed sounds a bit revolutionary" (Stevick 1967: 8) reveals that not only was the terminology inconsistent at the time, the entire concept of using authentic materials for language learning was not yet established. This interpretation matches Gilmore's claim that the prevalent teaching methods at the time "all imposed carefully structured (and therefore contrived) materials and prescribed behaviours on teachers and learners" (Gilmore 2007: 97), e.g. the New Method and the Audiolingual Method (ibid.).

Stevick appears to remain consistent in his diction after 1971. In 1989, he employs the term in alignment with the then prevalent discursive pattern:

> As Bert reads authentic materials written by and for Chinese people, he is not only picking up how the purely linguistic elements fit together; he is also finding out what meanings exist in Chinese life that do not exist in his native culture, and how some of these meanings are connected to one another […]. (Stevick 1989: 26-27)

By the time, the academic EFL discourse on authenticity had, of course, evolved significantly.

After deciding on Stevick (1971) as the first item of the academic EFL discourse on authenticity the relatively short time period from 1967 to 1971 is not considered sufficient to make informed statements about the explicit negotiation of authenticity – or the lack thereof – before Stevick (1971). The fact that merely one journal is looked at (*TESOL Quarterly*) further diminishes the validity of the method. The British journal *ELTJ* is investigated to confirm or reject the assumption that authenticity was not a subject of explicit negotiation prior to 1971. Between the journal's first issue in 1946 and 1971 only one article is found, which features the term *authentic/authenticity*. That article is Spicer (1968), which is relatively late considering that the preceding 22 years did not bring forth a text containing the term. In fact, some of the titles in *ELTJ* might suggest a fitting context for the term to occur but lack it throughout, e.g.:

Hornby, A. S. (1949). An approach towards real conversation. *ELT J* III (8), 199-206.

Phelps, Gilbert (1949). English idiom and English culture. *ELT J* III (4), 85-96.

Hornby, A. S. (1952). Situations – artificial or natural? *ELT J* VI (4), 118-124.

Lee, William R. (1963). Grading. *ELT J* XVII (3), 107-112.

Spicer (1968) uses the term *authenticity* in a surprisingly explicit manner:

> [I]deally, teaching materials should possess the following basic qualities:
>
> 'Authenticity': Whatever is presented to the pupils, whether linguistic or cultural material, should be an authentic representation of the language or civilization of the foreign country.
>
> 'Clarity': [...]
>
> 'Intrinsic value': [...]
>
> 'Practicality': [...]
>
> 'Appropriateness': [...] (Spicer 1968: 16-17)
>
> Recorded materials can provide the teacher and pupils with an authentic model [...]; many different voices; and a wide selection of varieties and styles of language. (Spicer 1968: 18)
>
> The materials must, of course, also be soundly based linguistically, authentic in their presentation of language and culture, and of immediate appeal to children of the age-range concerned. (Spicer 1968: 20)

The amount and explicitness of negotiation is comparable to Stevick (1971). The importance accorded to the concept is considerable given that it is the first of five basic qualities laid out for teaching materials. However, in comparison with Stevick (1971), Spicer's definition of authenticity is not quite as clear:

> Swahili-language materials [...] are authentic, in the sense that they were written by East Africans for East Africans [...]. (Stevick 1971: 190)
>
> [S]tudents know that they are working with something which was intended as communication among speakers of the language, and which therefore carries an unquestionable authenticity. (Stevick 1971: 369)

Ultimately, what tilts the decision in favor of Stevick (1971) as the first item in the discourse is the fact that his statements have been found to be referenced by another author (Paulston 1974: 359) who specifically invokes Stevick's definition of the term. Stevick has a high author status. His statements being cited by Paulston (1974) is a sign of recognition, this being a consensus in academic discourse theory (Hyland 2000: 37) and bibliometrics (Maheswarappa 1997: 6; Andrés 2009: 56-57; Meara 2012).

4.5.5.1.3 Notable absence of the term

In my study of *TESOL Quarterly*, concordances of *authentic* were of primary interest. In the process, however, passages were found where the term is notably absent. I define *notable absence* as textual instances where one would expect the term *authentic/authenticity* to be used – by today's standard. This applies predominantly to descriptions of textual authenticity because, to date, textual authenticity is the most consolidated concept of authenticity. Passages of notable absence, thus, feature expressions synonymous with textual authenticity, or paraphrases of the concept.

The discovery of such passages is in most cases fortuitous. The descriptions by O'Neill/Scott and Crystal/Davy (O'Neill/Scott 1974: vi; Crystal/Davy 1975: ix–x) – quoted in chapter 4.5.5.1) are examples of notable absence, though not in academic publications. Early works by Stevick have also been shown to feature notable absence: "One choice is between sequenced and unsequenced materials" (Stevick 1957: 61-62); "using such texts unedited, unmitigated and unembalmed" (Stevick 1967: 8).

The following instances were found in *TESOL Quarterly*:

Literature will increase all language skills because literature will extend linguistic knowledge by giving evidence of extensive and subtle vocabulary usage, and complex and exact syntax. It will often represent in a general way the style that can properly stand as a model for students. (Povey 1967: 41-42)

[O]therwise the most effective ESL reading material would be those items we created ourselves to the specific linguistic architecture of levels of difficulty. Such works more often become readers without any element of literature in them. The simplified stories from the classics are justified by a similar appeal to language necessity, but they are usually only a thin reminder of what was once a significant book. (Povey 1967: 43)

in preparing beginning and intermediate reading texts for use in the overseas ESL classroom we must exercise close controls. We will now suggest the principles upon which we build this control [...] First, we will examine how we can adapt the still-rather-conventional uncontrolled text to some degree of control over sound and grammatical patterns. Second, let's assume an ideal situation in which we can compose our own reading text with the necessary controls built into it. (MacLeish 1968: 44)

Povey and MacLeish differ completely in their approaches to fostering reading skills. Povey advocates authentic literature, MacLeish is in favor of creating simplified texts. What both have in common is that they omit the word *authentic*, while referring to the very characteristics of textual authenticity. MacLeish uses "uncontrolled" as a synonym. Povey speaks of "literature", which – according to later definitions – would be a subcategory of authentic text. It appears that in the late 1960s *authentic/authenticity* was far from being a common technical term in EFL and that, indeed, Stevick (1971) may have paved the way for its use and its explicit negotiation.

Throughout the 1970s sporadic instances of notable absence persist. The last examples I found are from 1977:

[D]oes traditional simplification really promote learning by providing for a smooth and orderly progression to 'full' English, as it is supposed to do? The present paper attempts to answer this question (Honeyfield 1977: 431)

The result [of simplification] may be material lacking in cohesion, and hence readability-material which inadequately represents the semantic and rhetorical systems of normal English. (Honeyfield 1977: 435)

communicative structure is an essential feature of original, unsimplified material (Honeyfield 1977: 436)

I believe, however, that we must keep in mind the terminal objective, which is for students to read 'unsimplified material'. (Honeyfield 1977: 436)

Honeyfield, whose article is titled "Simplification" (1977), never speaks of *authentic/authenticity*. Interestingly, the article is cited many years later by Nation/Deweerdt, who choose a similar title for their article: "A defence of simplification" (2001). Not only does the latter article use the term *authentic/authenticity*[56], but it does so giving the impression that it hails from Honeyfield (1977): "Graded readers that are simplified from literary texts written for native speakers are criticised for being unauthentic (Honeyfield 1977)" (Nation/Deweerdt 2001: 56). The two articles are thematically similar but while Honeyfield (1977) does not use the term, Nation/Deweerdt (2001) use it 14 times in their article – even when referring to Honeyfield. This comparison of the two articles reinforces the assumption that notable absence decreases over time.

In the same year as Honeyfield (1977), an EFL textbook appears which features similar parts of notable absence: *A technical reader for advanced students* (Broughton 1977). This book targets learners who are already proficient in the English language but who need practice in reading articles in technical English. Such texts may be part of their higher education or work training. They span fields as varied as medicine, plumbing, or electronics. The book relies exclusively on authentic texts. In the preface, the pedagogic rationale is laid out:

> The passages are all written by experts in their particular fields, who have, however, directed them at the educated lay-man rather than at members of their own professions. For this reason a surprisingly wide range of material can be presented here, moving the learner forward on a broad front [...]. In order that the student should experience the genuine article, no editorial alterations have been made [...]. Exercises have been set as a means of directing the student's attention to various aspects of usage: some aim to broaden his vocabulary, active or passive; others ask him to wrestle with specific words or phrases; others invite him to crystallise whole sections in his own words [...]. (Broughton 1977: preface)

The book does not really fall into the category of ESP (English for Specific Purposes). The variety of topics, along with the explanations above, suggests that "the foreign student who has completed a normal English language course" (ibid.) should generally benefit from this advanced learning material. It is interesting to see that the word *genuine* is chosen instead of *authentic*. Though the use is intuitive rather than informed, it shows that Widdowson's use of the term is not unparalleled. Widdowson introduces the term *genuine* to denote textual authenticity in 1976. Broughton (1977) is published so shortly after that he is unlikely to be informed by Widdowson's article.

To demonstrate the likeness of Broughton's wording to that of O'Neill/Scott (1974) and Crystal/Davy (1975), I reiterate the latter two:

> Since it is true that in order to understand English spoken at normal speed, the student must be exposed to 'real' English, it must also be true that the structures, patterns and vocabulary cannot be artificially graded. [...] Students' experience of spoken English is frequently confined to recordings of rehearsed conversations spoken below normal speed by trained actors. This is not what the student hears when he arrives in an English speaking country.

---

56 To remind the reader: I use *authentic/authenticity* in italics to refer to any lexeme of that word family. The term *unauthentic* is therefore included.

Students need a truly representative sample of real spoken English. 'Viewpoints' provide this. (O'Neill/Scott 1974: vi)

We attach particular importance to the naturalness of our data, which has not been edited in any way. We have not come across commercially available material that is so informal or realistic, and it is in this respect that we hope the main contribution of this book will lie. (Crystal/Davy 1975: ix–x)

The publications by O'Neill/Scott (1974), Crystal/Davy (1975), and Broughton (1977) have two things in common. One, they are learning materials of which the instances of notable absence are found, respectively, in the preface of the books. The passages can all be regarded as promotional texts. Two, all three books are published after Stevick (1971), so it would be hypothetically possible for them to use the word *authentic/authenticity* referring to Stevick. However, the question of readership must be considered. These texts target either teachers or learners of EFL, making them elements of the non-academic EFL discourse (cf. chapter 4.4.4). While the academic discourse negotiates terminology explicitly, O'Neill/Scott (1974), Crystal/Davy (1975), and Broughton (1977) aim for comprehensibility besides a certain level of persuasion. Even if their authors are aware of Stevick (1971), they must assure non-academics will understand what awaits them in the book. In conclusion, Honeyfield (1977) and Broughton (1977) are the latest texts found in my research to contain notable absence. While Honeyfield represents the academic discourse, Broughton's book belongs to the non-academic genre.

It is crucial to state that instances of notable absence are easily overlooked. It would be problematic to infer more than a vague tendency from the findings. This tendency lies in a gradual decrease of notable absence over time. Descriptions of textual authenticity seem more and more likely to actually use the term *authentic/authenticity* after one to two decades of terminological inconsistency. Early on during my research, I began to keep my eyes peeled for instances of notable absence in the literature under scrutiny, and I researched more literature published after 1977 than before. It is clear that notable absence will exist later than 1977, but it appears that throughout the 1970s *authentic/authenticity* establishes itself as a technical term and then quickly emanates to the non-academic circles. Cross-fertilization between academia and non-academia must also be considered. Nowadays, instances of notable absence are assumed to be virtually non-existent in both the academic and the non-academic contexts. Especially textbook publishers who advertise their materials use the term *authentic/authenticity* extensively. Such promotional texts are found in the prefaces of EFL textbooks, in advertising brochures, or on the websites of the publishing houses.

An early example of such a promotional text is a textbook by Walter published only five years after Broughton (1977): *Authentic reading – A course in reading skills for upper-intermediate students* (1982). The term is already contained in the title. The preface reads as follows:

'Authentic Reading' offers upper intermediate students a selection of authentic texts and a series of exercises specially designed to improve their reading skills. [...] There are 24 texts, all of them taken from authentic British and American sources. [...] Three of the texts have been adapted slightly; the changes are of the sort a native speaker would expect in an abridged novel. (Walter 1982: 12)

Walter uses the term *authentic/authenticity* consistently and often. The tone is obviously quite commendatory. Today, the term is employed abundantly in EFL advertising – "it is rare to find textbooks that do not claim to contain authentic texts" (Morton 1999: 177). However, the term no longer refers exclusively to textual authenticity but to various concepts. The following examples are symptomatic of this trend:

Through ELLIS' engaging, digital media, learners receive exposure to authentic language contexts and natural language use. (ELLIS Digital Learning Program 2015)

Each book is built around grade-level content that reflects the true academic classroom. 12 content-based thematic chapters. Authentic multicultural literature. (Scott Foresman ESL Sunshine Edition 2015)

Learners are exposed to a wide variety of language in authentic contexts and provided with the tools they need to produce their very own English. (Cambridge Your Space 2016)

These authentic examination papers provide candidates with an excellent opportunity to familiarise themselves with the content and format of the exam and to practise exam techniques. (Cambridge English First 2 2016)

The task is made more authentic by putting these questions before the text, in order to encourage candidates to read them first and then scan the text to find each answer. (Cambridge English. Preliminary. Handbook for teachers 2012: 10)

All texts are based on authentic situations. (Cambridge English. Preliminary. Handbook for teachers 2012: 30)

The best preparation for the Listening paper is exposure to, and engagement with, authentic spoken English at an appropriate level of difficulty. Classroom discussion activities provide a good authentic source of listening practice [...]. (Cambridge English. Preliminary. Handbook for teachers 2012: 31)

The Official Past Paper Packs have been especially designed by Cambridge English to provide teachers everything they need to give students authentic practice for their Cambridge Examination. (Official Past Paper Packs 2016)

Our course focuses especially on using authentic materials, the latest technologies and activities from the world of coaching. (Teaching Business English course 2016)

What's new: Even more choice and variety of authentic topics (New Inspiration 2016)

The podcasts offer authentic listening practice for you to use with – or recommend to – your business English students. (The Business Podcasts 2016)

These are all authentic and unscripted recordings, and expose students to real English as it is being used around the world today. (Global Coursebook 2016)

This apparently strong inclination of EFL advertisers to use the term *authentic/authenticity* is partially explainable by the question of targeted readership. Since the term connotates positive qualities in both academic and non-academic contexts, and since it is part of the colloquial discourse, it lends itself to marketing purposes with a target group of largely non-academic professionals, i.e. foreign language teachers. This target group is usually not familiar with the different concepts of authenticity discussed in academia.

4.5.5.1.4 Summary – early use of the term

An analysis of different text types has provided complex insights into the starting phase of the EFL discourse on authenticity. I have applied different methods to the different genres.

Lewkowicz (2000) and Gilmore (2007) make statements about the early years of authenticity in EFL, thereby providing a rough historical orientation. Both refer to Widdowson (1976) as the starting point of the discourse (e.g. "It was not until the late 1970s that Widdowson initiated a debate on the nature of authenticity" Lewkowicz 2000: 45).[57]

Indeed, the snowball method has not yielded relevant texts before 1976. To investigate the time prior to Widdowson a corpus study was conducted. The two journals *ELTJ* (first issue in 1946) and *TESOL Quarterly* (first issue in 1967) were extensively searched for articles containing the term *authentic/authenticity*. One of these articles references Stevick (1971) as a source conceptualizing authenticity. Stevick (1971), after a text-based analysis, emerges as the first element of the discourse.

A byproduct of sorts is the discovery of what I have termed *notable absence*. It appears that descriptions of textual authenticity used to be more terminologically inconsistent than they are today. During the 1960s and 70s, authors seemed more likely to forgo the term *authentic/authenticity* in such instances, using synonymous adjectives ("unsequenced" Stevick 1957: 61-62, "unedited" Stevick 1967: 8, "real" O'Neill/Scott 1974: vi etc.) or paraphrasing the concept as a whole. Notable absence is found in writings of academic EFL and non-academic EFL.

Gilmore's assertion that the "issue of authenticity" emerged in the 1970s, "culminated" in CLT, "and paved the way for the reintroduction of authentic texts" (Gilmore 2007: 97) is largely correct, but it does not distinguish between authenticity as a term and authenticity as a concept. Such a distinction is necessary, however, if one is interested in finding out whether the changes referred to were terminological or conceptual, or both.

In the previous chapters, the term is investigated as an emerging lexical unit in the EFL discourse. There is evidence that the term emerges in the academic discourse before being adopted in learning materials. Earl Stevick plays an important role in the term's introduction into the academic discourse. His publications contain instances of notable absence up to 1971, when he uses and explicitly negotiates the term arguably for the first time ever. Stevick goes on to deploy the term in later publications. Throughout the 1970s instances of notable absence continue to occur in both the academic and the semi-informed discourse. In the academic circle, these instances coexist with an increasing number of concordances of *authentic/authenticity*. No such concordances have been found in

---

57 Actually, both refer to Widdowson (1979) but, as mentioned before, Widdowson's statements on authenticity had already been published three years earlier and the monograph from 1979 is only a reprint.

learning materials from the 1970s. Only three texts taken from the sector of learning materials have been analyzed, which is obviously not enough to come to a conclusion. However, these texts were retrieved via the snowball method, which was used in the hope of finding concordances of *authentic/authenticity*. While the texts do contain clear descriptions of textual authenticity, the term is not used, which means that notable absence is discovered. Walter (1982) is the first textbook author to use the term "authentic". During the 1970s, the term is applied sporadically by EFL scholars describing different concepts. One gradually evolving pattern, however, is the consistent denotation of textual authenticity.

4.5.5.2 Authenticity and CLT

In order to compile the document selection a clear temporal line of demarcation is drawn. Stevick (1971) is identified as the first text in the chronology. This is possible because the focus is put on terminology, not on concepts. The conceptual discourse is too complex to be definitively demarcated in a similar manner. It is a truism that authenticity coincides with Communicative Language Teaching (CLT) but, here too, a distinction must be made between the term and the corresponding concepts of authenticity.

The question is to what extent the emergence of CLT is congruent with the conceptual and/or terminological emergence of authenticity. To that end, sources from the given time frame can be analyzed. These are for the most part internal accounts from within the CLT movement and they are often self-proclaimed or self-referential. These writings lend themselves to a comparison with later statements made by scholars who retrospectively emphasize the connection between CLT and authenticity. The latter kind is often found among the authors in the academic EFL discourse on authenticity. (Gilmore 2007: 97) (see above) is not the only author by far to link authenticity to CLT.

The theoretical groundwork for CLT is largely provided by influential linguists of the time, most prominently by Dell Hymes and Michael A.K. Halliday. Hymes challenges the form-focused approaches to conceiving of language competence such as Noam Chomsky's generative grammar:

> We break irrevocably with the model that restricts the design of language to one face toward referential meaning, one toward sound, and that defines the organization of language as solely consisting of rules for linking the two. Such a model implies naming to be the sole use of speech, as if languages were never organized to lament, rejoice, beseech, admonish, aphorize, inveigh [...]. A model of language must design it with a face toward communicative conduct and social life. (Hymes 1972: 278)

> It remains that the present vision of generative grammar extends only a little way into the realm of the use of language. [...] There are several sectors of communicative competence, of which the grammatical is one. Put otherwise, there is behavior, and, underlying it, there are several systems of rules reflected in the judgements and abilities of those whose messages the behavior manifests. (Hymes 1972: 281)

From these statements it is evident that a broad conceptual change is advocated (e.g. "We break irrevocably with [...]" (ibid.)) toward a new perspective which focuses on the use of language rather than on its formal features. Halliday advances practical considerations as early as in 1964:

> Teaching 'in' a language is a remarkably effective means of teaching a language [...].

> At the opposite end of the scale from learning a language through being taught some other subject in that language is the use for language teaching purposes of descriptive statements 'about' the language. To say that German has three genders, masculine, feminine and neuter; that in French the pronoun as complement occurs in the verbal group preceding the verb; that the RP accent of English has six simple vowel phonemes: these are observations 'bout' the languages concerned. They have an essential place in the 'total' scheme of teaching these languages. But frequently these and similar statements about languages are offered as if they represented the obvious and most effective means of imparting the language skills.

> It is true that there is one category of pupil who can make effective use of statements about a language: this is the sophisticated adult learner, especially one with experience of using and learning about several languages. [...] But such learners are relatively rare, perhaps extremely rare. [...] [A]n hour spent in teaching the facts of grammar, of phonology or of lexis, is not an hour of teaching the language. Teaching a language involves conjoining two essential features: first, the learner must 'experience' the language being used in meaningful ways, either in its spoken or in its written form; and secondly, the learner must himself have the opportunity of performing, of trying out his own skills, of making mistakes and being corrected. These are the essence of language learning; and teaching about a language does not contribute directly to either of them. (Halliday/McIntosh/Strevens 1964: 253-254)

Halliday/McIntosh/Strevens, thus, critique the status quo of language teaching and, much like Hymes, promote fundamental changes. Note that these early proponents of communicative approaches do not use the term *authentic/authenticity*. Neither does Hans H. Stern who, in 1983, takes a look back at the recent developments:

> From the mid-seventies the key concept that has epitomized the practical, theoretical, and research preoccupations in educational linguistics and language pedagogy is that of communication or communicative competence. [...] The various trends [...] and the concept of communicative competence have merged in the idea of communicative language teaching as a central focus for new thought and fresh approaches in language pedagogy in the early eighties.(Stern 1983: 111)

Not only the early proponents adopt a tone of paradigmatic shift, but also Stern reinforces the notion of a turning point commenting from the perspective of an observer who is looking back. Thus, the emergence of CLT was, in a certain way, marked by a high degree of demarcation – unlike the emergence of authenticity (as a term and as a concept).

Proponents of CLT deemed themselves part of a movement (Brumfit 1983: v), and the process was politically supported by the Council of Europe. This political dimension yielded a relatively closed circle of discursive contributors: those authors who belonged to the convened expert group.

> 'Communicative Language Teaching' has in recent years become a fashionable term to cover a variety of developments in syllabus design and, to a lesser extent, in the methodology of teaching foreign languages. Teachers and applied linguists wishing to examine the fundamental arguments underlying these developments have had to rely on the publications of the Council of Europe [...] (Brumfit/Johnson 1979: ix)

While the composition of the group changed over time, their most influential members were arguably John Trim, Jan van Ek, and David Wilkins (Trim 2007: 15). The circle expanded quickly beyond the expert group but remained confined to a relatively small number of authors in the early stages (see below). A collective feeling of historic achievement further strengthened the identification process:

> Many approaches to language teaching begin life as reactions to old approaches. Their starting point is often a belief in how languages should 'not' be taught, in how the old approaches have failed. Only after a while do the new approaches gain a more positive existence, as they begin to develop their own ideas as to what the task of language teaching involves. One way in which we might begin to consider 'communicative language teaching' [...] is therefore to ask 'what is it a reaction against?' (Johnson 1982: 5)

> In traditional, structurally-oriented, foreign language teaching the subject matter to be taught is usually given such priority that the methodology has been mainly geared to avoidance of errors [...] In communicative foreign language teaching, however, with its stress on developing the learner's capacity to negotiate meaning in the foreign language, these interaction processes obviously become much more vital. (Dolle/Willems 1984: 87-88)

Dolle/Willems are not instantly identified as CLT pioneers. As if to claim discursive relevance from the start, their article begins with a quote from Keith Johnson, who is amongst the most renowned authors in the field (Dolle/Willems 1984: 87). The general perception of CLT as an identifiable movement becomes apparent in the following lines by Richards/Rogers:

> The work of the Council of Europe; the writings of Wilkins, Widdowson, Candlin, Christopher Brumfit, Keith Johnson, and other British applied linguists on the theoretical basis for a communicative or functional approach to language teaching; the rapid application of these ideas by textbook writers; and the equally rapid acceptance of these new principles by British language teaching specialists, curriculum development centers, and even governments gave prominence nationally and internationally to what came to be referred to as the Communicative Approach, or simply Communicative Language Teaching. (The terms 'notional-functional' and 'funtional approach' are also sometimes used.) (Richards/Rodgers 2001: 154-155)

The terms *notional* and *functional* were typically used in the context of syllabus design (e.g. Wilkins 1976) but did not stand the test of time. They soon gave way to *communicative*. In Stern (1983), institutional stepping stones and seminal moments in research from 1970 to 1980 are listed and elaborated to outline the development of CLT. All innovations within this decade (e.g. Silent Way, Community Language Learning) are subsumed under "Communicative Approaches". Only three publications are portrayed as central to the evolution of CLT (Stern 1983: 111-113):

van Ek, Jan A. (1975). *The threshold level in a European uni/credit system for modern language learning by adults*. Strasbourg: Council of Europe.

Wilkins, David. A. (1976). *Notional syllabuses*. London: Oxford University Press.

Widdowson, Henry G. (1978). *Teaching language as communication*. Oxford: Oxford Univ. Press.

In addition, retrospective as well as synchronous accounts of the movement were published, reinforcing the impression of a concerted operation ("At present, the communicative tide is in full flood." Trim 1983: 70). These early retrospections were often contained in self-proclaimed CLT manuals with titles such as these (emphases added by L.W.):

Munby, John (1978). *Communicative syllabus design*. Cambridge University Press.

Widdowson, Henry G. (1978). *Teaching language as communication*. Oxford: Oxford Univ. Press.

Brumfit, Christopher; Johnson, Keith (eds.) (1979). *The communicative approach to language teaching*. Oxford: Oxford University Press.

Piepho, Hans-Eberhard (1979). *Kommunikative Didaktik des Englischunterrichts Sekundarstufe I*. Theoretische Begründung und Wege zur praktischen Einlösung eines fachdidaktischen Konzepts. 11. Limburg: Frankonius.

Littlewood, William (1981). *Communicative language teaching*. Cambridge: Cambridge University Press.

Brumfit, Christopher (ed.) (1983). *Learning and teaching languages for communication*. London: Centre for Information on Language Teaching and Research for British Association for Applied Linguistics.

Johnson, Keith; Porter, Don (1983). *Perspectives in communicative language teaching*. London, New York: Academic Press.

Brumfit, Christopher (1984). *Communicative methodology in language teaching*. Cambridge, New York: Cambridge University Press.

Willems, Gerard M.; Riley, Philip (1984). *Communicative foreign language teaching and the training of foreign language teachers*. Nijmegen: Interstudie Institute for Teacher Education.

Widdowson (1978) and Brumfit (1983) use the noun *communication*, not the adjective *communicative*. They are nevertheless considered to thereby refer to the movement of CLT.

The relatively closed circle of authors resulted partly from the political influence described above. The writings are often cross-referential within the circle, which is mirrored in some edited volumes. For instance, Brumfit/Johnson (1979) contains articles from authors, of which many have already been mentioned here: Brumfit, Johnson, Widdowson (four articles), Wilkins (two articles), Candlin, Trim, van Ek, Hymes, Halliday, J.P.B. Allen, Keith Morrow, Leonard Newmark, Richard Allwright. Another example is to be found in the preface to Munby (1978):

> In the preparation of this book I was influenced at the macro-level by the sociolinguistic writings of Dell Hymes and Michael Halliday, and at a more micro-level by the work of, in particular, Henry Widdowson, David Wilkins and Christopher Candlin. (Munby 1978: vi)

What is observable is that the conceptual innovation of CLT was spearheaded by a number of authors whose names crop up redundantly, which is likely a typical pattern of emerging movements.

The fast consolidation of the term *communicative/communication* may have played a beneficial role in the subsequent success of the approaches advocated. Without plunging too deep into the terminological analysis of *communicative/communication*, it is safe to say that the term evolved considerably faster and more smoothly than did the term *authentic/authenticity*, which to date must be considered a floating signifier. However, the connection of the two terms is abundant in the later literature. As mentioned before, this connection is made in the brief historical accounts of Lewkowicz and Gilmore. The former states that in "applied linguistics the notion emerged in the late 1970s at the time when communicative methodology was gaining momentum and there was a growing interest in teaching and testing 'real-life' language" (Lewkowicz 2000: 43). Gilmore says that the "issue of authenticity reappeared in the 1970s [...] This culminated in the approach which, at least in EFL circles, still holds sway today – Communicative Language Teaching – and paved the way for the reintroduction of authentic texts" (Gilmore 2007: 97). The following examples do not take an equally historical approach but merely serve to illustrate terminological co-occurrence. They are given chronological sequence (emphases added by L.W.):

> [W]e introduced a **communicative** language teaching approach coupled with the exclusive use of **authentic** materials [...]. (Kienbaum/Russell/Welty 1986: 7)

> The **communicative** approach has no single source and certainly exists in no single version. [...] [P]erhaps the majority of language classrooms it is manifested at least in the form of two lowest common denominators: emphasis on the spoken language and use of **authentic** texts. (Little/Devitt/Singleton 1988: foreword)

> It is the purpose of this book to re-examine some of the basic principles on which the **communicative** approach is founded, to show why **authentic** texts should be at the centre of the foreign language learning process [...]. (Little/Devitt/Singleton 1988: foreword)

> The relentless push since the mid-1970s towards **communicative** approaches to language teaching has brought along with it what some might characterize as a trend and others as a stampede supporting the use of **authentic** sources of language data in ESL textbooks and in classroom materials [...]. (Adams 1995: 1)

> With the onset of the **communicative** movement a greater awareness of the need to develop students' skills for the real world has meant that teachers endeavour to simulate this world in the classroom. One way of doing this has been to use **authentic** materials [...]. (Guariento/Morley 2001: 347)

> **Communicative** classrooms generally feature: [...] Use of **authentic** (nonpedagogic) texts and communication activities linked to 'real-world' contexts (Wesche/Skehan 2002: 208)

> In language teaching, there is an enduring 'cult of **authenticity**' that originated with the **communicative** language teaching (CLT) movement of the late 1970s. (Day/Bamford 2009 [Day, Richard (1998). Extensive reading in the second language classroom. Cambridge: Cambridge University Press. 53-61.]: 234)

> [T]he term [**authentic/authenticity**] moved to a central, if contested, position with the development of **communicative** language teaching from the 1970s onwards [...]. (Badger/MacDonald 2010: 578)

> [T]o expose students to natural language in a variety of situations, adherents of **CLT** advocate the use of **authentic** language materials. (Larsen-Freeman/Anderson 2011: 126)

This terminological co-occurrence of *communicative/communication* and *authentic/authenticity* is very commonly found from the mid-1980s onward. However, it was extremely rare during the earlier period when CLT established itself. Badger's statement (2010) is, thus, absolutely accurate in that it describes a simultaneous emergence of *authentic/authenticity* as a term and CLT as a movement. The terminological alignment did not arise until much later. Most of the seminal works in CLT from the 1970s and early 1980s actually lack the term *authentic/authenticity* completely. One exception is, of course, Widdowson (Widdowson 1978: 80-81). The other is Wilkins, who brings together both terms probably for the first time ever:

> In a context where we are emphasizing the communicative purpose of language and the immediate usefulness of the language being learned, the acquisition of comprehension skill poses a particular problem. [...] [M]uch more attention needs to be paid to the acquisition of a receptive competence and that an important feature of materials designed to produce such a competence would be authentic language materials. (Wilkins 1976: 78-79)

Wilkins continues to pursue this connection and may be considered the initiator of a merging process leading to today's perception that authenticity is all but inextricable from CLT, both conceptually and terminologically:

> [C]ommunicativity may be seen to lie in the priority of conversational interaction over other modes of language behaviour, [...] in the use of 'authentic' as opposed to 'non-authentic' materials, [...] in the desire to base learning on genuine communication rather than on participation in pedagogically motivated and structured activities. (Wilkins 1983: 24)

However, Widdowson contradicts Wilkins's idea in the same year:

> [T]his shift of emphasis [that came with CLT] has had the effect of identifying objectives more closely with aims. One result of this is the widespread (and I believe mistaken) belief that if language is to be taught 'for' communication it has necessarily to be presented 'as' communication, that every classroom activity must bear the hallmark of 'authenticity'. No doubt the title of my own book (Widdowson 1978 [Teaching language as communication]) has made its own contribution to this misconception, and I wish now that I had chosen the more accurate and less misleading title 'Teaching language 'for' communication'. (Widdowson 1983: 30)

Widdowson also takes a backward look in 1998 and rebuts the connection between CLT and the use of authentic materials:

> It is not the case that communicative language teaching focuses on meaning whereas the benighted structuralist approach did not: It focuses on pragmatic meaning in context rather than semantic meaning in the code. And the focus on pragmatic meaning does not require the importation of authentic language use into the classroom [...]. (Widdowson 1998: 715)

He is equally forthright about this point in a retrospective account in 2007, this time suggesting a wide-spread misconception of what Dell Hymes put forth:

> And here we come to another popular notion about CLT that, like the neglect of grammar, runs counter to Hymes' proposals, namely the notion that the language presented to learners must be 'authentic' or 'real'. This, of course, goes with the assumption that the objective of CLT is to replicate native speaker norms and develop communicative competence rather than capability. (Widdowson 2007: 218)

In conclusion, the temporal demarcation of authenticity does not lend itself to a simple alignment with the emergence of CLT. The deceptive element here is that, indeed, the term *authentic/authenticity* emerged roughly at the time when the concept of CLT came up. However, the denotations of *authentic/authenticity* were highly heterogeneous at the time. Widdowson (1976; 1978), for example, was specifically opposed to applying the term to materials. What is more, the terminological connection between authenticity and CLT remained sporadic until the mid-1980s when at least one denotation of *authentic/authenticity* became less contentious: texts and materials (usually from native speakers for native speakers).

Interestingly, the term *communicative/communication* overtook *authentic/authenticity* at a high pace as regards the transition from a floating signifier to a moment, the latter of which denotes a signifier with a stable denotation (cf. chapter 4.1). The word *communicative* has a more straight-forward meaning than *authentic*, which is extremely dependent on syntactical context. It may also be the case that the CLT movement, which was quite self-conscious at the time, underwent a discursive process of self-labeling which led to the adjective *communicative* prevailing over *functional* and *notional*. During the 1980s, few authors referred to the movement as anything other than *communicative*.

4.5.5.3 Concluding remarks on temporal demarcation

To summarize my approaches to a temporal demarcation of the EFL discourse on authenticity: two methodological means have been employed to analyze a historical time frame which very roughly ranges from 1945 to 1985. First, I sifted through all articles in *TESOL Quarterly* from the journal's inception to when Widdowson (1976) first used the term in a publication title. This helped trace the term on a text level basis as opposed to looking only at works carrying the term in the title. A similar, if less comprehensive, method was assumed investigating articles in *ELTJ*, which was founded in 1945. In *ELTJ*, only three articles per year were picked at random and word-searched (75 articles in sum) because using the word-search function required previous downloading of the file, making the process more involved.

Second, I investigated the common notion that authenticity has been closely tied to Communicative Language Teaching (CLT) from the very beginning. This question was addressed coming from two different directions – the CLT perspective and the authenticity perspective. The CLT perspective encompasses writings from within the CLT movement as well as retrospective descriptions of it. Of interest was primarily how CLT evolved and what role the term *authentic/authenticity* played in that process. The authenticity perspective provided information on how the *authenticity experts*, namely the authors within the document selection, connect the term to CLT. These statements typically come from texts published long after the 1970s, discussing the CLT movement retrospectively. In brief, the line of temporal demarcation is drawn as follows:

In 1971, Stevick was arguably the first EFL scholar to define authenticity in a clear and explicit manner. His publication, although *authentic/authenticity* does not appear in the title, marks the chronological beginning of the academic EFL discourse on authenticity. The academic EFL discourse on authenticity starts here. Before 1971, but also a number of years after, the term was either notably absent or it was used rather casually and unsystematically. Both phenomena, notable absence and casual use, decreased gradually over the next two decades. 1971 is certainly not the precise year when Communicative Language Teaching was born. To state that CLT and authenticity emerged simultaneously – as many authors do – is only a rough approximation. Stern actually sees the foundation of CLT in as early as 1951:

> The pioneer effort in Europe was the linguistic research project on 'francais fondamental', begun in France in 1951. [...] It was based on the thought that, at an elementary level of language use, a learner requires above all the spoken language of everyday life in concrete situations. (Stern 1983: 161)

The term *authentic/authenticity* was not very common in the early publications of CLT and its denotations were too heterogeneous to allow for a perfect congruence with the communicative innovations of the time. Rather, some of the later concepts of authenticity – but not all of them – were strongly advocated by the CLT movement during its early years.

5 Chronological analysis of the academic EFL discourse on authenticity

In this chapter, insights are drawn from a text level analysis of the documents that constitute the academic EFL discourse on authenticity. Thus far, an extensive literature review (chapter 2) and a bibliometric study (chapter 4.5.3) have been conducted. The former approach served to identify basic concepts of authenticity, which I have arranged to form a new taxonomy. Bibliometric approaches have yielded numbers of productivity and citation which largely remain to be interpreted. The temporal demarcation of the discourse required a more historical approach, which served to dispel a perceived congruence of authenticity and CLT (cf. chapter 4.5.5.2). An extensive electronic word search within articles of two EFL journals was conducted to discover early occurrences of the term *authentic/authenticity* (cf. chapter 4.5.5.1).

The bibliometric study, the analysis of the two journals, and the brief historical study were instrumental in detecting the body of documents which constitutes the academic EFL discourse on authenticity. At the basis of the whole study lies a more in-depth analysis, namely a text level discourse analysis of statements which explicitly negotiate authenticity. In the following chapters, the order of presentation and analysis is mainly chronological as opposed to the mainly systematic approach taken in the literature review. The systematic overview of concepts is, however, serviceable in the upcoming process. The concepts are frequently referred to, thereby providing a thematic structure. Another underpinning to the chronological study are bibliometric findings in terms of productivity and citation numbers. The findings of the productivity analysis conducted in chapter 4.5.3 are reiterated at relevant moments, for example pointing out that a given author is highly prolific in the discourse. The method of citation analysis was presented in the same chapter but the corresponding analysis is part of the upcoming chronological study. Citation counts help to highlight statements or publications in the discourse that are particularly well-received. Lastly, the various discourse analytical aspects expounded in chapters 4.2 and 4.3 are referred to at different stages throughout the analysis. Questions of authorial stance, authorial style, author status etc. are discussed at moments in the analysis when these contextual aspects facilitate an interpretation of statements that is more differentiated than what a simple literature review would engender.

The selection of documents is too large to present statements from each text in the forthcoming analysis. My primary research interest of determining what is deemed authentic in EFL entails a degree of prioritization that reflects relevance in the discourse. As a result, occasional omissions are made because, otherwise, the diversification of concepts would be enormous and their representation would suggest an undue equality of discursive relevance between all concepts.

Omissions are always the result of a two-step inquiry. The first step is to identify texts which have very low numbers of received citations. This usually means a maximum of one other text in the document selection citing it. In many cases the element is not cited at all. The second step is an inquiry of the text for noteworthy qualities. Such qualities include displays of typical patterns in the discourse. For instance, if a concept typical of the given time period is discussed, then to briefly mention the text or statement underscores the trend. Another noteworthy quality is of course relevance by virtue of substance. For example, Decke-Cornill (2004) provides an insightful categorization of concepts along with an interesting commentary displaying metadiscursive awareness. The text is useful for the comparison of conceptual categorizations that is put forth in chapter 2.1. It is, however, not cited by any of the other authors. All in all, noteworthy qualities can override the fact that a given text does not receive any citations within the discourse.

5.1   On my role as an analyst

When a discourse analysis is conducted, it is important to describe the role of the analyst with reference to the discourse under scrutiny. In the case at hand, the study itself becomes a contribution to this same discourse.

> [T]heoretical consistency demands that discourse analysts consider and make clear their position in relation to the particular discourses under investigation and that they assess the possible consequences or their contribution to the discursive production of our world. (Jørgensen/Phillips 2002: 22)

I shall make clear my "position in relation to the particular discourses under investigation" (ibid.) insofar as the given information on myself has a potential bearing on my research and my way of presentation. The point is addressed after responding to the second requirement put forth in the quote above: predictions on the "consequences or their contribution to the discursive production of our world" (ibid.). These are, naturally, difficult to make. Although I do contribute to the discourse by writing and publishing this book, the impact on the discourse is assumed to be relatively small. In order to notably influence the discourse some decisive criteria apply. These criteria include author status, which is quite low in my case rendering discursive impact of my writing all but negligible. Substance is expected to play a minor role in this regard.

By and large, the influence on the discourse is marginal compared to the influence on me and my career as a scholar. Besides factual autobiographical information, matters of personality and motivation arise. As is the case for any other contributor to the discourse, the following questions must be regarded:

- Why do the members of specific professional communities use language the way they do?

- How do these professionals manipulate professional genres to achieve their corporate objectives?

- How do these professionals 'bend generic norms' to achieve their 'private intentions' in addition to, and within, the framework of shared generic conventions? (Bhatia 2012: 250)

In my case the achievement of "corporate objectives" or "private intentions" (ibid.) is not so much contingent on a specific use of language or on a manipulation of the professional

genre. Having a book published requires obvious standards of quality. A bending of generic norms – except for plagiarism – is not conducive to this goal in any conceivable
way. Quality standards include a certain conformity with professional conventions. These
conventions pertain predominantly to the aspects of language, academic rigor, and relevance. Whereas conventional language is a general prerequisite, variation in rigor and
relevance impinge on the degree of impact this work will have on me as an individual.
However, even the best results in terms of rigor and relevance are not likely to notably
influence the discourse on authenticity at large due to a relatively low degree of author
status.

Before moving on to the chronological in-depth analysis of the discourse, a brief note
shall be made on the aspect of authorial style. Within the discourse, there is remarkable
variation in this regard, which is roughly to be seen as a range between descriptive approaches and conceptual approaches (cf. chapter 4.3.1). As a contributor to the discourse,
I must decide where to position myself stylistically. Since my study employs means of
discourse analysis, it veers strongly towards a descriptive style of presenting information.
This includes a high amount of referencing while disallowing the display of authorial
stance. As Jørgensen remarks, "a critical evaluation can be carried out at a later stage in
the analysis" (Jørgensen/Phillips 2002: 21). In the final chapter of this book – chapter 7
– some statements are made in this regard.

5.2   Chronological analysis by decade

In chapter 3, I suggested a typology of conceptual authenticity, which I referred to as a
taxonomy. Clarity and systematic distinctness with regard to the different concepts was
at the center of that endeavor. Only briefly did I broach questions of chronology. The
newly created document selection renders possible an enhanced contextualization of all
the concepts by means of the discourse analytical and bibliometric methods presented. In
what follows, I give a detailed account of how the concepts evolved over time. The analysis proceeds in largely chronological order along the individual texts of the document
selection. Texts are clustered in time periods to provide structure and a better overview.
A guideline with regard to thematic structure and terminology is the taxonomy of conceptual authenticity, which I have put forward (figure 5).

These categories are the research parameters which underlie the upcoming analysis.
Every statement that defines authenticity or works towards a definition of authenticity
can – ideally – be allocated to one of the categories. The allocation is often straight-forward. In such cases I usually do not mention the category. In more difficult cases it is
critical to discuss the issue of allocation.

Beside the allocation to concepts, another sort of allocation is occasionally helpful,
namely a grouping by thematic context. During the 2000s, for example, authenticity is
frequently discussed in the context of corpus linguistics, which is promoted following the
technological advancements of the time. Corpora are considered a source of authenticity.
The concept invoked by the given authors is almost exclusively textual authenticity. The

context of corpus linguistics is important to explain the temporary influx of the concept alongside a new perspective on textual authenticity (cf. chapter 5.2.4).

Concept	Subdivision	
1. Textual authenticity		
2. Authenticity of text reception		
3. Real-world authenticity	a) Typical activities of native-speakers	
	b) Typical activities of the learners in the future	
4. Classroom authenticity		
5. Authenticity of individual behavior		
6. Cultural authenticity	a) Behavioral cultural authenticity	
	b) Ethnographic cultural authenticity	

A taxonomy of conceptual authenticity in EFL (cf. figure 5 in chapter 3.7)

The following chapters are structured rather loosely so as to allow for flexibility of focus. Each decade is introduced in a couple of sentences so as to provide general context and advance-organize the chapter. The introduction is followed by a list of all the texts from the respective decade. The ensuing main part describes the discursive developments within the given time frame and ends with a short conclusion.

5.2.1 1971–79 – the early years

This period of time has already been under scrutiny in search of a starting point of the discourse. An analysis of *TESOL Quarterly* and *ELTJ* has yielded insights in terms of frequency and meaning of the term *authentic/authenticity*. These insights are of interest now that the most important contributions to the discourse are investigated in depth. The first decade of the discourse displays a low degree of activity compared to later decades. Eight publications negotiate the term explicitly:

Number of citations received	Publication	Citations made	Type of publication
0	Stevick, Earl W. (1971). *Adapting and writing language lessons*. Washington, DC: Foreign Service Institute.	None	Book
28	Widdowson, Henry G. (1976). The authenticity of language data. In: Fanselow, John F.; Crymes, Ruth H. *On TESOL '76*. Washington, D.C.: TESOL, 261-270.	None – no bibliography	Article in edited volume
7	Wilkins, David A. (1976). *Notional syllabuses*. London: Oxford University Press.	None	Book
5	Gutschow, Harald (1977). 'Authentizität' und 'Aktualität' in Texten für den Fremdsprachenunterricht. *Zielsprache Deutsch* 4/1977, 2-11.	None	Article in journal
10	Morrow, Keith (1977). Authentic texts and ESP. In: Holden, Susan. *English for specific purposes*. London: Modern English Publications, 13-15.	None – no bibliography	Article in journal
4	Geddes, Marion; White, Ron (1978). The use of semi-scripted simulated authentic speech and listening comprehension. *Audio-Visual Language Journal* 16 (3), 137-145.	Wilkins (1976)	Article in journal
28	Widdowson, Henry G. (1978). *Teaching language as communication*. Oxford: Oxford University Press.	None	Book
2	Beile, Werner (1979). Authentizität und Hörverstehen. In: Heuer, Helmut (ed.). *Dortmunder Diskussionen zur Fremd-sprachendidaktik. Kongressdokument-ation der 8. Arbeitstagung der Fremdsprachendidaktiker Dortmund 1978*. Dortmund: Lensing, 232-234.	None – no bibliography	Article in edited volume

Figure 10: The early years

Textual authenticity emerges as a common concept in the early years. One reason for listing this concept as the first category in the taxonomy is the fact that it occurred so early. While the authors in *TESOL Quarterly* and *ELTJ* use the term to denote the concept without explaining, the first definitions are presented by the authors in the discourse.

151

However, from the very beginning alternative denotations occur in the form of statements that explicitly challenge the concept of textual authenticity, or at least put forward a different understanding of it.

5.2.1.1 Detailed analysis

Wilkins is the first to give an explicit definition of textual authenticity using the term *authentic language materials*:

> [Learners] are not accustomed to hearing (or reading) the language as it is produced by native speakers for native speakers. This suggests that in language courses generally, but in courses based on a notional syllabus in particular, much more attention needs to be paid to the acquisition of a receptive competence and that an important feature of materials designed to produce such a competence would be authentic language materials. By this is meant materials which have not been specially written or recorded for the foreign learner, but which were originally directed at a native-speaking audience. (Wilkins 1976: 78-79)

The definition includes both written and spoken text, and it includes a native-speaker element. The first definition of textual authenticity is thus very similar to later definitions (cf. chapter 2.2 for an analysis of the various definitions).

The concept, however, is challenged by others right from the beginning. Stevick, whom I have identified as the presumptive originator of the term, does not conceive of authenticity in such a straight-forward way:

> Even 'real' communication in a foreign language may or may not be 'authentic'. If it is in the language that for the two interlocutors would be the natural one to use at that time, on that topic, then it is authentic; otherwise it is not. One of the peculiar skills, and a mark of dedication of a good language teacher (provided of course that he could be communicating with the student more easily in some other language) is his ability and willingness to carry on communication that is at the same time real and non-authentic. One of the mistakes of the unskilled teacher is to assume that because communication is not authentic, it can at best be realistic. (Stevick 1971: 31)

This description seems to focus on spoken interaction while omitting written text. At a different point, Stevick also applies the term to written materials: "One advantage in texts taken from such sources is that students know that they are working with something which was intended as communication among speakers of the language, and which therefore carries an unquestionable authenticity" (Stevick 1971: 369). Stevick describes authentic text as a means likely to provide *strength*, i.e. the topical relevance of a lesson to the learners: "[T]o what extent will the students be able to use the content of this lesson immediately, in a lifelike way?" (Stevick 1971: 46). According to him a sentence like "The book is on the table." (ibid.) has less strength than "I need a taxi." (ibid.) because the latter translates better into real life situations. This may be seen as a precursor to Task-Based Language Teaching (TBLT). He also says that materials should be "authentic both linguistically and culturally" (ibid.) but does not explain this distinction. All in all, Stevick, who performs terminological groundwork, puts forth a number of tentative conceptualizations, which appear to be connected but still denote slightly different things. Yet, his deliberations all apply to the concept of textual authenticity.

Textual authenticity is also commented on by Morrow (1977). Like Widdowson, whose view is presented shortly, Morrow considers the use of authentic materials as beneficial in ESP courses. In his definitions, however, Morrow appears to contradict himself by first propounding a definition of authentic text and then contending that authenticity can never occur in the classroom.

> An 'authentic text' is a stretch of real language, produced by a real speaker or writer for a real audience and designed to convey a real message of some sort. In other words it is 'not' a made-up text produced by an imaginary speaker or writer for an imaginary audience and designed to practise specific language points rather than to convey real information. (Morrow 1977: 13)

> A particular speaker talking to a particular audience at a particular time in a particular situation will use particular language [...]. If the situation changes in the slightest way the language used will also change, and this fact ultimately makes the concept of 'authentic' in language teaching terms unattainable. For the language we present as 'authentic' is authentic only to the very particular situation in which it was first used. By using it in a classroom for teaching purposes, we are destroying this authenticity [...]. (Morrow 1977: 14)

Unfortunately, later authors tend to refer to such intricate concepts in a simplistic manner. In one case, Gilmore (2007) quotes Morrow's statement from page 13 leaving out what is added on page 14:

> At least eight possible inter-related meanings emerge from the literature. Authenticity relates to:
>
> (i) the language produced by native speakers for native speakers in a particular language community (Porter & Roberts 1981; Little, Devitt & Singleton 1989);
>
> (ii) **the language produced by a real speaker/writer for a real audience, conveying a real message (Morrow 1977**; Porter & Roberts 1981; Swaffar 1985; Nunan 1988/9; Benson & Voller 1997) (Gilmore 2007: 98; emphasis added by L.W.)

By not indicating a page number – "Morrow 1977" (ibid.) – Gilmore creates the impression that Morrow's article provides a simple definition of textual authenticity and nothing more on the topic, when Morrow actually concludes that authenticity is unattainable in the English language classroom. Overall, Gilmore's method of allocating multiple authors to concise definitions must be critiqued for it often fails to reflect the complexity of the different conceptualizations. Stevick (1971) and Morrow (1977) illustrate the intricacies of the issue from the very beginning. While simple definitions of textual authenticity do exist, e.g. (Wilkins 1976: 78-79), Stevick (1971) and Morrow (1977) put forth elaborate concepts without committing to concise definitions, as Gilmore (2007) suggests.

A two-pronged definition is propounded by Geddes/White:

> The term 'authentic discourse' is employed in at least two senses. Firstly, it is used to refer to language which was originally written or spoken for a non-pedagogical purpose and which was, in its original context, a genuine act of communication. Secondly, it is employed to refer to language produced for a pedagogical purpose, but exhibiting features which have a high probability of occurrence in genuine acts of communication. (Geddes/White 1978: 137)

The second part of the definition is a clear expansion of the concept compared to the aforementioned more restrictive definitions. According to Geddes/White (1978) "[L]anguage produced for a pedagogical purpose, but exhibiting features which have a high probability of occurrence in genuine acts of communication" (ibid.) can be authentic. Very few definitions in the discourse are compatible with this statement.

The role of the native speaker in the definitions of textual authenticity, thus far, appears rather unimportant. Stevick (1971), Morrow (1977), and Geddes/White (1978) do not link authenticity to native speakers. Wilkins (1976) speaks of authentic materials being "originally directed at a native-speaking audience" (Wilkins 1976: 78-79) but he does not put much emphasis on this aspect. The two German publications of the decade contain definitions of textual authenticity that attach greater importance to the native speaker element:

> Strictly speaking, anything is authentic that is produced by native speakers.[58] (Gutschow 1977: 3)

> If a listening text is described as 'authentic speech', the listener must be able to rely on the speakers being native speakers who do not speak with a language teaching purpose but with a desire to express communicative needs.[59] (Beile 1979: 232)

It is conceivable that Stevick, Morrow and Geddes/White, who are all native speakers, do not include a native-speaker element in their definitions because either they take it for granted or they want to avoid giving an impression of condescension toward non-native speakers. All the same, there is a remarkable variation in how textual authenticity is defined during the first decade of the discourse.

The level of variation increases further as Widdowson's statements are considered. Widdowson makes an important contribution to the early discourse on authenticity, presenting two texts in the first decade – 1976 and 1978. Widdowson (1976) challenges textual authenticity as a concept by explicitly stating that text itself should not be referred to in terms of *authentic/authenticity*:

> I am not suce [sic] that it is meaningful to talk about authentic language as such at all. I think it is probably better to consider authenticity not as a quality residing in instances of language but as a quality which is bestowed upon them, created by the response of the receiver. Authenticity in this view is a function of the interaction between the reader/hearer and the text which incorporates the intentions of the writer/speaker. We do not recognize authenticity as something there waiting to be noticed, we realize it in the act of interpretation. [...] [A]uthenticity has to do with appropriate response. [...] Authenticity, then, is achieved when the reader realizes the intentions of the writer by reference to a set of shared conventions. It follows from this definition that a discourse may be written in conformity

---

58 Original: "Im strikten Wortsinne ist alles authentisch, was Sprachgebraucher mit Deutsch als Muttersprache produzieren." (Gutschow 1977: 3)

59 Original: "Wird ein Tonbandtext als ‚authentische Alltagssprache' beschrieben, muß der Zuhörer sich darauf verlassen können, daß die Sprecher ‚native speakers' sind und daß sie mit keiner fremdsprachendidaktischen Absicht sprechen, sondern um ihre eigenen kommunikativen Bedürfnisse innerhalb einer echten Sprechsituation auszudrücken." (Beile 1979: 232)

with a set of conventions, but still lack the quality of authenticity for particular readers. [...] [I]f I treat a poem as a sample of language for grammatical analysis, the poem is still a genuine poem but it is not authentic as a poem since I do not treat it like one. [...] The fact that the data is genuine is irrelevant. (Widdowson 1976: 263-264)

Widdowson's reference to and critique of the prevalent understanding of authenticity reveals a Saussurean thought pattern as opposed to the "Piercean view [...] of language as something which stands to somebody for something in some respect or capacity" (Badger/MacDonald 2010: 581). Instead of indicating that he, personally, conceives of authenticity in a certain way, Widdowson suggests that the prevalent *signifié* attached to authenticity as a *signifiant* should lose this connection.

The notion of *appropriate response* as well as the newly developed dichotomy of *genuineness* versus *authenticity* are expanded in Widdowson's second publication (1978). These new ideas are often referenced by later authors. They are integral to the second category of my taxonomy: authenticity of text reception (chapter 3.2). In the same article (1976), Widdowson goes on to condone the grading of text suggesting that such means of simplification do not hinder but facilitate authenticity in many cases:

> Our next task is to process our material, to prepare it pedagogically in some way so as to bring the learner to the point when he is capable of responding to the genuine discourse we have selected in authentic fashion. This is where the 'doctoring' comes in, the pedagogic tampering with data that the 'authentic data' school complains about. My argument would be that the pedagogic process must necessarily involve some kind of tampering in order to bring learners to the point at which they can realize the authenticity of the language by appropriate response. [...] As teaching proceeds, the filter can be adjusted to allow more stylistic features to appear until the learner is eventually confronted with genuine samples. In this way I believe we can, by sound pedagogic practice, achieve the desired aim of making genuineness correspond with authenticity. (Widdowson 1976: 266-267)

Widdowson concludes that "[t]here is no such thing as authentic language data. Authenticity is realized by appropriate response and the language teacher is responsible for designing a methodology which will establish the conditions whereby this authenticity can ultimately be achieved" (Widdowson 1976: 270). It is important to mention that the entire article is written with ESP (English for specific purposes) courses in mind, so it is not clear to what extent the new concepts lend themselves to a generalization. It is also unclear whether the contrivance of text for EFL purposes is seen as reconcilable with authenticity, now that Widdowson condones the grading (or simplifying) of text that is originally genuine.

Widdowson (1978) contains a reification of those new concepts. In this monograph, Widdowson devotes a few pages to the topic. What others call *authentic text* Widdowson calls *extracts* or *genuine instances of language use*:

> The extract is quite simply a piece of genuine discourse, an actual instance of use. Since it is precisely the ability to cope with genuine discourse that we are aiming to develop in the learner, it would seem on the face of it that the extract ought to be the preferred kind of reading passage. There are, however, certain complications. [...] The extracts are, by definition, 'genuine' instances of language use, but if the learner is required to deal with them in a way which does not correspond to his normal communicative activities, the they cannot be said to be 'authentic' instances of use. Genuineness is a characteristic of the passage

itself and is an absolute quality. Authenticity is a characteristic of the relationship between the passage and the reader and it has to do with appropriate response. One of the difficulties about extracts, then, is that although they are genuine, the fact that they are presented 'as' extracts imposed on the learner for language learning purposes necessarily reduces their authenticity. (Widdowson 1978: 80)

In the following quote, Widdowson uses the word *to authenticate* for the first time. It corresponds with his notion of appropriate response and furthers the idea that authenticity can only be the result of an individual process within the learner:

[T]he learner may simply not feel himself in any way engaged by the text being presented to him and so may refuse to authenticate it by taking an interest. This means, among other things, that the topic of the discourse has to be one which will appeal to the learner in some way. (Widdowson 1978: 80-81)

Finally, Widdowson adds to the issue of grading (or simplifying) text by expounding the problems of authentic text being often too difficult for learners to understand. Such difficulties, he claims, will obstruct the process of authentication:

[E]ven if the learner is motivated to read a particular extract and is ready to give an authentic response, he will be denied the opportunity if the linguistic difficulty of the passage is such that he cannot process it. [...] Clearly a genuine instance of use cannot be authenticated if it consists of syntactic structures and lexical items which the learner just has not the competence to comprehend. (Widdowson 1978: 82)

Widdowson's statements about authenticity, authentication, genuineness, and appropriate response are commonly quoted in later publications throughout the discourse, confirming Widdowson's status as the outstanding expert in the field. The bibliometric data shows that Widdowson's texts on the topic are referenced 121 times within the discourse. The author who receives the second most citations is Michael P. Breen with 36. These numbers are elaborated in detail in chapters 5.3.1 and 5.3.2. Widdowson's first article in the discourse (1976) is republished as a chapter in Widdowson's monograph *Explorations in applied linguistics* (1979), which heightens the article's exposure. Most authors refer to the monograph (1979), that is published by Oxford University Press, instead of the original but less prominent article (1976). The monograph is not featured in the document selection because none of the other chapters negotiate authenticity.

Widdowson's second text in the chronology, the monograph from 1978, has a word index but *authenticity* is not listed as a headword, unlike in Widdowson's later monographs (1990; 2003). Neither are his coinages *genuineness* and *appropriate response*. It suggests that the terms are not yet of central concern to Widdowson but are treated as side issues of sorts.

Widdowson's understanding that authenticity is the result of a negotiation between author and reader is remarkably akin to coeval trends in cognate disciplines. In chapter 5.2.1, societal developments of the time are linked to the general idea of learner-orientation, an idea that is clearly visible in Widdowson's concept. Two interdisciplinary developments in the humanities can provide a closer contextual backdrop for Widdowson's theories, one from linguistics and one from literary studies. The differentiation between genuineness and authenticity bears a strong affinity with that of cohesion and coherence in text linguistics. The corresponding theories were developed roughly at the same time. In both cases – genuineness/authenticity and cohesion/coherence – the former term denotes a certain objective quality of text, while the latter term refers to the desirable outcome of a dynamic process between two or more individuals. Here is a short description of cohesion followed by an explanation of coherence:

> The concept of cohesion is a semantic one; it refers to relations of meaning that exist within the text, and that define it as a text. Cohesion occurs where the interpretation of some element in the discourse is dependent on that of another. The one presupposes the other, in the sense that it cannot be effectively decoded except by recourse to it. When this happens, a relation of cohesion is set up, and the two elements, the presuppposing and the presupposed, are thereby at least potentially integrated into a text. (Halliday/Hasan 1976: 4)

> By and large, coherence of texts, I feel, should be thought of in very broad terms, as constituting some kind of 'rational totality' which the speaker tries to transmit – for one reason or another – to a listener. In order to get the message across, it is not enough for the speaker to be able to envisage this 'rational totality' in his own mind; he also has to try and dress it into a verbal message which will enable the listener to construct as closely identical a picture as possible of the speaker's underlying message via the verbal signs. Such an attempt of its result will rely a great deal on the mutual understanding between the participants in the communicative situation: shared presuppositions, the particular context-of-situation, their attitudes to one another etc. (Enkvist 1978: 103)

Widdowson, who was engaged in linguistic theory and had many publications in this discipline, appears to apply the same dichotomous pattern to his conceptualization of genuineness versus authenticity. Widdowson/Seidlhofer, incidentally, contribute to an edited volume by linguists Wolfram Bublitz, Uta Lenk, and Eija Ventola in 1999. The title of the book is *Coherence in spoken and written discourse*, Widdowson/Seidlhofer's contribution is: *Coherence in summary: The contexts of appropriate discourse* (1999). Some formulations are reminiscent of what Widdowson says about genuineness and authenticity:

> 'Cohesion', then, is a textual property and has to do with how linguistic elements relate by virtue of their lexical or grammatical features. But again the occurrence of cohesive devices are data which have to be interpreted as discourse evidence before you can make coherent sense of them. [...] [T]extual cohesion provides no guarantee of discourse coherence. (Widdowson/Seidlhofer 1999: 207)

The second coeval trend of the time, which appears to be reflected in Widdowson's concepts, is the literary notion of reader response theory, or *Rezeptionsästhetik* (*e.g.* Iser 1975: 253-276).

> One theorist, namely Hans Robert Jauss, is especially associated with the theory. He is concerned with the general response to literature in terms of reception-aesthetics [...] [T]he idea holds that the reader has a contribution to make in the process. So there is a kind of balance and co-operation between text and what it provides and what the reader contributes. However, all readers are different and therefore may be supposed to bring a different response to any text. (Cuddon 1991: 777-778)

Jauss and his colleague Wolfgang Iser (both at the University of Constance) developed this theory in the 1970s to overcome the former understanding that a given text transfers objective information (Kuester 2007: 363). Widdowson's idea of concentrating on the interactive dimension between reader and text instead of ascribing inherent qualities to the text bears analogies to these influential theories of literary thought. The phenomenon being commonly referred to as *reader-response theory* (Kuester 2007: 363), there exists even a terminological resemblance to Widdowson's notion of *appropriate response*. Jauss's and Iser's publications predate Widdowson's theorem by a few years.

5.2.1.2 Conclusion

In the early years of the discourse, textual authenticity emerges as the central concept tied to the term *authentic/authenticity*. It is introduced through casual use rather than by explicit statements in the discourse. Collocations such as *authentic materials* or *authentic text* or *authentic language* are intuitive and likely perceived as self-explanatory so that many authors do not feel a necessity to define the term. Instances of casual use have been found predominantly in articles of *TESOL Quarterly* and *ELTJ* between 1968 and 1978 (cf. chapter 4.5.5).

The explicit negotiation of the term begins presumably in 1971 (Stevick). During the 1970s, all authors who negotiate the term explicitly confirm textual authenticity as the primary concept. However, definitions vary. Wilkins (1976), Gutschow (1977), Beile (1978), and Geddes/White (1978) provide definitions that are fairly concise and straightforward, whereas Stevick (1971) and Morrow (1977) have more intricate understandings of the term. Wilkins, Gutschow, and Beile include a native speaker element in their definitions, which the other authors do not. Geddes/White state that there can be two definitions, one of which includes contrived text. Morrow sees textual authenticity as situational and, hence, as unachievable in the classroom. Stevick, who is the first to make explicit statements about authenticity in 1971, provides elaborations that are difficult to summarize. One way of gauging authenticity, according to Stevick, is to ask: "[T]o what extent will the students be able to use the content of this lesson immediately, in a lifelike way?" (Stevick 1971: 46). Example sentences are given that carry more authenticity than others. Thus, Stevick's thoughts remain barely within the realm of textual authenticity, though they may border on other concepts of authenticity, e.g. real-world authenticity.

Widdowson (1976; 1978) is the only author to challenge the concept of textual authenticity in a fundamental manner. He contributes to the discourse with two separate texts, and provides an entirely new concept: authenticity of text reception (cf. chapters 2.2 and 3.2 for elaborations on the concept and its placement in the taxonomy). By way of implication, his statement shows that textual authenticity has been the most common denotation up to that point: "I am not suce [sic] that it is meaningful to talk about authentic language as such at all. I think it is probably better to consider authenticity not as a quality residing in instances of language but as a quality which is bestowed upon them" (Widdowson 1976: 263). Widdowson's new approach is in line with the *zeitgeist* across the philological disciplines, as outlined above. Although textual authenticity must be affirmed to emerge and prevail as the most common denotation of *authentic/authenticity* in the 1970s, this status is challenged from the very beginning. Widdowson's opposition is by far the most systematic and explicit in terms of challenging the imminent merger of term and concept. Other challenging factors are rather subtle and uncoordinated in that, for example, the casual use of the term remains rampant thereby maintaining denotative heterogeneity, as has been shown in the analysis of *TESOL Quarterly* and *ELTJ* (chapter 4.5.5). However, even the explicit statements made by the authors in the discourse feature a high degree of inconsistency across the authors. Outside of Widdowson's statements, however, a consensus is observable in the fact that some sort of textual authenticity is referred to whenever the term *authentic/authenticity* is used.

In chapter 4.5.5.2, the congruence of authenticity and Communicative Language Teaching (CLT) is called into question. Two of the CLT movement's main actors, Wilkins and Widdowson, have been shown to have diverging notions of authenticity. If the assumption is that authentic materials were a unanimous element of CLT, then Widdowson's ideas would refute this to a certain extent.

Before moving on to the 1980s, some remarks on the topic of author status are required. All four authors, Stevick, Wilkins, Widdowson, and Morrow, have a relatively high general status, as they each are commonly associated with the CLT movement. Wilkins, Widdowson, and Morrow, for example, are featured in the widely received volume by Brumfit/Johnson (1979). In the context of authenticity, however, Widdowson stands out a little, especially from a present-day perspective. Widdowson's unparalleled status can be attributed to many factors, one of which is the sheer quantity of contributions to the topic of authenticity. Other biographical factors come in, such as his prolific output in the field of linguistics. Widdowson has, furthermore, always been associated with reputable institutions (University of London, University of Essex, University of Edinburgh, University of Vienna) and publishers (most notably Cambridge University Press). His conceptual and partly normative style of writing may have added to the status. Almost never does he work empirically and he often references renowned authors from other fields of the humanities. His propensity to create new terminology is typical of philosophy rather than of EFL.

One interesting institutional factor comes into play confirming the statuses of Widdowson and Morrow. In 2009, their texts (Widdowson 1976; Morrow 1977) are republished in Hedge/Andon/Dewey's edited multi-volume *English language teaching*, which compiles seminal articles in EFL. The two texts appear in the section *Authenticity and simplification in learning materials* which comprises seven articles in sum (Hedge/Andon/Dewey 2009: vi):

Widdowson, Henry G. (1976). The authenticity of language data. In: Fanselow/Crymes (eds.), 261-270.

Morrow, Keith (1977). Authentic texts and ESP. In: Holden (ed.), 13-15.

Davies, Alan (1984). Simple, simplified and simplification. What is authentic? In: Alderson/Urquhart (eds.), 181-195.

Breen, Michael P. (1985). Authenticity in the language classroom. *Applied Linguistics*, 6(1), 60-70.

Simensen, Aud Marit (1988). Adapted readers. *Reading in a Foreign Language,* 4(1), 41-57.

Clarke, David F. (1989). Communicative theory and its influence on materials production. *Language Teaching,* 22(2), 73-86.

Day, Richard; Bamford, Julian (1998). The cult of authenticity and the myth of simplification (Originally a chapter in the book: Day, Richard; Bamford, Julian (1998). *Extensive reading in the second language classroom.* Cambridge University Press.)

This selection might create the impression of a canon. The Routledge publication is henceforth taken into consideration as I proceed with my chronological investigation of the discourse. Only one text in it, Simensen (1989), is not part of the document selection.

With the first period, the early years, text-level insights into each of the eight texts have been afforded. This comprehensive coverage is deemed necessary because the texts lay the foundation of the discourse. As the discourse grows considerably over time, texts are analyzed more selectively.

5.2.2 The 1980s – decade of textual authenticity

During the 1980s, textual authenticity becomes a somewhat consolidated concept of authenticity. In the context of Task-Based Language Teaching (TBLT), however, an increasing number of authors deal with the question what sort of tasks should be called *authentic*. A controversy occurs between two opposing concepts, neither of which is particularly related to textual authenticity.

The productivity of the discourse increases considerably as of 1980. As many as 33 publications contain statements which explicitly negotiate authenticity. These are the texts of the document selection published between 1980 and 1989:

Number of citations received	Publication	Citations made	Type of publication
2	Henrici, Gert (1980). Authentischer Fremsprachenunterricht. Einige An-merkungen. *Bielefelder Beiträge zur Sprachlehrforschung* 2, 123-134.	None	Article in journal
2	Petersen, Hans (1980). Objektivierung und Vergegenwärtigung als Kategorien des Fremdsprachenunterrichts. In: Au-thentizität und Lehrbarkeit [thematic issue]. *Der fremdsprachliche Unterricht* 14/1980, Heft 55, 193-205.	None	Article in journal

3	Weijenberg, Jan (1980). *Authentizität gesprochener Sprache in Lehrwerken für Deutsch als Fremdsprache.* Heidelberg: Groos.	Beile (1979), Gutschow (1977)	Book
2	Beile, Werner (1981): Authentizität aus anderer Sicht. *Der fremdsprachliche Unterricht,* 15 (57), 61-62.	None – no bibliography	Article in journal
8	Grellet, Françoise (1981). *Developing reading skills. A practical guide to reading comprehension exercises.* Cambridge, New York: Cambridge University Press.	None	Book
5	Porter, Don; Roberts, Jon (1981). Authentic listening activities. *ELT Journal,* 36(1), 37-47.	None	Article in Journal
1	Beeching, Kate (1982). Authentic material 1. *British Journal of Language Teaching* 20 (2), 17-20.	Widdowson (1976)	Article in journal
5	Candlin, Christopher N.; Edelhoff, Christoph (1982). *Challenges: Teacher's Guide.* London: Longman.	Widdowson (1978)	Book
2	Lynch, Anthony J. (1982). 'Authenticity' in language teaching: Some implications for the design of listening materials. *British Journal of Language Teaching* 20 (2), 9-16.	Widdowson (1976)	Article in journal
1	Alexander, Richard (1983). How authentic can (and should) 'authentic' texts be? In: Kühlwein, Wolfgang (ed.). *Texte in der Sprachwissenschaft, Sprachunterricht und Sprachtherapie. Bd. 4.* Tübingen: Narr, 87-88.	None	Article in edited volume
1	Lee, William R. (1983). Some points about 'authenticity'. *World Language English,* 2(1), 10-14.	None – no bibliography	Article in journal
1	Rivers, Wilga M. (1983). *Communicating naturally in a second language.* New York: Cambridge University Press.		Book
4	Widdowson, Henry G. (1983). *Learning purpose and language use.* Oxford, New York: Oxford University Press.	Widdowson (1976; 1978)	Book
7	Davies, Alan (1984). Simple, simplified and simplification. What is authentic? In: Alderson, Charles J.; Urquhart, A. H. (eds.). *Reading in a*	Widdowson (1976; 1978)	Article in edited volume

	foreign language. Harlow: Longman, 181-195.		
1	Joiner, Elizabeth G. (1984). Authentic texts in the foreign language classroom: Focus on listening and reading. Monterey, CA: Defense Language Institute. *ERIC Document Reproduction Service No. ED 274153,* 3-24.	Rivers (1983)	Article via ERIC
3	Löschmann, Marianne & Löschmann, Martin (1984). Authentisches im Fremdsprachenunterricht. *Deutsch als Fremdsprache* 21/1984, 41-47.	Beile (1981), Edelhoff (1985), Gutschow (1977)	Article in journal
36	Breen, Michael P. (1985). Authenticity in the language classroom. *Applied Linguistics,* 6(1), 60-70.	Candlin/Edelhoff (1982), Widdowson (1976; 1978)	Article in journal
5	Edelhoff, Christoph (1985). Authentizität im Fremdsprachenunterricht. In: Edelhoff, Christoph (ed.). *Authentische Texte im Deutschunterricht.* München: Hueber, 7-30.	None	Article in edited volume
1	Richards, Jack C.; Platt, John Talbot; Weber, Heidi (1985). *Longman dictionary of applied linguistics.* Harlow: Longman.	None – no bibliography	Entry in dictionary
3	Seliger et al. (1985). *Language Testing* 2(1).	None	Approx. 7 articles in journal
9	Swaffar, Janet K. (1985). Reading authentic texts in a foreign language: A cognitive model. *Modern Language Journal* (69.1), 15-34.	Grellet (1981), Rivers (1983)	Article in journal
2	Beile, Werner (1986). Authentizität als fremdsprachendidaktischer Begriff. Zum Problemfeld von Texten gesprochener Sprache. In: Ehnert, Rolf; Piepho, Hans-Eberhard (eds.). *Fremdsprachen lernen mit Medien.* München: Hueber, 145-162.	Beile (1979; 1981), Edelhoff (1985), Gutschow (1977), Henrici (1980), Petersen (1980), Piepho (1977), Wejenberg (1979, 1980)	Article in edited volume
7	Rings, Lana (1986). Authentic language and authentic conversational texts. *Foreign Language Annals* 19 (3), 201-208.	Wilkins (1976), Swaffar (1985), Löschmann/Löschmann (1984), Weijenberg (1980)	Article in journal
1	Rück, Heribert (1986). Fetisch ‚authentischer Text'? *Neusprachliche Mitteilungen aus Wissenschaft und Praxis,* 39(3), 165.	None – no bibliography	Article in journal
8	Kienbaum, Barbara E.; Russell, A. J.; Welty, S. (1986). Communicative competence in foreign language	None – no bibliography	Article via ERIC

	learning with authentic materials. Calumet, Indiana. *ERIC Document Reproduction Service No. ED 275200*, 2-36.		
8	Hutchinson, Tom; Waters, Alan (1987). *English for specific purposes. A learning-centred approach.* Cambridge: Cambridge University Press.	None	Book
12	Little, David; Devitt, Seán; Singleton, David (1988). *Authentic texts in foreign language teaching. Theory and practice.* Dublin: Authentik.	Suggestions for further reading but no citations and no bibliography	Book
2	Little, David; Singleton, David M. (1988). Authentic materials and the role of fixed support in language teaching: Towards a manual for language learners. Dublin: Trinity College. *ERIC Document Reproduction Service No. ED 316033*, 3-30.	None	Article via ERIC
4	Nunan, David (1988b). *The learner-centred curriculum. A study in second language teaching.* Cambridge, New York: Cambridge University Press.	Candlin/Edelhoff (1982)	Book
10	Rogers, Carmen Villegas; Medley, Frank W. (1988). Language with a purpose. Using authentic materials in the foreign language classroom. *Foreign Language Annals* 21 (5), 467-478.	Geddes/White (1978), Grellet (1981), Joiner (1984), Rings (1986)	Article in journal
5	Clarke, David F. (1989). Communicative theory and its influence on materials production. *Language Teaching,* 22(2), 73-86.	Breen (1985), Davies (1984), Geddes/White (1978), Grellet (1981), Hutchinson/Waters (1987), Widdowson (1976; 1978), Wilkins (1976)	Article in journal
8	Nostrand, Howard Lee (1989). Authentic texts and cultural authenticity: An editorial. *Modern Language Journal* 73 (1), 45-52.	None	Article in journal
12	Nunan, David (1989). *Designing tasks for the communicative classroom.* Cambridge; New York: Cambridge University Press.	Candlin/Edelhoff (1982), Porter/Roberts (1981)	Book

Figure 11: Decade of textual authenticity

A remarkable number of eight publications are written in German indicating an active discourse in the German-speaking academy. Unfortunately, none of them refers to English publications in the discourse and only one of the English publications, Rings (1986), cites German articles. In the English-speaking discourse, Widdowson emerges as the favorite source to be cited. His two publications from the 1970s are referenced in eight publications during the 1980s. The following analysis begins with a focused discussion of textual authenticity before the newly emerging concepts are presented.

5.2.2.1 Detailed analysis

A brief glance at the titles of the publications reveals a heavy focus on textual authenticity – in written or spoken materials. Back in 1976, Widdowson expressed misgivings about an overemphasis: "Too exclusive a concern for 'authentic' language behaviour as communication [i.e. authentic text] can lead to a disregard of methodological principles upon which the pedagogy of language teaching must depend" (Widdowson 1976: 261). As shown in the preceding chapter, Widdowson is in favor of grading authentic materials. In 1980, Maingay states:

> The advantages of the use of such authentic material in the L2 reading class have been widely discussed, and I should like to consider a question which is often asked when this approach is advocated: 'Is there any way such material can be graded to take account of different levels of reading ability?' (Maingay 1980: 217)

She proceeds to conclude dogmatically that "[t]he use of authentic texts precludes any attempt at systematic grading on a structural basis" (Maingay 1980: 218). In this manner Maingay sets the tone for an evolving orthodoxy that authentic materials carry intangible values and, thus, should not be tampered with. Porter/Roberts (1981) see a similar value in authentic listening materials: "The need for and usefulness of authentic materials have been increasingly acknowledged in recent years. But should we stop there, with the linguistic characteristics of authenticity? It is our belief that there is much more involved" (Porter/Roberts 1981: 39). A growing enthusiasm with authentic materials can be perceived in such statements. A number of authors discuss the question whether the grading of text is beneficial or problematic. A theoretical approach is taken by Davies (1984), who deliberates on various aspects of grading and simplification. He also presents a differentiated terminology for different types of simplification. Being informed by Widdowson (1976; 1978) he condones practices of grading authentic text:

> It is not that a text is understood because it is authentic but that it is authentic because it is understood. In teaching our concern is with simplification, not with authenticity. Everything the learner understands is authentic for him. It is the teacher who simplifies, the learner who authenticates. (Davies 1984: 191)

Nonetheless, the support of textual authenticity continues to prevail, as the first three monographs in the chronology deal with authentic texts and materials: Kienbaum/Russell/Welty (1986), Little/Singleton/David (1988), Little/Devitt/Singleton (1988). Rück (1986) is critical of this development going so far as to call it a "fetish" (*Fetisch authentischer Text*). Clarke concurs seeing "[a]uthenticity of materials as a growing moral imperative" (Clarke 1989: 74). These statements describe a general trend that is epitomized by Grellet who claims: "It is important to use authentic texts whenever possible" (Grellet 1981: 7).

The issue of grading text remains controversial throughout the decade. Those authors, who are in favor, tend to merely condone the approach rather than strongly advocate it. It seems that the grading of authentic text is regarded by many as a necessary compromise. Others maintain it is unacceptable, as has been demonstrated. What is a consensus among the authors is that authentic text, which has been graded, can no longer be called *authentic*. The general prevalence of textual authenticity over other concepts of authenticity is reflected in Richards/Platt/Weber (1985), which is the first encyclopedia in applied linguistics to feature an entry for authenticity. The entry reads:

> the degree to which language teaching materials have the qualities of natural speech or writing. Texts which are taken from newspapers, magazines, etc, and tapes programmes, etc, are called authentic materials. When a teacher prepares texts or tapes for use in the classroom, he/she often has to use simplified examples. (Richards/Platt/Weber 1985: 22)

Here, a relative definition of textual authenticity is given rather than an absolute one, which is unusual (cf. chapter 2.2 for elaborations). For the purpose at hand, the quote shall merely serve to manifest the compelling presence of textual authenticity over alternative concepts. I will go on to show that the latter do exist in the 1980s, but their resonance remains low.

Beside the issue revolving around authentic material and the grading of it, two completely different concepts are put forth. The first of the two is the notion of authentic assessment. An entire issue of the journal *Language Testing* is dedicated to this topic in 1985. The issue is referred to by Bachman five years later as a milestone in the field:

> This search for 'authenticity' continues to be a major consideration in language testing [...]. The importance of this consideration to language testing was recognized in the convening of an international conference in 1984 whose focus was authenticity, and the dedication of an entire issue of the journal 'Language Testing' to the publication of the papers from this meeting ('Language Testing' 2, 1, June 1985). (Bachman 1990: 301)

Interestingly, none of the authors refer to any of the pre-existing literature on authenticity. The bibliographies of the different articles are built around aspects of testing and assessment. To a minor extent they feature well-known linguists such as Chomsky, Hymes, Levinson etc. Without going into too much detail, the different articles seem to have slightly diverging understandings of the term *authentic/authenticity*. Indicative of this diffusion is the announcement made in the foreword of the issue. Here, an attempt is made at including all possible concepts:

> In discussions of communicative language testing, questions relating to the issue of authenticity – of tasks, of texts, of content, of setting – form a recurrent theme. The implications of these questions for practical testing are many. Just what are the features of authentic language use that we need to embody in our tests, and with what degree of delicacy? What is the most appropriate method of assessing authentic or near-authentic performance? (Foreword 1985: 1)

It is also implied that the notion of authenticity is not new to the context of language testing. However, I have been unable to find earlier accounts of assessment being referred to as *authentic*. In the issue of *Language Testing* (1985), some notable statements can be found that are in line with the concept of real-world authenticity:

> In the field of language testing, the criterion of authenticity is most usually applied to the nature of the linguistic content of tests. [...] But my focus in this paper will not be on authenticity of content but on authenticity of task: The question I wish to consider is to what extent can a testing task be made authentic, so that it constitutes an example of normal and natural language behaviour on the part of both examiner and candidate. (Spolsky 1985: 32-33)

> A major problem in discussing authenticity in language testing is the 'like/as argument'. Just about any test or testing procedure, be it a cloze or an oral interview, can be argued to be a lot 'like' real-life language behaviour, to require examinees to do much 'as' they would do in non-testing situations. (Stevenson 1985: 41)

While conclusive definitions may be missing, the first step is made toward a growing presence of authentic assessment in the 1990s, and a new concept seems afoot. The authors seem unaware that the term *authentic/authenticity* has been subject of negotiation for over 10 years. By not making connections to the already existing literature on authenticity in EFL, the term *authentic testing/assessment* is on the cusp of creating a separate discourse. What Jørgensen states about external influences bears particular relevance here: "[B]ecause a discourse is always constituted in relation to an outside, it is always in danger of being undermined by it, that is its unity of meaning is in danger of being disrupted by other ways of fixing the meaning of the signs" (Jørgensen/Phillips 2002: 27-28). Academic discourse is normally less susceptible to these processes than other discursive formations because citations and references have a stabilizing function. This function is, however, missing with *authentic/authenticity* in the context of assessment. Instead of drawing on EFL concepts of authenticity, it is probable that colloquial understandings of authenticity are appropriated. The issue of authentic assessment is under further scrutiny as the chronological analysis proceeds.

The conceptual contribution made by the issue of *Language Testing* (1985) lies arguably in the promotion of real-world authenticity, as I have termed it. To reiterate:

> [M]y focus in this paper will not be on authenticity of content but on authenticity of task: The question I wish to consider is to what extent can a testing task be made authentic, so that it constitutes an example of normal and natural language behaviour [...]. (Spolsky 1985: 32-33)

The inception of real-world authenticity most probably took place three years earlier in Candlin/Edelhoff (1982) who focus on

> [...] the authenticity of the task that the materials offer as possibilities to the learner and to the teacher. [...] It is not enough [...] simply to present learners with a range of connected text-types if they are asked to perform fundamentally inauthentic tasks with the texts. One doesn't read a bus ticket or a train timetable in order to learn something about English grammar; you read them to check if the bus conductor has sold you the correct ticket [...]. (Candlin/Edelhoff 1982: 9)

Neither the statements in Candlin/Edelhoff (1982) nor the ones in *Language Testing* (1985) are as widely received as the statements made by David Nunan a few years later, who describes the same concept:

[W]e need to take account of what we might term activity authenticity (in contrast with authenticity of input which has already been considered). While there is general acknowledgement that authentic materials have a place in the classroom, the issue of activity authenticity is less widely recognised. [...] [T]he authenticity issue involves much more than simply selecting texts from outside the arena of language teaching, [...] the processes to which the learner submits aural and written texts and the things he or she is required to do with the data should also be authentic. [...] Certain activities might only remotely resemble the sorts of things learners are required to do in the real world. (Nunan 1989: 60)

Candlin/Edelhoff (1982) are cited four times, the articles in *Language Testing* (1985) are referenced three times in the discourse. Nunan (1989) is cited 12 times and may be falsely perceived as the originator of real-world authenticity. After all, Nunan is commonly associated with the highly influential technique of Task-Based Language Teaching (TBLT). He would later (2004) declare real-world authenticity a central tenet of TBLT.

The second concept, which is not concerned with authentic materials, is presented by Breen (1985). Breen has been accorded a category of his own in my taxonomy based on the statements made in this publication (1985) – classroom authenticity. Contrary to some of the preceding authors, Breen is relatively clear about his understanding of the term. A number of statements shall demonstrate this:

[A]n authentic learning task in the language classroom will be one which requires the learners to communicate ideas and meanings 'and' to meta-communicate about the language and about the problems and solutions in the learning of the language. In sum, tasks can be chosen which involve the learners not only in authentic communication with texts and with others in the classroom, but also about learning and for the purpose of learning. (Breen 1985: 66)

[T]he essential contribution of the classroom is that it is an almost unique social context where people meet for the explicit purpose of learning something—from others for themselves. Learning is the main psychological and social function of a classroom. In some senses, what is learned in a classroom—the subject matter which is worked upon—can be seen as quite independent of the social or interpersonal reality which the classroom itself provides. In a language classroom, the subject matter is communication. In this way, perhaps a language classroom is doubly unique! Its content is the learning of how to communicate in a new language, and—as with all other classrooms—it is essentially a social environment wherein people come to communicate for and about new knowledge. Therefore, perhaps the most socially appropriate and authentic role of the classroom situation is to provide the opportunity for public and interpersonal sharing of the content of language learning, the sharing of problems within such content, and the revealing of the most effective means and strategies to overcome such problems. [...] [G]iven the actual social potential of a classroom, the contrivance of 'other worlds' within it may not only be inauthentic but also quite unnecessary. (Breen 1985: 67)

The authenticity of the classroom is that it is a rather special social event and environment wherein people share a primary communicative purpose: learning. The language classroom can exploit this social potential by expecting and encouraging learners to share their own learning processes and experiences. Perhaps one of the main authentic activities within a language classroom is communication about how best to learn to communicate. (Breen 1985: 67-68)

These are Breen's conclusive remarks towards the end of the article. To him, authenticity is achieved when the learners communicate about the very topic of learning the foreign language.

The statements are preceded by a number of interesting thoughts, which equally resonate in the later discourse. Most notably, Breen uses the term *authentic* extensively in collocations with *task*, creating two categories. If the learner "is asked to do something which most people would never do in the 'real world'" (i.e. to fill gaps in a cloze), it is still possible "that such apparently inauthentic language-using behaviour might be authentic language 'learning' behaviour" (Breen 1985: 65). The two categories are therefore: "authentic communication task" and "authentic learning task" (ibid.). Breen goes on to propound his ultimate understanding of authenticity (see quotes above), but the main effect on the subsequent discourse is the terminological combination of *authentic/authenticity* and *task*.

What Breen also offers is a catalogue of concepts, which is the first of its kind:

In the daily life of the classroom, the teacher is continually concerned with four types of authenticity. These may be summarized as follows (Breen 1985: 61):

1 Authenticity of the texts which we may use as input data for our learners.

2 Authenticity of the learners' own interpretations of such texts.

3 Authenticity of tasks conducive to language learning.

4 Authenticity of the actual social situation of the language classroom.

In chapter 2.1, Breen's categorization is compared to the ones by Decke-Cornill (2004) and Gilmore (2007). The fourth point on the list is the one he clearly advocates.

Lastly, Breen weighs in on the grading of text:

[I]t seems to me that [...] pedagogic or contrived texts are likely to distort the target language data and, thereby, deprive the learner of two things: first, direct access to the actual conventions of target language use and, second, the opportunity to apply his own prior knowledge of the real conventions of communication which underlie his own mother tongue. My own main point would imply that learners—because they are learners—are themselves likely to 'filter out' what is inaccessible and, indeed, to distort any particular text in order to make it serve them in the development of new knowledge. An interesting conclusion from this would be that it may be quite unnecessary to adapt texts in any way or to devise 'pedagogic' texts at all! (Breen 1985: 69)

I treat this point as a side issue because Breen only mentions it in a footnote. It serves to illustrate the comprehensive nature of his article in terms of discussing the different aspects of authenticity. Breen (1985) probably provides the most holistic account and commentary on the topic up to that point in time.

Breen (1985) is the single most cited texts in the discourse. The article is referenced in as many as 36 publications. At first glance, this is astonishing because it is Breen's only contribution to the topic and it is only an 11-page article. Breen is also not comparable to Widdowson and Wilkins with regard to general author status. However, many other factors combine to yield an enormous degree of exposure. The periodical *Applied Linguistics*, published by *Oxford University Press*, is one of the most prestigious journals in the discipline. Although Breen references relatively few texts, the ones he invokes are amongst the most influential in the field of authenticity. Most notably, Breen responds to Widdowson (1976 and 1978) with unprecedented rigor. Thus far, only Davies (1984) has taken account of these two important texts. What is more, the title of Breen's publication, *Authenticity in the language classroom*, suggests an exhaustive discussion of the topic as opposed to titles that suggest a narrower focus.

A number of interesting characteristics on the text level can be identified and may help explain why Breen (1985) has become such a pivotal element in the discourse. First, Breen's elaborations are comprehensive and concise at the same time. He is aware that, at the time, textual authenticity has become the prevalent denotation. He accounts for this reality by opening as follows: "I would like to begin by providing a particular example of an authentic text" (Breen 1985: 60). He then goes on to contradict the notion that textual authenticity is of primary importance. Still, using it as a starting point is important to achieve discursive relevance. Breen then discusses four different types of authenticity which he presents in the form of a categorization. He speaks about the grading of authentic text, and he creates a new collocation: *authentic task*. Second, Breen describes a concept as authentic that has never carried that name. It is the first time that a concept of authenticity has nothing to do with text. Third, Breen's proposed concept is in line with the principles of Communicative Language Teaching (CLT). Multiple times he invokes "the communicative potential of the classroom" demanding that the learners be free to choose the topics for conversation. It is more of an assumption on Breen's part that these topics are likely to revolve around the very aspects of learning the language – it is not a precept. In essence, the concept is learner-oriented, which is a central idea of CLT. Four, Breen's authorial style is highly conceptual. He provides background information about authenticity in EFL, but he eventually advocates a specific concept of authenticity in an all but normative manner. The article is marked by pointed argumentation and clear – albeit non-explicit – expressions of approval and disapproval. Breen's bibliography comprises only nine works, two of which are by Widdowson and two by himself. Breen uses exclamation marks to put emphasis on points made, which is an idiosyncratic means.

5.2.2.2 Conclusion

The 1980s can be regarded as the decade of textual authenticity. No author contributing to the discourse ignores this concept, even if their approach is opposed to it or focuses on a different concept. A number of publications expound the benefits and possibilities of authentic materials in the form of written documents, listening materials, or videos. The first monographs carrying the term in the title are published and all of them head in a rather practical direction: Kienbaum/Russell/Welty (1986), Little/Singleton (1988), Little/Devitt/Singleton (1988). Weijenberg (1980), which is a monograph in German, analyzes the authenticity of textbook language, suggesting that dialogues in learning materials should reflect natural language use.

A counter movement of sorts, which has been started by Widdowson (1976; 1978), is emphatically resumed by Breen (1985). While Breen makes strong conceptual claims, others take on the role of critical observers writing in a rather descriptive style: Davies

(1984), Rück (1986), Clarke (1989). Breen introduces the new collocation of *authentic task*. The collocation itself will prove more influential than Breen's actual concept. The latter is labeled *classroom authenticity* in chapter 3 of this book, forming a category of its own in the taxonomy. Breen remains almost the lone representative of this concept, as very few of the later statements in the discourse fit the category. Breen (1985) is one of three texts from the 1980s that are republished in Hedge/Andon/Dewey's (eds.) *English language teaching* (2009): Davies (1984), Breen (1985), Clarke (1989). Breen's article is the single most cited publication in the discourse.

Authentic task is not the only new collocation. A pair of collocations is put forth in an issue of the journal *Language Testing* (1985): *authentic testing* and *authentic assessment*. The corresponding concepts are not conclusively defined and are scarcely informed by the EFL discourse on authenticity. The discussions about authentic assessment tend to form an all but isolated discourse. Statements that approximate a definition of authentic assessment appear to be in line with what I have termed *real-world authenticity* in my taxonomy (cf. chapter 3). The concept is introduced as early as in 1982 by Candlin/Edelhoff (see above) and picked up in 1989 by Nunan (see above) becoming a mainstay of TBLT. The continuing development of this concept becomes a focal point in the later chronology.

5.2.3 The 1990s – broad adoption of Widdowson's concept

During the 1990s, Widdowson resonates with a growing number of authors in the discourse. At least one of his works is cited in 15 of 26 publications in this decade – not counting his own publications from the 1990s, in which he cites himself (1990; 1994; 1996; 1998a; 1998b). Widdowson's appeal is noticeable on the conceptual level. The following texts on authenticity appear between 1990 and 1999:

Number of citations received	Publication	Citations made	Type of publication
21	Widdowson, Henry G. (1990). *Aspects of language teaching.* Oxford: Oxford University Press.	Breen (1985), Widdowson (1976)	Book
6	Bachman, Lyle F. (1990). *Fundamental considerations in language testing.* Oxford: Oxford University Press.	Seliger et al. (1985)	Book
11	Bacon, Susan M.; Finnemann, Michael D. (1990). A study of the attitudes, motives, and strategies of university foreign language students and their disposition to authentic oral and written input. *The Modern Language Journal* 74 (4), 459.	Nostrand (1989), Kienbaum/Russell/Welty (1986), Rogers/Medley (1988)	Article in journal
5	Arnold, Ewen (1991). Authenticity revisited: How real is real? *English for Specific Purposes,* 10, 237-244.	Breen (1985), Hutchinson/Waters (1987),	Aricle in journal

		Nunan (1989), Widdowson (1978)	
1	Bachman, Lyle F. (1991). What does language testing have to offer. *TESOL Quarterly* 25 (4), 671-704.	Bachman (1990), Widdowson (1978)	Article in journal
3	Herron, Carol; Seay, Irene (1991). The effect of authentic oral texts on student listening comprehension in the foreign language classroom. *Foreign Language Annals* 24 (6), 487-495.	Bacon/Finneman (1990), Kienbaum/Russell/Welty (1986), Nostrand (1989), Rogers/Medley (1988)	Article in journal
0	Weller, Franz Rudolf (1992). Wie ‚authentisch' ist ‚idiomatisches' Französisch? Anmerkungen zu zwei unklaren Begriffen der Fremdsprachendidaktik. *Fremdsprachen Lehren und Lernen* 21, 117-139.	Alexander (1983), Beile (1986), Gutschow (1977), Henrici (1980), Little/Devitt/Singleton (1988), Löschmann/Löschmann (1984), Petersen (1980), Piepho (1977), Rück (1986), Widdowson (1976)	Article in journal
7	Kramsch, Claire J. (1993). *Context and culture in language teaching.* Oxford: Oxford University Press.	Breen (1985), Little/Singleton (1988), Löschmann/Löschmann (1984), Nostrand (1989), (Widdowson 1976; 1990)	Book
2	Young, Dolly J. (1993). Processing strategies of foreign language readers: Authentic and edited input. *Foreign Language Annals* 26 (4), 451-468.	Davies (1984), Kienbaum/Russell/Welty (1986), Swaffar (1985)	Article in journal
3	McNeill, Arthur (1994). What makes authentic materials different? The case of English language materials for educational television. In: n.a. *Papers presented at the Annual International Language in Education Conference, Hong Kong.* n.a., 314-326.	Bacon/Finnemann (1990), Beeching (1982), Lynch (1982), Kienbaum/Russell/Welty (1986), Little/Devitt/Singleton (1988), Nostrand (1989), Widdowson (1976)	Article in edited volume
11	Taylor, David (1994). Inauthentic authenticity or authentic inauthenticity? http://www.tesl-ej.org/wordpress/issues/volume1/ej02/ej02a1/, access date: 08/15/2014.	Bachman (1990), Breen (1985), Kramsch (1993), Morrow (1977), Nunan (1989), Seliger et al. (1985), Widdowson (1976; 1990), Wilkins (1976)	Article in online journal
4	Widdowson, Henry G. (1994). The ownership of English. *TESOL Quarterly* (28/2), 377-389.	None	Article in journal
2	Adams, Thomas W. (1995). What makes materials authentic? *ERIC Document Reproduction Service No. ED 391389*, 1-8.	Breen (1985), Geddes/White (1978), Morrow (1977), Nunan (1989), Rogers/Medley (1988),	Article via ERIC

		Taylor (1994), Widdowson (1976)	
1	Dunkel, P.A. (1995). Authentic second/foreign language listening texts: Issues of definition, operationalization, and application. In: Byrd, Patricia (ed.). *Material writers' guide*. Boston: Heinle and Heinle, 95-106.	Geddes/White (1978), Herron/Seay (1991), Nostrand (1989), Porter/Roberts (1981), Rings (1986), Rogers/Medley (1988), Weijenberg (1980)	Article in edited volume
13	Lee, Winnie Yuk-chun (1995). Authenticity revisited: text authenticity and learner authenticity. *ELT Journal,* 49(4), 323-328.	Bachman (1990), Bacon/Finneman (1990), Breen (1985), Widdowson (1976)	Article in journal
4	Bachman, Lyle F.; Palmer, Adrian S. (1996). *Language testing in practice. Designing and developing useful language tests*. Oxford; New York: Oxford University Press.	Widdowson (1978; 1983)	Book
0	Kramsch, Claire (1996). Wem gehört die deutsche Sprache? *Die Unterrichtspraxis / Teaching German* 29 (1), 1.	Widdowson (1990; 1994)	Article in journal
0	Long, Michael H. (1996). Authenticity and learning potential in L2 classroom discourse. *University of Hawaii Working Papers in ESL,* 14(2), 127-149.	Arnold (1991), Breen (1985), van Lier (1996), Widdowson (1976; 1996), Wilkins (1976), Wong (1995)	Article in journal
1	O'Malley, J. Michael; Pierce, Lorraine Valdez (1996). *Authentic assessment for English language learners*. Reading, Massachusetts: Addison-Wesley Pub. Co.	None	Book
11	van Lier, Leo (1996). *Interaction in the language curriculum. Awareness, autonomy and authenticity*. New York: Longman.	Breen (1985), Widdowson (1976; 1990)	Book
10	Widdowson, Henry G. (1996). Comment: authenticity and autonomy in ELT. *ELT Journal,* 50(1), 67-68.	None	Article in journal
4	Cook, Guy (1997). Language play, language learning. *ELT Journal*, 51, 224-231.	None	Article in journal
1	Little, David (1997). Responding authentically to authentic texts: A problem for self-access language learning? In: Phil Benson; Peter Voller (eds.). *Autonomy and independence in language learning*. London; New York: Longman, 225-236.	Breen (1985), Widdowson (1978)	Article in edited volume

11	Peacock, Matthew (1997). The effect of authentic materials on the motivation of EFL learners. *ELT Journal,* 51(2), 144-156.	Bacon/Finneman (1990), Kienbaum/Russell/Welty (1986), Little/Devitt/Singleton (1988), Morrison (1989), Swaffar (1985)	Article in journal
4	Chavez, Monika (1998). Learner's perspectives on authenticity. *IRAL – International Review of Applied Linguistics in Language Teaching* 36 (4), 277-306.	Bacon/Finneman (1990), Davies (1984), Nostrand (1989), Rings (1986), Rogers/Medley (1988), Swaffar (1985), Weijenberg (1980), Young (1993)	Article in journal
1	Day, Richard; Bamford, Julian (1998/2009). The cult of authenticity and the myth of simplification. In: Hedge, Tricia; Andon, Nick; Dewey, Martin (eds.). *English Language Teaching 5.* 233-245.	Breen (1985), Davies (1984), Grellet (1981), Lee (1983), Richards/Platt/Weber (1985), Swaffar (1985), Widdowson (1976; 1978)	Chapter in a book
11	Widdowson, Henry G. (1998a). Context, community, and authentic language. *TESOL Quarterly* (32/4), 705-716.	Cook (1997), Widdowson (1990)	Article in journal
1	Widdowson, Henry G. (1998b). Communication and community: The pragmatics of ESP. *English for Specific Purposes* 17 (1), 3-14.	Widdowson (1983; 1990; 1994)	Article in journal
0	Chapelle, Carol A. (1999). Theory and research: Investigation of 'authentic' language learning tasks. In: Egbert, Joy; Hanson-Smith, Elizabeth (eds.). *CALL environments.* Alexandria, VA: TESOL. 101-115.	None	Article in edited volume
0	Johnson, Keith (1999). Authenticity. In: Johnson, Keith; Johnson, Helen (eds.). *Encyclopedic dictionary of applied linguistics.* Oxford: Blackwell, 24-25.	Breen (1985), Widdowson (1976; 1990)	Entry in encyclopedia
1	Kohonen, Viljo (1999). Authentic assessment in affective foreign language education. In: Arnold, Jane (ed.). *Affect in language learning.* Cambridge: Cambridge University Press, 279-294.	O'Malley/Pierce (1996)	Article in edited volume

Figure 12: Broad adoption of Widdowson's concept

The productivity of the discourse remains stable but does not increase compared to the previous decade (1980s: 33 publications; 1990s: 31 publications). Widdowson's early works (1976; 1978; 1983) function as a conceptual lynchpin. However, the authors in the discourse engage very differently with Widdowson's concepts. Meanwhile, Widdowson has four publications during the 1990s. These are presented first because they provide and interesting backdrop for the coeval developments in the discourse.

5.2.3.1 Detailed analysis

Widdowson's terminology and his advocated concepts differ from his earlier writings (1976; 1978). In Widdowson (1990), the term *authentic/authenticity* is suddenly employed to denote communication. In some statements, this seems to pertain to spoken interaction in the classroom:

> [I]f learners are aiming to communicate naturally, they need to be prepared for this by being involved in natural communicative language use in the classroom. In short, the language of the classroom has to be authentic. (Widdowson 1990: 44)

> I would prefer to retain the term to refer to the normal language behaviour of the user in pursuit of a communicative outcome [...]. (Widdowson 1990: 46)

Although there is no collocation of *authentic* and *communication*, the new concept appears to be about natural, meaningful communication between individuals in the classroom. The following quote corroborates this perception, yet it mentions a pitfall of the concept:

> [I]f authenticity is to be defined as natural language behaviour (and it is hard to see how else it might be defined) there is also the difficulty that learners will naturally incline to draw on their own language in any situation that calls for uncontrived linguistic communication. (Widdowson 1990: 45)

An interesting issue is raised here. For the first time in the discourse, an understanding of authenticity is put forth that may be informed by notions of philosophical existentialism. The idea is later expanded by van Lier (1996). The inherent problem is commented on by Decke-Cornill (2004). Both will be discussed in chronological order.

The old concept of authenticity coming from appropriate response is not dismissed in Widdowson (1990). This notion is predicated on reading materials which are to be authenticated by the learners in a constructivist process. Whether authenticity can actually be achieved as a result of this process is now called into question, which is a novelty:

> Authenticity of language in the classroom is bound to be, to some extent, an illusion. This is because it does not depend on the source from which the language as an object is drawn but on the learners' engagement with it. (Widdowson 1990: 44-45)

> To the extent that language learners, by definition, are deficient in competence they cannot authenticate the language they deal with in the manner of the native speaker. The language presented to them may be a genuine record of native speaker behaviour, genuine, that is to say, as textual data, but to the extent that it does not engage native speaker response it cannot be realized as authentic discourse. (Widdowson 1990: 45)

The concept itself is not new, as can be seen by a similar passage from 1978:

> To present someone with a set of extracts and to require him to read them not in order to learn something interesting and relevant about the world but in order to learn something about the language being used is to misrepresent normal language use to some degree. The extracts are, by definition, 'genuine' instances of language use, but if the learner is required to deal with them in a way which does not correspond to his normal communicative activities, then they cannot be said to be 'authentic' instances of use. (Widdowson 1978: 80)

The statement from 1978 does not go so far as to suggest that authenticity is impossible to achieve. Thus, the conclusion in Widdowson (1990 – see above) that authentication is not possibly yielded through the use of authentic materials has never been this clearly stated. In this publication (1990), Widdowson advances two diverging concepts of authenticity and expounds problems for both of them. It becomes questionable whether authenticity is still seen as a positive quality. In 1994, Widdowson is even more forthright about these difficulties. This time, he invokes cultural aspects:

> Over recent years, we have heard persuasive voices insisting that the English presented in the classroom should be authentic, naturally occurring language, not produced for instructional purposes. Generally, what this means, of course, is language naturally occurring as communication in native-speaker contexts of use, or rather those selected contexts where standard English is the norm: real newspaper reports, for example, real magazine articles, real advertisements, cooking recipes, horoscopes, and what have you. Now the obvious point about this naturally occurring language is that, inevitably, it is recipient designed and so culturally loaded. It follows that access to its meaning is limited to those insiders who share its cultural presuppositions and a sense of its idiomatic nuance. Those who do not, the outsiders, cannot ratify its authenticity. In other words, the language is only authentic in the original conditions of its use, it cannot be in the classroom. The authenticity is non-transferable. And to the extent that students cannot therefore engage with the language, they cannot make it their own. It may be real language, but it is not real to them. It does not relate to their world but to a remote one they have to find out about by consulting a dictionary of culture. It may be that eventually students will wish to acquire the cultural knowledge and the idiomatic fluency which enable them to engage authentically with the language use of a particular native-speaking community by adopting their identity in some degree, but there seems no sensible reason for insisting on them trying to do this in the process of language learning. On the contrary, it would seem that language for learning does need to be specially designed for pedagogic purposes so that it can be made real in the context of the students' own world. (Widdowson 1994: 384)

The quote begins with an acknowledgement that the use of authentic text has been widely championed in the discourse, which corresponds with Rück's observation of a "fetish" (Rück 1986: 165). The fact that such texts are "culturally loaded" (Widdowson 1994: 384 – quote above) is problematized by Widdowson, while it is seen as one of the primary assets by other authors. The proponents of cultural authenticity are presented in due course. Widdowson is not concerned about authentic text being linguistically too difficult, but about its cultural content so that "access to its meaning is limited to those insiders who share its cultural presuppositions" (Widdowson 1994: 384 – quote above).

According to Widdowson, the factor of culture is not limited to implications for the use of materials but extends to the question of whether learners should be taught by native speakers or non-native speakers:

> For the context of learning, contrived within the classroom setting, has to be informed in some degree by the attitudes, beliefs, values and so on of the students' cultural world. And in respect to this world, of course, it is the native-speaker teacher who is the outsider. To the extent that the design of instruction depends on a familiarity with the student reality which English is to engage with, or on the particular sociocultural situations in which teaching and learning take place, then nonnative teachers have a clear and, indeed, decisive advantage. (Widdowson 1994: 387)

The term *authentic/authenticity* is not used in this statement. However, the line of argumentation is analogous to the one above. The cultural factor hinders processes of authentication when authentic materials are used regardless of linguistic difficulties. The same logic is applied to proceedings in the classroom when native-speaker teachers conduct lessons in EFL.

Widdowson's concepts of authentication and appropriate response are thus expanded. They now have a bearing not only on the use of materials but also on the teacher as a person. The case is reiterated by Widdowson in 1996:

> [T]he language which is real for native speakers is not likely to be real for learners: indeed one might argue that logically it cannot be, for learners have by definition not yet learned how to make it so. They belong to another community and do not have the necessary knowledge of the contextual conditions which would enable them to authenticate English in native-speaker terms. (Widdowson 1996: 67-68)

> Teachers who come from the same community as their learners, of course, have this experience in common. They are therefore naturally in a better position to construct the relevant classroom contexts and make the learning process real than are teachers coming from a different linguistic and cultural background – for example those from an English-speaking community. (Widdowson 1996: 68)

It appears that Widdowson expands the range of what authenticity impinges on. At the same time, his statements become more straightforward and practice-oriented over the years. The straightforwardness of the two quotes above includes controversial content. This controversy is alleviated by means of hedging techniques so as to preempt reader opposition: "[T]he language which is real for native speakers is not **likely** to be real for learners: indeed **one might argue** that **logically** it cannot be" (ibid.). In chapter 4.2.1, examples are given to illustrate how Breen (1985) uses very similar techniques of authorial stance. In 1998, Widdowson makes the same statement as the one just analyzed. This time, however, the hedging is abandoned: "[T]he language that is authentic for native speaker users **cannot possibly** be authentic for learners" (Widdowson 1998: 711). Not only is hedging abandoned, it is replaced by boosting (cf. chapter 4.2.1 for theoretical elaborations on authorial stance). Widdowson appears to become more forthright and precise about the different issues pertaining to authenticity.

The publication (1998a) features statements that are increasingly redundant and serve to reify the practical implications of his deliberations in the previous writings. This includes very precise positioning on what sort of materials are to be used:

> [T]he solution [...] is not to foist authentic user text on the learners because, in the absence of the appropriately corresponding contexts that make it authentic, learners cannot engage with this either. On the contrary, they are more likely to be alienated by it. The solution must lie in some kind of pedagogic artifice whereby language is contrived to be both engaged with and learned from. (Widdowson 1998: 713)

Contrived and simplified materials are, thus, presented as the solution to the problems Widdowson identified in earlier writings but about which he had remained partly vague and non-committal.

Widdowson adds one further dimension to his concepts of authentication and appropriate response. Having discussed reading materials and the teacher being a native speaker or a non-native speaker, he now talks about which tasks are apt to yield authentication. The statements are again underpinned by the cultural factor:

> Tasks are designed to have designs on the learners: to induce learners to use language they can learn from. If such tasks are to engage learners in this way, their design must take account of the interests, attitudes, and dispositions of the learners, but these will relate to their own familiar cultural contexts and concerns, not those of the unfamiliar foreign community whose language they are learning but whose reality they are in no position to relate to. The whole point of language learning tasks is that they are specially contrived for learning. They do not have to replicate or even simulate what goes on in normal uses of language. Indeed, the more they seek to do so, the less effective they are likely to be. [...]

> [E]xcept in certain specific cases, there is no way of anticipating [...] encounters in any very precise way. The learners have to learn to fine-tune the appropriate patterns of contextual response for themselves. The purpose of teaching is to get learners to invest in a general capacity for further learning, not to rehearse them in communicative roles [...].

> As TESOL professionals, we need to make language and language learning a reality for learners, and we cannot do so by bland reference to 'real English'. It can only be done by contrivance, by artifice. And artifice, the careful crafting of appropriate language activities, is what TESOL is all about. Note that I say appropriate, not authentic. (Widdowson 1998: 714-715)

Widdowson does not use the word *authentic* until the last sentence of these deliberations. By the time the word occurs, it is made clear that a different adjective is chosen to apply to Widdowson's conceptualization: *appropriate*. The explicit avoidance of the term *authentic* implies that Widdowson is aware of how the term has been used by other authors in recent years. Widdowson's statements come at a time when the idea of task authenticity has gained great momentum in the context of Task-Based Language Teaching (TBLT). Widdowson now dismisses those techniques as "rehearsing" (Widdowson 1998: 714-715) – quote above). Proponents of TBLT usually speak of authenticity referring to *real-world tasks*:

> [W]e need to take account of what we might term activity authenticity (in contrast with authenticity of input which has already been considered). [...] Certain activities might only remotely resemble the sorts of things learners are required to do in the real world. (Nunan 1989: 60)

> Evaluating the authenticity of second language tasks relies on an analysis of the correspondence between a second language learning task and tasks that the learner is likely to encounter outside the classroom. (Chapelle 1999: 102)

> Authenticity through real world targets: [A] task might be said to be authentic if it has a clear relationship with real world needs (Guariento/Morley 2001: 349-350)

> Task authenticity refers to tasks that closely mirror communication in the world outside the classroom. (Nunan 2004: 212)

In 1998, Widdowson (quote above) likely knows that it would be confusing if he used the word *authentic* referring to tasks that contradict the current trend and that also contradict a somewhat established use of the term. Widdowson (1998b), once more, propounds an approach which runs counter to the trend. 20 years earlier he opposed textual authenticity, now he speaks out against real-world authenticity (terminology corresponding to the taxonomy in chapter 3).

In chapter 5.2.2, the emergence of real-world authenticity is traced and a very early statement by Candlin/Edelhoff (1982) is found. Almost paradoxically, their conceptualization refers to Widdowson, as they focus

> [...] on the authenticity of the task that the materials offer as possibilities to the learner and to the teacher. [...] It is not enough [...] simply to present learners with a range of connected text-types if they are asked to perform fundamentally inauthentic tasks with the texts. One doesn't read a bus ticket or a train timetable in order to learn something about English grammar; you read them to check if the bus conductor has sold you the correct ticket [...]. This is what Henry Widdowson refers to as 'authenticating' a text [...]. (Candlin/Edelhoff 1982: 9)

The rather vague ideas put forth by Widdowson in his early works appear to have an interesting effect. Authors like Candlin/Edelhoff (1982) reify these ideas in a way that Widdowson would later be opposed to. In the process, the term *authentic/authenticity* is appropriated by the advocates of real-world approaches, so that Widdowson, in 1998, opts for a different term to label his concepts: *appropriate*.

In his four publications of the 1990s, Widdowson expands his concept of authentication by incorporating aspects of teacher and task. In the meantime, Widdowson's old concept, which applies to the use of authentic materials, has been broadly adopted throughout the discourse. To reiterate, Widdowson writes in 1978:

> Genuineness is a characteristic of the passage itself and is an absolute quality. Authenticity is a characteristic of the relationship between the passage and the reader and it has to do with appropriate response. [...]

> [T]he learner may simply not feel himself in any way engaged by the text being presented to him and so may refuse to authenticate it by taking an interest. This means, among other things, that the topic of the discourse has to be one which will appeal to the learner in some way. (Widdowson 1978: 80-81)

The following quotes from the 1990s are all inspired by Widdowson's concept. The series of statements merely serves to illustrate how entrenched Widdowson's idea has become in the discourse.

> [T]here is no guarantee at all that authentic materials mean authentic interaction or authentic communication. (Arnold 1991: 241)

> [I]t has become a commonplace to say that authenticity does not lie in the text but in the uses speakers and readers make of it. (Kramsch 1993: 178)

> Inauthentic uses can reduce genuine texts to mere citation forms. (Long 1996: 129)

> [T]here is a difference between the instances of language (texts) and the uses to which they are put. Unfortunately the fact remains that many writers, as we have seen, use the term 'authenticity' to refer to the texts themselves. (Taylor 1994: 5)

> [Authenticity] has nothing to do with the origination of the linguistic material brought into the classroom [...]. (van Lier 1996: 127)

[I]t is important to enable learners to respond authentically to authentic texts. (Little 1997: 225)

All of these excerpts echo Widdowson's old concept (1976; 1978). Lee (1995), who is second only to Widdowson (1990) in citations received during the decade, draws on the same principle:

In this paper, 'text authenticity' is defined in terms of the origin of the materials, while 'learner authenticity' refers to the learner's interaction with them, in terms of appropriate responses and positive psychological reaction. (Lee 1995: 323)

The general consensus is that textual authenticity bears little value as long as the material is not used in ways that allow the learners to authenticate it.

Few authors draw on Widdowson as meticulously as do Day/Bamford (1998). The authors engage in a critical analysis of Widdowson's distinction between simple accounts (e.g. motherese, Pidgin languages) and simplified (i.e. graded) versions of authentic text (Widdowson 1978: 88-91). They go on to complement this binary distinction with the textual category of the *simple original*: "The second type of simplified material is text written specifically for second language learners. Writing an original text from scratch for an audience of language learners has been termed a 'simple original'" (Day/Bamford 2009 [Day, Richard (1998). Extensive reading in the second language classroom. Cambridge: Cambridge University Press. 53-61.]: 237). While Day/Bamford (1998) merely graze Widdowson's concept of authentication, they extensively respond to his more text-based elaborations. The two authors arguably provide one of the most in-depth analyses of textual authenticity by categorizing methods and degrees of simplification along with their implications for foreign language learning and teaching. In concluding, Day/Bamford (1998) use the term *authentic* in an unusual manner:

[S]econd language learners need a variety of excellent material written especially for them. Because of its communicative intent, such material would be authentic and appropriately simple in language and concept. Such material might properly be called 'language learner literature' [...]. (Day/Bamford 2009 [Day, Richard (1998). Extensive reading in the second language classroom. Cambridge: Cambridge University Press. 53-61.]: 241)

If a definition of textual authenticity is to be extrapolated, it would contradict basically all other definitions in that it describes contrived text as authentic, provided it has a communicative intent.

This publication is the last to be republished in the Routledge multi-volume edited by Hedge/Andon/Dewey (2009). However, none of the other authors in the discourse cites Day/Bamford (1998), which may be owed to the fact that *The cult of authenticity and the myth of simplification* is only a chapter in the monograph *Extensive reading in the second language classroom* (Day/Bamford 1998). Hence, this valuable contribution to the discourse is easily overlooked. The notion that contrived text can be authentic goes equally unnoticed so that the discursive impact of Day/Bamford (1998) remains small at best. This could change due to the republication in Hedge/Andon/Dewey (eds. 2009) but thus far it has not, meaning that even after 2009 no publication in the discourse mentions Day/Bamford. Elaborations on Hedge/Andon/Dewey (eds. 2009) and its role in the discourse are made in the next chapter of this chronology, which covers the 2000s. With regard to Day/Bamford (1998) no increased exposure appears to have accrued from the republishing.

Another development during the 1990s is the (tenuous) adoption of Widdowson's concepts in the context of authentic assessment. It has been shown that, until the late 1980s, authentic assessment formed an all but isolated discourse not informed by any of the conceptual theories advanced within the EFL discourse on authenticity.

Bachman publishes a monograph (1990) and an article (1991) in quick succession, both of which broach the issue of authentic assessment. The monograph continues to draw on authors within the niche of language assessment, if reference is made at all. Bachman sees

> [...] two main approaches to defining and operationalizing authenticity that have evolved in recent years. [...]

> What I will call the 'real-life' (RL) approach to defining authenticity essentially considers the extent to which test performance replicates some specified non-test language performance. [...] The RL approach has been the dominant one for the past ten years in the area of testing oral proficiency in a foreign language [...].

> The other approach to defining test authenticity, which I will call the 'interactional/ability' (IA) approach, is in keeping with both the mainstream approach to measuring language as a mental ability and the current view of communicative language use [...]. (Bachman 1990: 301-302)

Bachman's primary source for this conceptualization is John L.D. Clark (Bachman 1990: 303-304), who scarcely speaks of authenticity, though. Bachman's terminological choice puts a label on pre-existing concepts with little regard for the history of the term *authentic/authenticity*. Authentic language tests are essentially described as being integrative (as opposed to discrete-point testing) and direct (as opposed to indirect). The latter applies to testing that replicates non-test language performance, which makes it akin to the non-classroom approach that underlies real-world authenticity (cf. chapter 2 for a distinction between classroom authenticity and real-world authenticity). A slight difference can be recognized in that authentic assessment accepts a stronger deviation from real-world behavior due to the formal test criteria (Bachman 1990: 305):

> In summary, the 'real-life' approach defines language proficiency as the ability to perform language tasks in non-test situations, and authenticity as the extent to which test tasks replicate 'real-life' language use tasks. (Bachman 1990: 307)

If a replication of real-life language use tasks is described as authentic, then authentic assessment can be seen as a replication of a replication. Still, Bachman's definition would fall under real-world authenticity.

An explicit adoption of Widdowson's concepts in the context of authentic assessment is found in Bachman (1991). For the first time in the discourse Widdowson is invoked in the context of assessment:

> What we call interactional authenticity is essentially Widdowson's (1978) definition of authenticity and is a function of the extent and type of involvement of task takers' language ability in accomplishing a test task. The different areas of language knowledge and the different strategies can be involved to varying degrees in the problem presented by the test

task. In contrast to situational authenticity, where the focus is on the relationship between the test task and nontest [sic] language use, interactional authenticity resides in interaction between the test taker and the test task. (Bachman 1991: 691)

This interpretation hardly reflects Widdowson's (1978) postulations. The "involvement of task takers' language ability in accomplishing a test task" (Bachman – quote above) is not easily matched with Widdowson's notion that "[a]uthenticity is a characteristic of the relationship between the passage and the reader and it has to do with appropriate response" (Widdowson 1978: 80).

Bachman (1991) citing Widdowson (1978) without a page reference makes it difficult to trace the exact ideas that are drawn upon. A similar problem occurs in Bachman/Palmer (1996) who mention Widdowson briefly in a footnote: "Widdowson (1978, 1983) discusses authenticity in language teaching materials and exercises" (Bachman/Palmer 1996: 41). The reference must, once more, be considered tokenistic, since the authors show no intention of incorporating Widdowson in their conceptualizations. Bachman's (1990; 1991; 1996) and Palmer's (1996) rapprochement to the EFL discourse on authenticity is, therefore, not very explicit or precise. Widdowson is cited (Bachman 1991: 691; Bachman/Palmer 1996: 41) but a conceptual kinship with real-world authenticity is discernible, which contradicts Widdowson's ideas.

Lewkowicz (2000) shows more eagerness to bridge the conceptual gap between authentic assessment and understandings of the term in the EFL discourse. Many references to Widdowson are made in her article that is discussed later in the chronology. Another publication on authentic assessment during this decade, O'Malley/Pierce (1996), is not connected to the discourse by means of citations.

In addition to the notions of authentication and the development within the field of assessment, one rather marginal emergence shall be mentioned. Kramsch (1993) discusses authenticity in the context of culture; she coins the term *cultural authenticity* (Kramsch 1993: 178) developing a concept predicated on authentication:

> For example, a German menu is a genuine piece of cultural realia, but if I use it in the classroom to practice reading prices or to learn the endings of adjectives, I have not used it in the way the restaurant management had intended, nor the way native customers do when they go to that restaurant. [...] The teacher's task is precisely to give the learner the means of properly authenticating a text like a German menu. (Kramsch 1993: 178-179)

This concept is referred to as marginal because Kramsch herself is tentative in advocating the concept. Her thoughts are marked by ambivalence and problematization taking account of the prevalent theorems by Widdowson and Breen (cf. chapter 2.8 for a conceptual analysis of cultural authenticity). Nevertheless, Kramsch (1993) is cited a solid six times in the discourse. As mentioned before, the mere use of a new collocation such as *authentic task* (Breen 1985) can have a strong discursive impact, which may unfold nearly regardless of the corresponding elaborations. Such an effect may be expected as Kramsch speaks of *cultural authenticity*. As a generally well-known author Kramsch is likely to receive more attention than many other authors in the discourse. Her segment on cultural authenticity is formally comparable to Day/Bamford's on textual authenticity (1998). Both are easily overlooked since they are, respectively, a chapter in a monograph that does not carry the term *authentic/authenticity* in its title. Author status may partly account for Kramsch (1993) being cited six times as opposed to Day/Bamford (1998) who remain completely unnoticed (numbers do not include self-citation). Kramsch (1993) is one of the few authors to cite both English and German (Löschmann/Löschmann 1984) texts in the discourse. She is actually the only author who contributes to the discourse in both languages (German: Kramsch 1996). Weller (1992) is the first German publication to cite English works within the discourse, namely Widdowson (1976) and Little/Devitt/Single-ton (1988). Thus, a certain degree of exchange between the English and the German discourse is maintained during the 1990s after Rings (1986) was the first author to cite works in both languages.

One contribution to the discourse, that stands out, is van Lier (1996). Van Lier is one of the most conceptually substantial contributors to the discourse. He argues in a similar vein as Widdowson (1976; 1978) and Breen (1985). He also pursues a similarly conceptual style that features few references. His common ground with Widdowson and Breen is the opposition to real-world authenticity (my taxonomy), which he takes to an extreme. The following statement, which I have referenced twice before, is the most pronounced one in this regard:

> In a curious way, it seems to me that the traditional language lessons of the grammar translation type which I remember from my school days might lay greater claim to that sort of authenticity than some of the so-called communicative classrooms that I have had occasion to observe in recent years. I must emphasize that the old lessons seem to have been authentic 'for me', although they may well have been inauthentic for some of my class mates, although they may well have been inauthentic for some of my class mates.

> Authentication is basically a personal process of engagement, and it is unclear if a social setting could ever be clearly shown to be authentic for every member involved in it. However, given the privileged status of the teacher, it is reasonable to suggest that a teacher's authenticity may stimulate authenticity in the students as well. In terms of language teaching methods, one cannot say that any particular teaching method is more likely to promote authenticity than any other, regardless of whether or not it promotes the use of 'genuine' materials. Rather, the people in the setting, each and every one individually for himself or herself, as well as in negotiation with one another, authenticate the setting and the actions in it. When such authentication occurs en masse, spontaneously or in an orchestrated fashion (socially constructed authentication, so to speak), we may well have the most authentic setting possible. A good teacher may be able to promote such authenticity. It may be easier to achieve it in some settings than in others. (van Lier 1996: 128)

No other author considers the process of authentication to be so universally applicable and so open-ended. To consider the grammar-translation method as potentially authentic is a complete outlier in the discourse. Van Lier refers not only to Widdowson and Breen but also draws on linguistics as well as on existentialist philosophy as he lays out his thoughts on authenticity. Terminologically, he adopts Widdowson's diction by speaking of "genuine materials" and "authentication" (ibid.).

Toward the close of the decade an encyclopedia is published 14 years after Rich-ards/Platt/Weber's (1985), i.e. Johnson/Johnson (1999 – *Encyclopedic dictionary of applied linguistics*). The encyclopedia differs from the Longman dictionary in size and makeup. Individual entries are written by different authors, who are indicated, and they are significantly longer than those in Richards/Platt/Weber (1985). The entry for *authenticity* is written by editor Keith Johnson himself and features a bibliography, which is not the case for all entries. The four bibliographical references are Breen (1985) and Widdowson (1976; 1984; 1990). The entry is an accurate account of the different concepts beginning with textual authenticity and presenting the concepts by Breen and Widdowson. Thus, the descriptions go far beyond authentic materials – unlike in Richards/Platt/Weber (1985). Yet, they do not incorporate the most recent publications on the topic. Not only is van Lier (1996) missing, the latest publication considered is actually Widdowson (1990). Widdowson's recent conceptual expansion of authentication (see above) is thus unaccounted for. Consequently, Johnsons's concluding words depict a position that is accurate but does not reflect the status quo of the discourse in the late 1990s: Widdowson "captures the common argument against the necessity for authenticity, and opens the way for the simplification, and other doctoring of texts for reasons of pedagogic presentation – clarifying and giving salience to selected language points, for example" (Johnson 1999: 24).

5.2.3.2 Conclusion

The 1990s are the time when more and more authors acknowledge the conceptual expansion of authenticity spurred by Widdowson (1976; 1978) and Breen (1985) during the previous decades. A majority of the authors refer to writings by Widdowson. As many as 16 of 35 publications refer to Breen (1985), one of them being Widdowson (1990). The fact that Widdowson (1990) refers to Breen (1985) is particularly notable. Widdowson uses very few references in all of his publications in the discourse.

As an author, only Widdowson is quoted more often than Breen, which is not surprising given the fact that he has published more widely than anyone else on the subject. The proliferation of Widdowson's and Breen's concepts is manifested in an increased acceptance of the idea that textual authenticity is not of overriding importance. Rather, the nature of engagement with such materials becomes prevalent, which was christened *authentication* or *appropriate response* by Widdowson in the late 1970s. While this notion begins to catch on, Widdowson (1990; 1994; 1996; 1998a; 1998b) remains prolific as a contributor to the discourse. He applies the concept of authentication to new aspects such as tasks and the teacher (native speaker or non-native speaker?). Van Lier (1996) draws on Widdowson most thoroughly claiming all but universal applicability of his concept. The incremental awareness of Widdowson's and Breen's commentaries has, however, not led to a diminished use of *authentic/authenticity* for denoting textual authenticity. Unlike for the early years, when I looked at the EFL discourse at large by scanning all publications in *TESOL Quarterly*, the casual use of *authentic/authenticity* can no longer be under scrutiny here because this would be a massive task which cannot be undertaken by an individual. Yet, a general observation is that the traditional notions of textual authenticity are still viral manifesting themselves in the ubiquitous collocations *authentic text(s)* and *authentic material(s)*, which occur in publication titles seven times.

5.2.4 The 2000s – persistent diversity

There has been an expanding conceptual range during the 1990s and the diversification of concepts remains unabated in the 2000s. A heightened awareness of this development prompts some authors to write synthetic literature reviews attempting to represent all nuances of the growing discourse. In the meantime, technological advancements create a new context in which the term *authentic/authenticity* occurs very frequently. The publications appearing in the 2000s are:

Number of citations received	Publication	Citations made	Type of publication
2	Kramsch, Claire J.; A'Ness, Francine; Lam, Wan Shun Eva (2000). Authenticity and authorship in the computer-mediated acquisition of L2 literacy. *Language Learning & Technology* 4 (2), 78-104.	Breen (1985), Grellet (1981), Hutchinson/Waters (1987), Kramsch (1993), Nunan (1989), Widdowson (1990)	Article in journal
1	Lewkowicz, Jo A. (2000). Authenticity in language testing: some outstanding questions. *Language Testing*, 17(1), 43-64.	Bachman (1990; 1991), Bachman/Palmer (1996), Breen (1985), Lynch (1982), Peacock (1997), Seliger et al. (1985), van Lier (1996), Widdowson (1976; 1978; 1990; 1996; 1998b)	Article in journal
1	MacDonald, Malcolm N.; Badger, Richard; White, Goodith (2000). The real thing? Authenticity and academic listening. *English for Specific Purposes* 19(3), 253-267.	Breen (1985), Cook (1997), Hutchinson/Waters (1987), Lee (1995), Nunan (1989), Taylor (1994), Widdowson (1976, 1978, 1996)	Article in journal
0	Rixon, Shelagh (2000). Authenticity. In: Michael Byram et al. (eds.). *Routledge encyclopedia of language teaching and learning.* London; New York: Routledge, 68-69.	Breen (1985), Candlin/Edelhoff (1982), Widdowson (1978)	Entry in encyclopedia
3	Widdowson, Henry G. (2000). On the limitations of linguistics applied. *Applied Linguistics* 21 (1), 3-25.	None	Article in journal
16	Guariento, William; Morley, John (2001). Text and task authenticity in the EFL classroom. *ELT Journal*, 55(4), 347-353.	Breen (1985), Little/Devitt/Singleton (1988), Porter/Roberts (1981), Wilkins (1976), Widdowson (1978)	Article in journal
0	Nation, I.S.P.; Deweerdt, Jean Paul (2001). A defence of simplification. *Prospect* 16 (3), 55-65.	Widdowson (1976)	Article in journal
3	Alptekin, Cem (2002). Towards intercultural communicative competence in ELT. *ELT Journal* 56 (1), 57-64.	Widdowson (1998a)	Article in journal

0	Amor, Stuart (2002). *Authenticity and authentication in language learning.* Frankfurt am Main; New York: Peter Lang.	Bachman (1990), Beile (1986), Breen (1985), Edelhoff (1985), Gutschow (1977), Kramsch (1993), Morrison (1989), Nunan (1989), Peacock (1997), van Lier (1996), Widdowson (1978; 1990; 1996)	Book
5	Rost, Michael (2002). *Teaching and researching listening.* Harlow, New York: Longman/Pearson.	Breen (1985), Taylor (1994)	Book
1	Day, Richard (2003). Authenticity in the design and development of materials. In: Renandya, Willy A. (ed.). *Methodology and materials design in language teaching.* Singapore: SEAMEO Regional Language Centre, 1-11.	Not available	Article in edited volume
2	Widdowson, Henry G. (2003). *Defining issues in English language teaching.* Oxford: Oxford University Press.	None	Book
0	Brown, H. Douglas (2004). *Language assessment.* New York: Pearson/Longman.	Bachman/Palmer (1996)	Book
2	Day, Richard (2004). A critical look at authentic materials. *The Journal of AsiaTEFL* 1 (1), 101-114.	Bacon/Finnemann (1990), Clarke (1989), Day/Bamford (1998), Lee (1995), Little/Devitt/Singleton (1988), Morrison (1989), Nunan (1988b), Peacock (1997), Swaffar (1985)	Article in journal
0	Decke-Cornill, Helene (2004). Die Kategorie der Authentizität im mediendidaktischen Diskurs der Fremdsprachendidaktik. In: Bosenius, Petra (ed.). *Interaktive Medien und Fremdsprachenlernen.* Frankfurt am Main: Peter Lang. 17-27.	Breen (1985), Kramsch (1993), Little/Singleton (1988), Widdowson (1976)	Article in edited volume
8	Gilmore, Alex (2004). A comparison of textbook and authentic interactions. *ELT Journal,* 58(4), 363-374.	Widdowson (1998a)	Article in journal
3	Kilickaya, Ferit (2004). Authentic materials and cultural content in EFL classrooms. *ITESLJ* 10 (7). http://iteslj.org/Techniques/Kilickaya-AutenticMaterial.html, access date: 06/20/2016.	Chavez (1998), Guariento/Morley (2001)	Article in online journal

2	Mishan, Freda (2004). Authenticating corpora for language learning. *ELT Journal,* 58(3), 219-227.	Hutchinson/Waters (1987), Morrow (1977), van Lier (1996), Widdowson (1978, 1983, 1998a, 2000)	Article in journal
1	Nunan, David (2004). *Task-based language teaching.* Cambridge (UK); New York (NY): Cambridge University Press.	Candlin/Edelhoff (1982), Porter/Roberts (1981)	Book
0	Davies, Alan (2005). *A glossary of applied linguistics.* Edinburgh: Edinburgh University Press.	None – no bibliography	Entry in encyclopedia
9	Mishan, Freda (2005). *Designing authenticity into language learning materials.* Bristol, UK; Portland, OR: Intellect.	Arnold (1991), Breen (1985), Clarke (1989), Davies (1984), Grellet (1981), Hutchinson/ Waters (1987), Kramsch/ A'Ness/Lam (2000), Lee (1995), Little (1997), Little/Devitt/Singleton (1988), Morrow (1977), Nostrand (1989), Swaffar (1985), Taylor (1994), van Lier (1996), Widdowson (1978, 1983, 1990, 1998, 2000)	Book
1	Seargeant, Philip (2005). More English than England itself. The simulation of authenticity in foreign language practice in Japan. *International Journal of Applied Linguistics* 15 (3), 326-345.	Breen (1985), Lee (1995), van Lier (1996), Widdowson (1976, 1978, 1996)	Article in journal
2	Tan, Melinda (2005). Authentic language or language errors? *ELT Journal,* 59(2), 126-134.	None	Article in journal
3	Berardo, Sacha Anthony (2006). The use of authentic materials in the teaching of reading. *The Reading Matrix* 6 (2), 60-69.	Breen (1985), Davies (1984), Guariento/Morley (2001), Peacock (1997), Widdowson (1990)	Article in journal
3	MacDonald, Malcolm N.; Badger, Richard; Dasli, Maria (2006). Authenticity, culture and language learning. *Language and Intercultural Communication,* 6(3-4), 250-261.	Alptekin (2002), Breen (1985), Gilmore (2004), Guariento/Morley (2001), Lee (1995), Taylor (1994), Widdowson (1976; 1990)	Article in journal
2	Tatsuki, Donna (2006). What is authenticity? In: Newfields, Tim (ed.). *Authentic communication: Proceedings of the 5th Annual JALT PanSIG Conference.* Shizuoka, Japan: n.a., 1-15.	Breen (1985), Day (2004), Guariento/Morley (2001), Lee (1995), MacDonald/Badger/Dasli (2006), Nunan (1988b), Taylor (1994), Widdowson (1990; 1998a)	Article in journal

1	Thornbury, Scott (2006). *An A-Z of ELT.* Oxford: Macmillan Education.	None – no bibliography	Entry in encyclopedia
10	Gilmore, Alex (2007). Authentic materials and authenticity in foreign language learning. *Language Teaching,* 40(02), 97-118.	Arnold (1991), Bachman/Palmer (1996), Bacon/Finneman (1990), Breen (1985), Clarke (1989), Cook (1997), Gilmore (2004), Grellet (1981), Guariento/Morley (2001), Hutchinson/Waters (1987), Kienbaum/Russell/ Welty (1986), Kohonen (1999), Kramsch (1993), Lee (1995), Lewkowicz (2000), Little/ Devitt/Singleton (1988), Mishan (2005), Morrison (1989), Morrow (1977), Nunan (1989), Peacock (1997), Porter/Roberts (1981), Rings (1986), Rogers/Medley (1988), Rost (2002), Swaffar (1985), van Lier (1996), Widdowson (1976; 1978; 1994; 1996; 1998a; 2003)	Article in journal
0	Shomoossi, Nematullah; Ketabi, Saeed (2007). A critical look at the concept of authenticity. *Electronic Journal of Foreign Language Teaching* 4 (1), 149-155.	Breen (1995), Day (2004), Dunkel (1995), Guariento/ Morley (2001), Lee (1995), MacDonald/Badger/Dasli (2006), Nunan (1988b), Rings (1986), Rogers/Medley (1988), Taylor (1994), Tatsuki (2006), Widdowson (1998a)	Article in online journal
0	Allan, Rachel (2008). Can a graded reader corpus provide 'authentic' input? *ELT Journal,* 63(1), 23-32.	Mishan (2004)	Article in journal
1	Dantas-Whitney, Maria; Rilling, Sarah; Savova, Lilia (2009). *Authenticity in the language classroom and beyond: adult learners.* Alexandria, VA: TESOL.	Gilmore (2007), Grellet (1981), Guariento/Morley (2001), Mishan (2005), Morrow (1977), Seargeant (2005), Widdowson (1998a; 2003)	Book
0	Farrell, Thomas S. C. (2009). *Teaching reading to English language learners.* Thousand Oaks: Corwin Press.	None	Book

1	Roberts, Celia; Cooke, Melanie (2009). Authenticity in the adult ESOL classroom and beyond. *TESOL Quarterly* 43 (4), 620-642.	Breen (1985), Cook (1997), Kramsch (1993), Taylor (1994), Widdowson (1998a)	Article in journal
1	Tamo, Daniela (2009). The use of authentic materials in classrooms. *Linguistic and Communicative Performance Journal* 2 (1), 74-78.	Clarke (1989), Guariento/Morley (2001), Widdowson (1990)	Article in journal
1	Waters, Alan (2009). Ideology in applied linguistics for language teaching. *Applied Linguistics* 30 (1), 138-143.	Clarke (1989), Hutchinson/Waters (1987), Widdowson (2003), Wilkins (1976)	Article in journal

Figure 13: Persistent diversity

The productivity of the discourse stays constant for the third straight decade (35 publications). Widdowson's abiding presence is mirrored in the fact that his coinage *authentication* appears in the titles of two publications (Amor 2002; Mishan 2005). Certain concepts of authenticity see a temporary upswing as electronic corpora facilitate new ways of using authentic text. The following analysis begins with a look at how electronic corpora influence the discourse on authenticity. Widdowson remains an important actor as he comments on this new trend. The analysis then continues with a more conceptual focus because nearly all the concepts of the taxonomy experience modifications during this decade, which increases the diversification.

5.2.4.1 Detailed analysis

Widdowson (2000) has one of the earliest contributions to the discourse in this decade. His publication is discussed alongside some other writings, because Widdowson reacts to a new development, of which some of the other publications are symptomatic. The new development in question is the rise of corpus linguistics, which now emanates into the EFL discourse on authenticity. Corpora are not an overall new phenomenon but the technological possibility of saving and sifting large amounts of textual data was not readily available until late in the 20th century. Different ways of using corpora are pursued in EFL, and naturally, many of them are linked to concepts of authenticity during the first decade of the 21st century. After all, the idea of corpus linguistics is to analyze language as it is genuinely used by speakers and writers. In the following definition of *corpus* Sampson actually invokes authenticity:

> A 'corpus', in the context of computational linguistics, is simply a sizeable machine-readable sample of a language, which will commonly be constructed using random-sampling techniques in such a fashion as to form a 'fair cross-section' of authentic usage for the language as a whole or for some particular genre. [...] [T]he one feature uniting the diverse findings of corpus linguistics is that they depend on access to quantities of authentic language data, and could not meaningfully be established on the basis of the invented example sentences which play a central role in some areas of linguistics. (Sampson 1992: 181)

Most approaches in EFL make use of corpora as a source of authentic text. The quantifiability of structures and words allows for a measurement of frequency and, as a result, the extrapolation of idiomaticity from vast textual data. At the turn of the century, Widdowson testifies to the recent developments as follows:

> There is now a fairly widespread conviction that linguistics should concern itself not with idealized constructs but with the reality of language as people actually experience it: as communication, as the expression of identity, as the means for the exercise of social control. (Widdowson 2000: 4-5)

Linguistic findings of this nature are apt to inform an analysis of textbook language, which is what Gilmore (2004) pursues. He conducts an empirical study from which "it seems clear that there have been substantial differences in the past between coursebook dialogues and their authentic equivalents" (Gilmore 2004: 370-371). Gilmore then raises the following question: "[T]o what extent should we deprive students of exposure to natural language?" (ibid.). Barbieri/Eckhardt (2007) are forthright about this question asserting that "[c]orpus-based texts are by definition authentic, and as such naturally lend themselves to input flood and input enhancement" (Barbieri/Eckhardt 2007: 335).[60] "L2 instructional materials should reflect the findings of empirical, corpus-based research" (Barbieri/Eckhardt 2007: 338). Amor concurs stating that an "extensive spoken language corpus specifically designed for EFL teaching would be a great step forward towards using genuine material and would make it much easier to plan authentic tasks" (Amor 2002: 86). Amor devotes two chapters to the alleged value of corpora in his monograph *Authenticity and authentication in language learning* (2002).

Such ideas are by no means new, and they have even occurred within the EFL discourse on authenticity:

> The aim of this project, namely to investigate the authenticity of textbook dialogues, suggests that a comparison between textbook dialogues and authentic speech material would be worthwhile. An 'impressionistic' analysis of textbook dialogues can be a sensible approach. By and large, however, these approximations get caught up in detail, and they depend too much on the appraisal of the analyst. If rigorous textbook analysis is the aim, then a linguistic and corpus-based method is preferable.[61] (Weijenberg 1980: 6-7)

Weijenberg's study is written in German which is likely the main reason it is not cited by the other proponents of corpus-informed textbook design. At the time, such analyses were

---

60 Barbieri/Eckhardt (2007) are not featured in the document selection because their negotiation of the term is negligible in quantity and quality.

61 Original: "Das konkrete Ziel des Projekts, Lehrwerkdialoge auf ihre Sprachauthentizität hin zu prüfen, legt es nahe, den Versuch zu unternehmen, einen Vergleich zwischen authentischem Sprachmaterial und Lehrwerkdialogen durchzuführen. [...] [Eine] ‚impressionistische' Analyse von u.a. Lehrwerkdialogen kann m.E. als sinnvoller Ansatz im Rahmen der Lehrwerkkritik angesehen werden. Insgesamt bleiben diese Annäherungsweisen jedoch im Detail stecken, sie hängen allzusehr von der Einschätzung des Beurteilers ab [...]. Wird also, wie in der vorliegenden Untersuchung, auf Lehrwerkanalyse oder -forschung gezielt, so dürfte eine linguistische, korpusorientierte Verfahrensweise [...] zu bevorzugen sein." (Weijenberg 1980: 6–7)

obviously more involved than today. The corpus used by Weijenberg, for example, consisted of analog audio tapes which were transcribed onto paper. Considering such lengthy procedures, it is not surprising how eager linguists and EFL scholars are to use computer corpora at the turn of the century. The value of the corpus-based approach for EFL may have been recognized decades earlier, but the facilitation of computer technology has caused this new surge.

Textbook design is only one area that purportedly benefits from corpus linguistics. Some authors go further advocating what is called data-driven learning (DDL):

> Data-driven learning (DDL) refers to the use of a corpus of texts with concordancing software, to find answers to linguistic questions. The learner inputs the target word or words into the software and all examples from the corpus are returned, usually in a keyword in context (KWIC) format, with the target word in the middle of the line [...]. These lines can then be sorted in a variety of ways that may help to reveal patterns in meaning and usage. (Allan 2008: 23)

Mishan, who adheres most tenaciously to Widdowson's concept of authentication, sees great potential here. She is in favor of creating

> [...] conditions that enable learners to 'authenticate' the corpus data through some sort of engagement with it. Of the corpus-based pedagogies to have been developed, the most authentic [...] is the methodology known as data-driven learning (DDL), a methodology which sees learners engaging with the corpus via research tasks. [...] [T]he most authentic DDL activity (in that historically, lexicography was one of the corpus's original functions) – researching and writing a dictionary definition. (Mishan 2004: 222-223)

Allan comes to a similar conclusion – actually referring to Mishan (2004):

> [DDL] can be viewed as a task-based approach [...]. Not only does it use authentic input, but it is a 'pedagogical application of a research method' (Mishan 2004: 222) – an authentic task in its own right. (Allan 2008: 24)

However, it must be noted that Mishan's (2004) idea of authentication is different from what Widdowson says on the topic. To him, the problem of decontextualized language cannot be overcome by the learners, which – consequently – hinders processes of authentication:

> Now that we know what real language looks like, the argument runs, we expose learners to it and rid our classrooms of contrivance. [...] [W]hat is not taken into account is the pedagogic perspective, the contextual conditions that have to be met in the classroom for language to be a reality for the learners. [...] The contextual authenticity from which textual features originally derived cannot be ratified by language learners precisely 'because' they are learners and do not know (yet) how to do it. (Widdowson 2000: 7)

In his second publication of the decade, Widdowson reiterates his position:

> [N]ow that the findings of corpus linguistics are becoming available, non-native teachers 'do' have direct access to the facts of actual usage, and so can now learn to recognize authenticity when they see it. [...] The difficulty here [...] is that the concordance will only reveal usage as recurring patterns in the text that people produce. It will not reveal the actuality of use, the discourse process whereby meanings are pragmatically achieved under various contextual conditions. (Widdowson 2003: 155)

Whereas Gilmore (2004) (as well as Barbieri/Eckhardt (2007)) promotes the use of corpora to render textbook language more authentic, Mishan (2004) and Allan (2008) praise the benefits of DDL where learners themselves actually work with corpora. Wilcox/Morrison/Oaks argue: "With such an array of computer tools and materials available, it is time to begin more aggressively to consider specific uses of corpora technology in the classroom" (Wilcox/Morrison/Oaks 1999: 419). The corresponding article *Computer corpora and authentic texts: Toward more effective language teaching* (1999) is not included in the document selection because the term *authentic text* is used as a consolidated concept rather than being explicitly negotiated.

Widdowson (2000; 2003) makes a case against both approaches corpus-informed textbook design and DDL. It is interesting to see how his concept of authentication is appropriated by Mishan (2004) and interpreted in ways which he, himself, is opposed to. This difference in interpretation, if not misinterpretation, is equally perceivable in Mishan (2005), though she does not speak about DDL here (cf. chapter 2.2.2.4 for a closer analysis of Mishan's monograph of 2005). Widdowson is opposed to ideas that are associated with his own term – *authentication*. This discursive pattern recurs after some of Widdowson's statements from the 1990s are antithetical to what Candlin/Edelhoff understand by *authentication* in 1982 (cf. chapter 5.2.2). Both Candlin/Edelhoff (1982) and Mishan (2004; 2005) refer to Widdowson's early works. Unlike in the case of Candlin/Edelhoff (1982), however, Mishan is also familiar with Widdowson's later thoughts. In her piece on DDL she actually quotes Widdowson (2000):

> Appearance, to coin a phrase, really does matter. And because of this, 'the texts which are collected in a corpus have only a reflected reality' (Widdowson 2000: 7), for 'Reality [...] does not travel with the text' (Widdowson 1998[62]: 711-12). The reality, the authenticity, of text is tarnished by transposition.

> Part of the problem is that because of the form a corpus takes, a core aspect of authenticity - context - is in effect lost in the transition from source to electronic data; this data is 'decontextualised language which is why it is only partially real' (Widdowson 2000). (Mishan 2004: 220)

Mishan's proposal for classroom practice is, therefore, a conscious contradiction of Widdowson's recent stand.

Widdowson does not add much to his conceptualization of authenticity during this decade. Rather, he appears to anticipate developments in the discourse. His statements on the role of corpora in EFL predate those by Gilmore (2004), Mishan (2004), and Allan (2008). Two of these three authors, Gilmore and Mishan, refer to works by Widdowson. Mishan (2004) even cites Widdowson (2000).

A completely different way of utilizing corpora in EFL is proposed by Tan (2005). Tan is the first and only author who considers learner language authentic. Instead of using corpora that are constituted of native-speaker use from contexts outside the classroom she investigates what is uttered by learners of English during the lessons: "The common conclusion is that learner data illustrate examples of 'overuses', 'underuses', or 'misuses' of

---

62   In my bibliography: Widdowson (1998b).

the target language" (Tan 2005: 126-127). Tan pleads for a new legitimacy of learner language under the premise of English as a lingua franca (ELF):

> The impression given from learner corpora research is that learner language is flawed because it contains usages which are considered unnatural and inauthentic when compared to native language usage. However, if we were to examine the 'authenticity' criteria by which researchers base their claims, we would find that it is very much based on imperialistic assumptions about the ownership of English, rather than the present role of English as a lingua franca. [...]

> [W]hat NS [i.e. native-speaking] English teachers employed in NNS [non-native-speaking] countries tend to label as language 'errors' might not really be errors, but simply examples of 'authentic' or 'real' language use [...] (Tan 2005: 128-129)

> My suggested definition of 'authentic' language use is meant to signal an acknowledgement of the present role of English as a lingua franca [...]. (Tan 2005: 133-134)

Tan's definition enters into the category of textual authenticity, yet it is not represented in the taxonomy put forth earlier in this study. The definition is an outlier in that it adds a component of non-native speaker production, which thus far has been one of the few aspects all authors exclude from their definitions of textual authenticity. Nonetheless, Tan's statements show how diversified the different understandings of textual authenticity are.

All in all, corpus-informed approaches appear to be linked to authenticity by virtue of their fundamental purpose: to represent naturally occurring language with all its facets and potential flaws. This realness is seen by many authors as a legitimating factor in establishing linguistic norms. The aspect of corpus linguistics is not addressed in the systematic overview part of this study because it is a phenomenon that influences conceptualizations but not a concept in and of itself. It is represented in this chronology for it is conjoined with the technological developments of a certain time period.

Widdowson (2000; 2003) has been shown to refute the idea of using corpora in the ways just outlined. In his publication of 2003, he returns to the general issue of authentication. While Widdowson's statements become increasingly redundant with regard to content, his forthrightness is unprecedented:

> [Every] text is designed to be accessible to, and acceptable to, a like-minded reader. And if **you** can identify with this assigned reader, then you confirm your common communal values, and ratify **your role as insider**. You then 'authenticate' the text as a discourse which is expressive of a particular community which you belong to. There is thus the creation of a solidarity between writer and reader, and a kind of **conspiracy** against those who cannot fill the position of assigned reader: the writer makes allusions to things which are particular, specific indeed, to a closed community of like-minded people. If you cannot ratify the role of assigned reader, **you become an outsider, excluded, alienated** from the text. Either **you** cannot authenticate it, and no coherent discourse is derived from the text. Or you authenticate it on your own terms, and assert your own discourse, **which may have little convergence** with that of the writer's original intention. (Widdowson 2003: 66) (emphases added by L.W.)

Hyland investigates instances of self-mention, which means the author writing in the first person. Self-mention is categorized under authorial stance (Hyland 2005: 181). The use of the second person in academic writing, however, is uncharted territory. It is presumably a stance feature symptomatic of conceptual style and largely irreconcilable with descriptive writing. Here (Widdowson 2003: 66), it creates a certain directness of delivery by addressing the reader personally. Drastic metaphors evoked by words like *conspiracy* and *outsider* increase the intensity. They are rather uncharacteristic of academic writing. In the last sentence of the quote above, the hedging device *may* is employed. As explained, this strategy is used to defuse controversial statements, thereby preempting reader opposition. Stylistic idiosyncrasies of the sort just outlined are likely accepted when applied by an individual of high author status, and may otherwise confuse or even antagonize the reader (Cecchetto/Stoinska 1997: 150-151).

Lewkowicz, as mentioned in the analysis of the previous decade, discusses authentic assessment while invoking Widdowson's theories. She thus forges a nexus between the EFL discourse on authenticity and what has nearly grown into an isolated discursive formation: the EFL discourse on authentic assessment. As Lewkowicz discusses authentication, she displays some criticism of Widdowson's position:

> [Widdowson] argued that genuine texts would only be considered authentic after undergoing a process of authentication, a process which he suggested may only be truly accessible to the native speaker. He failed to account for the way language learners could progress towards being able to authenticate texts, or to describe the native speaker. (Lewkowicz 2000: 45)

Such criticism of Widdowson's concept is very rare in the discourse. Authors in favor of using authentic text in the classroom usually do not cite Widdowson, or they cite Widdowson's early works (1976; 1978) where authentication is conceived as reconcilable with textual authenticity. Lewkowicz does not commit to a certain concept. Instead, she provides an extensive literature review that presents and discusses authenticity not only in the context of assessment. Publications referenced are Lynch (1982), Breen (1985), Peacock (1997), van Lier (1996), and Widdowson (1976; 1978; 1990; 1996; 1998b). As an article on assessment Lewkowicz (2000) is distinct from Bachman (1991) and Bachman/Palmer (1996) in that the author engages with the different conceptualizations of authenticity in EFL and then applies them to the domain of assessment. As I have detailed in chapter 5.2.3, such connections are rather vague and superficial in both Bachman (1991) and Bachman/Palmer (1996). Gilmore (2007), whose article is discussed shortly, accommodates authentic assessment in his comprehensive depiction of authenticity in EFL. Both sides, the general authenticity discourse and the authentic assessment discourse, show a new willingness to connect to the other domain.

One other publication deals with authentic assessment during the 2000s: In Brown's (2004) monograph titled *Language assessment – principles and classroom practices* one chapter is devoted to authenticity (Brown 2004: 28). The concept advocated is based on real-world approaches, but what is more interesting from a discourse analytical perspective is that, once more, no reference is made beyond the field of assessment. Bachman/Palmer (1996) are the only authors cited in this context, as Brown asserts that "we explore many different types of task in this book [...] the principle of authenticity will be very much in the forefront" (Brown 2004: 28). Another publication discussing authentic assessment is Farrell (2009). The use of the term is also not connected to EFL theories but is actually rather intuitive (Farrell 2009: 95-96). The discourse on authentic assessment, thus, remains partly separate from the general EFL discourse on authenticity.

The decade of the 2000s yields elaborations on different concepts and in diverse contexts. Textual authenticity as a concept (my taxonomy) is revisited via corpus linguistics. Authentic assessment is another aspect that remains under discussion in this decade. Both developments have been portrayed.

A third topic are the contrary concepts of real-world authenticity and classroom authenticity, which are once more the backdrop for deliberations on tasks-based language teaching (TBLT). Guariento/Morley (2001) propound arguably the most extensive definition of task authenticity merging the prevalent real-world approaches with Breen's (1985) authentic classroom proposals. The following two types of authenticity are presented as being equally important (Guariento/Morley 2001: 350):

Authenticity through real world targets

[…] [A] task might be said to be authentic if it has a clear relationship with real world needs

[…]

Authenticity through classroom interaction

[...] [I]t is important that the choice and sequence of tasks are negotiated, and it is this very process of negotiation which is authentic.

Breen (1985) is cited by Guariento/Morley so as to warrant the second type. Very few authors really draw on the concept of classroom authenticity that is introduced and strongly championed by Breen (1985). Guariento/Morley's (2001) article is influential receiving by far the most citations in the decade (16 citations).

A new context of authenticity is broached as Rost (2002) discusses the term in conjunction with listening activities:

As is now well established in pragmatics, the closer a participant is to the 'control centre' on an interaction, the more immediate the purpose for the interaction, and therefore the more authentic and meaningful the discourse. If we accept the notion of discourse control as leading to authenticity, then for purposes of language education, those inputs and encounters that involve the students' own purposes for listening can best be considered authentic. In this sense, any source of input and interaction that satisfies the learner's search for knowledge and allows the learner the ability to control that search is authentic. (Rost 2002: 165)

This statement is reminiscent of Widdowson's concept of authentication, though it is applied to listening, not reading. Rost refers to Widdowson asserting that "authenticity is relative; what's relative to one listener may not be relative to another (cf. Widdowson, 2007)" (Rost 2002: 165). It is therefore problematic that Rost (2002) is listed by Gilmore under category "(vi) the social situation of the classroom" (Gilmore 2007: 98) instead of "(iii) the qualities bestowed on a text by the receiver, in that it is not seen as something inherent in a text itself, but is imparted on it by the reader/listener" (ibid.). This divergence in interpretation is a result of the growing conceptual complexity and diversification. In general, however, the grouping of entire publications under single categories can hardly do justice to the complex discussions and considerations presented by the authors in the discourse.

Rost, beyond linking authenticity to listening activities, acknowledges a discursive pattern in stating that "['g]enuineness', 'realness', 'truthfulness', 'validity', 'reliability', 'undisputed credibility', and 'legitimacy' are just some of the concepts involved when we talk about authenticity" (Rost 2002: 165). The statement is indicative of a meta-discussion on authenticity, which continues in the years going forward. Authors increasingly comment on the fact that authenticity as a term conjures up manifold concepts and that this effect potentially influences the use of the term. An earlier example is found in Johnston (1999):

> The notion of 'authenticity' is commonly invoked in language learning, yet the field's understanding of its meaning is to a large extent purely intuitive. [...] Most language teaching professionals agree that it is desirable to aim for authenticity in the classroom [...]. (Johnston 1999: 60)

Such statements are meta-discursive but they are not considered discourse analytical as long as they occur rather unsystematically, as is the case in both instances above. Meta-discursiveness is not to be equated with descriptive style, which simply depicts what has been said about authenticity and which therefore marks the opposite of conceptual style (cf. chapter 4.3.1). Meta-discursiveness is in place when statements are made about the underpinnings and the formal/structural aspects of the discussion on authenticity as a term. Usually, such statements express notions that the term carries a positive connotation. Here are some examples to illustrate the influx of meta-discursiveness after the turn of the century:

> Authenticity stands for realness, credibility, warranty - the term is ethically connotated.[63] (Decke-Cornill 2004: 17)

> From any concordance for the words 'authentic' and 'authenticity', it will quickly emerge that authenticity is a positive attribute, collocating with desirable qualities such as purity, originality and quality, and valuable enough to earn credentials such as a certificate, a stamp, or a seal. (Mishan 2004: 219)

> Authenticity doesn't necessarily mean 'good', just as contrivance doesn't necessarily mean 'bad' [...] [T]erms such as 'authentic', 'genuine', 'real' or 'natural' and their opposites 'fake', 'unreal' or 'contrived' are emotionally loaded and indicate approval or disapproval whilst remaining ill-defined. (Gilmore 2007: 98)

> [D]iscourse promotes or proscribes language teaching ideas on the basis of ideological belief rather than pedagogical value. The debate about 'authenticity' vs. 'artificiality' in language teaching is a representative example of this tendency. (Waters 2009: 138)

> [W]e do think that the discourse related to authenticity is problematic. [...] [T]he concept of authenticity is used to justify more than it should [...]. (Badger/MacDonald 2010: 578-579)

---

63   Original: „Authentizität steht für Echtheit, Glaubwürdigkeit, Verbürgtheit – der Begriff ist ethisch konnotiert." (Decke-Cornill 2004: 17)

If a didactic design is authentic, the assumption goes, it is good. That authenticity supports language learning is often considered a given [...]. (Buendgens-Kosten 2013: 3)

Thaler (2007) facetiously establishes a top 10 of buzz words that are frequently used in the EFL discourse. *Authenticity*, which makes the list, is described as a principle worth striving for almost regardless of its meaning (Thaler 2007: 3).[64] What is new about such comments is that they address the terminological role of authenticity. Much earlier statements can be found which equally describe states of the discourse but which focus on conceptual aspects, not on terminological ones. Those statements are not considered meta-discursive in the sense described. Two examples:

> Over recent years we have witnessed an increasing concern on the part of the linguist with the communicative functioning of language. There is a feeling abroad that for a linguistic description to be adequate it must not reduce natural language to an algebraic system but should attempt to account for 'authentic' data, the language user's own experience of language in contexts of use. This movement towards an approximation to authenticity has its dangers: it can lead to a linguistics of anecdote, ad hoc observation, and a neglect of methodological principles upon which any systematic account must depend. (Widdowson 1976: 261)

> It is interesting to trace the elevation of 'authentic' materials to the level of what appears to be almost a categorical imperative, a moral 'sine qua non' of the language classroom. (Clarke 1989: 74)

Both authors use the term in italics, which hints at a certain awareness of terminological difficulties. Yet, meta-discursiveness refers to more explicit comments on the term itself. Similarly, the "fetish of authentic text" (Rück 1986) and the "cult of authenticity" (Day/Bamford 1998) describe the dogmatic adherence to a concept and do not so much refer to a terminological hype.

The 2000s is the decade of conceptual diversification: "The debate over the role of authenticity, as well as what it means to be authentic, has become increasingly sophisticated and complex over the years and now [i.e. in 2007] embraces research from a wide variety of fields" (Gilmore 2007: 97). This growing complexity prompts authors to offer synoptic accounts of the topic. Three of these have been presented as part of the systematic overview: Breen (1985), Decke-Cornill (2004), Gilmore (2007). Especially Gilmore is frequently cited by later authors. He, unlike Decke-Cornill, choses the form of a tabular representation, which is introduced with the words "[a]t least eight possible inter-related

---

64   Original: "Die Forderung nach Authentizität im Fremdsprachenunterricht ist eine dreifache. Zunächst müssen die Materialien konsequent authentisch sein, i.e. echt, mit dem Siegel des Ziellandes versehen, nicht didaktisiert eben. Dies bedeutet natürlich, dass ab dem 1. Lernjahr *Ulysses* von Joyce, aktuelle Wirtschaftsnachrichten und Fotogeschichten aus einschlägigen Herrenmagazinen eingesetzt werden. Dafür werden didaktisierte Texte, an der Progression orientierte Lehrbücher und grundsätzlich alle Krücken verbannt, die dem Schüler das Lernen erleichtern könnten. Sodann müssen Kommunikationssituation und Interaktionspartner authentisch sein, i.e. der Schüler mit seinen echten Bedürfnissen, privaten Interessen und spontanen Einfällen initiiert das Unterrichtsgespräch, und die Lehrkraft stellt unverfälscht ihre ehelichen Konflikte und privaten Obsessionen zur Diskussion." (Thaler 2007: 3)

meanings emerge from the literature. Authenticity relates to" (Gilmore 2007: 98). Gilmore uses the hedging device "possible" (ibid.) and remains cautious about a conclusive number of concepts ("[a]t least eight", ibid.) as well as clear-cut distinctions ("inter-related meanings", ibid.). Instead of providing definitions, it is merely stated what "[a]uthenticity relates to" (ibid.) eight different concepts. This strategic use of hedging is applied to preempt reader opposition due to controversial content. Interesting is the fact that so much authorial stance is employed within a purely descriptive passage where reader opposition is usually not to be expected. Apparently, statements on the topic of authenticity can be controversial even if they claim objectivity and descriptiveness. Thus, in Gilmore's case, the mere act of categorizing calls for a high degree of hedging. This discursive idiosyncrasy can be partly attributed to the positive qualities evoked by the term *authenticity*. The emergence of meta-discursive statements in the discourse indicates an increasing awareness of the problem.

Breen's (1985) synoptic account is of course much older than Decke-Cornill's (2004) and Gilmore's (2007). It is actually a small descriptive element in an otherwise strongly conceptual article. Breen lists four types of authenticity just to deconstruct them subsequently. Decke-Cornill's (2004) article is more descriptive but it also features conceptual statements. Gilmore's (2007) article is highly descriptive and even starts out with discourse analytical elements. It then becomes slightly more conceptual as it weighs various positions on the use of authentic materials, while terminological issues are no longer discussed. An extremely high number of references characterizes the work throughout, which is typical of descriptive style. The bulk of the article is actually a literature review.

The terminological question of authenticity is abandoned early on. Gilmore does not provide a conclusive definition. This absence of a new definition or concept is one of the main differences between Gilmore (2007) and Breen (1985). This non-committal approach comes at a time when various conceptual innovations have been attached to the term *authentic/authenticity*.

Gilmore's listing of eight concepts, which are each linked to publications, suggests that those publications are conceptual in style and committed to one specific concept. I have been critical of this simplistic attribution. Nevertheless, Gilmore's method shows that, up to that point in time, the bulk of publications have displayed affinities to certain concepts instead of describing the discourse. Obviously, Gilmore's (2007) article itself would be impossible to categorize in such a manner, as would Decke-Cornill's (2004).

Gilmore's categorization of publications may have an interesting effect within the discourse. It can be likened to the canonizing effect of the compilation provided by Hedge/Andon/Dewey (eds. 2009) in the same decade. What Gilmore's (2007) method suggests is that only those publications referenced within the list are considered noteworthy. This is significant given how widely received Gilmore's (2007) article is in the discourse. No publication is cited more often after 2007 (15 citations received).

The texts referenced by Gilmore are:[65]

Widdowson, Henry G. (1976). The authenticity of language data. In: Fanselow/Crymes (eds.), 261-270.

Morrow, Keith (1977). Authentic texts and ESP. In: Holden (ed.), 13-15.

Widdowson, Henry G. (1978). *Teaching language as communication.* Oxford: Oxford University Press.

Porter, Don; Roberts, Jon (1981). Authentic listening activities. *ELT Journal,* 36(1), 37-47.

Swaffar, Janet K. (1985). Reading authentic texts in a foreign language: A cognitive model. *Modern Language Journal* (69.1), 15-34.

Breen, Michael P. (1985). Authenticity in the language classroom. *Applied Linguistics,* 6(1), 60-70.

Little, David; Devitt, Seán M.; Singleton, David M. (1989). *Learning foreign languages from authentic texts.* Dublin: Authentik.[66]

Nunan, David (1988a). *Syllabus design.* Oxford: Oxford University Press.

Nunan, David (1989). *Designing tasks for the communicative classroom.* Cambridge, New York: Cambridge University Press.

Arnold, Ewen (1991). Authenticity revisited: How real is real? *English for Specific Purposes,* 10, 237-244.

Bachman, Lyle F. (1991). What does language testing have to offer. *TESOL Quarterly* 25 (4), 671-704.

Kramsch, Claire J. (1993). *Context and culture in language teaching.* Oxford: Oxford University Press.

Lee, Winnie Yuk-chun (1995). Authenticity revisited: text authenticity and learner authenticity. *ELT Journal,* 49(4), 323-328.

Bachman, Lyle F.; Palmer, Adrian S. (1996). *Language testing in practice. Designing and developing useful language tests.* Oxford, New York: Oxford University Press.

van Lier, Leo (1996). *Interaction in the language curriculum. Awareness, autonomy and authenticity.* New York: Longman.

---

65   Inaccuracies on Gilmore's part have been changed: Widdowson (1979) is a reprint of Widdowson (1976). Kramsch (1998), as Gilmore cites it, is not in his bibliography, but must be Kramsch (1993). Benson/Voller (1997), as Gilmore cites it, is an edited volume which contains only one contribution that discusses authenticity: Little (1997).

66   This title is a reprint of the book *Authentic texts in foreign language teaching* (Little/Devitt/Singleton 1988).

Little, David (1997). Responding authentically to authentic texts: a problem for self-access language learning? In: Benson/Voller (eds.), 225-236.

Lewkowicz, Jo A. (2000). Authenticity in language testing: some outstanding questions. *Language Testing,* 17(1), 43-64.

Guariento, William; Morley, John (2001). Text and task authenticity in the EFL classroom. *ELT Journal,* 55(4), 347-353.

Rost, Michael (2002). *Teaching and researching listening.* Harlow, New York: Longman/Pearson.

For comparison, these are the texts compiled in Hedge/Andon/Dewey (eds. 2009):

Widdowson, Henry G. (1976). The authenticity of language data. In: Fanselow/Crymes (eds.), 261-270.

Morrow, Keith (1977). Authentic texts and ESP. In: Holden (ed.), 13-15.

Davies, Alan (1984). Simple, simplified and simplification. What is authentic? In: Alderson, J. C.; Urquhart, A. H.: Reading in a Foreign Language, 181-195.

Breen, Michael P. (1985). Authenticity in the language classroom. *Applied Linguistics,* 6(1), 60-70.

Simensen, Aud Marit (1988). Adapted readers. *Reading in a Foreign Language,* 4(1), 41-57.

Clarke, David F. (1989). Communicative theory and its influence on materials production. *Language Teaching,* 22(2), 73-86.

Day, Richard; Bamford, Julian (1998). The cult of authenticity and the myth of simplification. (Originally a chapter from the book Day, Richard; Bamford, Julian (1998). *Extensive reading in the second language classroom.* Cambridge University Press.)

Three texts from Gilmore (2007) are also featured in Hedge/Andon/Dewey (eds. 2009): Widdowson (1976), Morrow (1977), Breen (1985). These three are indeed essential to the discourse on authenticity. Gilmore (2007) and Hedge/Andon/Dewey (eds. 2009) may be viewed by recipients as literary canons on authenticity – irrespective of the authors' intentions.

One synoptic account during the 2000s, which has not yet been mentioned, is given in MacDonald/Badger/Dasli (2006):

> Four types of authenticity have been proposed within the literature of applied linguistics: text authenticity (e.g. Guariento & Morley, 2001), competence authenticity (e.g. Canale & Swain, 1980), learner authenticity (Widdowson, 1979), and classroom authenticity (Breen, 1985; Taylor, 1994). We argue that this typology reflects the binary conceptualisation of the term: the first three types are derived from an authenticity of correspondence; the last is derived from an authenticity of genesis. (MacDonald/Badger/Dasli 2006: 251)

Note that this is the only account where the authors explicitly speak of a *typology*. All four types of authenticity are laid out in short subchapters of half a page respectively. While text authenticity, learner authenticity, and classroom authenticity are common concepts, competence authenticity is a surprising addition. The corresponding description fails to link Canale's and Swain's (1980) model of language competence to authenticity in a convincing manner. The only sentence in MacDonald/Badger/Dasli (2006) to contain the term – in this case *to authenticate* – is one that has little to do with authenticity: "What 'authenticates' a learner's ability to communicate in another language is derived from its correspondence to interactions which take place between idealised native speakers or between native speakers and non-native speakers" (MacDonald/Badger/Dasli 2006: 252). Canale/Swain (1980) use the term *authentic/authenticity* but do not negotiate it explicitly or use it in combination with *competence*. The compound *competence authenticity* is created by MacDonald/Badger/Dasli (2006) and remains slightly vague as a concept.

The typology is another indication that synopses of authenticity are deemed necessary to react to the diversification of concepts. It has been mentioned that the mere act of categorizing requires authorial stance. In the vibrant discourse on authenticity, a categorization or typology amounts to a bold claim. Referencing is one means of authorial stance apt to strengthen a claim:

> [A]ppropriate textual practices are crucial to the acceptance of claims. Explicit reference to prior literature is a substantial indication of a text's dependence on contextual knowledge and thus a vital piece in the collaborative construction of new knowledge between writers and readers. The embedding of arguments in networks of references not only suggests an appropriate disciplinary orientation, but reminds us that statements are invariably a response to previous statements and are themselves available for further statements by others. (Hyland 2000: 21)

In the cases of MacDonald/Badger/Dasli (2006) and Gilmore (2007) whole publications are referenced suggesting an implicit literary canon, although this effect is likely unintentional.

The synoptic account by Decke-Cornill (2004), which is detailed in chapter 2.1, lacks the discursive reach of other publications probably for the reason of being written in German. In this chapter, it serves as further evidence for the emergence of descriptiveness and meta-discursiveness in the EFL discourse on authenticity. The following publications of the 2000s are symptomatic of this development:

- Decke-Cornill (2004)
- MacDonald/Badger/Dasli (2006)
- Gilmore (2007)
- Hedge/Andon/Dewey (eds. 2009)

Hedge/Andon/Dewey (eds. 2009) is a text compilation under the heading *Authenticity and simplification in learning materials*. The context being limited to materials means that no claim is laid to a full conceptual coverage of authenticity.

Three disciplinary encyclopedias come out during the 2000s:

Byram, Michael et al. (ed.) (2000). *Routledge encyclopedia of language teaching and learning*. London, New York: Routledge.

Davies, Alan (2005). *A glossary of applied linguistics*. Edinburgh: Edinburgh University Press.

Thornbury, Scott (2006). *An A-Z of ELT*. Oxford: Macmillan Education.

All three of these contain an entry for *authenticity*, which points to the solidified status of authenticity as a term. The encyclopedias differ, however, greatly in various respects. Byram et al. (2000) is by far the most voluminous of them and its entries are contributed by a large number of authors. The entry for *authenticity* is written by Shelagh Rixon. It is two pages long and features a short bibliography of five titles, two of which are Widdowson (1978) and Breen (1985). The entry offers an elaborate description of the different concepts as well as a brief insight into the discourse on authenticity. Davies (2005) and Thornbury (2006) are published in single authorship. Davies's entry for *authenticity* is unconventional. It is short enough to be quoted here in full length:

> Authenticity
>
> A somewhat heretical requirement (in the 1970s and 1980s) for language teaching materials that became associated with communicative competence developments. The idea seems to have been that for the best results, learners need to be placed in as naturalistic an environment as possible. The rationale, which was rarely made explicit, was that the best language learning takes place among young children learning their L2, and therefore what second language teaching should do is, as far as possible, to replicate that environment. The deliberate pursuit of authenticity contained its own failure, since by definition authenticity must be non-deliberate. No doubt informal SLL could use authenticity, but only if it remained informal and therefore beyond the reaches of planning and organising. (Davies 2005: 12)

In terms of authorial style the entry is highly conceptual, which is uncharacteristic of encyclopedias. The entry divulges its author's positioning within a controversial debate. Arguments are put forth to support a certain perspective instead of laying out various viewpoints and concepts in a descriptive manner. Other entries in Davies (2005) are entirely descriptive corresponding to the tacit set of stylistic rules that is in place for the encyclopedic text genre. The stylistic anomaly in Davies (2005) is likely owed to the discursive characteristics which make the discourse on authenticity such a dynamic one, as detailed in chapter 4.3.3: Firstly, the term is a floating signifier. Secondly, one or more of the term's possible denotations are subject to controversy as regards their value for language learning. These aspects seem so powerful that they can override stylistic convention as is the case in Davies (2005).

Thornbury (2006), in his entry for *authenticity*, pursues the conventional descriptive approach. The entry covers different concepts but remains less scrupulous than Byram et al. (2000).

5.2.4.2 Conclusion

The years 2000 to 2009, as mentioned, bring about an increased diversification of concepts denoted as *authentic*. Some authors in the discourse react to this development by providing synoptic accounts of the different concepts. Most of these, but not all, are written in a descriptive rather than in a conceptual style. The referencing of whole publications when describing a concept may – accidentally or intentionally – have a canonizing effect because it creates the impression that a given publication is pivotal in developing a concept while others remain unmentioned. Such techniques are used by MacDonald/Badger/Dasli (2006) and Gilmore (2007). Another potential canon is created by Hedge/Andon/Dewey (eds. 2009) who republish seminal texts of EFL. Their section *Authenticity and simplification in learning materials* does not notionally apply to all concepts of authenticity. It consists of seven articles, which is quite selective.

The diversification of concepts yields not only literature reviews and synopses in descriptive authorial style. It also prompts authors to deliberate on potential causes. Such thoughts commonly allude to connotational factors playing a role. In this study, comments on the connotation of the term *authentic/authenticity* are referred to as *meta-discursiveness*. The comments are mostly short and make assumptions about what authenticity as a term conjures up. By using meta-discursiveness authors display a certain degree of awareness of connotation and its possible effects. The goal of meta-discursiveness is to inform but it may also invest the author with credibility and an air of impartiality.

Synopsis, descriptiveness, and meta-discursiveness show a tendency to co-occur during the 2000s, e.g. in Gilmore (2007) or in Waters (2007). They are each part of a new development, which may be seen as a reaction to the conceptual diversification. Incidentally, the diversification is not a new or sudden emergence. It accompanies the discourse throughout its chronology. Nonetheless, with the growth of the literary body at large, the diversification reaches new heights during the 1990s and 2000s.

The second most important development of the decade is the influence that corpus linguistics exerts on the discourse. The technological advancements of the past decades have created possibilities to amass text in form of corpora which are then analyzable with the help of electronic search tools. Provided that the texts contained in a corpus meet the criteria of textual authenticity, the technology offers potentially authentic applications for EFL purposes. Some authors see authentic text corpora as a means to achieve objective criteria of textual authenticity through concordancing. New insights into frequency and idiomaticity are apt to inform textbook design. Learners may also benefit more directly, if concordancing becomes a classroom activity, as is proposed by advocates of data-driven learning (DDL), e.g. Mishan (2004). Corpus linguistics and authenticity become so intertwined that even corpora of learner language, which are naturally marked by a high number of errors, are considered authentic merely on the grounds that they reflect real language use. Widdowson, who is the most prolific contributor to the discourse, speaks out against the use of corpora in EFL (2000; 2003).

In the meantime, the term *authenticity* is featured in all three disciplinary encyclopedias that appear during the decade. The presence of the term underscores its status as an established *terminus technicus* in applied linguistics and EFL. The entry for *authenticity* in Davies (2005) strays from the stylistic conventions for encyclopedias. It appears that the term is so controversial that, even in an encyclopedia, it is commented on in a highly conceptual and argumentative manner by the author.

5.2.5 The 2010s – a new trend?

From 2010 to 2014, it is slightly more difficult to identify discursive trends because the time period is relatively short and no insights are gained as to which of the publications are – or rather will be – widely received in the discourse. It appears that one specific development, that began around the turn of the century, continues. Also, the general pattern of conceptual diversification persists. This pattern is as old as the discourse itself. These are the texts on authenticity published between 2010 and 2014:

Number of citations received	Publication	Citations made	Type of publication
0	Badger, Richard; MacDonald, Malcolm N. (2010). Making it real: Authenticity, process and pedagogy. *Applied Linguistics,* 31(4), 578-582.	Badger (2006), Breen (1985), Gilmore (2007), Roberts (2009), Widdowson (1976)	Article in journal
1	Dantas-Whitney, Maria; Rilling, Sarah (2010). *Authenticity in the language classroom and beyond: children and adolescent learners.* Alexandria, VA: TESOL.		Book
0	Leitzke-Ungerer, Eva (2010). Authentizität. In: Surkamp, Carola (ed.). *Metzler-Lexikon Fremdsprachendidaktik.* Stuttgart; Weimar: Metzler, 10-11.	Gilmore (2007), Widdowson (1978)	Entry in encyclopedia
0	Mishan, Freda (2010). Task and task authenticity: Paradigms for language learning in the digital era. In: Mishan, Freda; Chambers, Angela (eds.). *Perspectives on language learning materials development.* Oxford; New York: Peter Lang, 149-172.	Davies (1984), Gilmore (2007), Guariento/Morley (2001), Mishan (2005), Nunan (1989, 2004), van Lier (1996), Widdowson (1978; 1998)	Article in edited volume
0	Trabelsi, Soufiane (2010). Developing and trialling authentic materials for business English students at a Tunisian university. In: Tomlinson, Brian; Masuhara, Hitomi (eds.). *Research for materials development in language learning.* London: Continuum, 103-120.	Bachman (1990), Bacon/Finneman (1990), Breen (1985), Kramsch (1993), Kramsch/A'Ness/Lam (2000), Little/Devitt/Singleton (1988), Mishan (2005), Swaffar (1985)	Article in edited volume
0	Nikitina, Larisa (2011). Creating an authentic learning environment in the foreign language classroom. *International Journal of Instruction,* 4(1), 33-46.	None	Article in journal

0	Joy, John L. (2011). The duality of authenticity in ELT. *Journal of Language and Linguistic Studies,* 7(2), 7-23.	Arnold (1991), Breen (1985), Chavez (1998), Davies (1984), Guariento/Morley (2001), Kim (2000), Lee (1995), Little/Devitt/Singleton (1988), Mishan (2004), Morrow (1977), Nunan (1989), Rogers/Medley (1988), Taylor (1994), Thornbury (2006), van Lier (1996), Widdowson (1976; 1978)	Article in journal
1	Khalili Sabet, Masoud (2012). The impact of authentic listening materials on elementary EFL learners' listening skills. *IJALEL* 1 (4), 216-229.	Adams (1995), Bacon/Finnemann (1990), Berardo (2006), Breen (1985), Chavez (1998), Gilmore (2004), Guariento/Morley (2001), Herron/Seay (1991), Kilickaya (2004), Kim (2000), Lee (1995), McNeill (1994), Mishan (2005), Morton (1999), Peacock (1997), Rings (1986), Rogers/Medley (1988), Rost (2002), Widdowson (1978; 1996)	Article in journal
1	Kramsch, Claire (2012). Authenticity and legitimacy in multilingual SLA. *Critical Multilingualism Studies* 1 (1), 107-128.	Widdowson (1994)	Article in journal
0	Henry, Alastair (2013). Digital games and ELT: Bridging the authenticity gap. In: Ushioda, Ema (ed.). *International perspectives on motivation.* Basingstoke, Hampshire: Palgrave Macmillan, 133-155.	Gilmore (2007)	Article in edited volume
1	Buendgens-Kosten, Judith (2013). Authenticity in CALL: three domains of 'realness'. *ReCALL,* 25(02), 1-14.	Breen (1985), Edelhoff (1985), Mishan (2005), Widdowson (1998a)	Article in journal
0	Chan, Jim Yee Him (2013). The role of situational authenticity in English language textbooks. *RELC Journal* 44 (3), 303-317.	Gilmore (2004), Guariento/Morley (2001)	Article in journal
0	Liddicoat, Anthony; Scarino, Angela (2013). *Intercultural language teaching and learning.* Chichester, West Sussex, UK; Malden, MA: Wiley-Blackwell.	Alptekin (2002), Arnold (1991), Widdowson (1978)	Book

0	McKay, Sandra (2013). Authenticity in the language teaching curriculum. In: Chapelle, Carol (ed.). *The encyclopedia of applied linguistics*. Oxford: Blackwell, 299-302.	Dantas-Whitney/Rilling/Savova (2009), Dantas-Whitney/Rilling (2010), Day (2003), Mishan (2005), Nunan (1989), Roberts/Cooke (2009), Widdowson (1998), Wilkins (1976)	Entry in encyclopedia
1	Pinner, Richard (2013a). Authenticity and CLIL: Examining authenticity from an international CLIL perspective. *International CLIL Research Journal* 2 (1), 44-45.	Gilmore (2007), Little/Devitt/Singleton (1988), Morrow (1977), Peacock (1997), Widdowson (1990)	Article in journal
1	Pinner, Richard (2013b). Authenticity of purpose: CLIL as a way to bring meaning and motivation into EFL contexts. *Asian EFL Journal* 15 (4), 138-159.	Bachman/Palmer (1996), Gilmore (2007), Morrow (1977), Peacock (1997), van Lier (1996), Widdowson (1990)	Article in journal
0	Barekat, Behzad; Nobakhti, Hamed (2014). The effect of authentic and inauthentic materials in cultural awareness training on EFL learners' listening comprehension ability. *TPLS* 4(5), 1058-1065.	Guariento/Morley (2001), Rogers/Medley (1988), Rost (2002)	Article in journal
0	Buendgens-Kosten, Judith (2014). Key concepts in ELT. Authenticity. *ELT Journal,* 68(4), 457-459.	Alptekin (2002), Breen (1985), Buendgens-Kosten (2013), Edelhoff (1985), Mishan (2005), Gilmore (2004), Gilmore (2007), Lee (1995), Tan (2005), Widdowson (1976; 1978)	Article in journal
0	Clavel-Arroitia, Begona; Fuster-Marquez, Miguel (2014). The authenticity of real texts in advanced English language textbooks. *ELT Journal,* 68(2), 124-134.	Guariento/Morley (2001), Gilmore (2004), Hutchinson/Waters (1987), Little/Devitt/Singleton (1988), Tamo (2009), Widdowson (1978; 1998b; 2000)	Article in journal
0	Al Azri, Rahid Hamed; Al-Rashdi, Majid Hilal (2014). The effect of using authentic materials in teaching. *International journal of scientific and technology research,* 3(10), 249-254.	Bacon/Finneman (1990), Baniabdelrahman (2006), Berardo (2006), Breen (1985), Gilmore (2007), Guariento/Morley (2001), Kienbaum/Russell/Welty (1986), Kilickaya (2004), Kim (2000), Lee (1995), Little/Devitt/Singleton (1988), MacDonald/Badger/Dasli (2006),	Article in journal

		McNeill (1994), Mishan (2005), Nunan (1988b), Peacock (1997), Rost (2002), Tatsuki (2006), Taylor (1994), Widdowson (1990; 1996)	
0	Siegel, Aki (2014). What should we talk about? The authenticity of textbook topics. *ELT Journal*, 68(4), 363-375.	Gilmore (2004), Widdowson (1990)	Article in journal
0	Pinner, Richard (2014). The authenticity continuum: Towards a definition incorporating international voices. *English Today*, 30(04), 22-27.	Gilmore (2007), Morrow (1977), Peacock (1997), Pinner (2013a), Pinner (2013b), Tan (2005), van Lier (1996), Widdowson (1978; 1990; 1996)	Article in journal
0	Creese, Angela; Blackledge, Adrian; Takhi, Jaspreet Kaur (2014). The ideal 'native speaker' teacher: Negotiating authenticity and legitimacy in the language classroom. *Modern Language Journal*, 98(4), 937-951.	Kramsch (1998; 2012)	Article in journal
0	Zhafarghandi, Amir Mahdavi; Barekat, Behzad; Homaei, Sepideh (2014). A survey of Iranian EFL teachers' and learners' perceptions toward authentic listening materials at university level. *Advances in Language and Literary Studies* 5 (4), 184-197.	Adams (1995), Bacon/Finnemann (1990), MacDonald/Badger/White (2000), Berardo (2006), Breen (1985), Chavez (1998), Clarke (1989), Gilmore (2004), Guariento/Morley (2001), Herron/Seay (1991), Khalili Sabet (2012), Kilickaya (2004), Kienbaum/Russell/Welty (1986), Kim (2000), Lee (1995), McNeill (1994), Nostrand (1989), Nunan (1989), Peacock (1997), Rings (1986), Rost (2002), Taylor (1994), Widdowson (1976; 1978; 1990; 1996; 1998a), Young (1993)	Article in journal

Figure 14: A new trend?

At first glance, the number of texts seems remarkable – 24 in only five years, when the previous decades produced 33, 31, 35 (in chronological order). However, a boom cannot be inferred from these numbers. Meara observes a much greater growth in output for the subject of vocabulary acquisition in EFL:

> Readers who have been working in this field for some time will realize that there has been a huge growth in output over the last 20 years. When I first started working on vocabulary

acquisition back in the 1970s, there were perhaps half a dozen relevant papers published each year. Now, a single year's publications amounts to nearer 120 papers – a twenty-fold increase in outputs – and many more people are involved with this work. (Meara 2012: 7-8)

A twenty-fold increase is not to be ascribed to a single cause. Beside the increasing popularity of the subject (vocabulary), the growth of the EFL body of literature at large must be taken into consideration. The EFL discourse on authenticity should be regarded in the same context. If anything, the seemingly consistent output numbers of the 1980s (33), the 1990s (31), and the 2000s (35) must be interpreted as a gradual decline in interest. The uptick as of 2010 is likely more of a stabilization than a veritable boom.

The following analysis sheds light on the latest developments in the discourse. Towards the end, questions are raised on whether a new trend is discernible.

5.2.5.1 Detailed analysis

A considerable number of publications conduct scrupulous literature reviews on the subject of authenticity. Trabelsi (2010) traces the term etymologically and consults dictionaries for general definitions before giving an overview of the existing literature in the discourse. He cites Bachman (1990) thereby invoking considerations from the context of authentic assessment. Badger/MacDonald (2010) display meta-discursive awareness as they reference and discuss an interesting article by Alan Waters: *Ideology in applied linguistics for language teaching* (2009). Waters' article is presented shortly. To give a textual example of meta-discursiveness in Badger/MacDonald: "[W]e do think that the discourse related to authenticity is problematic. [...] [T]he concept of authenticity is used to justify more than it should" (Badger/MacDonald 2010: 578-579). Waters (2009) is among the most discourse analytical texts on authenticity. He analyzes the role of authenticity as an ideological concept. The publication is mentioned in this chapter, although it is published in 2009. It epitomizes the growing meta-discursive awareness in the discourse, a development that got under way approximately at the turn of the century and remains robust until the end of this chronology.

The increase in literature reviews of authenticity accompanies the emergence of meta-discursiveness. Knowledge of the existing literature often leads to the insight that the term is used differently by different authors, which is then discussed. Another instance of rigorous literature review is found in Khalili Sabet (2012). He limits his review to textual authenticity and recognizes that even this seemingly straight-forward concept is controversially debated in the discourse. Khalili Sabet does not comment on the controversy itself but proceeds to speak about how authentic listening materials can be used (Khalili Sabet 2012: 218-220). Thus, he does not engage in meta-discursiveness as I conceive of it. Mishan (2010) features a literature review comparable to Khalili Sabet's (2012), though hers is confined to authenticity in the context of tasks (Mishan 2010: 151-152). Buendgens-Kosten (2013) focuses on CALL (computer-assisted language learning) in her literature review chapters "Use of 'authenticity' in contemporary research literature" and the "Notion of authenticity" (Buendgens-Kosten 2013: 273-274). In Buendgens-Kosten's article meta-discursiveness is found: "If a didactic design is authentic, the assumption goes, it is good. That authenticity supports language learning is often considered a given […]" (Buendgens-Kosten 2013: 274).

Similar patterns of literature review and/or meta-discursiveness are present in Joy (2011), Al Azri/Al-Rashdi (2014), Clavel-Arroitia/Fuster-Marquez (2014), Pinner (2014), Zhafarghandi/Barekat/Homaei (2014). What the literature reviews have in common is that they are structured around authenticity. Some focus on a certain concept or domain, e.g. textual authenticity in Khalili Sabet (2012) or tasks in Mishan (2010). By and large, however, authenticity appears to be increasingly perceived as a thematic sub-field of EFL by the authors in the discourse. A bibliometric feature resulting from the heightened rigor in literature reviews is that a higher number of references is made within the discourse. In the post-2000 period, as many as 12 publications cite ten or more works from the discourse. Half of these are from 2010 or later. Only one earlier publication (Weller 1992) contains this many references. Obviously, the number of works to draw on increases over time. Still, the vast disparity between the pre- and post-2000 period is considered indicative here. Furthermore, some extreme examples from the later period show that the term *authentic* was likely used as a search word and basically all hits were referenced: Al Azri/Al-Rashdi (2014) – 21 citations within the discourse; Zhafarghandi/Barekat/Homaei (2014) – 28 citations within the discourse. Both these publications cite many more articles which carry *authentic* in the title. Those publications are not included in the document selection either because they do not negotiate the term explicitly or because they come from online blogs and similar sources where the peer review processes are obscure.

While such extreme examples of referencing emerge as of 2010, there remain instances when no connection is made to the existing literature on authenticity. Nikitina, who links authenticity to drama techniques in the EFL classroom, refers to none of the authors in the discourse when writing:

> In the context of foreign language pedagogy, the need for authenticity is well recognized. The dominant approach to language teaching – the communicative method – demands that the use of 'real life' language is promoted in the classroom. In order for the real world language to emerge there is a need to create authentic learning situations. (Nikitina 2011: 34)

This understanding of authenticity clearly falls into the category of real-world authenticity (cf. taxonomy in chapter 3). It appears that descriptions of authenticity, which are scarcely or not at all linked to the discourse by means of citation, veer toward real-world authenticity. This is typically the case with texts on authentic assessment: Seliger et al. (1985), Bachman (1990), O'Malley/Pierce (1996), Kohonen (1999), Farrell (2009), Brown (2004). It may be assumed that the concept of real-world authenticity is more intuitive than other concepts of authenticity. It may tally with the colloquial understanding of the word.

The observation that authenticity is increasingly perceived as a thematic field within EFL is buttressed by the fact that it appears in the series *Key concepts in ELT* that is featured irregularly in the issues of *ELTJ* (*English Language Teaching Journal*). The article *Key concepts in ELT: Authenticity* is written by Buendgens-Kosten (2014). The series differs from entries in EFL dictionaries in that the focus is conceptual rather than terminological. Unlike headwords in an EFL dictionary, the key concepts may have less concise titles such as *Task repetition in ELT* (ELT Journal 66:3) or *Age and the critical period hypothesis* (ELT Journal 63:2). Still, the texts are written in descriptive style and thereby resemble the entries in EFL dictionaries. Two of the latter appear between 2010 and 2014: *Metzler-Lexikon Fremdsprachendidaktik* (2010 – Stuttgart: Metzler) and *The encyclopedia of applied linguistics* (2013 – Oxford: Blackwell). Leitzke-Ungerer's entry *Authentizität* in the Metzler dictionary (2010) is informed and concise. It is written in descriptive style. The Blackwell dictionary (2013) is a multi-volume encyclopedia, the extensiveness of which is unprecedented. Its entries are more like journal articles not only in size but – as in the case of authenticity – also in style. McKay, who writes the entry (or article) *Authenticity in the language teaching curriculum*, provides definitions of textual authenticity before segueing into passages that feature strong conceptual style (cf. chapter 4.3.1):

> What is needed in classrooms is practice in interactional encounters in which the learners discuss topics that matter to them in their daily lives. This is the kind of **authentic voice** that a classroom, with carefully chosen topics and tasks, can engender. […]

> Authenticity in the language classroom, then, has less to do with matching the classroom with the 'real' world and more to do with making the classroom a community of learners where students are given the opportunity to interact with a text or with others in the classroom 'about matters of importance to them'. (McKay 2013: 301) (emphasis added by L.W.)

The term *authentic voice* is actually a new coinage that is used frequently by McKay without referencing. The entry (or article) is introduced by an abstract, which is equally uncharacteristic of encyclopedias especially since it features self-mention – a discursive means of authorial stance (Hyland 2005: 181) (cf. chapter 4.2.1):

> In closing **I question** the current devotion to authenticity as it is presently defined and offer an alternative view of authenticity, one that characterizes the classroom as a community of learners in which students interact with texts and peers about topics/concerns that are important to them. (McKay 2013: 299) (emphasis added by L.W.)

The fact that McKay (2013) is nominally part of an encyclopedia is misleading, yet the clear advocacy of a concept makes the text an interesting contribution to the discourse. McKay is one of the very few authors who support the concept I refer to as *authenticity of individual behavior* in the taxonomy presented in chapter 3. Catering to the learners' interests when selecting topics for communication is in line with this learner-oriented concept. McKay is not the only author to assume this approach. Siegel applies the same rationale to textbook topics:

> Furthermore, the discussion on textbook authenticity has focused on language 'per se' and has overlooked the authenticity of topics, what people actually talk about in their daily lives. In particular, little is known about which topics L2 users typically converse about in the L2. (Siegel 2014: 365)

Authenticity of individual behavior, as I define it, is not achieved unless the learners' interests are really met. Choosing textbook topics based on assumed learner preferences is difficult in this regard because assumptions are made by the textbook designers instead of leaving the choice to the learners. After all, Breen (1985) assumes that the most authentic topic for learners to discuss in class is not one originating from the so-called real world but is the very question of how to learn a language:

> [...] [A] language classroom [...] is essentially a social environment wherein people come to communicate for and about new knowledge. Therefore, perhaps the most socially appropriate and authentic role of the classroom situation is to provide the opportunity for 'public' and 'interpersonal' sharing of the content of language learning, the sharing of problems within such content, and the revealing of the most effective means and strategies to overcome such problems. (Breen 1985: 67)

Interestingly, Pinner (2013b) describes authenticity as the exact opposite of what Breen (1985) suggests: "To put it simply, authentic language is language where something other than language for its own sake is being discussed" (Pinner 2013: 151). Pinner proposes an "authenticity of purpose" (title of the publication) which he considers to be best attained in classes of content and language-integrated learning (CLIL). He argues in the same vein as McKay (2013) and Siegel (2014) asserting that "there is a greater need in language teaching for the content to have a focused topic which is authentic and relevant to the students" (Pinner 2013: 144). "This increased authenticity is hypothesised to lead to an increase in engagement and motivation in the learning" (Pinner 2013: 138).

As explained in chapters 2.4 and 3.5, authenticity of individual behavior is an almost elusive concept. The concept can veer between real-world authenticity (e.g. Siegel 2014) and classroom authenticity (e.g. Breen 1985) based on what is assumed to best engage the learner. The elusiveness is highlighted by the different approaches taken by different authors trying to choose topics that appeal to the learners. Nevertheless, to conceive of authenticity in this purely learner-oriented manner reveals an understanding of the term that has not surfaced for a longer period in the discourse and is now displayed by various authors (McKay 2013; Pinner 2013b; Siegel 2014). The one author who pursues authenticity of individual behavior most rigorously is actually Henry (2013) who refers to authenticity as a psychological concept:

> [...] [A]uthenticity is the experience of being true to one's self in doing something that fits with who we feel we are, and which coheres with our own particular view of the world. In this sense experiences of authenticity are linked to other emotions and sensations, such as pleasure, satisfaction, contentedness and self-esteem. And, just as with other affective dimensions of motivation, we will be encouraged to do something if we believe that the activity is authentic and involves things that cohere or are congruent with our sense of self (Henry 2013: 141)

Henry proceeds to elaborate on the implications which this understanding of authenticity has for the EFL classroom:

> [...] [B]ecause as individuals we orient towards activities that provide us with feeling of self-congruence and authenticity [...] teachers need to provide students with greater opportunities for creativity and meaningful self-expression. (Henry 2013: 151)

Authenticity of individual behavior appears to emerge as a central concept. The four authors who advocate the concept (Henry 2013; McKay 2013; Pinner 2013b; Siegel 2014) do not really have a common point of reference, although both Henry and Pinner refer to theories of motivation by Zoltán Dörnyei. What is more, the four publications are almost coeval so they do not cite one another. Given that all four carry the term *authentic/authenticity* prominently in their respective titles, it will be interesting to see whether a conceptual impact will be felt in the future discourse.

Conceptually, the time between 2010 and 2014 yields descriptions and commentaries that touch on all existing concepts. As for textual authenticity, an interesting development can be observed. Two authors in the discourse, Trabelsi (2010) and Kramsch (2012), challenge the notion that authentic text must be produced by a native speaker. Current societal phenomena such as globalization and the rise of the Internet are the driving forces behind a redefinition of authenticity:

> According to the classical view, authenticity is considered a property of the NS [...]. Today, especially with the Internet, the authenticity wheel has in a sense come full circle, from cherishing the prerogative of the NA as sole 'producer' of authentic texts [...] to conflating authenticity with 'authorship' [...], which is the right of any Internet user regardless of his/her native language (i.e. whether he/she is NS or NNS). (Trabelsi 2010: 116)

> If authenticity means 'with a recognizable origin,' then the monolingual NS was that origin. If legitimacy means 'authorized by a recognizable authority,' then the monolingual NS was that authority. Globalization is reshuffling the cards. Now that not monolingualism, but multilingualism is slowly becoming the coin of the global realm, authenticity and legitimacy become an issue. (Kramsch 2012: 115)

Many definitions of textual authenticity omit the native-speaker element, as is detailed in chapter 2.2.2. The earliest example of such a definition is put forth by Morrow. In his account, the communicative intent is emphasized:

> An 'authentic text' is a stretch of real language, produced by a real speaker or writer for a real audience and designed to convey a real message of some sort. In other words it is 'not' a made-up text produced by an imaginary speaker or writer for an imaginary audience and designed to practise specific language points rather than to convey real information. (Morrow 1977: 13)

However, such definitions beg the question whether the omission is made on purpose. Morrow (ibid.) may as well consider it a given that authentic text is produced only by a native speaker. Trabelsi (2010) and Kramsch (2012) are the first to be explicit about the possibility of authentic text being produced by non-native speakers. Their line of argumentation, which invokes global developments, entails that the definition applies to English exclusively, as Trabelsi reasons: "[U]p to 80 per cent of communication in English takes place between NNS. In summary, the new approach of authenticity implies a kind of 'linguistic equality' between NS and NNS" (Trabelsi 2010: 116). It is a therefore a novelty that a definition of textual authenticity does not necessarily extend to languages other than English. The applicability of the definitions to other languages may be compromised. At the same time, the definitions are more open and inclusive by explicitly incorporating text produced by non-native speakers.

The inclusive definition of textual authenticity is contradicted by Liddicoat/Scarino: "Most importantly, [authentic materials] are produced within the cultural context of native speakers and are imbued with the assumptions, values, and ways of communicating of that culture" (Liddicoat/Scarino 2013: 95). The native speaker element is thus described as a central asset of authentic materials. However, the statement by Liddicoat/Scarino is not really a definition of textual authenticity because the non-linguistic qualities of materials are emphasized. The statement rather pertains to cultural authenticity and, more precisely, to what I have termed ethnographic cultural authenticity in chapter 3. This concept is pursued whenever authentic materials are primarily seen as cultural artefacts by the author. Liddicoat/Scarino (2013) use the term *authentic/authenticity* not only for materials but also for how these are used. One example is "[a]uthenticity of conditions: the conditions for language use need to be reflective of the conditions for use of the resource in the 'real world'" (Liddicoat/Scarino 2013: 95). The elaborations by Liddicoat/Scarino thus reflect notions of both cultural authenticity and real-world authenticity.

An equally eclectic view of authenticity is found in Mishan (2010) who applies the term to different kinds of tasks:

> At the pedagogical end of the spectrum, 'authentic tasks' might include a range of classic information gap activities. Further along the continuum come games and play, which [...] are an intrinsic part of both the human experience and of language learning. At the 'real-life' end, come any number of everyday tasks – corresponding with 'e-pal' via email or chat, talking about the meaning or emotional impact of a film or song, making a podcast, writing a blog or story and so on. (Mishan 2010: 152)

The spectrum described is almost large enough to conceptually cover classroom authenticity ("pedagogical end" – ibid.) and real-world authenticity ("'real-life' end" – ibid.).

5.2.5.2 Conclusion

What becomes evident is that the period from 2010 to 2014 brings about uses of the term *authentic/authenticity* that fall into various categories of the conceptual taxonomy established in chapter 3. As seen in Liddicoat/Scarino (2013) and Mishan (2010), conceptual heterogeneity can even occur within a single publication.

Authenticity of text reception, which is based on Widdowson's ideas, is the only concept that has not been mentioned in the detailed analysis. Indeed, Widdowson's later position that authentic text should not be used in the EFL classroom because it hinders authentication (Widdowson 1996: 67-68) is not shared by any of the authors between 2010 and 2014. However, his earlier position that authentic text requires appropriate activities so learners can engage with it (Widdowson 1978: 80, 1976: 263-264) is found lurking in many statements (e.g. Liddicoat/Scarino 2013: 95). Still, such statements are often closer to other concepts, e.g. to real-world authenticity, so that elements of Widdowson's notions were neglected in the analysis. Widdowson's general influence on the discourse persists as 16 of 23 texts refer to him in the period under scrutiny (not counting Dantas-Whitney/Rilling 2010 because the book was unavailable to me).

On the conceptual level, the most interesting observations include the emergence of authenticity of individual behavior as well as a remarkable redefinition of textual authenticity. Authenticity of individual behavior, which is a concept rarely invoked in the previous decades, is pursued by four different authors. The contexts in which the different conceptualizations occur are quite different (Henry 2013: computer games; McKay 2013: interaction among learners; Pinner 2013b: CLIL; Siegel 2014: textbook topics) and no common point of reference – in the literal sense – has been identified. All four authors are, however, eager to intrinsically engage learners by catering to their interests and personal characteristics. The lack of common context or reference between the four publications suggests a conceptual coincidence, and it will be interesting to see whether their notions are drawn upon in the future discourse.

The second conceptual co-occurrence applies to textual authenticity. Trabelsi (2010) and Kramsch (2012), respectively, plead for an inclusion of the non-native speaker as a potential producer of authentic text. Definitions of textual authenticity have previously either made clear that authentic text be a result of communication within native speaker communities or they have simply not mentioned this aspect. For the first time in the discourse, such an explicitly inclusive definition is proposed (Trabelsi 2010; Kramsch 2012). Unlike with authenticity of individual behavior (Henry 2013; McKay 2013; Pinner 2013b; Siegel 2014), the conceptual co-occurrence of Trabelsi (2010) and Kramsch (2012) has an identifiable origin. Trabelsi (2010) draws upon Kramsch's earlier works (1993; 2000) extensively during his conceptualizations. Though the topic of non-native speaker text is not discussed in Kramsch (1993; 2000) – at least not with reference to authenticity – the general ideas expressed in these publications go in the same direction. The conceptual co-occurrence of Trabelsi (2010) and Kramsch (2012) is therefore less coincidental than that of Henry (2013), McKay (2013), Pinner (2013b), and Siegel (2014).

Two structural developments in the discourse have emerged since the turn of the century and continue until 2014. The first of these is a tendency toward more extensive literature reviews on the topic of authenticity. The second development is the growing phenomenon of meta-discursiveness, which is marked by commentaries on authenticity as a term. Such commentaries tend to highlight the positive connotation that the term carries. Both developments intertwine. Many of the literature reviews use the term *authentic/authenticity* as a guiding line and compare conceptual (and possibly judgmental) statements made by other authors on aspects of authenticity. Such literature reviews can be said to display a certain degree of meta-discursiveness in themselves. Commentaries on connotation are oftentimes embedded in them. It may be the case that meta-discursive awareness actually arises from a sound knowledge of the literature.

Literature reviews and meta-discursiveness are indications that authenticity is increasingly perceived as a thematic field. *Authenticity* is also featured under the rubric *Key concepts in ELT* in the year 2014. The rubric has appeared in *ELT Journal* since 1993. The two EFL dictionaries that come out during the final period under scrutiny both contain an entry for authenticity. However, one of them, McKay (2013) in Blackwell's *The encyclopedia of applied linguistics*, is more of an article written in largely conceptual style than an encyclopedic entry. Leitzke-Ungerer's entry *Authentizität* (2010) in the *Metzler-Lex-ikon Fremdsprachendidaktik* is rather conventional – since descriptive – in style. What is remarkable about the latter is that primarily English sources are cited. In fact, the only German text cited is one written by Leitzke-Ungerer herself. Since Weller (1992), all German publications have drawn on English texts on authenticity.

As stated earlier, it is difficult to identify trends during this short period in the discourse. The appearance of multiple statements advocating authenticity of individual behavior is one example where it is more plausible to assume a coincidence rather than a discursive pattern. Furthermore, bibliometric insights are limited because it is unknown which of the texts will resonate in the discourse. The number of citations that a given publication receives has served as useful information in the earlier decades but is naturally missing in this final period of the chronology.

5.3 Summary of the chronological analysis

This chapter consists of subchapters, the first of which elaborates on the methodological approach taken during the chronological analysis (chapter 5.3.1). These elaborations are presented here and not in the methodological chapters because they are so specific and practical that they are best exemplified referring to different parts within the analysis. Next, some interesting findings of citation analysis are presented in chapter 5.3.2. What follows in chapters 5.3.3 is a conceptual synopsis of the chronological analysis. This summary is primarily structured by the different concepts established as parts of the taxonomy in chapter 3.

5.3.1 Bibliometrics informing discourse analysis: Productivity and citation

Unlike Meara (2012), who is one of the very few authors (if not the only one) in EFL to employ bibliometrics, I use the method merely to complement my discourse analytical approach. Bibliometric aspects have therefore accompanied the entire chronological analysis. Often these aspects were made explicit, but they also informed sporadic issues of prioritization. For example, no publication which receives a considerable number of citations is left unmentioned. Conversely however, a low number of received citations does not bar a publication from being presented and discussed in the analysis. Obviously, substance and relevance override a lack in discursive resonance. What is more, some works are part of a certain trend. At times, I even mentioned texts that are not included in the document selection, if their presence underscores a certain development in the discourse.

The academic EFL discourse on authenticity unfolds across different publication formats. The document selection I have compiled is therefore not homogeneous in format and consequently more difficult to analyze by means of bibliometrics. The method is usually applied only to journal articles (e.g. Meara 2012).

With regard to productivity the difficulties lie in measuring the contributions of single authors to the discourse because some publish a number of articles (e.g. Pinner 2013a; 2013b; 2014) whereas others publish one book on the topic (e.g. van Lier 1996). Entries in EFL dictionaries are different yet again. Only very striking instances of accumulation can thus be seen as indicative of high productivity, which is for example the case with Widdowson who contributes to the topic in ten different writings.

With regard to citation the bibliometric method must also be adjusted to the circumstance of dealing with different formats. It is for example not sufficient to look at the bibliographies of the publications, which is typically done in bibliometric research. Especially monographs that show up in a bibliography may not be cited in the context of authenticity. For example, Nunan (1988b) and Nunan (1989) appear to be generally popular publications that are frequently referenced but rarely do the citations refer to the statements concerning authenticity. Also Wilkins (1976) is often cited in other contexts, as are some monographs by Widdowson as well as Kramsch (1993). Only if a publication is cited due to its statements on authenticity is it credited with receiving a citation in my analysis.

The citation analysis has of course led to my discovery of new publications, which means that the process also functioned as a snowball method. Every time a new text was found, all other texts were searched to see whether they cite it. After a while, no new discoveries were made. It appears that a point of saturation was reached.

It must be mentioned that some texts appeared promising but were not available at my institution. Usually, these texts are cited by at least one author in such a way that an explicit negotiation of authenticity is to be expected within them. In some cases, the title of the publication raises similar expectations. These texts are included in the document selection and would be interesting to look at. There is, however, no guarantee that they offer valuable contributions to the discourse. In the list of documents, they are indicated as "not available".

5.3.2 Findings of citation analysis

Chapters 5.2.1 through 5.2.5 present findings of citation analysis that are diachronic, meaning that the patterns observed span longer periods or that they become pertinent only in contrast to other periods in the discourse. The patterns were therefore not – or only swiftly – mentioned in the different chapters of the chronological analysis. Some findings of productivity analysis, which are rather basic and superficial, are presented in chapter 4.5.3, prior to the chronological analysis. The following chapters describe findings of citation analysis, which by comparison are more insightful.

5.3.2.1 Amplification

An interesting diachronic pattern can be revealed through citation analysis. Two examples of this pattern are given:

A solid number of four authors cite an article that predates Stevick (1971): *Textes et documents authentiques au niveau 2* by Daniel Coste (1970). Since the article is in French, it is not investigated in my study. It is remarkable that four English and German publications cite Coste (1970) while Stevick (1971) does not receive any citations. Breen (1985) is the first of the four authors to cite Coste (1970). Given Breen's enormous impact in the discourse, it is possible that other authors would have overlooked Coste, if Breen had not cited him.

Similar dynamics could be at work concerning Cook (1997). This publication is also cited four times. Widdowson (1998b) is the first of the four in the chronology. His bibliography consists of only three items: Cook (1997), a novel by Toni Morrison, and a monograph by himself (Widdowson 1990). Widdowson speaks of Cook in a commendatory manner: "language play, as my colleague Guy Cook (1997) has argued so convincingly, is also a part of reality" (Widdowson 1998: 714). The three other authors who cite Cook (1997) cite Widdowson (1998b) as well. In other words, no author cites Cook (1997) without citing Widdowson (1998b). It is thus very likely that the other authors who cite Cook have discovered his work via Widdowson.

The dynamics described could be spoken of in terms of amplification. If a rather low-profile publication is cited in a highly exposed publication, then the former's impact may be amplified in the discourse. Obviously, instances of amplification differ in degree and are never the lone cause of a high number of citations received by a publication. Sometimes, strong indications of amplification can be found, and sometimes, the evidence is rather tenuous. There is, for example, more evidence rendering the amplification of Cook (1997) probable than that of Coste (1970).

Beside the two examples of amplification that I have just given, there may be a third example that would be far more consequential. One must wonder how Breen (1985) receives such a massive number of citations. Considering that Widdowson generally cites very few sources, his citation (Widdowson 1990) of Breen (1985) is noticeable. Only one author in the discourse cites Breen (1985) before Widdowson (1990) does. It is therefore possible that Widdowson (1990) functions as an amplifier for Breen (1985). All in all, a certain effect of amplification seems not improbable.

5.3.2.2 EFL dictionaries

One striking outcome of the citation analysis is that EFL dictionaries (or encyclopedias) are very rarely cited. Richards/Platt/Weber (1985) and Thornbury (2006) receive one citation apiece, while the other dictionaries are not cited by any of the authors in the discourse. Since terminology plays such a central role in the discourse on authenticity, one would expect more authors to consult the different EFL dictionaries while in the process of negotiating authenticity.

EFL dictionaries are in some respect comparable to EFL manuals in that they are

> [...] conservative exemplars of current disciplinary paradigms. They are seen as places where we find the tamed and accepted theories of a discipline, where 'normal science' is defined and acknowledged fact is represented. (Hyland 2000: 105)

Hyland proceeds to describe disciplinary manuals, which he calls *textbooks*, as less prestigious than other academic text genres:

> [...] [T]extbooks [are set] apart from the more prestigious genres through which academics exchange research findings, dispute theories and accumulate professional credit. Thus, while the research article is a highly valued genre central to the disciplinary construction of

new knowledge, the textbook simply represents an attempt to reduce the multivocity of past texts to a single voice of authority. (Hyland 2000: 105)

Arguably, EFL dictionaries contain the same "tamed and accepted theories" (ibid.) as manuals. If one applies Hyland's thoughts on prestige to EFL dictionaries, then it is not surprising that authors are reluctant to reference them. After all, "citing the work of others is not simply an issue of accurate attribution, but also a significant means of constructing an authorial self" (Hyland 2000: 37). It is of course possible that the EFL dictionaries are consulted for basic orientation but not cited by some of the authors in the discourse.

5.3.2.3 The German discourse

Productivity analysis shows that the German discourse on authenticity is particularly active during the 1970s and 80s. Citation analysis adds a number of noteworthy details.

None of the first six German publications cites an English publication from the discourse on authenticity: Gutschow (1977), Henrici (1980), Petersen (1980), Löschmann/Löschmann (1984), Edelhoff (1985), Beile (1986). Three German publications are not counted because they do not have a bibliography: Beile (1979; 1981), Rück (1986). Things change after 1990. All four German publications that appear between 1990 and 2014 cite English works from within the discourse, the first of which is Weller (1992). Lana Rings, who writes in English, actually cites German writings from the discourse as early as in 1986. Other authors who cite German publications while writing in English are Kramsch (1993), Amor (2002), and Buendgens-Kosten (2013; 2014). Edelhoff (1982; 1985) and Kramsch (1993; 1996; 2000; 2012) are the only authors who make contributions to the discourse in both languages.

Although the sample size is small, there seems to be a growing exchange between the English and the German EFL discourse on authenticity. Especially publications written in German today are unlikely to ignore the English-speaking discourse on authenticity. The fact that texts in German did not cite English publications in the 1970s and 1980s points to a certain self-sufficiency during that period. Rings (1986) citing German texts reinforces the impression. This phenomenon of self-sufficiency, besides productivity, is an indication that the German-speaking discourse was highly active at the time.

5.3.2.4 Electronic literature research

The later in the chronology the more works from the discourse are cited by the authors. In part, this pattern is a corollary of the growing body of literature to draw on as the discourse progresses. However, a vast disparity is identified between the pre-2000 and the post-2000 period. Some of the later bibliographies are most likely the result of extensive literature research with the help of ever-evolving electronic search functions. Online databases continue to expand and search engines become increasingly elaborate. It is probable that many authors have used *authentic* as a search word in all periods of the discourse. Yet, today's possibilities make it easier to find greater amounts of relevant literature.

Striking examples of extensive bibliographies are Al Azri/Al-Rashdi (2014) – 21 citations within the discourse – and Zhafarghandi/Barekat/Homaei (2014) – 28 citations within the discourse. Both bibliographies contain sources retrievable exclusively online where issues of peer review and academic rigor appear unresolved, e.g. "Martinez, A.G. (2002). Authentic materials: An overview. Free resources for teachers and students of English, Karen's Linguistics Issues, 1-7." (Al Azri/Al-Rashdi 2014: 254). Gilmore's (2007) impressive bibliography is likely another instance where the benefits of electronic literature research are taken advantage of.

As search functions become ever more elaborate and databases ever larger and better connected, it becomes easier to find literature of interest. This is particularly true in the EFL discourse on authenticity because the term itself can be used as a search word and oftentimes explicit negotiation is already recognizable in the title of the publication. Later publications in the discourse clearly benefit from these possibilities.

5.3.2.5 An egalitarian discourse?

A very tentative assumption is made in this chapter, namely that the EFL discourse on authenticity is more egalitarian than other thematic discourses in the field. The numbers yielded by the citation analysis do not entirely correspond to one basic pattern of academic discourses: "Several studies have shown that most publications produced in a field are seldom cited, while a few are cited by many authors" (Crane 1972: 70).

The pre-eminence of Henry G. Widdowson is of course uncontested and the number of citations received by Breen (1985) is staggering. Still, it appears that many other texts receive solid attention in the discourse judging by the citation numbers. This relatively broad distribution of citations may be partially owed to the fact that the discourse as such is rather small. The EFL discourse on vocabulary acquisition, that is investigated by Paul Meara (2012), produces approximately 120 articles per year (Meara 2012: 7-8), which does not include monographs and edited volumes on the topic. It is therefore impossible for a scholar to read all potentially relevant publications. The discourse on authenticity is – by comparison – almost manageable in its entirety. As a result, authors in search of literature need not be as selective as in thematic discourses that are more productive. For example, Al Azri/Al-Rashdi (2014) and Zhafarghandi/Barekat/Homaei (2014) seem almost indiscriminate citing every publication on authenticity they can find (cf. chapter 5.2.5). The terminological criterion, which likely entails a word search for *authentic*, requires a minimum of complementary criteria. In some cases, only the most recent works may be of interest, which narrows down the number of search results considerably. An equally simple word search for *vocabulary acquisition*, by contrast, is not likely to yield satisfactory results unless a number of additional search criteria are applied. Consequently, scholars in the field of vocabulary acquisition may be more inclined to use the snowball method, thus looking for works that are frequently cited, or they may to some extent rely on author status as an indication that a publication is worth reading.

These deliberations are speculative and merely aim at raising awareness for how individuals may go about researching literature within the EFL discourse on authenticity.

It would be worthwhile looking deeper into the issue of literature search, since it may be assumed to have a bearing on power structures within the discourse.

5.3.3 Conceptual summary of the chronological analysis

This chapter is structured chronologically as well as conceptually. A somewhat flexible structure is needed so that conceptual developments over time can be represented most coherently. A continual point of reference throughout this chapter is the taxonomy (chapter 3) with its different concepts of authenticity.

The first explicit statements on authenticity found in the discourse fall within the realm of textual authenticity (Stevick 1972; Wilkins 1976; Gutschow 1977; Morrow 1977; Geddes/White 1978; Beile 1979). A real consensus on what constitutes an authentic text is neither found in the early years of the discourse nor at any later point. Widdowson (1976; 1978) challenges the general concept so fundamentally that I choose to accord his propositions a separate concept: authenticity of text reception. The concept is based on the following premise:

> I think it is probably better to consider authenticity not as a quality residing in instances of language but as a quality which is bestowed upon them, created by the response of the receiver. Authenticity in this view is a function of the interaction between the reader/hearer and the discourse as incorporating the intentions of the writer/speaker. (Widdowson 1976: 263)

During the 1980s, the productivity of the discourse increases, spawning at least two new concepts which accompany – but never replace – textual authenticity and authenticity of text reception. Textual authenticity continues to play a preponderant role but according to Breen "the focus shifts towards authenticity of tasks or learning behaviours required in relation to whatever data are offered" (Breen 1985: 64). The label *task authenticity* proves unfit as a conceptual description because two completely antagonistic approaches claim to constitute it. The first approach consists in what I term real-world authenticity, namely the idea that activities should resemble communicative situations that typically occur outside the classroom (Candlin/Edelhoff 1982; Seliger et al. 1985; Nunan 1989). This understanding of authenticity is present in conceptualizations of authentic assessment (Seliger et al. 1985) and Task-Based Language Teaching (TBLT – Nunan 1989). The opposite approach is most notably propounded by Breen (1985):

> [...] [G]iven the actual social potential of a classroom, the contrivance of 'other worlds' within it may not only be inauthentic but also quite unnecessary. [...] The authenticity of the classroom is that it is a rather special social event and environment wherein people share a primary communicative purpose: learning. [...] Perhaps one of the main authentic activities within a language classroom is communication about how best to learn to communicate. (Breen 1985: 67-68)

The idea of having learners communicate about the learning process is a very concrete and practical understanding of authenticity. It is not echoed in the subsequent discourse. However, Breen (1985) is the most cited publication in the discourse and his more general ideas are eagerly adopted: One, tasks and behaviors can be referred to as *authentic* instead of texts and materials. Two, the EFL classroom lays claim to an authenticity in its own right as opposed to the so-called real world.

Although real-world authenticity and classroom authenticity emerge during that period, it is textual authenticity that stays at the helm conceptually, and even prompts commentators to detect a "fetish of authentic text" (Rück 1986 – title of the publication) seeing "[a]uthenticity of materials as a growing moral imperative" (Clarke 1989: 74).

In the following decade, more and more authors display notions of authenticity informed by Henry G. Widdowson (1976; Widdowson 1978). It becomes a truism that it is not sufficient to present learners with authentic texts but that authenticity depends on the engagement of the learner who interacts with the material (Arnold 1991: 241; Kramsch 1993: 178; Long 1996: 129; Taylor 1994: 5; Lee 1995: 323; van Lier 1996: 127; Little 1997: 225 – cf. chapter 5.2.3 for quotes). Even experts in authentic assessment begin to draw on Widdowson, though some of the citations appear rather tokenistic (e.g. Bachman/Palmer 1996: 41) and the conceptualizations remain closer to real-world authenticity than authenticity of text reception.

In the meantime, Widdowson publishes six texts that contain contributions to the discourse (1990; 1994; 1996; 1998a; 1998b). He reifies his old concept of authentication (or appropriate response) which vaguely stipulates that learners must be put in a position to authenticate the texts they work with in class (Widdowson 1976; 1978). Most importantly, the use of authentic text is cast as a hindrance to processes of authentication. Widdowson uses a style of writing that I refer to as conceptual – as opposed to descriptive – and employs means of authorial stance (cf. chapter 4.2.1). Widdowson also suggests that learners are unlikely to authenticate a native speaker teacher and should be taught by professionals who share their mother tongue (Widdowson 1994: 387, 1996: 68). The concept of authentication is thereby extended beyond text reception. Authentication as a completely learner-oriented theorem is adopted by van Lier (1996) who claims all but universal applicability of the concept and implies that even formal grammar teaching can be authenticated, if a given learner is accordingly inclined (van Lier 1996: 128). Van Lier's emphasis on learner-orientation and his reference to existentialist philosophy (van Lier 1996: 13) align his deliberations with what I have called authenticity of individual behavior.

Around the turn of the century, the emergence of electronic corpus linguistics causes a resurgence of textual authenticity. Some authors suggest comparing corpora of authentic language to corpora of textbook language (Gilmore 2004; Barbieri/Eckhardt 2007). An alignment of the two genres is aimed at, whereby textbook language would become more idiomatic, hence more authentic. Another approach is to use concordancing software in class and engage the learners in corpus analysis (Mishan 2004; Allan 2008). The term *authentic/authenticity* is frequently used in these contexts because the texts that constitute the corpora are produced by native speakers and are not produced for language learning purposes. Widdowson is opposed to the use of corpora because language becomes decontextualized in the process, which according to him renders an authentication on the receiver's part impossible (Widdowson 2003: 155).

The 2000s can be called the decade of diversification not because many new concepts are created but because the whole spectrum of concepts accumulated over the decades is on display. A side effect of this accumulation is that authors question how so many different concepts can be linked to a single term. Extensive literature reviews are conducted more frequently and an increased meta-discursive awareness is observable with a growing number of authors as of the year 2000 (cf. chapter 5.2.4).

From 2010 to 2014, the discourse remains conceptually heterogeneous. An interesting co-occurrence lies in the fact that as many as four authors appear to promote the rarely invoked concept that is authenticity of individual behavior (Henry 2013; McKay 2013; Pinner 2013b; Siegel 2014). A common denominator of their advocacies is the notion that "there is a greater need in language teaching for the content to have a focused topic which is authentic and relevant to the students" (Pinner 2013: 144). Henry reasons psychologically:

> [...] [B]ecause as individuals we orient towards activities that provide us with feeling of self-congruence and authenticity [...] teachers need to provide students with greater opportunities for creativity and meaningful self-expression. (Henry 2013: 151)

The understanding of authenticity held by the four authors is in line with van Lier's (1996), but only Pinner (2013b) references him.

Another remarkable occurrence on the conceptual level relates to textual authenticity. Two authors, Trabelsi (2010) and Kramsch (2012), make an explicit case for the inclusion of a non-native speaker element in the definition of textual authenticity. The lingua franca aspect is alluded to by Trabelsi (Trabelsi 2010: 116) supporting the idea that text produced by non-native speakers should be called authentic.

One concept of the taxonomy which has not been mentioned in this summary is cultural authenticity. Unlike other concepts, cultural authenticity is never concisely defined and it is scarcely championed in an explicit manner. Rather, the notion of cultural authenticity underpins many statements without being pursued in a more elaborate manner. One of the earlier examples is found in Nostrand (1989):

> Suppose that one of our objectives as humanists is to impart an empathic understanding of a foreign culture, and that we want to pursue authenticity to its limits. [...] Students should certainly practice [...] by means of exercises where they study in depth a small, manageable corpus of authentic examples. They need to learn by experience how responsible generalizations are created. (Nostrand 1989: 50)

Authentic texts – or *authentic examples* in Nostrand's wording – are valued for their cultural benefits instead of their linguistic ones. Kramsch (1993) actually coins the term *cultural authenticity* but does not commit to a conceptual definition (Kramsch 1993: 177-184). The rather subtle presence of cultural authenticity proves consistent in the discourse as Liddicoat/Scarino write in 2013: "Most importantly, [authentic materials] are produced within the cultural context of native speakers and are imbued with the assumptions, values, and ways of communicating of that culture" (Liddicoat/Scarino 2013: 95).

To conclude, textual authenticity is a prolific concept in the early period of the discourse (Stevick 1971; Gutschow 1977; Morrow 1977; Geddes/White 1978; Beile 1979). It remains robust until today. The concept is altered immensely by Widdowson's notions of authentication and appropriate response so that a separate category is created: authenticity of text reception (Widdowson 1976/1978/1983). During the 1980s, some understandings of authenticity are completely detached from texts and materials. According to one understanding, activities in the EFL classroom are to reflect real-world procedures (real-world authenticity – Candlin/Edelhoff 1982; Seliger et al. 1985; Nunan 1989). Another understanding entirely opposes the real-world approach and asserts the authenticity of the classroom wherein "the contrivance of 'other worlds' [...] may not only be inauthentic but also quite unnecessary" (classroom authenticity – Breen 1985: 67). Widdowson's conceptual influence is increasingly felt during the 1990s. Many authors agree that it is not enough to bring authentic materials into the EFL classroom but that learners must be assisted in engaging with the materials (cf. chapter 5.2.3). Widdowson himself makes a number of new contributions to the discourse in that period (1990; 1994; 1996; 1998a; 1998b). He openly speaks out against the use of authentic materials in EFL settings. He also suggests that learners will have difficulties engaging in EFL classes conducted by English native speakers. In Widdowson's words, learners cannot authenticate native speaker materials or native speaker teachers (cf. chapter 5.2.3). Van Lier (1996) creates a strong form of authentication, as it were. He considers authentication a completely individual process within the learner, one that impinges on all aspects of language learning (authenticity of individual behavior). In the meantime, the concept of cultural authenticity evolves rather inconspicuously.

The different concepts of authenticity accumulate over time. By the year 2000, all the concepts in my taxonomy (cf. chapter 3) have come into existence. They continue to co-exist until today in varying contexts and proportions. Textual authenticity gains presence in the context of corpus linguistics. The general idea that corpora of authentic text can be analyzed and used for the benefit of language teaching occurs during the early years of the new millennium (Amor 2002; Gilmore 2004; Mishan 2004; Tan 2005; Allan 2008). It becomes increasingly difficult to identify conceptual trends in the discourse, partly because citation analysis fails to provide information about which texts are most widely received in the discourse. A certain correlation may exist between a number of late articles that champion authenticity of individual authenticity (Henry 2013; McKay 2013; Pinner 2013b; Siegel 2014).

None of the concepts which I have extrapolated from the discourse and established as components of the taxonomy in chapter 3 seem to disappear over time. They are created at different times in the chronology of the discourse but from the moment of nascency each concept shows its own kind of resilience. Even cultural authenticity, which is predicated on essentialist notions and may thus appear somewhat outdated, resurfaces in 2013 (Liddicoat/Scarino 2013: 95). Nevertheless, certain temporary upswings of single concepts are recognizable. At times, trends can be linked to contextual conditions. For example, Widdowson's concept of authentication (authenticity of text reception) is not dissimilar to coeval movements in the academic fields of literature and linguistics (cf. chapter 5.2.1). By and large, textual authenticity is the most consistent concept over the decades. Even very pointed and unyielding critiques delivered by the most influential actor in the discourse (e.g. Widdowson 1978: 80, 1983: 30) do not prevent numerous other authors from treating authenticity as a textual quality.

6 The history of authenticity in EFL and beyond

The academic EFL discourse on authenticity, which has been presented and analyzed, is historical in that it consists of statements made in the past. The temporal demarcation of the discourse may suggest that authenticity is a fairly new phenomenon that did not exist before the 1970s. This assumption is inaccurate on two accounts. Firstly, the term *authentic/authenticity* existed long before 1970, yet it was used primarily outside of EFL. Secondly, many EFL concepts of authenticity existed long before 1970, which means that these approaches to language teaching are not new but simply used to bear different names – if they had any. Thus, the term existed and the concepts existed but, prior to the 1970s, they had not merged within EFL. The discourse depicted in the previous chapters can therefore be seen as a merging process between one preexisting *signifiant* (authenticity as a term outside of EFL) and a number of preexisting *signifiés* (EFL concepts).

6.1 The history of authenticity as a term outside of EFL

This chapter deals with authenticity as a preexisting *signifiant*, meaning that the term *authentic/authenticity* is scrutinized for the time before it entered the EFL discourse. The representations in this chapter are fairly condensed. They are intended to give an impression of what the term denoted in different contexts prior to its insertion into the EFL discourse.

The English adjective *authentic* is partly a borrowing from French, partly a borrowing from Latin (Oxford English Dictionary (online) 2016). Trilling asserts that there exist "violent meanings which are explicit in the Greek ancestry of the word 'authentic'. 'Authenteo': to have full power over; also, to commit a murder. 'Authentes': not only a master and a doer, but also a perpetrator, a murderer, even a self-murderer, a suicide" (Trilling 1972: 131). Over the centuries, the aspects of violence fade while the aspects of power persist. This process results in the term's increasing application to written documents:

> This sort of agency develops in the direction of power, held by someone to do something. What is primarily meant is the authority which is contained in certain pieces of writing such as a testament, a borrower's note, or a letter. Contracts that are handwritten or signed are, until today, the basic forms of authentic expression.[67] (Stegemann 2014: 41)

In jurisdiction, the *authentica interpretatio* of a statute means an official interpretation of the text issued by the statute's legislator so as to afford it the status of law (Lethen 1996: 209-210). This objectification of authenticity is prevalent in the medieval period and is existing to date. The authenticity of legal documents is still referred to in these terms and it is not difficult to see how this translates into the use of the term for texts and materials

---

67   Original: "Im Weiteren entwickelt sich die Art dieser Urheberschaft und bedeutet zusehends die Macht, die jemand hat, um etwas zu tun. Gemeint ist dabei vor allem die Autorität, die ein Schriftstück von eigener Hand hat, wie etwa ein Testament, ein Schuldschein oder ein Brief. Handschriftliche oder mit eigener Hand unterschriebene Verträge sind bis heute die Grundform authentischer Äußerungen." (Stegemann 2014: 41)

in EFL. Objectified authenticity is increasingly accompanied by descriptions of human behavior in the wake of Enlightenment:

> Tracing the use of the term 'authenticity' it becomes evident that a change occurs in Western Europe since the 17th century. The general understanding moves from the authorization of objects and texts to representations which are perceived as real and which are ultimately attributed to qualities of individuals. The individual must be unique.[68] (Noetzel 1999: 11)

Two contextual strands of authenticity have developed, the first of which refers to objects, the second of which refers to individuals. "In the 20th century, new meanings of the term emerge owing to its use in various academic disciplines" (Noetzel 1999: 19).[69] Many of these meanings belong to the second strand denoting human behavior, and philosophy becomes a highly influential discipline in this respect. Without going into detail two succinct accounts of Heidegger's conceptualization shall be given:

> 'Who I am depends upon my possibility to choose and to become what I am' expands Heidegger's notion of *Eigentlichkeit* (authenticity). And the equally determinate possibility 'to forego normal choice and to adopt those offered me by the world or other people' captures the kernel of his *Uneigentlichkeit* (inauthenticity). (Kaelin 1988: 58)

> For Heidegger [...] any given mode of [...] existence can be assessed in terms of what he calls authenticity or inauthenticity. We can always ask of any given individual whether the choices she makes between different possible modes of existence and the way she enacts or lives them out are ones through which she is most truly herself, or rather ones in which she neglects or otherwise fails to be herself. (Mulhall 2005: 32)

Authenticity thus refers to the notion that an individual uses their freedom of choice to make decisions that are expressive of their true self, as opposed to adopting "those [behaviors] offered me by the world or other people" (Heidegger in Kaelin 1988 – quote above). Though the philosophical understanding of authenticity with all its implications is considerably more complex and contested, it is this basic idea that is perceived by posterity as being quintessentially linked to existentialism. Van Lier (1996) is the only author in the EFL discourse on authenticity to draw on this concept explicitly:

> I take as my starting point the existentialist definition of 'authentic': an action is authentic when it realizes a free choice and is an expression of what a person genuinely feels and believes. An authentic action is intrinsically motivated. Inauthentic action is taken because everyone else is doing them, they 'ought' to be done, or in general they are motivated by external factors. (van Lier 1996: 13)

---

68 Original: "Folgt man dem Gebrauch des Begriffs ‚Authentizität' [...], dann wird deutlich, daß die seit dem 17. Jahrhundert in Westeuropa zu beobachtende Wortverwendung sich von einem allgemeinen Verständnis der Autorisierung von Dingen und Texten zu einer Kennzeichnung für echt gehaltene Repräsentationsverhältnisse wandelt, die [...] schließlich auch auf Eigenschaften der Individuen Anwendung findet. Die Individuen müssen unverwechselbar sein." (Noetzel 1999: 11)

69 Original: "Im 20. Jahrhundert entstehen nun neue Bedeutungsinhalte des Begriffs, die vor allem auf die Ausweitung seiner Benutzung im Rahmen zahlreicher wissenschaftlicher Disziplinen zurückzuführen sind." (Noetzel 1999: 19)

Beside philosophy, the terminological and conceptual opposition between authenticity and inauthenticity is negotiated within the scholarly discourses of psychology, education, and ethnology (Noetzel 1999: 12).[70] In chapter 2.8, the ethnological understanding of authenticity is sketched because it appears to inform the EFL concept of cultural authenticity.

These brief insights do not lay claim to a comprehensive representation of how the term *authentic/authenticity* has evolved over centuries. Rather, glimpses are offered so as to outline meanings of the term in different contexts and in different periods of time. Connections between historical uses of the term and its use in today's EFL context are based on assumption and should be seen as mere indications that instances of conceptual kinship can be identified. This chapter is historical for it describes the diachronic use of the term *authentic/authenticity*. The following chapter illustrates periods in EFL history when practices of foreign language teaching were in line with what would likely be called *authentic* today.

6.2 The history of textual authenticity as an EFL concept

This chapter deals with authenticity as a preexisting concept (i.e. a *signifié*), which implies that the idea of using authentic materials existed long before the communicative turn (Mishan 2005: 3-10). Since textual authenticity is the most consolidated concept of authenticity in EFL, I focus on this concept while paying less attention to the other concepts contained in the taxonomy of authenticity (chapter 3). Tracing the concept of textual authenticity means to investigate the history of language teaching in order to find out when and in what way authentic materials were used. As the history of language teaching and learning is several thousand years long (see e.g. Kelly 1969) it is obviously not possible to look at aspects of authenticity everywhere and for the whole period of time. Therefore, one needs to limit the investigation both locally and temporally. Locally, the focus is on Germany, which comprises the German-speaking regions of central Europe. The timeframe under scrutiny begins in 1668 which is the year the first institutionalized English lessons were documented in Germany (Klippel 1994: 458). The timeframe ends with the emergence of the EFL discourse on authenticity, an emergence that roughly coincides with the onset of Communicative Language Teaching (CLT), as I detailed in chapter 4.5.5.2. Some background information is given on English language teaching and learning in Germany prior to 1668. In order to illuminate the use of authentic materials over time a broader historical context is often considered necessary so as to explain under which circumstances the given developments played out.

---

70 Original: "Im Prozeß der Verwissenschaftlichung der Debatten über das Individuum und seiner Repräsentationen sickert die Unterscheidung Authentizität/Inauthentizität in viele Disziplinen ein, wobei insbesondere Psychologie, Pädagogik, Philosophie und Ethnologie an einer spezifischen Erweiterung des Vokabulars der Authentizität arbeiten." (Noetzel 1999: 12)

The aim of the following descriptions is not to provide a comprehensive account of textual authenticity in the history of EFL. Such an investigation would require a considerably higher degree of differentiation and would consequently be very extensive. For the interest of this study it is mostly sufficient to identify broad trends in language learning and teaching and to question what role textual authenticity played at the given point in time. To that end, the secondary sources used are Klippel (1994), Hüllen (2005), Macht (1986), Schröder (1969; 1985), and Howatt/Widdowson (2004). Some primary sources in the form of learning materials are also scrutinized. It is not the case that these materials are representative of entire periods or historical developments. They are always used as examples with the important caveat that other materials were also available and used, and that those other materials often took quite different approaches to the facilitation of language learning. Context is provided in terms of how popular the different materials were at the time, and in terms of who used them.

6.2.1 Before 1600

Konrad Schröder (1969) makes plausible suppositions about English language teaching in Germany having started in the Middle Ages when the Hanse trade network was in full bloom. German business men traveling to London would likely prepare themselves by learning short phrases geared to their specific needs. Thus, an assumed starting point goes as far back as to the mid-13th century. Due to the ongoing exchange within the Hanse, Schröder speculates about veritable English language classes being established for business people during the 15th and 16th centuries. Some teachers of such classes may even have been employed by universities (Schröder 1969: 12-16).

For the 16th century, Schröder highlights the political and religious status of cities like Basel during the Protestant Reformation. Basel university attracted many Englishmen who offered private lessons of English within the institution. Motives for local students to learn English may have been diverse: reading English treatises, interacting with the incoming Englishmen, prospective trips to England, affinity for languages etc. (ibid.).

In 16th century Europe, national languages were on the rise, which also promoted the learning of English as a foreign language, though on a very small scale. Schröder remarks that the development manifested itself in the growth of national literatures, which in turn shows how these languages were deemed not merely a practical necessity but an art form. This is valid specifically for Italian and French. The classical languages were no longer unchallenged as the sole holders of sublime thought and expression:

> Everywhere, national languages were attributed a value in their own right [...]. The study of a foreign language meant the appropriation of the values and the culture of a neighboring nation. The learner would thereby further his own wisdom and repute.[71] (Schröder 1969: 17)

---

71 Original: "Überall wird der Muttersprache und der neueren Fremdsprache nun ein eigener Wert beigemessen [...]. Wer neuere Sprachen lernt, macht sich damit Werte zu eigen, erschließt sich Geist und Welt der national verselbständigten Nachbarkultur und gewinnt damit selbst an Weisheit und an Ansehen." (Schröder 1969: 17)

6.2.2 17th century

During the 17th century Latin lost its supremacy as the language of international communication in Europe. Humanism and the Reformation favored the respective first languages which also meant that these languages became generally more attractive to be learned as a foreign language. While the new international language was French (followed by Italian), English – too – saw a notable influx (Schröder 1969: 19). The age of Enlightenment also influenced the European educational systems after the Thirty Years' War. As national languages came to the fore, Latin gradually lost its status as a productive literary language. The educated nobleman became the ideal replacing the scholar, and an increase in travel and mobility required the knowledge of languages (Hüllen 2005: 63). It was considered essential for educated men to be able to converse in a foreign language (Klippel 1994: 45).

First records of textbooks for English date back to the second half of the 17th century in Germany, as Tellaeus (1665) is the earliest publication listed in Schröder's comprehensive bibliography of early EFL textbooks. The place of publication is the then German city of Straßburg (Schröder 1975: 255, 1975: XIII). The earliest account of institutionalized English language teaching dates from the year 1668 at a *Gymnasium* (secondary school) in Korbach (Klippel 1994: 458). Further documents testify to courses of English language teaching at Greifswald University in 1686 and at the Wolfenbüttel knights' academy in 1687. In comparison, French was taught quite commonly at universities and knights' academies (Hüllen 2005: 47).

> The real breakthrough for the English language came towards the end of the [17th] century in Germany where an interest, almost an obsession, grew up round the dramatic works of English literature, and particularly Shakespeare. (Howatt/Widdowson 2004: 68)

Though Howatt/Widdowson speak of a breakthrough, it was of course French, not English, that had established itself as a European *lingua franca*. At the time when English learning materials emerged in Germany the most common book type for learning French was the grammar book which often came with a dialogue section and a vocabulary section. The dialogues, likely, were to be memorized by the learners (Hüllen 2005: 48), which was a long-standing tradition dating back to the learning of Latin in the 9th century (*Kasseler Glossen* and *Pariser Gespräche*). Usually, there was no connection between the grammar section and the dialogue section. The dialogues were made up by the author, which in modern terminology would make them inauthentic samples of text (Hüllen 2005: 48).

The increase in travel and the gradual decline of Latin did not lead to a decline of formalistic grammar study. This is partially due to the resounding impact of the *Grammaire générale et raisonnée* (Antoine Arnauld and Claude Lancelot), a French grammar book published in 1660. Hüllen describes the book as highly influential with regard to how language as such was conceived (Hüllen 2005: 70-72). The study of grammar was proclaimed by the authors of the book as being conducive to universal processes of the human mind. The core idea was that of a universal grammar which lead to an ever more common practice of contrastively analyzing two or more languages. According to Hüllen, this orthodoxy permeated the European continent for a long time to come. In France, the impact was such that the *collèges* taught French grammar increasingly in contrast with Latin, which was considered to possess the most universal of grammars. Internationally, language learning was spurred by the movement in general. However, approaches to learning and teaching were separated from practical needs. Latin resurged and methodologies in modern languages highlighted formal grammar study and contrastive analyses. Learning a language became an end in itself, which was in line with the emerging movement of neo-humanism (*Neuhumanismus* – Hüllen 2005: 72).

In the following, a close look is taken at an early textbook. Questions of authenticity receive particular attention.

Offelen (1687)

Henry Offelen's book *A double grammar for Germans to learn English and for Englishmen to learn the German tongue* (1687–title abridged) was one of the first English textbooks. It was similar to French (and other) textbooks of the time in that it contained both grammar sections and dialogues. The importance of grammar is stressed in the preface:

> I endeavoured to expound everything clearly; therefore I translated all Latin words belonging to the grammar into German; for whereas no man is able to learn any language perfectly without the knowledge thereof; on the contrary, any man that understands them well can easily obtain and learn them; I added all difficulties and rules that may be found in this language [...]. (Offelen 1687: preface)

Offelen (1687) contains grammar, dialogues, and a literary section that at the time was often referred to as *chrestomathy*. The latter section includes literary and scholarly texts from British authors who were popular at the time. Some examples are *Hero and Leander* (poem by Christopher Marlowe), *Parthenissa* (romance by Roger Boyle of Orrery), *Man's mortality* (theological/philosophical treatise by Richard Overton), *A dissertation concerning the pre-existency of souls* (theological/philosophical treatise–author unknown), *The parable of the dove* (political satire–author unknown).

Treatises outnumber literary texts, which reflects the general interest of Germans at the time. Most German readers of English texts were far more interested in academic and scientific writing than in English literature (Klippel 1994: 45). England was venerated for its political and theological thought, and for its advancement in the sciences (Schröder 1985: 53-54). The English Civil War and the subsequent Glorious Revolution galvanized intellectuals throughout Europe. Overton (*Man's mortality* – see above), for example, was a pamphleteer during the English Civil War.

Offelen (1687) also contains some texts in Latin. One of them is a defense of Sir Francis Walsingham, principal secretary to Queen Elizabeth I. The fact that Latin texts are featured is an indication that the focus of the book is on content as much as it is on language. The garnering of cultural knowledge seems intertwined with the learning of the English language, sometimes the former is even prioritized.

Very sporadically, one can find little notes on the side margin of the text. These notes are explanatory, applying to content rather than language. Next to the Marlowe text, for example, it says: "Here you must note nothing can be hid from true love" or "Here the author pitieth Leander & decrieth the fish" (Offelen 1687: literary section). These rare annotations may be the first commentaries ever in an EFL textbook (though they were not uncommon in legal or theological texts). They may be regarded as elements of scaffolding:

> Learning is 'assisted performance', and this happens when someone with more knowledge – say a parent or a teacher – helps the learner to progress. This help is called 'scaffolding', a kind of supportive framework for the construction of knowledge, and the scaffolding is only removed when the learners can appropriate the knowledge for themselves. (Harmer 2007: 59)

The annotations in Offelen (1687) may be a precursor to the much later practice of annotating and simplifying text linguistically.

By today's definition, the philosophical and literary texts in Offelen (1687) are authentic, while the dialogues are not. The texts were chosen primarily for their content, as is indicated by the fact that some texts in Latin are included.

6.2.3 18th century

The 18th century is characterized by Hüllen as the *silent age* (*stille Periode* – Hüllen 2005: 63) because it was not marked by one dominant method. Rather, it lay at the interface between humanism and neo-humanism (*Neuhumanismus*–Hüllen 2005: 72). The former is linked to the aim of reading scholarly literature. Neo-humanism made its mark on language learning through the notion that learning the structures of languages has a universal benefit for the human mind (Hüllen 2005: 72).

As Klippel points out, the few language pedagogical writings of the time made different statements about how best to learn a foreign language (Klippel 1994: 85-86). Michaelis (1758) stressed the efficiency of content-focused practice in the form of casual speaking and extensive reading. He harshly admonished an overemphasis on grammar (Klippel 1994: 86). The spectrum of approaches becomes evident with Prager (1764), who did not weigh in on the discussion but whose grammar book catered mainly to scholars and thus strongly foregrounded the formal study of grammar rules. Prager's book was published after Michaelis had voiced his thoughts but it must have been this sort of learning that Michaelis was so averse to. Köster (1763) saw the perfect method in the balance between form-focused study and practice.

The lack of a widely accepted method was, of course, also due to the low degree of institutionalization that marked English language learning:

> Before 1800 most modern language learners were individual scholars trying to gain a reading knowledge of the language by studying the grammar and applying this knowledge to the interpretation of texts with the use of a dictionary. Most of them were highly educated men and women who were trained in classical grammar and knew how to apply the familiar categories to new languages. (Howatt/Widdowson 2004: 151)

The enthronement of George I of Hanover as King of England in 1714 prompted a heightened interest in the English language among Germans (Hüllen 2005: 64). Even so, English was still learned very sporadically in the 18th century. England was revered as a country of scientific and academic accomplishment, but also the interest in English literature was increasing (Klippel 1994: 55). A differentiation of learning motives is sketched by Schröder for Italian, French and English before 1800 (Schröder 1985: 53-57). Italian was esteemed almost exclusively for its aesthetic value, which meant an interest in original literature by Italy's renowned writers. French, in speaking and writing, had become a *sine qua non* for anyone who aspired to mingle with the noble ranks throughout Europe. The effect trickled down to school systems and curricula where French held its hegemony for centuries. French was a prerequisite to the extent that sometimes learners of English would translate texts from French into English (Schröder 1985: 57). Lastly, English was regarded as a language of science and philosophy. Reading theological, political, medical, mathematical etc. treatises by British authors in the original was by far the most common motive for learning the language. The Leipzig book fair, which was held in the middle of the century, faced a demand in English scientific books that exceeded the demand in literature (Klippel 1994: 46-47). Beginning in the late 17th century, German academic scholars in theology and philosophy read sources in English. By the mid-18th century, English reading proficiency had become all but indispensable for these academics. Schröder considers the reading of English philosophers as one of the main motives for learning English in the German academic setting of the 18th century (Schröder 1969: 23). As a spoken language and also as a literary language English was not considered on a par with French and Italian, at least during the first half of the century.

However, Schröder also mentions the availability of English literature translated into German from 1680. Milton, Gray, Young, Thomson, and Richardson were most popular, later Percy, Shakespeare, Scott, and Byron. Germans grew enamored with these authors throughout the 18th century and started emulating their style. Academics with an interest in literature were likely to learn English. At the end of the century English literature was no longer considered aesthetically inferior to French and Italian (Schröder 1969: 23-24). Original versions of English literature were available from the middle of the 18th century in Germany creating a new stimulus to study the language:

> The growing influence of English *belles lettres* on learning motivation and course design becomes manifest from the beginning of the 18th century; between 1760 and 1840 the literary domain is the prime stimulus for (adult) EL studies, as can be seen from the great number of texts published in English by German publishers during that time […]. (Schröder 1985: 51)

In the second half of the 18th century proclamations can be found which praise the English language for more than granting access to scientific and philosophical writings. Both Ehlers (1766) and Witzendorf (1763) highlight aesthetic values which formerly were attributed mainly to French and Italian. English rhetoric is even put in line with that of the Ancient Greeks and Romans. What is more, the disposition of the English people is likened to that of the Germans in that both peoples are claimed to display a strong affinity for structure and discipline (*Gründlichkeit* – Schröder 1985: 54-55). Schröder emphasizes, however, that with regard to oral proficiency, English did not compare to the prestige that French continued to carry (Schröder 1969: 24).

In Germany the demand for original English texts grew throughout the 18th century. German editors reacted to this demand by reprinting texts on a large scale from 1770 onwards. There was a scarcity of book imports from England. The reprints did not only cover literature but also biographies, travel diaries, and philosophical treatises, thereby reflecting the broad interest in English publications (Klippel 1994: 44-45).

Both treatises and literature are authentic texts according to modern definitions. To gain an understanding of how textual authenticity was used for language learning purposes, a look is taken at learning and teaching materials of the time.

6.2.3.1 Grammar books

As for teaching and learning materials, Klippel remarks that teachers often created and published their own textbooks. Such books usually contained both grammar rules and selections of original English literary or scientific texts (which today would be called *authentic*). The books were used by teachers to teach English, but more commonly they were used for individual self-study (Klippel 1994: 61-62).

Johann König's *A complete English guide for high Germans* (1706) combined many of the then current approaches to textbook design. The book contains sections of pronunciation, homophones, idioms, grammar, words, dialogues, and letter writing. However, it does not contain literary or scientific works (Hüllen 2005: 64-65).

Section V of the book is titled *Familiar dialogues* (König 1748: 299-352). It displays interactions, each of which is between two people who converse about topics considered realistic and relevant to people's everyday encounters. The entire section is split into two columns. On the left the English dialogue plays out while being rendered in German on the right. The translations are precise and every sentence is put in the same line as the English original. Single dialogues are one to three pages long, the topics apparently reflect practical needs: *At rising in the morning*, *With a taylor*, *With a merchant about a bill of exchange*. The dialogues are largely uncommented but on the English side one can sometimes find alternative formulations behind words or sentences – the German translation is never varied:

Is Mr. N. within? (at home?) – Ist Herr N. zu Hause?

or

Do you sleep? Are you asleep? – Schlaffet ihr?

Single turns are kept uniformly short:

Good Morrow, (t'ye) Sir.
Welcome Sir, your Servant.
How d'ye do this Morning?
Very well. At your Service.
How is it with you?
Pretty well, God be thanked.
I am glad to see you (in good Health) well.
I am obliged to you.
How dos (the Gentleman) your Brother do?

Section VI is *A London-Guide, of the Curiosities to be seen in and about London* (König 1748: 353-392). The split columns for English and German, as in the preceding chapter, are maintained throughout this section. The section functions like a travel guide being mainly informative in nature. The section starts with information about history, art, culture etc., then it segues into another stretch of dialogues which is still under the heading "Wegweiser durch London" (guide to London). This time, the dialogues mirror the content previously provided, as if to give examples of how to apply the newly acquired knowledge. The first of these dialogues, for instance, is "Between a German and a Hollander". It features a German telling a Dutchman about London and its people, the conversation being held in English (right column still in German):

> Sir, will you have me to give you a Description of London, the Metropolis of England and one of the chief Cities in Europe?

> That's a Thing I am desirous of.

> I must tell you then in the first Place that London is situated in the 52. Degree of North Latitude in the County of Middlesex, and that it is watered by the Thames, the most famous River in England.

Unlike in the dialogue section, this conversation shows a disproportion in turn length, the Dutchman merely giving brief prompts while the German talks extensively. The dialogue can be seen as a mix between travel guide and conversation. Comparing the dialogues to the previous section, it is evident that König applies some sort of sequencing as a progression is made from short turns to longer and more linguistically complex turns in the dialogues.

The subsequent dialogues provide new information about England, revolving around holidays, currency, and proceedings that apparently differ from Germany (e.g. posting letters). The prominent agent in these conversations seems to be an Englishman explaining his country's idiosyncrasies to a German. Utterances by the German are very limited and mostly in the form of queries.

Almost two thirds of the cultural guide section are in the form of dialogues. Together with the dialogue section this amounts to 78 pages of spoken interaction. No textual authenticity is featured in König's book (1706) meaning that no text is included that is culled from literary or academic sources. The dialogues are obviously contrived. However, at least two other concepts of authenticity are clearly identifiable: real-world authenticity and cultural authenticity. Real-world authenticity appears in the form of predictions about the learner's future activities. The dialogues are structured around situations a German traveler is likely to encounter in England. This understanding of authenticity is similar to what proponents of task-based language learning advocate:

> While there is general acknowledgement that authentic materials have a place in the classroom, the issue of activity authenticity is less widely recognised [...]. Certain activities might only remotely resemble the sorts of things learners are required to do in the real world. (Nunan 1989: 60)

Dialogues, in themselves, cater to the *real world* by mirroring communicative situations. The topics of the dialogues in König (1706) increase the sense of practicality that is at the core of real-world authenticity.

Cultural authenticity features as a constant theme in König's book. The book, being a combination of learning material and travel guide, displays an essentialist understanding of culture, which is of course typical of that time. Still, the method pursued by König is quite in line with the concept of cultural authenticity in the academic EFL discourse on authenticity:

> Suppose that one of our objectives as humanists is to impart an empathic understanding of a foreign culture, and that we want to pursue authenticity to its limits [...]. Authentic examples and anecdotes can produce understanding [...]. (Nostrand 1989: 50)

While König's book (1706) does not contain any instances of authentic text, it clearly displays elements that are labeled *authentic* centuries later in the EFL discourse.

6.2.3.2 Chrestomathies

Beside grammar books, translations and chrestomathies became more common during the 18th century. Both types of books were often published by teachers. Translations may have been used contrastively, complementing the work with original versions. Their emergence is indicative of an increased interest in British culture at large.

Chrestomathies were typically used by educated adults for self-study. One of the earliest examples is a text collection by John Tompson titled *English miscellanies consisting of various pieces of divinity, philosophy, morals, politicks and history* (1737) (Schröder 1969: 53). Another early chrestomathy is Valett's *Englisches Lesebuch nebst einer Sprachlehre für Anfänger* (1791). The book is divided into two parts – prose and poetry. While the latter is inherently literary, the former includes dialogues along with letters and narratives. Unlike the contrived dialogues in other textbooks, however, many of the dialogues in Valett are taken from Shakespeare, which makes them authentic by modern definitions. Valett explicitly states in the preface that all dialogues were selected based on moral value and stylistic refinement. Schröder sees Valett as a precursor to the more literary approaches gaining momentum in the 19th century (Schröder 1985: 58).

Chrestomathies contain authentic texts by nearly all definitions of textual authenticity (cf. chapter 2.2.2 for a close analysis of text genres). Valett (1791) stresses the moral value of the texts as well as their entertaining contents. He is also aware of the linguistic difficulties that come with the texts. To alleviate the problem, he carefully selects and sequences the different components, as is claimed in the preface to his book (Schröder 1985: 58). Valett (1791) recommends his book be used for EFL teaching both at school and at university. Another chrestomathy, *Handbuch der Englischen Sprache und Literatur* by Nolte/Ideler (1793), explicitly targeted advanced learners in *Gymnasium*, Germany's higher-tier secondary school (Klippel 1994: 178-179). It is therefore probable that at least some English teachers used chrestomathies in institutional settings by the end of the 18th century.

At the interface between aesthetics and practicality lay the genre of letter writing. Some of the textbooks – Valett (1791) for example – contain a separate section for letters. At the time, letters were seen both as a literary genre as well as something one had to learn for reasons of pragmatics. Some textbook authors advertised them for their stylistic elegance: "some elegant and very curious letters" – Arnold 1718 (Schröder 1975: 18). As of 1767, the publication of the letters by Lady Mary Wortley Montagu inspired textbook authors (Schröder 1985: 57).

Letters may be considered to combine different concepts of authenticity. They are textually authentic, provided that they are real letters and not imitations written by textbook authors. They are culturally authentic because they qualify as cultural artefacts. And they promote real-world authenticity in that they reflect practical needs of the learner. After all, writing letters was an important skill at the time.

6.2.4 1800–1881

The 19th century is often characterized as a time of formalistic language study:

> Nineteenth-century textbook compilers were mainly determined to codify the foreign language into frozen rules of morphology and syntax to be explained and eventually memorised. Oral work was reduced to an absolute minimum, while a handful of written exercises, constructed at random, came as an appendix to the rules. (Titone 2000: 265)

> When once the Latin tongue had ceased to be a normal vehicle for communication, and was replaced as such by the vernacular languages, then it most speedily became a 'mental gymnastic', the supremely 'dead' language, a disciplined and systematic study of which was held to be indispensable as a basis for all forms of higher education. [...] And when under the pressure of circumstance a modern foreign language had to be found a place in the school curriculum as a serious timetable subject, it was considered natural, right and proper that it should be taught along these patterned lines that had proved their worth. (Mallinson 1966: 8)

At the end of the 18th century, a French textbook was published that was so successful that it would also influence the way English was taught and learned during the 19th century: Johann Valentin Meidinger's *Practische Französische Grammatik wodurch man diese Sprache auf eine ganz neue und sehr leichte Art in kurzer Zeit gründlich erlernen kann* (1783). Meidinger's book focuses on systematic grammar explanations. The novelty about Meidinger (1783) lies in the interspersed exercises which require the learner to translate single sentences from their first language into the foreign language applying the newly acquired grammar structure. The translation activities thus follow a precise grammatical progression (Klippel 1994: 143).

Meidinger's method for learning French was often adapted for English and was influential in the first half of the 19th century. In 1809, Wilhelm von Humboldt called for a method of language learning that would benefit the human mind even if the language itself was forgotten in the long run (Macht 1986: 19). Language was increasingly conceived of as a system of rules. The learning of the rules would help develop intellectual capacities in the learner. As of 1810, secondary schools could only employ teachers who had passed a state exam, which gradually dismissed the *Sprachmeister*. The latter were usually native speakers that were untrained as teachers. The new guild of teachers oftentimes had not learned English at school or university. In many cases their skills were confined to what had been acquired through self-study, entailing that reading and grammar were stressed as opposed to communication. Humboldt's educational ideal preferred language learning methods that were in line with how Latin and Greek were learned (Macht 1986: 19-21).

The overarching method to emerge from these circumstances became known as the grammar-translation method:

> The central feature [of the grammar-translation method] was the replacement of the traditional texts by exemplificatory 'sentences'. [...] Grammar-translation textbooks were graded, though not in the modern sense exactly, and presented new grammar points one-by-one in an organized sequence. Each step needed appropriate examples, and specially devised sentences were simpler than samples from 'reputable authors' which contained extra difficulties for the pupils. (Howatt/Widdowson 2004: 152)

As English became increasingly relevant as a school subject, the grammar-translation method, which was deemed fit for younger learners and the requirements of institutionalized language teaching, established itself in the 19th century. The first textbook of this kind was Fick (1793) (Howatt/Widdowson 2004: 151-152).

Methods in the 19th century were more diverse than it appears. The age was marked by complexity and coexistence, not by a sweeping hegemony of grammar and translation (Macht 1986: 10). Klippel emphasizes the variety of EFL textbooks between 1770 and 1840 (Klippel 1994: 100-101). Yet, a general trend toward different forms of grammar-translation was discernible.

T.S. Williams's book *Theoretisch-practische englische Schul-Grammatik* (1836) was explicitly intended as a school book. It is highly grammar-oriented. Macht sees it as the second well-received book representative of the Meidinger method after Fick (1793). The book contains many exercises which uniformly consist of German sentences to be translated into English (Macht 1986: 39-44). This type of exercise was becoming prevalent at the time (Klippel 1994: 390). Authentic text is not found in the book. English sentences serve exemplification and are likely made up by the author (Macht 1986: 39-44). In chapter 3 of this study, the different concepts of authenticity are presented. They are shown to yield a large conceptual spectrum. However, it is difficult to find any of the concepts pursued in the book by Williams (1836).

Nevertheless, textual authenticity continued to play a big role in EFL. During the first half of the 19th century, more and more chrestomathies were published. These would often comprise a multitude of genres. Schröder sees *Praktische Englische Sprachlehre für Schulen und Privatunterricht* by Burckhardt/Jost (1826) as a typical example. The volume encompasses anecdotes, fables, historical accounts, philosophical reflections, letters, dialogues, newspaper articles, and literature both in prose (e.g. Washington Irving) and in verse (predominantly Shakespeare). All texts are authentic including the dialogues which are in part taken from Arthur Murphy's *Three weeks after marriage* (Schröder 1985: 60-61). Considering the range of genres, it seems that textual authenticity is in fact one of the guiding principles.

The EFL focus slowly shifted toward literary works during the 19th century. The most successful chrestomathy is Ludwig Herrig's *The British classical authors* (1948), which saw reprints being used well into the second half of the 20th century (Klippel 2005: 196-

197). Shakespeare became the most popular English writer to be read in 19th century Germany. Throughout the century many of his works were published as annotated versions serving mainly the adult self-study learner. Annotated books from other popular writers such as Byron, Thomson, or Milton were equally available. Goldsmith's *The Vicar of Wakefield* became a bestseller – with a special dictionary to accompany the novel. The annotations and supportive devices that come with these books indicate their purpose of aiding language learning (Schröder 1985: 60-62). Among the many annotated versions that came out in the 19th century Schröder mentions one edition of James Thomson's *Seasons* referring to the book as an "easy reader" (Schröder 1985: 61). The edition actually dates back to 1798. Simplified versions of authentic text were not common at the time but the influx of annotated versions testifies to an increased awareness of the difficulties that come with textual authenticity. Annotated versions were probably also a result of the higher demand and the concomitant competition among textbook authors. Klippel, who analyzed secondary school documents of the time, describes an established canon of literary works that were used very commonly in English language classrooms in the second half of the 19th century (Klippel 1994: 303). Not only literary classics were available with annotations. Speeches by William Pitt the Elder and William Pitt the Younger are printed and annotated in a textbook by Winkelmann (1883). The publication illustrates that authentic spoken text is also used for language learning, though in its almost literary form of political speeches. Schröder's bibliography of EFL textbooks (1975) mentions Pitt as authors and Winkelmann as co-author, which suggests that the speeches themselves are unaltered (Schröder 1975: 205).

By and large, textual authenticity appears as a central pillar of EFL in 19th century Germany. Literature – besides being textually authentic – is also considered a vessel of cultural authenticity. One concept of authenticity identifiable in earlier textbooks (e.g. König 1706) is real-world authenticity, for example in the form of situational dialogues. This concept may have been weakened during the 19th century by an emphasis on classic literature on the one hand and grammar-translation on the other. This is the case especially in situations where classroom practice approximated the following characterization of the grammar-translation method:

> Although the grammar-translation method started out as a simple approach to language learning for young schoolchildren, it was grossly distorted in the collision of interests between the classicists and their modern language rivals. Intrinsically, as we shall see later, the method is so ordinary that it is sometimes difficult to see what all the fuss was about. Each lesson had one or two new grammar rules, a short vocabulary list, and some practice examples to translate. Boring, maybe, but hardly the horror story we are sometimes asked to believe. However, it also contained seeds which eventually grew into a jungle of obscure rules, endless lists of gender classes and gender-class exceptions, self-conscious 'literary' archaisms, snippets of philology, and a total loss of genuine feeling for living language. (Howatt/Widdowson 2004: 156)

No concept of authenticity applies to these practices. Van Lier (1996) conceives of authenticity as the result of an individual process within the learner. He is, however, an absolute exception depicting the grammar-translation method as potentially authentic:

In a curious way, it seems to me that the traditional language lessons of the grammar translation type which I remember from my school days might lay greater claim to that sort of authenticity than some of the so-called communicative classrooms that I have had occasion to observe in recent years. I must emphasize that the old lessons seem to have been authentic 'for me', although they may well have been inauthentic for some of my class mates, although they may well have been inauthentic for some of my class mates. (van Lier 1996: 128)

The Prussian system established by Wilhelm von Humboldt consisted of two main school types on the secondary level. English was rarely taught in the higher tier, the *Gymnasien*, for they strongly represented Humboldt's humanistic ideal which prioritized the classical languages (Howatt/Widdowson 2004: 156; Hüllen 2005: 76). English was often taught with the grammar-translation method. The lower tier was again divided into the quite prestigious *Realgymnasien* and the lower-aspiring *Oberrealschulen* (Howatt/Widdowson 2004: 156). "The breakthrough in modern-language teaching reform in Germany came in the 'Realgymnasien' which were prestigious enough to matter but sufficiently 'expendable' for change to be permitted" (Howatt/Widdowson 2004: 156).

English being taught at *Realschule* seems logical because the language became more and more useful as opposed to the classical languages. However, the method of grammar-translation was perceived as a mismatch. Hüllen describes its implementation at *Realschule* as a concession to the humanistically inclined government. To a certain extent the notions of usefulness and practicality were simply incongruent with the German *Zeitgeist* of Weimar Classicism and Romanticism which remained powerful under Humboldt. Scientific and technological innovations, along with a growing internationalization, slowly strengthened the spirit of efficacy and pragmatism in language learning during the course of the century and may have contributed to what today is known as the Modern Language Reform of 1882 (Hüllen 2005: 76-77).

6.2.5 1882 until the emergence of *authentic/authenticity* as a term (approx. 1970)

Wilhelm Vietor's book *Der Sprachenunterricht muss umkehren!* (*Language teaching must start afresh!* – 1882) is closely associated with the reform throughout Europe. Other important contributors were Paul Édouard Passy (France), Otto Jespersen (Denmark), and Henry Sweet (England). The reformers championed practical proficiency in the foreign language. To achieve this, they saw fit what became known as the Direct Method. Target language use with little regulation lay at the core of this method. At the beginners' stage, imitative pronunciation drills became common. Later, explanations in the target language dominated, while translations and formalistic grammar teaching became less frequent (Hüllen 2005: 106). Meaning was to be gleaned and produced on the sentence level rather than on the word level. Oral activities tended to precede written ones, all of this happening with minimal resort to the mother tongue. Proponents of the method found arguments in the latest psychological findings of the time. Detractors would highlight the forfeiture of systematicity and insight which purportedly resulted from devaluing grammar as well as the mother tongue. The Direct Method was slow to catch on. Even in its moderate form it would not find broad implementation until the Prussian school reform of 1925 (Hüllen

2005: 104-108). More comprehensive accounts of the reform movement are provided by Hüllen (ibid.) and by Howatt/Widdowson (2004: 187–209).

By and large, the movement marks a shift toward what I have termed real-world authenticity:

> The Reform Movement was founded on three basic principles [...]: the primacy of speech, the centrality of the connected text as the kernel of the teaching-learning process, and the absolute priority of an oral classroom methodology. (Howatt/Widdowson 2004: 189)

These principles reflect the demands of communication outside the classroom, thereby matching definitions of real-world authenticity. One such definition is articulated by Nunan:

> Task authenticity refers to tasks that closely mirror communication in the world outside the classroom. (Nunan 2004: 212)

The increased sense of usefulness also promoted English as a school subject:

> By the end of the 19th century, French and English had acquired the recognition necessary to become relevant for the *Abitur*. Teaching these languages was considered educationally useful. New economic developments, in which the young German empire wanted to partake, made an active knowledge of the two languages appear indispensable.[72] (Hüllen 2005: 114)

The Prussian School Reform of 1924 brought important changes about. As for foreign language learning, the reform paper was strongly influenced by the Direct Method, at the core of which lay pronunciation and speaking activities, inductive and functional grammar, and the renunciation of rote learning (Hüllen 2005: 110-121). The main focus of the reform was on national culture (*Kulturkunde*), which was later distorted into patriotism and self-adulation by the national socialists (*Folientheorie* – roughly translatable as blueprint theory or template theory). In EFL, the focus manifested itself in the contrasting of the own culture with the target culture. Familiarization with the target culture was to be achieved through the reading of literature so as to become acquainted with the fine arts of the respective foreign countries: "Reading lies at the center of modern language learning. The reception of complete works or extracts from these should begin as early as possible" (extract of the reform paper in Hüllen 2005: 118).[73] Thus, literature became the medium of cultures. National cultures were taught as homogeneous reservoirs of personal characteristics and literary style.

Two concepts of authenticity are clearly visible in the approaches promoted by the Prussian School Reform: textual authenticity and cultural authenticity. Textual authenticity in the form of literature was not new. Cultural authenticity, however, had never figured

---

72   Original: "Das Französische und Englische hatten sich im 19. Jahrhundert allgemeine Anerkennung als abiturfähige Schulfächer verschafft, weil mit ihrer Lehre ein erzieherischer Nutzen verbunden werden konnte. Damals neue wirtschaftliche Entwicklungen, an denen das junge Deutsche Reich teilnehmen wollte, ließen die aktive Kenntnis dieser beiden Sprachen als unabdingbar erscheinen." (Hüllen 2005: 114)

73   Original: "Die Lektüre steht im Mittelpunkt des neusprachlichen Unterrichts. Das zusammenhängende Lesen ganzer Werke oder selbständiger Abschnitte daraus soll möglichst früh einsetzen" (Hüllen 2005: 118).

so prominently. The concept is informed by essentialist notions and pursued in a contrastive manner, as explained above. A modern-day description of cultural authenticity that corresponds with the tenets of the reform is provided by Liddicoat/Scarino: "Most importantly, [authentic materials] are produced within the cultural context of native speakers and are imbued with the assumptions, values, and ways of communicating of that culture" (Liddicoat/Scarino 2013: 95). The use of literature with the explicit goal of garnering knowledge about the given target culture causes a merger of two concepts of authenticity – textual and cultural authenticity.

The educational policies of the Third Reich had a surprisingly moderate influence on language teaching practice (Hüllen 2005: 130). Unlike other languages, predominantly French, English did not suffer marginalization as a school subject. It became the first foreign language in most secondary schools as of 1937/38 thus reversing the traditional order (Lehberger 2003: 612). Adjustments were for the most part confined to content:

> New textbooks did not appear until 1937/38. Their ideological content varied. Some books highlighted England as a political role-model with regard to history and character (British Empire, national pride, willingness to sacrifice). Other books went further by directly propagating the politics and ideology of national socialism (colonial and territorial claims, race ideology). As with other periods in the history of language teaching, not even during the time of National Socialism did theoretical precepts lead to a complete implementation in the classroom.[74] (Lehberger 2003: 613)

Instructional methods remained largely in line with the prevailing approaches that had established themselves since the school reform of 1924. Language, unlike content subjects, was not prone to political indoctrination, as Hüllen summarizes: "Pronunciation stayed pronunciation, vocabulary stayed vocabulary, grammar stayed grammar" (Hüllen 2005: 130).[75] Certain authors were censored but English, being a Germanic language, was generally preferred over French, which was historically laden with hostility (Hüllen 2005: 127-130).

The end of World War II did not bring about much change. English was – except in the French occupied zone – cemented as the prioritized foreign language, especially when the *Hamburger Abkommen* of 1964 made it a compulsory subject in all secondary schools in West Germany (Hüllen 2005: 131-134). In post-war Germany EFL theory was initially influenced by a seminal publication by Adolf Bohlen (1957) who pursued the humanistic goal of learning the foreign language as *Bildungssprache* instead of conceiving of English as a practical means of communication (Hüllen 2005: 135–136). In practice, compelling

---

74 Original: "Neue Lehrbücher erscheinen sukzessive erst ab 1937/38, ihr ideologischer Gehalt ist unterschiedlich zu werten. Während Lehrbücher einiger Verlage sich in ihrer Politisierung auf die Hervorhebung der politischen Vorbildfunktion englischer Geschichte und Charakterzüge (Empire, Nationalstolz, Opferbereitschaft) beschränken, finden sich in anderen Lehrwerken die direkte Propagierung nationalsozialistischer Politik und Ideologie (Kolonial- und Gebietsansprüche, Rassenideologie). [...] Wie für andere Phasen in der Geschichte des Fremdsprachenunterrichts, so gilt selbst für die Zeit des Nationalsozialismus, dass eine völlige Gleichsetzung von theoretischen Zielsetzungen und Unterrichtspraxis nicht vorgenommen werden kann." (Lehberger 2003: 613)

75 Original: "Aussprache blieb (und bleibt) Aussprache, Vokabular blieb (und bleibt) im Kernbereich Vokabular, Grammatik blieb (und bleibt) Grammatik" (Hüllen 2005: 130).

external conditions such as the occupation of Germany, increased immigration, and growing internationalism counteracted Bohlen's maxims and provided the soil for more communicative approaches to language teaching. Hüllen sees unprecedented circumstances in effect as of the mid-1960s (Hüllen 2005: 140141)–. According to him, the bulk of language learning in Germany had previously followed the aims of either acquiring reading skills or conversing within elitist circles (Hüllen 2005: 135-142).

Around 1965 language learning theory and practice became experimental and varied (Hüllen 2005: 146). A common denominator was the chiefly functional approach as opposed to the pursuit of humanistic goals through language learning. Methods emerged which invoked scientific findings in the fields of linguistics and psychology. New technology was incorporated. EFL and applied linguistics became prolific academic disciplines (Hüllen 2005: 142-143; 146), and Communicative Language Teaching (CLT) arose.

The use of classic literature decreased, as "[m]any attempts to implement the communicative approach have found no use for literary texts" (Little/Devitt/Singleton 1988: 25). Schröder makes a similar observation regarding literature:

> Political thought post-1968 chastised the outdated literary canon for being bourgeois. In some German states it was completely abandoned. The results in literature pedagogy grew ever poorer. The reform of the upper grades in *Gymnasium* reinforced the decline. Today [i.e. in 1985] a Renaissance is under way, sparked by notions of nostalgia and restoration. Literature is back in fashion.[76] (Schröder 1985: 51-52)

An epitome of that old canon is Ludwig Herrig's anthology *The British classical authors* (1849) which was republished for over one hundred years (Klippel 2005: 196-197). The book's eventual decline roughly coincided with the developments just outlined. Klippel describes the temporary lull in the use of literature as follows:

> The use of literary texts in language teaching post-1945 is characterized by three phases. Until the early 1970s, literature was studied intensively in the advanced grades. A period ensued which favored non-fiction and journalistic prose, whereas classic literature was scarcely used. Since the late 1990s, literature has reemerged in the context of new theoretical developments.[77] (Klippel/Cillia 2016: 630)

---

76   Original: "Im Zuge der kulturpolitischen Denkprozesse der Jahre nach 1968 wurde der überkommene literarische Kanon als bildungsbürgerlich gebrandmarkt und in einer Reihe von Bundländern ganz zu den Akten gelegt. [...] [D]ie konkreten literaturdidaktischen Ergebnisse des Deutsch- und besonders des Fremdsprachenunterrichts wurden immer dürftiger. Die Oberstufenreform mit ihrer Grundkurs-Misere hat den Niedergang nur noch augenfälliger gemacht. Inzwischen bahnt sich – vor einem insgesamt nostalgisch-restaurativen Hintergrund – der Umschwung an [...]. [...] Literatur im engen Sinne ist wieder ‚in'." (Schröder 1985: 51–52)

77   Original: "Der Einsatz literarischer Texte im Fremdsprachenunterricht ist seit 1945 grob durch drei Phasen charakterisiert. Auf die Zeit intensiver Lektüre literarischer Werke im fortgeschrittenen Unterricht bin in die 1970er Jahre folgte eine Periode der Bevorzugung von Sachtexten und journalistischer Prosa, wenngleich im Englischunterricht wenige klassische literarische Texte weiter behandelt wurden. Seit den späten 1990er Jahren gewinnt

Gilmore, who takes an international perspective, considers slightly different circumstances. He identifies an eschewal of authentic texts in general:

> During the twentieth century [...], prevailing linguistic theories of the time spawned a multitude of methods such as the 'New Method' and the 'Audiolingual Method' (Richards & Rodgers 1986) which all imposed carefully structured (and therefore contrived) materials and prescribed behaviours on teachers and learners, leading to what Howatt (1984: 267[78]) refers to as a 'cult of materials' [...] The issue of authenticity reappeared in the 1970s [...] This culminated in the approach which, at least in EFL circles, still holds sway today – Communicative Language Teaching – and paved the way for the reintroduction of authentic texts (Gilmore 2007: 97)

It becomes evident that the different genres of authentic text must be distinguished. Schröder (1985) and Klippel (2016) speak of the classic literary canon being phased out as of 1968 – a development that largely corresponded with Communicative Language Teaching. Other genres of authentic text, such as non-fiction and newspaper articles, were actually trending up during that period (Klippel/Cillia 2016: 630). It is possible that modern literature saw a similar uptick in contrast to the old classics.

6.3 Summary

The preceding descriptions are lacking in historical detail due to the focus on conceptual authenticity. The rough sketching of trends allows for the tracing of textual authenticity as an EFL concept. At no point in time were authentic texts completely abandoned. This overview helps us gain a general understanding of when authentic texts were used, how they were used, and to what extent they were used. The historical chapters, therefore, lay no claim to comprehensiveness and/or fine detail. They are primarily intended to illustrate that concepts of authenticity existed prior to the term coming into existence. Yet they show that a more thorough study of the use of authentic texts in the history of language teaching and learning would be a very fruitful undertaking indeed. The notion that authenticity coincides with Communicative Language Teaching (CLT) is valid only in certain respects, as I detailed in chapter 4.5.5.2. While the term was not widely used before the 1970s, the corresponding concepts were in many cases not new at the time they became labeled *authentic*.

First and foremost, the concept of textual authenticity has been a mainstay of EFL. In chapter 2.2.3, the different text genres that fall within the concept are presented. Literary fiction is probably the most consistent genre of authentic text to be used in EFL over time. It probably never disappeared completely but went through periods when it was less fashionable. One such period was roughly between 1968 and 1985, as Schröder points out (Schröder 1985: 51-52 – see previous chapter).

---

die Literatur im Kontext neuerer theoretischer Entwicklungen erneut an Bedeutung [...]." (Klippel/Cillia 2016: 630)

78   Page numbers may differ because I use a later edition of the book.

The concept of cultural authenticity has been pursued with equally remarkable consistency in the history of EFL in Germany. It typically occurred in combination with textual authenticity, namely when literature and other authentic genres were used for learning and teaching English. A period of particular focus on cultural authenticity are the years following the Prussian School Reform of 1924. The reform papers display an extreme propensity to teach students about foreign cultures via the use of literature in the public schools. In these documents, the connection between literature and cultural learning is made explicit (Hüllen 2005: 118).

The third concept of authenticity that occurs sporadically, though not quite as consistently as the first two, is real-world authenticity. Many approaches in the history of EFL relied on the principle of approximating as closely as possible the tasks which the learner is likely to face in the future. To give one example, dialogue books, which were common for centuries, are based on this idea. Johann König's *A complete English guide for high Germans* (1706), for instance, contains dialogues that the author considers to mirror realistic situations: *With a taylor, With a merchant about a bill of exchange* (König 1748: 299-352).

Concepts of authenticity that appear not to have played a role in EFL before CLT emerged are predominantly authenticity of text reception and authenticity of individual behavior. Both concepts are essentially constructivist and learner-oriented. Authenticity of individual behavior is a rather vague concept, which makes it difficult to trace over time. Authenticity of text reception, on the other hand, may be affirmed to be an innovation that emerged alongside CLT.

Authenticity of text reception is predicated on the idea that the individual learner must be put in a situation where he or she can authenticate the given text. What this entails is that the text cannot be too difficult, that it should be appealing to the learner, and that the activities to be done with the text should be relevant to the learner. The following lines by Widdowson apply to extracts of authentic text:

> [E]ven if the learner is motivated to read a particular extract and is ready to give an authentic response, he will be denied the opportunity if the linguistic difficulty of the passage is such that he cannot process it. [...] Clearly a genuine instance of use cannot be authenticated if it consists of syntactic structures and lexical items which the learner just has not the competence to comprehend. (Widdowson 1978: 82)

> If we read a newspaper report, for example, we do so because we have an interest in its topic and as we read we associate the contents with our existing knowledge. We read what is relevant to our affairs or what appeals to our interests; and what is remote from our particular world we do not bother to read at all. To present someone with a set of extracts and to require him to read them not in order to learn something interesting and relevant about the world but in order to learn something about the language being used is to misrepresent normal language use to some degree. The extracts are, by definition, 'genuine' instances of language use, but if the learner is required to deal with them in a way which does not correspond to his normal communicative activities, then they cannot be said to be 'authentic' instances of use. (Widdowson 1978: 80)

Similar ideas may have existed in earlier decades, and possibly in earlier centuries. However, little evidence exists that the approaches were implemented on a scale comparable with the period following the communicative turn of the 1960s and 1970s. For example, one corollary of Widdowson's concept is the principle of using simplified versions of text:

> Our next task is to process our material, to prepare it pedagogically in some way so as to bring the learner to the point when he is capable of responding to the genuine discourse we have selected in authentic fashion. This is where the 'doctoring' comes in, the pedagogic tampering with data that the 'authentic data' school complains about. My argument would be that the pedagogic process must necessarily involve some kind of tampering in order to bring learners to the point at which they can realize the authenticity of the language by appropriate response. It is not enough to establish ends which are adequate: we must also establish adequate means of achieving them. (Widdowson 1976: 266)

Widdowson advocates what is otherwise known as simplification (or grading) as a form of textual scaffolding (e.g. Harmer 2007: 59). Simplification was not common practice during the time when English literature became readily available in Germany. One outlier appears to have been an edition of James Thomson's *Seasons* from 1798, according to (Schröder 1985: 61). A different form of scaffolding became very common during the 19th century: annotations. Widdowson's statement above (Widdowson 1976: 266), however, makes clear that annotations would not be considered sufficient to fit his conceptualization of authenticity. Beside the element of simplification, the idea that the content of the text must be of interest to the learner may have been emblematic of the *Zeitgeist*. The principle of learner-orientation in settings of EFL instruction may have gone hand in hand with a gradual change of values in German post-war society at large. The same principle is reflected in the advocacy of activities that engage the learners and render the text relevant to them.

Reinfried describes this principle as part of a paradigm shift:

> As early as in the 1970s, the conceptualization of the communicative method included a certain learner-orientation, although the term did not yet exist back then. Certain tasks and exercises made bolder attempts to incorporate the individual interests of the learners. One way of doing this was to encourage learners to share their opinions on various matters that occurred in the course book texts. Learners were provided useful chunks to that end. Another way was to prompt learners to speak about their personal interests and experiences, their preferences and aversions.[79] (Reinfried 2001: 4-5)

Authenticity *per se* cannot be said to be an innovation of CLT. In fact, a minority of the concepts which are today described as authentic are really new. Widdowson's concept of authentication – or authenticity of text reception, as I have called it – is a concept which probably did not play a big role in ELT before Widdowson put forward his thoughts.

---

79   Original: "Die kommunikative Methodenkonzeption beinhaltete schon in den siebziger Jahren Ansätze zu einer gewissen Lernerorientierung, obwohl es den Begriff damals noch nicht gab. [...] Darüber hinaus versuchten einige Aufgaben oder Übungen nun auch stärker, die individuellen Interessen der Schüler einzubeziehen. Dies geschah zum einen dadurch, dass Schüler aufgefordert wurden, ihre persönliche Meinung zu irgendwelchen Fragen, die in Lehrwerktexten angesprochen wurden, zum Ausdruck zu bringen. Dazu wurden ihnen auch entsprechende Redemittel zur Verfügung gestellt. Zum anderen wurden Schüler angeregt, sich über ihre persönlichen Interessen und Erfahrungen, ihre Vorlieben und Abneigungen zur äußern." (Reinfried 2001: 4–5)

Other concepts, most importantly textual authenticity, cultural authenticity, and real-world authenticity, have been present in the learning and teaching of EFL for centuries.

7 Six concepts of authenticity

This study investigates authenticity in EFL by means of discourse analysis. The EFL discourse on authenticity is an academic discursive formation that is idiosyncratic in some regards. Most notably, the explicit negotiation of a single term is what makes the discourse dissimilar from many other thematic fields in EFL.

The discourse analytical approach includes an investigation of aspects which tend to stay hidden and go unmentioned in ordinary literature reviews. The method applied in this study considers such aspects as authorial style, authorial stance, author status, and citations. This in-depth analysis reveals complex dynamics in the discourse which determine what gets to be called *authentic*. In this concluding chapter, the most important points are summarized. The summary is descriptive, yet it includes assumptions as to what the causes of certain developments and phenomena may be. At a later stage, I put forth a number of propositions relating to the future use of the term *authentic/authenticity*. These propositions are informed by the discourse analytical findings of this study, which sets them apart from the numerous statements in the discourse that suggest what authenticity should refer to. It is my hunch that many of those statements are influenced by the positive connotation which the term carries. Therefore, I must emphasize that none of my propositions makes any claim as to what constitutes, or contributes to, good practice in teaching and learning English as a foreign language.

The EFL discourse on authenticity, as I define it, consists of all statements that contribute to an explicit negotiation of the term *authentic/authenticity* in EFL (cf. chapter 4.4.3). This discourse emerges in the 1970s. While the earliest statements use the term to describe a certain type of texts and materials, Henry G. Widdowson challenges this paradigm (1976; 1978; 1983). His thoughts include a clear proposal that no texts at all should be referred to as authentic:

> Genuineness is a characteristic of the passage itself and is an absolute quality. Authenticity
> is a characteristic of the relationship between the passage and the reader and it has to do
> with appropriate response. (Widdowson 1978: 80)

Many authors put forth concepts of authenticity implying that these should be called authentic, but very few argue that specific concepts should not be called authentic, as does Widdowson. He proposes the term *genuine* as a replacement of sorts, to denote what is otherwise known as authentic text. The bibliometric data shows that Widdowson is by far the most frequently cited author in the discourse. Yet, his terminological proposal proves to be of little avail. Even authors who are demonstrably familiar with Widdowson's distinction continue to speak of authentic texts and authentic materials (e.g. Breen 1985). This shows that it is all but impossible for a single author – even if he is as influential as Widdowson – to deprive a concept of the term *authentic/authenticity*. However, Widdowson also propounds a new concept in the abovementioned statement, namely appropriate response, which he chooses to label *authentic*. This conceptual and terminological innovation actually catches on in the discourse. It may do so partially by virtue of

Widdowson's relatively high author status, which affords his writings considerable exposure in the field. It appears that the term *authentic/authenticity* is difficult to detach from a concept, while being more easily connected to new concepts.

I have created a category based on appropriate response that is authenticity of text reception. It is expounded in chapter 3 along with the other conceptual categories which constitute my taxonomy. As a starting point for the taxonomy three different categorizations are drawn upon. The most recent and most extensive of these three is Gilmore (2007). My taxonomy differs from Gilmore's list in one central aspect. It is entirely conceptual and it considers terminology only insofar as the term *authentic/authenticity* is used to denote the given concept in the discourse. Gilmore, by contrast, appears to group authors by collocation. For example, if two different authors use the collocation *authentic task*, they are grouped in the same category by Gilmore. This can be misleading, if one is not aware that the two authors may have completely different understandings of what authenticity means. The latter is the case with Bachman (1991) and Breen (1985):

> We define situational authenticity as the perceived relevance of the test method characteristics to the features of a specific target language use situation. Thus, for a test task to be perceived as situationally authentic, the characteristics of the test task need to be perceived as corresponding to the features of a target language use situation. (Bachman 1991: 690)

> [G]iven the actual social potential of a classroom, the contrivance of 'other worlds' within it may not only be inauthentic but also quite unnecessary. [...] The authenticity of the classroom is that it is a rather special social event and environment wherein people share a primary communicative purpose: learning. [...] [O]ne of the main authentic activities within a language classroom is communication about how best to learn to communicate. (Breen 1985: 67-68)

The two statements reveal notions of authenticity that are basically incompatible. Consequently, I do not conceive of *authentic task* as a concept or a meaning, but as a collocation that may refer to at least two different concepts. In the case of Bachman (ibid.) and Breen (ibid.), the former statement is largely in line with the concept of real-world authenticity, while the latter lays the foundation for what I have termed classroom authenticity.

Six concepts can be extrapolated from the discourse. They form the taxonomy represented in figure 15. I have shown how collocations may be misleading. Still, they can function as conceptual anchors to a certain extent. It appears that authenticity is particularly difficult to grasp if the noun is used outside of a collocation. For example, it is impossible to answer the question *What is authenticity?* in an objective and universal manner. A collocation such as *cultural authenticity* is still not easily defined but the realm of possible meanings is narrowed considerably. The adjective *authentic* is syntactically more prone to form collocations because it is mostly used as a modifier as in *authentic materials*. In the taxonomy above, the noun *authenticity* is embedded in different collocations which I have chosen or even created. The collocations in the taxonomy, thus, do not necessarily correspond to the ones used by the authors in the discourse.

1. Textual authenticity
2. Authenticity of text reception
3. Real-world authenticity
4. Classroom authenticity
5. Authenticity of individual behavior
6. Cultural authenticity

Figure 15: Six concepts of authenticity

The term *authentic/authenticity* is extremely context-dependent, almost to the point of being generic. The word is actually close in function to *consistent/consistency* (Will 2016: 87-88). Only collocations, syntax, and broader context can determine what something is consistent with thereby instilling meaning into the term. This applies similarly to both *consistent/consistency* and *authentic/authenticity*. The term *authentic/authenticity* on its own has little semantic value, which means that its denotation varies. However, the term's connotation appears not to vary so much: "What is invariably carried over from every day discourse to the academic field of language teaching is the extremely positive connotation of the terms 'authentic/authenticity'" (Will 2016: 88). Some authors mention this phenomenon:

> When we try to define 'authenticity', however, we notice that it is one of those words like 'real' (as in 'He's really real') that sounds good but leaves us wondering exactly what it means. (Bachman 1991: 689)

> 'Genuineness', 'realness', 'truthfulness', 'validity', 'reliability', 'undisputed credibility', and 'legitimacy' are just some of the concepts involved when we talk about authenticity. (Rost 2002: 165)

> Authenticity stands for realness, credibility, warranty – the term is ethically connotated.[80] (Decke-Cornill 2004: 17)

> From any concordance for the words 'authentic' and 'authenticity', it will quickly emerge that authenticity is a positive attribute, collocating with desirable qualities such as purity, originality and quality, and valuable enough to earn credentials such as a certificate, a stamp, or a seal. (Mishan 2004: 219)

---

80 Original: "Authentizität steht für Echtheit, Glaubwürdigkeit, Verbürgtheit – der Begriff ist ethisch konnotiert." (Decke-Cornill 2004: 17)

> [T]erms such as 'authentic', 'genuine', 'real' or 'natural' and their opposites 'fake', 'unreal' or 'contrived' are emotionally loaded and indicate approval or disapproval whilst remaining ill-defined. I would argue that, from the classroom teacher's perspective, rather than chasing our tails in pointless debate over authenticity versus contrivance, we should focus instead on learning aims (Gilmore 2007: 98)

> If a didactic design is authentic, the assumption goes, it is good. That authenticity supports language learning is often considered a given [...]. (Buendgens-Kosten 2013: 274)

The exact connotation of the word is difficult to pinpoint beyond a recognition that exclusively positive qualities appear to be evoked. As alluded to above, these positive qualities are equally present in the colloquial use of the term. Rosenbloom (2011), in her article for the *New York Times*, describes and exemplifies the publicly perceived value of authenticity:

> Authenticity seems to be the value of the moment, rolling off the tongues of politicians, celebrities, Web gurus, college admissions advisers, reality television stars. In recent months it's been cited by the likes of Katie Couric ('I think I love to be my authentic self,' she said on CBS); Secretary of State Hillary Rodham Clinton ('I believe in being as authentic as possible,' she told Glamour magazine); former Senator Rick Santorum of Pennsylvania (who on Fox described himself as 'being authentic') (Rosenbloom 2011: 1)

In the colloquial discourse, the positive connotation of authenticity may be used to valorize one's own position. In the EFL discourse, very similar dynamics may be at work, but the valorization applies to concepts rather than individuals. Such dynamics can ultimately lead to the development of an ideology at the expense of pedagogic value, as Alan Waters remarks:

> [D]iscourse promotes or proscribes language teaching ideas on the basis of ideological belief rather than pedagogical value. The debate about 'authenticity' vs. 'artificiality' in language teaching is a representative example of this tendency. (Waters 2009: 138)

More research is needed to find out about the origins and implications of connotations in the EFL discourse. It is possible that the positive connotation of authenticity plays a role in the term's proliferation and in the diversification of concepts.

The rapid proliferation of the term in EFL is depicted in chapter 4.5.5. The emergence of the term, however, is not identical with the emergence of the concepts that are attached to it. Chapter 6 provides a rough historical sketch of how certain concepts were pursued in EFL long before the term *authentic/authenticity* came up and before it began to denote these same concepts. Textual authenticity, cultural authenticity and real-world authenticity are particularly robust ideas in EFL history. It is a commonplace that authenticity came into being with Communicative Language Teaching (CLT). This is valid primarily for authenticity as a term entering the EFL discourse. However, many of the concepts have informed practical language learning and teaching for centuries. One concept of authenticity that can possibly be considered innovative is authenticity of text reception, as introduced by Widdowson in the late 1970s (cf. chapter 5.2.1).

What can be ultimately said about authenticity as an element in the EFL discourse is that it is not helpful to have a term attached to so many concepts. The problem is intensified by the fact that some of the concepts are mutually exclusive (real-world authenticity vs. classroom authenticity). However, it appears hardly possible to reverse the process of conceptual diversification that has taken place over the past decades. An unsuccessful initiative by Widdowson (1976; 1978) to rechristen textual authenticity as *genuineness* is symptomatic of such impossibility. It is all the more important that authors who use the term *authentic/authenticity* be precise about what they mean by it.

Terminological precision is best achieved through citations, which presupposes a sound knowledge of the discourse on authenticity. Given how many concepts are already attached to the term, one is likely to find statements supporting one's own understanding of authenticity. Since *authentic/authenticity* is today an established technical term, it is included in all the latest EFL dictionaries. Four of these feature entries for authenticity that provide accurate accounts of the discourse.[81] They also name sources – except for Thornbury (2006) – thereby serving as a good starting point for a literature review. Three EFL dictionaries cannot be recommended if one is in search of an unbiased and comprehensive overview of authenticity.[82] It appears that authenticity, partly due to its connotation, is such a contentious topic that even the otherwise descriptive genre of the EFL dictionary becomes prone to pedagogic argument and conceptual advocacy (cf. chapter 5.2.4). Beside EFL dictionaries, some articles take a comprehensive approach to presenting the discourse on authenticity in largely descriptive style. Gilmore (2007), Joy (2011), and Buendgens-Kosten (2014) each provide highly informed and nuanced overviews citing many relevant sources. When using the term *authentic/authenticity*, references are important because collocations are insufficient in providing due clarity and conceptual accuracy, as illustrated above. From a discourse analytical perspective, it is not advisable to pass on references and engage in new definitions instead, for such practice perpetuates the process of conceptual diversification.

The conceptual taxonomy put forth in this study (chapter 3) may be considered helpful in terms of orientation. The in-depth analysis of the discourse (chapter 5) provides differentiated insights into how the term *authentic/authenticity* has been linked to different concepts over the past 45 years.

---

81   These are:

      Johnson, Keith; Johnson, Helen (eds.) (1999). *Encyclopedic dictionary of applied linguistics*. Oxford: Blackwell.

      Byram, Michael et al. (eds.) (2000). *Routledge encyclopedia of language teaching and learning*. London: Routledge.

      Thornbury, Scott (2006). *An A-Z of ELT. A dictionary of terms and concepts*. Oxford: Macmillan.

      Surkamp, Carola (ed.) (2010). *Metzler-Lexikon Fremdsprachendidaktik*. Stuttgart: Metzler.

82   These are:

      Richards, Jack C.; Platt, John Talbot; Weber, Heidi (eds.) (1985). *Longman dictionary of language teaching and applied linguistics*. Harlow: Longman.

      Davies, Alan (2005). *A glossary of applied linguistics*. Edinburgh: Edinburgh University Press.

      Chapelle, Carol (ed.) (2013). *The encyclopedia of applied linguistics*. Oxford: Blackwell.

Bibliography

Adams, Thomas W. (1995). What makes materials authentic? *ERIC Document Reproduction Service* No. ED 391389, 1-8.

Al Azri, Rahid Hamed; Al-Rashdi, Majid Hilal (2014). The effect of using authentic materials in teaching. *International journal of scientific and technology research* 3 (10), 249-254.

Alderson, Charles J.; Urquhart, A. H. (eds.) (1984). *Reading in a foreign language.* Harlow: Longman.

Alexander, Richard (1983). How authentic can (and should) 'authentic' texts be? In: Kühlwein (ed.), 87-88.

Allan, Rachel (2008). Can a graded reader corpus provide 'authentic' input? *ELT Journal* 63 (1), 23-32.

Alptekin, Cem (2002). Towards intercultural communicative competence in ELT. *ELT Journal* 56 (1), 57-64.

Amor, Stuart (2002). *Authenticity and authentication in language learning. Distinctions, orientations, implications.* 85. Frankfurt am Main, New York: Peter Lang.

Andrés, Ana (2009). *Measuring academic research. How to undertake a bibliometric study.* Oxford: Chandos Publishing.

Appel, Joachim (1995). *Diary of a language teacher.* Oxford: Heinemann.

Arnold, Ewen (1991). Authenticity revisited: How real is real? *English for Specific Purposes* 10, 237-244.

Arnold, Theodor (1718). *A new English grammar (title abridged).* Hannover: Förster.

Bachman, Lyle F.; Palmer, Adrian S. (1996). *Language testing in practice. Designing and developing useful language tests.* Oxford, New York: Oxford University Press.

Bachman, Lyle F. (1991). What does language testing have to offer. *TESOL Quarterly* 25 (4), 671-704.

Bachman, Lyle F. (1990). *Fundamental considerations in language testing.* Oxford: Oxford University Press.

Bacon, Susan M.; Finnemann, Michael D. (1990). A study of the attitudes, motives, and strategies of university foreign language students and their disposition to authentic oral and written input. *The Modern Language Journal* 74 (4), 459.

Badger, Richard; MacDonald, Malcolm N. (2010). Making it real: Authenticity, process and pedagogy. *Applied Linguistics* 31 (4), 578-582.

Baker, Paul; Ellece, Sibonile (2011). *Key terms in discourse analysis.* New York: Continuum International Pub. Group.

Barbieri, Federica; Eckhardt, Suzanne E.B. (2007). Applying corpus-based findings to form-focused instruction: The case of reported speech. *Language Teaching Research* 11 (3), 319-346.

Barekat, Behzad; Nobakhti, Hamed (2014). The effect of authentic and inauthentic materials in cultural awareness training on EFL learners' listening comprehension ability. *TPLS* 4 (5), 1058-1065.

Basturkmen, Helen (2014). *English for academic purposes. Critical concepts in linguistics.* Abingdon (UK), New York: Routledge.

Burwitz-Melzer, Eva; Mehlhorn, Grit; Riemer, Claudia; Bausch, Karl-Richard; Krumm, Hans-Jürgen (eds.) (2016). *Handbuch Fremdsprachenunterricht.* 5. Auflage. Tübingen: Narr.

Bausch, Karl-Richard; Christ, Herbert; Krumm, Hans-Jürgen (eds.) (2003). *Handbuch Fremdsprachenunterricht.* Tübingen: A. Francke Verlag.

Beck, Rudolf; Kuester, Hildegard; Kuester, Martin (eds.) (2007). *Basislexikon anglistische Literaturwissenschaft*. Bd. 2930. Paderborn: Fink.

Beeching, Kate (1982). Authentic material 1. *British Journal of Language Teaching* 20 (2), 17-20.

Beile, Werner (1979). Authentizität und Hörverstehen. In: Heuer (ed.), 232-234.

Beile, Werner (1986). Authentizität als fremdsprachendidaktischer Begriff. Zum Problemfeld von Texten gesprochener Sprache. In: Ehnert/Piepho (eds.), 145-162.

Benson, Phil; Voller, Peter (eds.) (1997). *Autonomy and independence in language learning*. London, New York: Longman.

Berardo, Sacha Anthony (2006). The use of authentic materials in the teaching of reading. *The Reading Matrix* 6 (2), 60-69.

Bhatia, Vijay (2012). Professional written genres. In: Gee/Handford (eds.), 239-251.

Biber, Douglas (2006). *University language. A corpus-based study of spoken and written registers*. v. 23. Amsterdam, Philadelphia: J. Benjamins.

Bishop, Rudine Sims (2003). Reframing the debate about cultural authenticity. In: Fox/Short (eds.), 25-40.

Bohlen, Adolf (1957). *Moderner Humanismus*. Heidelberg: Quelle & Meyer.

Böhme, Hartmut; Scherpe, Klaus R. (1996). *Literatur und Kulturwissenschaften. Positionen, Theorien, Modelle*. Reinbek bei Hamburg: Rowohlt.

Bosenius, Petra (ed.) (2004). *Interaktive Medien und Fremdsprachenlernen. Beiträge des 6. Mediendidaktischen Kolloquiums an der Universität zu Köln im Oktober 2002. Mediendidaktisches Kolloquium. Bd. 17.* Frankfurt am Main: Peter Lang.

Bowen, J. Donald (1972). Contextualizing Pronunciation Practice in the ESOL Classroom. *TESOL Quarterly* 6 (1), 83.

Breen, Michael P. (1985). Authenticity in the language classroom. *Applied Linguistics* (6(1)), 60-70.

Broughton, Geoffrey (1977). *A technical reader for advanced students*. London: Macmillan.

Brown, H. Douglas (2004). *Language assessment. Principles and classroom practices*. New York: Pearson/Longman.

Brown, J. S.; Collins, A.; Duguid, P. (1989). Situated Cognition and the Culture of Learning. *Educational Researcher* 18 (1), 32-42.

Brumfit, Christopher (1983). Introduction: Applied lingistics and communicative language teaching. In: Brumfit (ed.), v–vi.

Brumfit, Christopher (ed.) (1983). *Learning and teaching languages for communication. Applied linguistic perspectives*. London: Centre for Information on Language Teaching and Research for British Association for Applied Linguistics.

Brumfit, Christopher; Johnson, Keith (1979). Preface. In: Brumfit/Johnson (eds.), ix–x.

Brumfit, Christopher; Johnson, Keith (eds.) (1979). *The communicative approach to language teaching*. Oxford: Oxford University Press.

Bublitz, Wolfram; Lenk, Uta; Ventola, Eija (eds.) (1999). *Coherence in spoken and written discourse. How to create it and how to describe it : selected papers from the International Workshop on Coherence, Augsburg, 24-27 April 1997.* Bd. new ser. 63. Amsterdam, Philadelphia: John Benjamins Pub.

Buendgens-Kosten, Judith (2013). Authenticity in CALL: three domains of 'realness'. *ReCALL* 25 (02), 272-285.

Buendgens-Kosten, Judith (2014). Key concepts in ELT: Authenticity. *ELT Journal* 68 (4), 457-459.

Burckhardt, G. F.; Jost, J. M. (1826). *Praktische Englische Sprachlehre für Schulen und Privatunterricht*. Berlin: n.a.

Byram, Michael (ed.) (2000). *Routledge encyclopedia of language teaching and learning*. London, New York: Routledge.

Byrd, Patricia (ed.) (1994). *Material writer's guide*. New York: Heinle & Heinle Pub.

Cambridge English. Preliminary. Handbook for teachers (2012). Cambridge, United Kingdom: University of Cambridge, ESOL Examinations.

Cambridge University Press (2016). Cambridge English First 2. http://www.cambridge.org/us/cambridgeenglish/catalog/cambridge-english-exams-ielts/cambridge-english-first-2, access date: 07/16/2016.

Cambridge University Press (2016). Cambridge Your Space. http://www.cambridge.org/us/cambridgeenglish/catalog/secondary/your-space, access date: 07/16/2016.

Cambridge University Press (2016). Official Past Paper Packs. http://www.mycambridge-shop.ch/PastPaperPacks/en>, access date: 07/16/2016.

Canale, Michael; Swain, Merrill (1980). Theoretical bases of communicative approaches to second language teaching and testing. *Applied Linguistics* I (1), 1-47.

Candlin, Christopher N.; Edelhoff, Christopher (1982). *Challenges. Teacher's guide*. London: Longman.

Cecchetto, Vittorina; Stoinska, Magda (1997). Systems of reference in intellectual discourse: a potential source of intercultural stereotypes. In: Duszak (ed.), 141-154.

Chan, Jim Yee Him (2013). The role of situational authenticity in English language textbooks. *RELC Journal* 44 (3), 303-317.

Chapelle, Carol (1999). Theory and research: Investigation of 'authentic' language learning tasks. In: Egbert/Hanson-Smith (eds.), 101-115.

Chapelle, Carol (ed.) (2013). *The encyclopedia of applied linguistics*. Oxford: Blackwell.

Chavez, Monika (1998). Learner's perspectives on authenticity. *IRAL – International Review of Applied Linguistics in Language Teaching* 36 (4), 277-306.

Clarke, David F. (1989). Communicative theory and its influence on materials production. *Language Teaching* 22 (2), 73-86.

Clavel-Arroitia, Begona; Fuster-Marquez, Miguel (2014). The authenticity of real texts in advanced English language textbooks. *ELT Journal* 68 (2), 124-134.

Cook, Guy (1997). Language play, language learning. *ELT Journal* 51 (3), 224-231.

Crane, Diana (1972). *Invisible colleges. Diffusion of knowledge in scientific communities*. Chicago: University of Chicago Press.

Creese, Angela; Blackledge, Adrian; Takhi, Jaspreet Kaur (2014). The ideal 'native speaker' teacher: Negotiating authenticity and legitimacy in the language classroom. *Modern Language Journal* 98 (4), 937-951.

Crystal, David; Davy, Derek (1975). *Advanced conversational English*. London: Longman.

Cuddon, J. A. (1991). *A dictionary of literary terms and literary theory*. 3rd ed. Oxford, Cambridge (USA): Blackwell Reference.

Dantas-Whitney, Maria; Rilling, Sarah; Savova, Lilia (2009). *Authenticity in the language classroom and beyond: adult learners*. Alexandria, VA: TESOL.

Dantas-Whitney, Maria; Rilling, Sarah (2010). *Authenticity in the language classroom and beyond: children and adolescent learners*. Alexandria, VA: TESOL.

Davies, Alan (1984). Simple, simplified and simplification. What is authentic? In: Alderson/Urquhart (eds.), 181-195.

Davies, Alan (2005). *A glossary of applied linguistics*. Edinburgh: Edinburgh University Press.

Davies, Alan (2009). Simple, simplified and simplification: What is authentic? In: Hedge/Andon/Dewey (eds.), 163-175.

Day, Richard (2004). A critical look at authentic materials. *The Journal of AsiaTEFL* 1 (1), 101-114.

Day, Richard; Bamford, Julian (2009). The cult of authenticity and the myth of simplification. In: Hedge/Andon/Dewey (eds.), 233-245. (Originally a chapter in the book: Day, Richard (1998). *Extensive reading in the second language classroom*. Cambridge: Cambridge University Press.)

Decke-Cornill, Helene (2004). Die Kategorie der Authentizität im mediendidaktischen Diskurs der Fremdsprachendidaktik. In: Bosenius (ed.), 17-27.

Del Lungo Camiciotti, Gabriella; Tognini Bonelli, Elena (eds.) (2004). *Academic discourse. New insights into evaluation*. Bd. Volume 15: Peter Lang.

Devarajan, G. (ed.) (1997). *Bibliometric studies*. Bd. 1. New Delhi: Ess Ess Publications.

Dolle, Dora; Willems, Gerard M. (1984). The communicative approach to foreign language teaching; the teacher's case. In: Willems/Riley (eds.), 87-102.

Dunkel, Patricia A. (1994). Authentic second/foreign language listening texts: Issues of definition, operationalization, and application. In: Byrd (ed.), 95-106.

Dunn, Opal (2006). Do boys as young learners of English need different language learning opportunities from girls? Can authentic picture books help? In: Enever/Schmid-Schönbein (eds.), 115-122.

Duszak, Anna (ed.) (1997). *Culture and styles of academic discourse*. Bd. 104. Berlin, New York: Mouton de Gruyter.

Egbert, Joy; Hanson-Smith, Elizabeth (eds.) (1999). *CALL Environments. Research, Practice, and Critical Issues*. Alexandria, Virginia: TESOL.

Ehlers, Martin (1766). *Gedanken von der zur Verbesserung der Schulen notwendigen Erfordernissen*. Altona.

Ehnert, Rolf; Piepho, Hans-Eberhard (eds.) (1986). *Fremdsprachen lernen mit Medien*. München: Max Hueber Verlag.

Ellis, Rod (2003). *Task-based language learning and teaching*. Oxford, U.K., New York: Oxford University Press.

Enever, Janet; Schmid-Schönbein, Gisela (ed.) (2006). *Picture books and young learners of English*. Bd. 14. 1st edition. Berlin, München, Wien, Zürich, New York: Langenscheidt.

Enkvist, Nils Erik (1978). Introduction: text, cohesion, and coherence. In: Östman (ed.), 101-108.

Fairclough, Norman (1989). *Language and power*. London, New York: Longman.

Fairclough, Norman (2015). *Language and power*. Third edition; Twenty-fifth anniversary edition. London, New York: Routledge, Taylor & Francis Group.

Fanselow, John F.; Crymes, Ruth H. (eds.) (1976). *On TESOL '76. Selections based on teaching done at the Tenth Annual TESOL Convention [in New York, NY March 2-7, 1976]*. Washington, DC: TESOL.

Farrell, Thomas S. C. (2009). *Teaching reading to English language learners. A reflective guide*. Thousand Oaks: Corwin Press.

Finocchiaro, Mary (1971). Myth and reality in TESOL: A plea for a broader view. *TESOL Quarterly* 5 (1), 3.

FM4 (2015). About Radio FM4. http://fm4.orf.at/radio/stories/about, access date: 10/10/2015.

Foreword (1985). *Language Testing* 2 (1), 1.

Foucault, Michel (1969). *L'archéologie du savoir*. Paris: Gallimard.

Foucault, Michel (1971). *L'ordre du discours*. Paris: Gallimard.

Fox, Dana L.; Short, Kathy Gnagey (eds.) (2003). *Stories matter. The complexity of cultural authenticity in children's literature*. Urbana, Ill.: National Council of Teachers of English.

Geddes, Marion; White, Ron (1978). The use of semi-scripted simulated authentic speech and listening comprehension. *Audio-Visual Language Journal* 16 (3), 137-145.

Gee, James Paul; Handford, Michael (eds.) (2012). *The Routledge handbook of discourse analysis*. London, New York: Routledge.

Geurds, Alexander (2013). Culture sketching: the authenticity quest in ethnographic museums. In: Geurds/van Broekhoven (eds.), 1-10.

Geurds, Alexander; van Broekhoven, Laura (eds.) (2013). *Creating authenticity. Authentication processes in ethnographic museums*. Bd. 42.

Gilmore, Alex (2004). A comparison of textbook and authentic interactions. *ELT Journal* 58 (4), 363-374.

Gilmore, Alex (2007). Authentic materials and authenticity in foreign language learning. *LTA* 40 (02), 97-118.

Gläser, Rosemarie (1995). *Linguistic features and genre profiles of scientific English*. Bd. 9. Frankfurt am Main, New York: P. Lang.

Gotti, Maurizio (2003). *Specialized discourse. Linguistic features and changing conventions*. v. 8. Bern, New York: P. Lang.

Gray, Bethany; Biber, Douglas (2012). Current conceptions of stance. In: Hyland/Guinda (eds.), 15-33.

Gregory, Michael; Carroll, Susanne (1978). *Language and situation. Language varieties and their social contexts*. London: Routledge & Kegan Paul.

Grellet, Françoise (1981). *Developing reading skills. A practical guide to reading comprehension exercises*. Cambridge, New York: Cambridge University Press.

Guariento, William; Morley, John (2001). Text and task authenticity in the EFL classroom. *ELT Journal* 55 (4), 347-353.

Gutschow, Harald (1977). 'Authentizität' und 'Aktualität' in Texten für den Fremdsprachenunterricht. *Zielsprache Deutsch* 4, 2-11.

Haas, Renate; Klein-Braley, Christine; Schrey, Helmut (eds.) (1985). *Literatur im Kontext. Festschrift für Helmut Schrey zum 65. Geburtstag am 6. 1. 1985*. Bd. 10. Sankt Augustin: Hans Richarz.

Halliday, Michael A.K. (1976). *The social interpretation of language and meaning*. London: Edward Arnold.

Halliday, Michael A.K.; Hasan, Ruqaiya (1976). *Cohesion in English*. no. 9. London: Longman.

Halliday, Michael A.K.; McIntosh, Angus; Strevens, Peter (1964). *The linguistic sciences and language teaching*. London: Longman.

Harmer, Jeremy (1983). *The practice of English language teaching*. London, New York: Longman.

Harmer, Jeremy (2007). *The practice of English language teaching*. 4th ed. Harlow: Pearson Longman.

Hedge, Tricia (2000). *Teaching and learning in the language classroom*. Oxford: Oxford University Press.

Hedge, Tricia; Andon, Nick; Dewey, Martin (eds.) (2009). *English language teaching. Major themes in education 5*. Bd. 5. New York: Routledge.

Henrici, Gert (1980). Authentischer Fremsprachenunterricht. Einige Anmerkungen. *Bielefelder Beiträge zur Sprachlehrforschung* 2, 123-134.

Henry, Alastair (2013). Digital games and ELT: Bridging the authenticity gap. In: Ushioda (ed.), 133-155.

Herrig, Ludwig (1852). *The British classical authors. Select specimens of the national literature of England from G. Chaucer to the present time. Poetry and prose*. Braunschweig: Westermann.

Herron, Carol; Seay, Irene (1991). The effect of authentic oral texts on student listening comprehension in the foreign language classroom. *Foreign Language Annals* 24 (6), 487-495.

Heuer, Helmut (ed.) (1979). *Dortmunder Diskussionen zur Fremdsprachendidaktik. Kongressdokumentation der 8. Arbeitstagung d. Fremdsprachendidaktiker Dortmund 1978*. Dortmund: Lensing.

Holden, Susan (ed.) (1977). *English for specific purposes*. London: Modern English Publications.

Honeyfield, John (1977). Simplification. *TESOL Quarterly* 11 (4), 431-440.

Howatt, Anthony P. R.; Widdowson, H. G. (2004). *A history of English language teaching*. 2nd edition. Oxford, New York: Oxford University Press.

Hughes; Annie (2006). The 'why', 'what' and 'how' of using authentic picture books and stories in the EYL classroom. Some practical considerations. In: Enever/Schmid-Schönbein (eds.), 151-163.

Hüllen, Werner (2005). *Kleine Geschichte des Fremdsprachenlernens*. Berlin: Erich Schmidt.

Hutchinson, Tom; Waters, Alan (1987). *English for specific purposes. A learning-centred approach*. Cambridge: Cambridge University Press.

Hyland, Ken (2000). *Disciplinary discourses. Social interactions in academic writing*. Harlow, New York: Longman.

Hyland, Ken (2005). Stance and engagement. A model of interaction in academic discourse. *Discourse Studies* 7 (2), 173-192.

Hyland, Ken; Guinda, Carmen Sancho (eds.) (2012). *Stance and voice in written academic genres*. Houndmills, Basingstoke, Hampshire, New York: Palgrave Macmillan.

Hymes, Dell (1972). On communicative competence. In: Pride/Holmes (eds.), 269-293.

Iser, Wolfgang (1975). Der Lesevorgang: Eine phänomenologische Perspektive. In: Warning (ed.), 253-276.

Johnson, Keith (1982). *Communicative syllabus design and methodology*. 1st ed. Oxford, New York: Pergamon Press.

Johnson, Keith (1999). Authenticity. In: Johnson/Johnson (eds.), 24-25.

Johnson, Keith; Johnson, Helen (eds.) (1999). *Encyclopedic dictionary of applied linguistics*. Oxford: Blackwell.

Johnson, Keith; Porter, Don (eds.) (1983). *Perspectives in communicative language teaching*. London, New York: Academic Press.

Johnston, Bill (1999). Theory and research: Audience, language use, and language learning. In: Egbert/Hanson-Smith (eds.), 55-64.

Joiner, Elizabeth G. (1984). *Authentic texts in the foreign language classroom: Focus on listening and reading*. Monterey, CA: Defense Language Institute.

Jørgensen, Marianne; Phillips, Louise (2002). *Discourse analysis as theory and method*. London, Thousand Oaks: Sage Publications.

Joy, John L. (2011). The duality of authenticity in ELT. *Journal of Language and Linguistic Studies* 7 (2), 7-23.

Kaelin, Eugene Francis (1988). *Heidegger's Being and Time. A reading for readers*. Tallahassee: University Presses of Florida; Florida State University Press.

Kaplan, Robert B. (ed.) (2002). *The Oxford handbook of applied linguistics*. New York, N.Y: Oxford University Press.

Keller, Reiner (2008). *Wissenssoziologische Diskursanalyse. Grundlegung eines Forschungsprogramms*. 2nd edition. Wiesbaden: VS, Verlag für Sozialwissenschaften.

Kelly, Louis G. (1969). *25 centuries of language teaching. An inquiry into the science, art, and development of language teaching methodology, 500 B.C.-1969.* Rowley, Mass.: Newbury House Publishers.

Kestemont, Mike; Daelemans, Walter; Sandra, Dominiek (2012). Robust rhymes? The stability of authorial style in medieval narratives. *Journal of Quantitative Linguistics* 19 (1), 54-76.

Khalili Sabet, Masoud (2012). The impact of authentic listening materials on elementary EFL learners' listening skills. *IJALEL* 1 (4), 216-229.

Kienbaum, Barbara E.; Russell, A. J.; Welty, S. (1986). *Communicative competence in foreign language learning with authentic materials. final project report.* Final project report. Calumet (USA): n.a.

Kierepka, Adelheid (2006). Children's approaches to authentic picture books in the primary EFL classroom. In: Enever/Schmid-Schönbein (eds.), 123-130.

Kilickaya, Ferit (2004). Authentic materials and cultural content in EFL classrooms. *ITESLJ* 10 (7). http://iteslj.org/Techniques/Kilickaya-AutenticMaterial.html, access date: 06/20/2016.

Klein-Braley, Christine (1985). A cloze-up on the c-test: A study in the construct validation of authentic tests. *Language Testing* 2 (1), 76-104.

Klippel, Friederike (1994). *Englischlernen im 18. und 19. Jahrhundert. Die Geschichte der Lehrbücher und Unterrichtsmethoden.* Münster: Nodus.

Klippel, Friederike (2005). Englische Literatur im Englischunterricht des 19. Jahrhunderts. In: Klippel/Hüllen (eds.), 185-209.

Klippel, Friederike; Hüllen, Werner (eds.) (2005). *Sprachen der Bildung - Bildung durch Sprachen im Deutschland des 18. und 19. Jahrhunderts.* Wiesbaden: Harrassowitz.

Klippel, Friederike; Doff, Sabine (2006). *Englischdidaktik. Praxishandbuch für die Sekundarstufe I und II.* 1st edition. Berlin: Cornelsen Scriptor.

Klippel, Friederike; Cillia, Rudolf de (2016). Geschichte des Fremdsprachenunterrichts in deutschsprachigen Ländern seit 1945. In: Burwitz-Melzer et al. (eds.), 625-631.

Klippel, Friederike (ed.) (2016). *Teaching languages – Sprachen lehren.* Münster, New York: Waxmann.

Kohonen, Viljo; Enkvist, Nils Erik (eds.) (1978). *Text linguistics, cognitive learning and language teaching.* Turku: Finnish Association for Applied Linguistics.

König, Johann (1748). *The true English guide for the Germans. Der getreue englische Wegweiser, oder kurtze doch gründliche Anleitung zur englischen Sprache für die Teutschen.* 5th edition. Leipzig: Charles Ludwig Jacobi.

Köster, Henrich Martin Gottfried (1763). *Anweisung die Sprachen und Wissenschaften vernünftig zu erlernen und ordentlich zu studieren.* Frankfurt am Main, Leipzig.

Kramsch, Claire J. (1993). *Context and culture in language teaching.* Oxford: Oxford University Press.

Kramsch, Claire (2012). Authenticity and legitimacy in multilingual SLA. *Critical Multilingualism Studies* 1 (1), 107-128.

Kuester, Martin (2007). Reception theory / reader-response theory – Rezeptionsästhetik. In: Beck/Kuester/Kuester (eds.), 363-364.

Kühlwein, Wolfgang (ed.) (1983). *Texte in der Sprachwissenschaft, Sprachunterricht und Sprachtherapie.* Tübingen: Narr (Forum Angewandte Linguistik, 4).

Landwehr, Achim (2008). *Historische Diskursanalyse.* 4. Frankfurt am Main: Campus.

Larsen-Freeman, Diane; Anderson, Marti (2011). *Techniques and principles in language teaching.* 3rd edition. Oxford, New York: Oxford University Press.

Lautamatti, Liisa (1978). Observations on the Development of the Topic in Simplified Discourse. In: Kohonen/Enkvist (eds.), 71-104.

Lee, William R. (1983). Some points about 'authenticity'. *World Englishes* 2 (1), 10-14.

Lee, Winnie Yuk-chun (1995). Authenticity revisited: text authenticity and learner authenticity. *ELT Journal* 49 (4), 323-328.

Lehberger, Reiner (2003). Geschichte des Fremdsprachenunterrichts bis 1945. In: Bausch/Christ/Krumm (eds.), 609-614.

Leitzke-Ungerer, Eva (2010). Authentizität. In: Surkamp (ed.), 10-11.

Lethen, Helmut (1996). Versionen des Authentischen: Sechs Gemeinplätze. In: Böhme/Scherpe, 205-231.

Lewkowicz, Jo A. (2000). Authenticity in language testing: some outstanding questions. *Language Testing* 17 (1), 43-64.

Liddicoat, Anthony; Scarino, Angela (2013). *Intercultural language teaching and learning.* Chichester (UK), Malden (USA): Wiley-Blackwell.

Little, David (1997). Responding authentically to authentic texts: a problem for self-access language learning? In: Benson/Voller (eds.), 225-236.

Little, David; Singleton, David M. (1988). *Authentic materials and the role of fixed support in language teaching: Towards a manual for language learners. CLCS Occasional Paper no. 20.* Dublin: Trinity College.

Little, David; Devitt, Seán; Singleton, David (1988). *Authentic texts in foreign language teaching. Theory and practice.* Dublin: Authentik.

Long, Michael H. (1996). Authenticity and learning potential in L2 classroom discourse. *University of Hawaii working papers in ESL* 14 (2), 127-149.

Löschmann, Marianne; Löschmann, Martin (1984). Authentisches im Fremdsprachenunterricht. *Deutsch als Fremdsprache* 21, 41-47.

Lynch, Anthony J. (1982). 'Authenticity' in language teaching: Some implications for the design of listening materials. *British Journal of Language Teaching* 20 (2), 9-16.

MacDonald, Malcolm N.; Badger, Richard; Dasli, Maria (2006). Authenticity, culture and language learning. *Language and Intercultural Communication* 6 (3-4), 250-261.

Macht, Konrad (1986). *Methodengeschichte des Englischunterrichts.* 35. Augsburg: Universität Augsburg.

MacLeish, Andrew (1968). Adapting and Composing Reading Texts. *TESOL Quarterly* 2 (1), 43.

MacMillan Publishing Company (2016). Global Coursebook. http://www.macmillanglobal.com/about/the-course, access date: 07/16/2016.

MacMillan Publishing Company (2016). New Inspiration. http://www.macmillaninspiration.com/new/, access date: 07/16/2016.

MacMillan Publishing Company (2016). The Business Podcasts. http://www.businessenglishonline.net/resources/podcasts/, access date: 07/16/2016.

Maheswarappa, B. S. (1997). Bibliometrics: An overview. In: Devarajan (ed.), 1-10.

Maingay, Susan M. (1980). Selection and grading of authentic material for the reading class. *ELT Journal* 34 (3), 217-221.

Mallinson, Vernon (1966). *Teaching a modern language.* London: Heinemann.

Mauranen, Anna (2004). Where Next? A summary of the round table discussion. In: Del Lungo Camiciotti/Tognini Bonelli (eds.), 203-216.

McKay, Sandra (2013). Authenticity in the language teaching curriculum. In: Chapelle (ed.), 299-302.

McNeill, Arthur (1994). What makes authentic materials different? The case of English language materials for educational television. In: n.a. *Papers presented at the Annual International Language in Education Conference, Hong Kong*. n.a., 314-326.

Meara, Paul (2012). The bibliometrics of vocabulary acquisition. An exploratory study. *RELC Journal* 43 (1), 7-22.

Meißner, Franz-Joseph; Reinfried, Marcus (eds.) (2001). *Bausteine für einen neokommunikativen Französischunterricht. Lernerzentrierung, Ganzheitlichkeit, Handlungsorientierung, Interkulturalität, Mehrsprachigkeitsdidaktik: Akten der Sektion 13 auf dem 1. Frankoromanistentag in Mainz, 23.–26.09.1998*. Tübingen: Narr.

Michaelis, Johann David (1758). Zerstreuete Anmerkungen über das Gedächtnis. In: *Nützliche Sammlungen*, 86-89.

Mishan, Freda (2004). Authenticating corpora for language learning. A problem and its resolution. *ELT Journal* 58 (3), 219-227.

Mishan, Freda (2005). *Designing authenticity into language learning materials*. Bristol (UK), Portland (USA): Intellect.

Mishan, Freda; Chambers, Angela (eds.) (2010). *Perspectives on language learning materials development*. Bd. 1. Oxford, New York: Peter Lang.

Mishan, Freda (2010). Task and task authenticity: Paradigms for language learning in the digital era. In: Mishan/Chambers (eds.), 149-172.

Morris, Charles W. (1946). *Signs, language and behavior*. New York: George Braziller.

Morrow, Keith (1977). Authentic texts and ESP. In: Holden (ed.), 13-15.

Morton, Robert (1999). Abstracts as authentic material for EAP classes. *ELT Journal* 53 (3), 177-182.

Mulhall, Stephen (2005). *Routledge philosophy guidebook to Heidegger and Being and time*. 2nd edition. London, New York: Routledge.

Munby, John (1978). *Communicative syllabus design*. Cambridge, New York: Cambridge University Press.

Murphy, Terrence P. (2006). 'Getting rid of that standard third party narrative voice': The development of James Kelman's early authorial style. *Language and Literature* 15 (2), 183-199.

Nation, I.S.P.; Deweerdt, Jean Paul (2001). A defence of simplification. *Prospect* 16 (3), 55-65.

Newfields, Tim (ed.) (2006). Authentic communication: Proceedings of the 5th Annual JALT PanSIG Conference. Shizuoka, Japan. Available online at http://jalt.org/pansig/2006/index.html, access date: 12/12/2013.

Nikitina, Larisa (2011). Creating an authentic learning environment in the foreign language classroom. *International journal of instruction* 4 (1), 33-46.

Noetzel, Thomas (1999). *Authentizität als politisches Problem. Ein Beitrag zur Theoriegeschichte der Legitimation politischer Ordnung. Univ., Habil.-Schr. Marburg, 1998*. 9. Berlin: Akad.-Verl.

Nostrand, Howard Lee (1989). Authentic texts and cultural authenticity: an editorial. *Modern Language Journal* 73 (1), 45-52.

Nunan, David (1988a). *Syllabus design*. Oxford: Oxford University Press.

Nunan, David (1988b). *The learner-centred curriculum. A study in second language teaching*. Cambridge, New York: Cambridge University Press.

Nunan, David (1989). *Designing tasks for the communicative classroom*. Cambridge, New York: Cambridge University Press.

Nunan, David (2004). *Task-based language teaching*. Cambridge (UK), New York (NY): Cambridge University Press.

Nützliche Sammlungen (1758). (editor unknown)

Offelen, Henry (1687). *A double grammar for Germans to learn English and for English-men to learn the German tongue.* London: Thompson.

Omaggio Hadley, Alice (1993). *Teaching language in context.* 2nd edition. Boston: Heinle & Heinle.

O'Malley, J. Michael; Pierce, Lorraine Valdez (1996). *Authentic assessment for English language learners. Practical approaches for teachers.* Reading, Massachusetts: Addison-Wesley Pub. Co.

O'Neill, Robert; Scott, Roger (1974). *Viewpoints. Interviews for listening comprehension.* London: Longman.

Östman, Jan-Ola (ed.) (1978). *Semantics and cohesion.* Bd. nr 41. Åbo: Åbo Akademi Foundation, Research Institute.

Oxford English Dictionary. Oxford (2016). http://public.oed.com/the-oed-today/rewriting-the-oed/collecting-the-evidence/, access date: 07/05/2016.

Oxford University Press (2016). *Teaching Business English Course.* http://www.oxfordtefl.com/oxford-tefl-courses/teacher-development/business-english, access date: 07/16/2016.

Palmer, Harold E. (1968). *The scientific study and teaching of languages.* Oxford: Oxford University Press.

Paran, Amos (2012). Language skills: questions for teaching and learning. *ELT Journal* 66 (4), 450-458.

Paulston, Christina Bratt (1974). Linguistic and communicative competence. *TESOL Quarterly* 8 (4), 347.

Peacock, Matthew (1997). The effect of authentic materials on the motivation of EFL learners. *ELT Journal* 51 (2), 144-156.

Pearson (2015). *ELLIS Digital Learning Program.* http://www.pearsonschool.com/index.cfm?locator=PSZu72, access date: 12/10/2016.

Pearson (2015). *Scott Foresman ESL Sunshine Edition.* http://www.pearsonschool.com/index.cfm?locator=PSZu72, access date: 12/10/2016.

Peirce, Charles S.; Weiss, Paul; Hartshorne, Charles (1932). *Collected papers of Charles Sanders Peirce. Volumes I and II: Principles of philosophy and elements of logic.* London: Belknap Press of Harvard U.P.

Pennington, Martha Carswell; Stevens, Vance (eds.) (1992). *Computers in applied linguistics. An international perspective.* Bd. 75. Clevedon (UK), Philadelphia: Multilingual Matters.

Petersen, Hans (1980). Objektivierung und Vergegenwärtigung als Kategorien des Fremdsprachenunterrichts. *Der fremdsprachliche Unterricht – Themenheft 'Authentizität und Lehrbarkeit'* 14 (55), 193-205.

Pho, Phuong Dzung (2013). *Authorial stance in research articles. Examples from applied linguistics and educational technology.* Basingstoke: Palgrave Macmillan.

Pinner, Richard (2013a). Authenticity and CLIL: Examining authenticity from an international CLIL perspective. *International CLIL Research Journal* 2 (1), 44-45.

Pinner, Richard (2013b). Authenticity of purpose: CLIL as a way to bring meaning and motivation into EFL contexts. *Asian EFL Journal* 15 (4), 138-159.

Pinner, Richard (2014). The authenticity continuum: Towards a definition incorporating international voices. *English Today,* 30(04), 22-27.

Pinner, Richard (2016). *Reconceptualising authenticity for English as a global language.* Bristol: Channel View Publications (Second language acquisition).

Porter, Don (1983). Some issues in communicative language teaching and their relevance to the teaching of languages in secondary schools. Prepared comments by Don Porter. In: Johnson/Porter (eds.), 38-43.

Porter, Don; Roberts, Jon (1981). Authentic listening activities. *ELT J* 36 (1), 37-47.

Povey, John F. (1967). Literature in TESL programs: the language and the culture. *TESOL Quarterly* 1 (2), 40-46.

Prager, Johann Christian (1764). *Englische Grammatik oder leichte und gründliche Anleitung zur Erlernung der Englischen Sprache.* Coburg: n.a.

Prator, Clifford H. (1969). Adding a Second Language. *TESOL Quarterly* 3 (2), 95.

Pride, J. B.; Holmes, Janet (eds.) (1972). *Sociolinguistics. Selected readings.* Middlesex, Baltimore: Penguin.

Reinfried, Marcus (2001). Neokommunikativer Fremdsprachenunterricht: Ein neues methodisches Paradigma. In: Meißner/Reinfried (eds.), 1-20.

Richards, Jack C.; Platt, John Talbot; Weber, Heidi (1985). *Longman dictionary of applied linguistics.* Harlow: Longman.

Richards, Jack C.; Rodgers, Theodore S. (2001). *Approaches and methods in language teaching.* 2nd ed. Cambridge, New York: Cambridge University Press.

Rings, Lana (1986). Authentic language and authentic conversational texts. *Foreign Language Annals* 19 (3), 201-208.

Rivers, Wilga M. (1983). *Communicating naturally in a second language.* Cambridge, New York: Cambridge University Press.

Rixon, Shelagh (2000). Authenticity. In: Byram (ed.), 68-69.

Roberts, Celia; Cooke, Melanie (2009). Authenticity in the adult ESOL classroom and beyond. *TESOL Quarterly* 43 (4), 620-642.

Rogers, Carmen Villegas; Medley, Frank W. (1988). Language with a purpose. Using authentic materials in the foreign language classroom. *Foreign Language Annals* 21 (5), 467-478.

Rosenbloom, Stephanie (2011). Authentic? Get Real. *New York Times.* http://www.nytimes.com/2011/09/11/fashion/for-only-the-authentic-cultural-studies.html?pagewanted=1&_r=2, access date: 27.04.2013.

Rost, Michael (2002). *Teaching and researching listening.* Harlow, New York: Longman/Pearson.

Rück, Heribert (1986). Fetisch ‚authentischer Text‘? *Neusprachliche Mitteilungen aus Wissenschaft und Praxis* 39 (3), 165.

Ruisz, Dorottya (2014). *Umerziehung durch Englischunterricht? US-amerikanische Reeducation-Politik, neuphilologische Orientierungsdebatte und bildungspolitische Umsetzung im nachkriegszeitlichen Bayern (1945-1955).* 28. Münster: Waxmann.

Sampson, Geoffrey (1992). Analysed corpora of English: A consumer guide. In: Pennington/Stevens (eds.), 181-200.

Sancho, Anthony R. (1972). Spanish: A New Approach for Bilingual Programs. *TESOL Quarterly* 6 (4), 333.

Saussure, Ferdinand de (1959). *Course in general linguistics.* New York: Philosophical Library.

Schröder, Konrad (1969). *Die Entwicklung des Englischunterrichts an deutschsprachigen Universitäten.* Ratingen: Henn.

Schröder, Konrad (1975). *Lehrwerke für den Englischunterricht im deutschsprachigen Raum 1665-1900. Einführung und Versuch einer Bibliographie.* Darmstadt: Wissenschaftliche Buchgesellschaft.

Schröder, Konrad (1985). Literatur in der Frühzeit des Englischunterrichts. In: Haas/Klein-Braley/Schrey (eds.), 51-71.

Scrivener, Jim (2012). *Classroom management techniques*. Cambridge, New York: Cambridge University Press.

Seargeant, Philip (2005). 'More English than England itself'. The simulation of authenticity in foreign language practice in Japan. *International Journal of Applied Linguistics* 15 (3), 326-345.

Seliger, Herbert W. (1985). Testing authentic language: the problem of meaning. *Language Testing* 2 (1), 1-15.

Shohamy, E.; Reves, T. (1985). Authentic language tests: where from and where to? *Language Testing* 2 (1), 48-59.

Shomoossi, Nematullah; Ketabi, Saeed (2007). A critical look at the concept of authenticity. *Electronic Journal of Foreign Language Teaching* 4 (1), 149-155.

Short, Kathy Gnagey; Fox, Dana L. (2003). The complexity of cultural authenticity in children's literature: Why the debates really matter. In: Fox/Short (eds.), 3-24.

Siegel, Aki (2014). What should we talk about? The authenticity of textbook topics. *ELT Journal* 68 (4), 363-375.

Spicer, A. (1968). The Nuffield Foreign Languages Teaching Materials Project. *ELT J* XXIII (1), 14-21.

Spolsky, Bernard (1985). The limits of authenticity in language testing. *Language Testing* 2 (1), 31-40.

Stegemann, Bernd (2014). *Kritik des Theaters*. 2nd edition. Berlin: Theater der Zeit.

Stern, Hans H. (1983). *Fundamental concepts of language teaching*. Oxford: Oxford University Press.

Stevenson, Douglas K. (1985). Authenticity, validity and a tea party. *Language Testing* 2 (1), 41-47.

Stevick, Earl W. (1957). *Helping people learn English. A manual for teachers of English as a second language*. Nashville: Abingdon Press.

Stevick, Earl W. (1967). The Modular Mousetrap. *TESOL Quarterly* 1 (3), 3.

Stevick, Earl W. (1971). *Adapting and writing language lessons*. Washington, DC: Foreign Service Institute.

Stevick, Earl W. (1989). *Success with foreign languages. Seven who achieved it and what worked for them*. New York: Prentice Hall.

Surkamp, Carola (ed.) (2010). *Metzler-Lexikon Fremdsprachendidaktik*. Stuttgart, Weimar: Metzler.

Swaffar, Janet K. (1985). Reading authentic texts in a foreign language: A cognitive model. *Modern Language Journal* (69.1), 15-34.

Swales, John M. (1990). *Genre analysis. English in academic and research settings*. Cambridge, New York: Cambridge University Press.

Sweet, Henry (1899). *A Practical Study of Languages*. London: Dent.

Tamo, Daniela (2009). The use of authentic materials in classrooms. *Linguistic and Communicative Performance Journal* 2 (1), 74-78.

Tan, Melinda (2005). Authentic language or language errors? Lessons from a learner corpus. *ELT Journal* 59 (2), 126-134.

Tatsuki, Donna (2006). What is authenticity? In: Newfields (ed.), 1-15.

Taylor, David (1994). Inauthentic authenticity or authentic inauthenticity? *TESL-EJ*. http://www.tesl-ej.org/wordpress/issues/volume1/ej02/ej02a1/, access date: 08/15/2014.

Thaler, Engelbert (2007). Top Ten der Fremdsprachendidaktik. *Praxis Fremdsprachenunterricht* (04/07), 3-5.

Thomas, Jimmy (1976). Translation, language teaching, and the bilingual assumption. *TESOL Quarterly* 10 (4), 403.

Titone, Renzo (2000). History: the nineteenth century. In: Byram (ed.), 264-270.

Tomlinson, Brian; Masuhara, Hitomi (eds.) (2010). *Research for materials development in language learning. Evidence for best practice*. London, New York: Continuum.

Tompson, John (1737). *English miscellanies consisting of various pieces of divinity, philosophy, morals, politicks and history*. Göttingen: n.a.

Trabelsi, Soufiane (2010). Developing and trialling authentic materials for business English students at a Tunisian university. In: Tomlinson/Masuhara (eds.), 103-120.

Trilling, Lionel (1972). *Sincerity and authenticity*. Oxford: Oxford University Press.

Trim, John L. M. (1983). Yes, but what do you mean by 'communication'? In: Brumfit (ed.), 70-81.

Trim, John L. M. (2007). *Modern languages in the Council of Europe 1954-1997*. Strasbourg: Council of Europe.

Ushioda, Ema (ed.) (2013). *International perspectives on motivation. Language learning and professional challenges*. Basingstoke: Palgrave Macmillan.

van Ede, Yolanda (ed.) (2004). *Authenticity*. Bd. 17,1/2. Münster: Lit.

van Ede, Yolanda (2004). Editorial. In: van Ede (ed.), 5-6.

van Lier, Leo (1996). *Interaction in the language curriculum. Awareness, autonomy and authenticity*. New York: Longman.

Walter, Catherine (1982). *Authentic reading. A course in reading skills for upper-intermediate students*. Cambridge: Cambridge University Press.

Warning, Rainer (ed.) (1975). *Rezeptionsästhetik. Theorie und Praxis*. Bd. 303: Literaturwissenschaft. München: W. Fink.

Waters, Alan (2009). Ideology in applied linguistics for language teaching. *Applied Linguistics* 30 (1), 138-143.

Weijenberg, Jan (1980). *Authentizität gesprochener Sprache in Lehrwerken für Deutsch als Fremdsprache*. Heidelberg: Groos.

Weller, Franz Rudolf (1992). Wie ‚authentisch' ist ‚idiomatisches' Französisch? Anmerkungen zu zwei unklaren Begriffen der Fremdsprachendidaktik. *Fremdsprachen Lehren und Lernen* 21, 117-139.

Wesche, Marjorie Bingham; Skehan, Peter (2002). Communicative, task-based, and content-based language instruction. In: Kaplan (ed.), 207-228.

White, Ronald V. (1974). The Concept of Register and TESL. *TESOL Quarterly* 8 (4), 401.

Whitman, Randal L. (1974). Teaching the Article in English. *TESOL Quarterly* 8 (3), 253.

Widdowson, Henry G. (1976). The authenticity of language data. In: Fanselow/Crymes (eds.), 261-270.

Widdowson, Henry G. (1978). *Teaching language as communication*. Oxford: Oxford University Press.

Widdowson, Henry G. (1979). *Explorations in Applied Linguistics*. Oxford: Oxford University Press.

Widdowson, Henry G. (1983). *Learning purpose and language use*. Oxford, New York: Oxford University Press.

Widdowson, Henry G. (1984). *Explorations in applied linguistics 2*. Oxford: Oxford University Press.

Widdowson, Henry G. (1990). *Aspects of language teaching*. Oxford: Oxford University Press.

Widdowson, Henry G. (1994). The ownership of English. *TESOL Quarterly* (28/2), 377-389.

Widdowson, Henry G. (1996). Comment: authenticity and autonomy in ELT. *ELT Journal* 50 (1), 67-68.

Widdowson, Henry G. (1998a). Communication and community: The pragmatics of ESP. *English for Specific Purposes* 17 (1), 3-14.

Widdowson, Henry G. (1998b). Context, community, and authentic language. *TESOL Quarterly* 32 (4), 705-716.

Widdowson, Henry G.; Seidlhofer, Barbara (1999). Coherence in summary: The contexts of appropriate discourse. In: Bublitz/Lenk/Ventola (eds.), 205-220.

Widdowson, Henry G. (2000). On the limitations of linguistics applied. *Applied Linguistics* 21 (1), 3-25.

Widdowson, Henry G. (2003). *Defining issues in English language teaching*. Oxford: Oxford University Press.

Widdowson, Henry G. (2007). Un-applied linguistics and communicative language teaching. *International Journal of Applied Linguistics* 17, 214-220.

Wikipedia (2015). https://en.wikipedia.org/wiki/FM4, access date: 10/10/2015.

Wilcox, Brad; Morrison, Timothy G.; Oaks, Dallin D. (1999). Computer corpora and authentic texts. Toward more effective language teaching. *Reading Research and Instruction* 38 (4), 415-423.

Wilkins, David A. (1976). *Notional syllabuses. A taxonomy and its relevance to foreign language curriculum development*. Oxford: Oxford University Press.

Wilkins, David (1983). Some issues in communicative language teaching and their relevance to the teaching of languages in secondary schools. In: Johnson/Porter (eds.), 23-37.

Willems, Gerard M.; Riley, Philip (eds.) (1984). *Communicative foreign language teaching and the training of foreign language teachers*. Nijmegen: Interstudie Institute for Teacher Education.

Will, Leo (2016). The authentic language teacher. In: Klippel (ed.), 75-90.

Winkelmann, n.a.; Pitt the Elder, William; Pitt the Younger, William (1883). *Ausgewählte Reden englischer Staatsmänner*. Leipzig: Renger.

Witzendorf, Alfred Friedrich von (1763). *Unterricht von den wahren Vorzügen in einem Schreiben an den durchlauchtigen jüngsten Prinzen von Mecklenburg-Strelitz*. Leipzig: n.a.

Young, Dolly J. (1993). Processing strategies of foreign language readers: Authentic and edited input. *Foreign Language Annals* 26 (4), 451-468.

Zhafarghandi, Amir Mahdavi; Barekat, Behzad; Homaei, Sepideh (2014). A survey of Iranian EFL teachers' and learners' perceptions toward authentic listening materials at university level. *Advances in Language and Literary Studies* 5 (4), 184-197.